Marijuana Boom

Marijuana Boom

THE RISE AND FALL OF COLOMBIA'S FIRST DRUG PARADISE

Lina Britto

UNIVERSITY OF CALIFORNIA PRESS

University of California Press
Oakland, California

Library of Congress Cataloging-in-Publication Data

Names: Britto, Lina, author.
Title: Marijuana boom : the rise and fall of Colombia's first drug paradise /
    Lina Britto.
Description: Oakland, California : University of California Press, [2020] |
    Includes bibliographical references and index. Manufactured in the United
    States of America
Identifiers: LCCN 2019030166 (print) | LCCN 2019030167 (ebook) |
    ISBN 9780520325456 (cloth) | ISBN 9780520325470 (paperback) |
    ISBN 9780520974265 (ebook)
Subjects: LCSH: Drug traffic—Colombia—History. | Drug control—
    Colombia—History.
Classification: LCC HV5840.C7 B75 2020 (print) | LCC HV5840.C7 (ebook) |
    DDC 364.1/336509861—dc23
LC record available at https://lccn.loc.gov/2019030166
LC ebook record available at https://lccn.loc.gov/2019030167

27   26   25   24   23   22   21   20
10   9   8   7   6   5   4   3   2   1

"Hurricane Winds: Vallenato Music and Marijuana Traffic in Colombia's
First Illegal Drugs Boom" is abridged here from the original, published in
Hispanic American Historical Review 95, no. 1 (2015): 71–102. Copyright 2015,
Duke University Press. All rights reserved. Republished by permission of the
copyright holder, Duke University Press. www.dukeupress.edu.

Para mi abuela Nina

CONTENTS

ILLUSTRATIONS

MAPS

FIGURES

ACKNOWLEDGMENTS

This book has been a labor of love about the region where I found my roots. I am grateful to all of my relatives and family friends who talked to me about the past and helped me to construct my own research landscape. I am especially in debt to my late grandmother Celinda Molina de Britto, known in town as Nina. Her love and intelligence were the forces that attracted me to the Guajira and sparked my curiosity about its history. Thanks to my aunts Marujita, Estela, and Juana Britto in San Juan del Cesar, and Elizabeth Machuca in Bogotá, for their wisdom, care, and affection. Along with my father, my aunts and uncles—Rodrigo, Arique, Rubén, and Jaime—taught me how to approach regional culture with passion and respect. Special thanks to Rubén, who assisted me in Riohacha during the first stages of my research, and recently organized events in San Juan and Riohacha for me to share my work with general audiences; to Rafael Enrique, a renowned storyteller and civic leader better known as Arique, who shared his knowledge and memories and drove me around in his jalopy, introducing me to people who provided me with valuable information and insights; and to my father, Luis Carlos, simply Luchy, who passed along his love for reading and writing and gave me a lifelong class on vallenato music—many times against my will. Forrest Hylton was my family during the years of research and dissertation writing and the person who prompted me to dare. Our love inspired me to undertake this project, and his generosity helped me to conduct preliminary research and sharpen the arguments of the PhD dissertation that serves as the foundation for this book. His son, Steele Miller, and mother, Peggy Celano, filled my days with joy. I cannot thank all of them enough for so many trips, laughs, and hugs.

At Universidad de la Cordillera, in La Paz, Bolivia, where I began this project as an MA thesis in anthropology, I am grateful to my classmates and professors, particularly Ramiro Molina Barrios, Rossana Barragán Romano, and Silvia Rivera Cusicanqui for introducing me to the depths of history. At New York University (NYU), where I became a historian, I am in debt to all my peers and mentors. Special recognition to Sinclair Thomson, my adviser during the first years in the program, and a generous friend and valuable interlocutor until today. I have benefited greatly from my adviser Barbara Weinstein, whose knowledge, enthusiasm, and optimism helped me navigate the rough waters of the profession; and from the marvelous Marilyn Young, giant historian and fairy godmother, who provided a model of how to be humane, brilliant, and fun. At Harvard University, where I began to transform the dissertation into this book, I received solid and steady support from Jorge Domínguez and the staff, mentors, and colleagues of the Harvard Academy for International and Area Studies. Thanks to all of them and especially to my dear friends Cristina Florea, Malgorzata Kurjanska, and Noora Lori, who along with Jen Fucelli helped sustain me through tectonic changes. At Northwestern University, where I became an educator, thanks to all my students for pushing me out of my comfort zone, especially to the graduate students who worked as TAs for some of the courses I taught while finishing the manuscript, Jayson Maurice Porter, Elsa de la Rosa, and Sarah-Louise Dawtry; and to the graduate students who took my seminar on modern Latin America during spring 2019 and whose brilliant discussions helped me rethink many of the central debates that I address in this book. My colleagues in the Department of History have taught me how to be a team player, while the staff have made possible every little (and big) thing. My greatest debts are to Helen Tilley and Mike Sherry, wise mentors and friends; Sarah Maza and Ed Muir, who read portions of this book and gave me relevant ideas for revision; Ken Alder and Laura Hein, lifesavers who provided me with unwavering support as chairs; the graduate students and faculty who attended the Chabraja Center's work-in-progress workshop in which I presented; and the staff and members of the Latin American and Caribbean Studies program, who bring the sunny disposition of the tropics to the Windy City.

The assistance of archivists and librarians was also indispensable. I thank the personnel of the Gilberto Alzate Avendaño Library in Political History, the library of the Universidad Nacional, the Biblioteca Nacional's Hemeroteca, the Luis Angel Arango Library, and the Archivo General de la Nación, all located in Bogotá; the libraries of the Universidad del Magdalena and Fundación ProSierra Nevada in Santa Marta; the Centro Cultural and Fondo Mixto para la Promoción de la Cultura y las Artes in Riohacha; and the Biblioteca Departamental del Cesar, Archivo Histórico del Cesar, and Fundación de la Leyenda Vallenata in Valledupar. The help of Jhon Jairo Ortiz and Ofelia Muñoz in the photographic archive of *El Espectador* in Bogotá was essential. Special thanks to William Renán, Alvaro Mercado, and Antonio Navarro at the Universidad del Magdalena in Santa Marta; Roberto Villanueva at the Defensoría del Pueblo in Maicao; Juan Carlos Gamboa at the Universidad Popular del Cesar; and Nelson Ramírez at the Biblioteca Departamental del Cesar in Valledupar. In the United States, I am grateful to the personnel at the National Archives in College Park, Maryland; the Fales Library and Tamiment Library at the Elmer Holmes Bobst Library at NYU; the Widener Library, Houghton Library, and Law School Library at Harvard University; Albert Nason and his team at the Jimmy Carter Presidential Library in Atlanta; Michael Evans and his collaborators at the National Security Archive in Washington, D.C.; Leigh Grissom and assistant registrars at the Center for Creative Photography at the University of Arizona in Tucson; and to Paula Covington and the staff of the Special Collection of Vanderbilt University's library in Nashville.

The financial support of the institutions that granted me fellowships for travel, research, publication, and living expenses was crucial. These include the Tinker Foundation; the Center for Latin American and Caribbean Studies and the Graduate School of Arts and Science at NYU; the Social Science Research Council, the Universidad de los Andes, the Open Society Foundation, and the International Development Research Center–Canada; the Woodrow Wilson National Fellowship Foundation and the Charlotte Newcombe Foundation; and the Alice Kaplan Institute for the Humanities and the Department of History at Northwestern University.

Friends and colleagues introduced me to people, accompanied me to interviews, called my attention to specific sources, shared materials, commented on my work at different stages, invited me to give talks or participate in podcasts, edited papers that helped me sharpen my ideas, or served as sources of inspiration and examples to follow. In the Guajira, I would like to thank César Arismendy, Roger Bermúdez, Adela Fonseca, Fredy González Zubiría, Wilder Guerra Curvelo, Natividad "Tivi" López, Martín López González, Miguel Ángel López Hernández, Abel Medina Sierra, Meña Melo, Gilberto Ospino, Luis Alfonso Pérez Guerra, and Emanuel Pichón Mora. In Medellín, thanks to Mario Arango, Oscar Calvo, Sebastián Gómez, and Byron White. In Bogotá, thanks to Mauricio Archila, Josefina Castro Daza, Adriana Corso, Martha Cecilia García, Catalina Muñoz, Eduardo Sáenz Rovner, Gonzalo Sánchez, and my editor at *El Espectador,* Fidel Cano Correa. In Europe and the United Kingdom, I extend my gratitude to Sean Brady, Christopher Fletcher, James Mills, Rachel Moss, and Lucy Riall. In different cities of the United States and Canada, I benefited from the collegiality of Peter Andreas, Ana María Bejarano, Charles Bergquist, Gerry Cadava, Isaac Campos, Joaquín M. Chávez, Margaret Chowning, Jorge Coronado, Valeria Coronel, Marcela Echeverri, Froylán Enciso, Ann Farnsworth-Alvear, Andreas Feldmann, Ada Ferrer, José Antonio Figueroa, Brodwyn Fischer, Caitlin Fitz, Lesley Gill, Paul Gillingham, Paul Gootenberg, Greg Grandin, Chris Gratien, Mark Hauser, Paula Ibarra, Luis van Isschot, Robert Karl, Jane Landers, Catherine LeGrand, Henri Lauzière, Emily Maguire, Aldo Marchesi, Amy Offner, Susan Pearson, Matthew R. Pembleton, Lara Putnam, Paul Ramirez, Pilar Riaño, Mary Roldán, Joan and Frank Safford, Ernesto Semán, Federico Sor, Alejandro Velasco, Abby Wasserman, Daniel Weimer, Kirsten Weld, and my accomplice and confidant A. Ricardo López-Pedreros. My gratitude goes to the mentors and fellows at the Social Science Research Council's Drugs Security and Democracy workshops in 2011 and 2012 for stimulating conversations and nights of *juerga.*

The help of assistants made possible the completion of several tasks. Thanks to Juan Sebastián Salgado, my cousins María Paula Zuleta and Vanesa Londoño, Gabe Levine-Drizin, and Alana Marie Toulin. The work of ESL editors saved me from errors of form and content. Thanks to Amanda Pearson and her team at Pearson Ink for polishing the manuscript to make my nonnative English more readable and enjoyable. I will always be grateful to my friend and colleague Daniel Immerwahr for his generosity at so many levels, but especially for introducing me to Kate Marshall, who turned out to be my editor extraordinaire at the University of California Press and who, along with her assistant, Enrique Ochoa-Kaup, led the team that transformed my ideas into the object you have in your hands.

Others welcomed me in their homes and brought human warmth, laughter, food, drinks, music, and prayers to the fieldwork and writing process. I have been very fortunate to count on Carlos Ortega, "Yors" González, "You" Henríquez, "Pupy" Romero, Orlando Mejía, "Conchita" Namen, Yelitza Guerra, Jairo Rosado, Luisa Bruges, Neila Esther Madero, Germán Aguilar Epieyú, Cristina Epieyú, and Sergio Cohen Epieyú in Riohacha, Maicao, and Uribia; Jorge Derpic, Bennet Campoverde, Sara Monsalve, Matt Komonchak, and Richard Matusow in New York City; Sandra Ocampo Kohn in Washington, D.C.; the late "Nueve" Lopera, "Joche" Restrepo, Patricia Monsalve, Alfonso Buitrago, "Pájara" Pérez, Mónica Fandiño, and Amanda and Gilma Orrego in Medellín; Lucas Jaramillo, Umberto Giangrandi, Teo Balve, and Angela Carrizosa in Bogotá; Natalia Ramírez Bustamante, Ana Villarreal, Daniel Pérez Becker, Alex Fattal, and Lars and Jennie Samoska in Boston and Cambridge; Mike and Holly Gransky and their extended family in Connecticut; and Yanilda María González, María del Rosario Acosta, Jana-Maria Hartmann, Kathleen Belew, Ana Arjona, Eudald Lerga, Lydia Barnett, Nick Valvo, Petra Cooper, and Karla Pariser in Chicago and Evanston. A toast to captains and crews of El Guanábano in Medellín and Rogers Park Social in Chicago. A bow to my shaman César Augusto Hernández for holding me in the light. And heartfelt thanks to my sisters Valentina Tabares, María Isabel Botero, and Isabel Cristina Botero for keeping me company rain or shine; to my brother Carlos Rafael Britto for always opening my mind to unconsidered possibilities; to my mother, Myriam Londoño Mora, for loving me and supporting me through thick and thin; and to my sweet Seth Gransky for teaching me the magical properties of kindness and patience, and for his love and help, which allowed me to complete the monumental task of finishing this book.

My greatest debt is, however, to everyone who allowed me to ask questions, turn on the recorder, and take notes during long conversations. Although I do not use the names of many of them, in order to protect their identities, I remember our exchanges by heart. The vitality of their memories, along with the soulful presence of *mi abuela* Nina, my godmother Amanda, my mentor Marilyn, and my dearest friend Carlos, all of whom passed away while I was bringing this book to life, guided me to reach this destination.

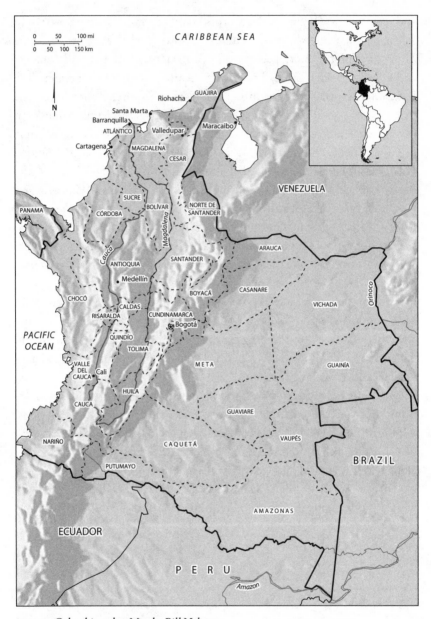

MAP 1. Colombia today. Map by Bill Nelson.

Introduction

FROM JUAN VALDEZ TO PABLO ESCOBAR, for the past half century at least, a *mestizo* man with a thick mustache has represented Colombia on the world stage. Valdez was a fictional character who during the 1960s and early 1970s promoted Colombian coffee to the international market. Escobar was a cocaine kingpin who in the 1980s and early 1990s led a war against his extradition to the United States. The inspiration for the Valdez character was the typical male farmer of the Andean interior. He wore a straw hat, a poncho, and *alpargatas* (rope-soled sandals), carried a machete, and was always accompanied by Conchita, a mule loaded with jute sacks of the precious bean. Escobar, in contrast, established his own visual referent. His curly hair, protruding belly, colorful shirts, dispassionate expression, and fleet of aircraft filled with tons of the profitable alkaloid have inspired so many telenovelas and movies that at this point he is as fictional as Valdez. And between the two icons extends the history of a country that in two decades transitioned from a coffee republic to a narcotics nation.

But before the bucolic Valdez yielded to the warmongering Escobar, marijuana traffickers partnered with US buyers in the early 1970s to flood North American cities and suburbs with the drug, thereby capitalizing on growing countercultural demand, and at the end of the decade these traffickers resisted the frontal attack of the state. Popularly known as *marimberos,* these pioneers of the drug trade came from the Guajira peninsula and the neighboring Sierra Nevada de Santa Marta, two areas in the northernmost section of the country's Caribbean coast that were considered as barely belonging to the nation-state. Although *marimberos* made Colombia the main supplier of US drug markets, and later became the first targets of the US-led "war on drugs" in South America, the boom they brought to life is a forgotten chapter of the innocent era before the cocaine industry car-bombed the country. After them other peoples in poor and isolated territories became involved in the cultivation, commercialization, and exportation of drugs, making Colombia one of the principal producers in the world and a problem for hemispheric security.

How did a peripheral region become the birthplace of the illicit drug trade that turned Colombia's coffee republic into a narcotics nation? And why did this first boom in illicit drugs not only decline but also fall into oblivion? These unanswered questions form this book's points of departure. For the past three decades, scholars, journalists, and artists have focused on untangling the ins and outs of the hydra of cocaine processing, trafficking, diplomacy, and war. Academic literature on the popularly known *bonanza marimbera,* however, is scant. Most existing works were produced at the time of the boom, when social scientists, politicians, and diplomats sought to explain a novelty for which there were no precedents and they had no framework. Between academic debates and ideological controversies, experts and stakeholders forged a consensus according to which this boom was a regional anecdote of the absence of the state in a frontier society and the result of the moral degeneration that US consumers and smugglers brought with them in their search for new sources of marijuana. Its decline, on the other hand, was interpreted as the logical outcome of boom-and-bust dynamics and of the takeover of the country by the cocaine cartels.[1]

In this book, I take a different approach and instead argue that the marijuana boom was as dramatic a turning point in the history of Colombia as the one that took place with coffee. Moreover, I find that the marijuana boom was also a critical component of hemispheric relations to the extent that it served as a training ground for the "war on drugs" in South America. Without denying the weakness of central governments in the marijuana region, or the crucial role US buyers played in stimulating this illicit export economy, I contend that the causes of the boom cannot be found in "the myth of the absence of the state," much less in external factors.[2] Instead, I examine and analyze the process of integration of the broader region that includes the Guajira peninsula and the Sierra Nevada de Santa Marta into national and international political, commercial, and cultural networks centered in the Andean interior and oriented toward the United States. I assert that the marijuana boom was the product of unintended consequences stemming from a series of state interventions that the Colombian government carried out in pursuit of agrarian development and nation-state formation.

From the early twentieth century into the late 1960s, these state-led reforms were implemented with support from US federal governments and private investors. The contradictory ways in which local, regional, national, and international interest groups coalesced in response to these state interventions created a new arena of contestation and accommodation that materialized in the marijuana boom of the 1970s.

Without disregarding boom-and-bust dynamics and the rapid expansion of the cocaine business as factors for the subsequent collapse in the marijuana export economy, I call attention to more important causes. In particular, the political and diplomatic struggles to define the state response to the growing drug traffic between Colombia and the United States better explain the decline. The criminalization of producers and traffickers and the militarization of the region between 1978 and 1980—a concerted initiative on the part of the Colombian and US governments—were deliberate strategies to sort out deep domestic crises unfolding in both countries in a context of increasing militarism as the Cold War escalated at the end of the 1970s. The marijuana region served as a laboratory for the US and Colombian governments to experiment with a novel approach to statecraft and international cooperation, an approach that assumed drug production and traffic to be security threats that warranted bilateral military interventions in peripheral areas where national sovereignty and US hemispheric hegemony were challenged. On the ground, the campaign of crop eradication and traffic interdiction prompted marijuana traffickers to develop mechanisms of survival that led to ferocious competition among them, so that their business practices morphed from reciprocity and solidarity to indiscriminate violence in the form of killings, robberies, and betrayals, making marijuana cultivation, commercialization, and exportation an expensive and less viable practice.

This book's publication happens to coincide with a sweeping change to marijuana policy throughout the world, from decriminalization to legalization. In Colombia, medical marijuana is legal (albeit not yet completely regulated), but recreational consumption is still prohibited and is a contentious matter. After years of toleration following the 1994 Constitutional Court order allowing individuals to possess a personal dosage, a presidential decree came into force on October 1, 2018, that prompted the National Police to conduct raids against recreational users. Months later, the Constitutional Court reversed the decision. In the meantime, excessive police activity and even brutality have not prevented activists and enthusiasts from regularly protesting through social media and direct action, including calling for *fumatones*—marathons of public marijuana smoking in designated parks. In the United States, at this writing twenty-six states and the District of Columbia have fully legalized marijuana. News about increasing tax revenues, growing incomes for small entrepreneurs and farmers, and even employment for veterans of the "war on terror" conflict with reports on the difficulties and challenges that producers, merchants, and consumers face in dealing with the gap between state and federal laws. But long before marijuana came in from the cold, an agrarian country in South America traveling a rugged road to industrialization and urbanization supplied the largest market in the world with tons of weed at a moment when youth challenged the US government's forms of domination and hegemonic projects at home and abroad one joint at a time.

Using a multiscale perspective on local, regional, national, and international developments; a commodity studies approach; and methods of political, cultural, and diplomatic history, this book addresses Colombia's forgotten history of its marijuana boom in the hope of decoding one of the greatest conundrums of our times: how and why illicit drug economies and cultures emerged in the Americas in the last quarter of the twentieth century, and how massive drug trafficking, and the violent structures that sustain it, was born.[3]

REGION AND NATION

In the national imaginary, the Guajira and Sierra Nevada de Santa Marta occupy a singular place. Precariously connected to the rest of the littoral and the Andean interior through overland trails, the peninsula and the mountain range became objects of inquiry, exploration, and inspiration for thinkers, entrepreneurs, and artists in search of spaces and peoples not yet fully integrated with the modern nation-state. It is not a coincidence that the first Colombian modernist novel, *Four Years Abroad Myself,* and the most famous work on the "magical realism" of Latin American modernity, *One Hundred Years of Solitude,* take place in the Guajira and the Sierra Nevada.

While much has been written about the landmark novel of Colombia's Nobel Prize winner, little has been said about the work of one of his mentors. Before there was Gabriel García Márquez, Colombia had Eduardo Zalamea Borda. It was Zalamea Borda who overcame Colombian literature's "sad provincial condition" to find the "authentically universal."[4] In *Cuatro años a bordo de mí mismo: Diario de los cinco sentidos* (Four Years Abroad

Myself: Diary of the Five Senses), Zalamea Borda tells the story of a young aspiring writer who, finding Bogotá "narrow, cold, disastrously built, with pretensions of a big city," travels to its antipode, the Guajira, where rumor has it that anyone can make "marvelous business" and get rich.[5] In search of women to love and pearls to buy, he finds a cosmopolitan world of contraband, sexual pleasure, and violence that transforms him forever. Published in 1934, almost a decade after Zalamea Borda left the Guajira, the book came out at the same time that Liberal president Alfonso López Pumarejo came to power with an ambitious modernization plan. In tune with its times, the novel was "a romantic wandering" that criticized development, and it became an instant classic and a best seller.[6] Two decades later, the first generation of nationally trained anthropologists began to study the peoples of the Guajira through a lens similar to what Zalamea Borda had used—that is, as an archaic human group confronting modernity.[7]

By then, Zalamea Borda was a successful diplomat, and he returned to the Guajira to advocate for its modernization. Under his leadership, a governmental commission attended an international meeting of the United Nations Educational, Scientific, and Cultural Organization (Unesco) in Paris in May 1960 to promote the Guajira as the setting of the pilot project in Latin America for Unesco's Desertification and Arid Zones program. Zalamea Borda and his team presented the Guajira as "a zone that should be treated as of high national interest" and requested the "scientific, technical, and financial assistance" of Unesco to pursue "the organization of a live economic and cultural frontier of DEEP PATRIOTIC SENSE" (capitals in the original). During the next few months, Bogotá, with the help of Washington, Unesco, the Rockefeller Foundation, and the Fulbright Commission, created the institutes that administered the program that would make the Guajira an "active coast in terms of the exploitation of maritime resources, tourism, international trade, and a future great export industry."[8] But no bureaucracy could compete with neighboring Venezuela's oil economy, and these international efforts to create a productive sector in the peninsula proved insufficient. For the rest of the 1960s the Guajira's indigenous people continued living in precariousness, depending on rich Venezuela for survival.[9]

Much like the Guajira, the Sierra Nevada exists as a liminal place in Colombia's imagination. Since the mid-nineteenth century, its unique ecosystems have enchanted visionaries who wished to colonize areas with abundant natural resources. In 1855, a young French anarchist named Élisée Reclus published the first modern account of the mountain range, a book that recounts the adventurous two years Reclus spent working on a tropical agriculture project he described as a "great whirlwind of work and commerce" involving a "brave people who live without preoccupation for the future."[10] Although Reclus's project failed and he returned to Europe empty-handed—to become the father of comparative geography—others followed his example and wrote about the socioeconomic potential of the Sierra Nevada.[11] Through governmental reports, chorographic commissions, and travelers' accounts, men of letters and science invented a "savage frontier" to which the state had to bring progress by supporting investors in agricultural enterprises.[12] This "otherness" had made the Sierra Nevada the cradle of modern anthropology and archaeology in Colombia by 1941, when another Frenchman, renowned ethnologist Paul Rivet, who lived in exile in Bogotá under the official auspices of the Liberal government, sent his Austrian mentee Gerardo Reichel-Dolmatoff and the latter's Colombian wife, Alicia Dussán, to found there a local branch of the National Institute of Ethnology (IEN).[13] During the next five years, the couple studied the four indigenous groups that lived in the Sierra Nevada's three watersheds, and concluded that they were on the verge of cultural extinction.[14] The ethnologists' *indigenismo* aimed to foster a more inclusive national culture by counteracting the beliefs of racial superiority that prevailed in Colombia's coffee republic.[15] However, their works represented the Sierra Nevada as a world that stood in opposition to the modern nation-state though it was swept by external forces out of its peoples' control.[16]

This nineteenth- and early-twentieth-century academic and artistic literature set the foundation for the official discourse that cast the Guajira and the Sierra Nevada as one of the nation's primitive alterities, its shadow, its other. It is no surprise that Macondo, the fictional town of García Márquez's *One Hundred Years of Solitude* and paragon of premodern isolation and endogamy, was located somewhere in the Sierra Nevada after the Buendía family migrated from the Guajira. But contrary to these discourses, the peninsula and the mountain range have been historically integrated into, and dependent on, linkages to national and international webs of trade, investment, and politics.[17] The prevalent idea of the Guajira and the Sierra Nevada as places and peoples without history is one more case of "Occidentalism," that is, a series of representational operations that separates the capitalist world into bounded units, disaggregates their relational histories, turns differences into hierarchies, and naturalizes these representations as factual realities.[18]

Once we widen our gaze to consider the larger region, this vision does not hold. Located in the most septentrional area of South America, with the islands and the isthmus to the north and west, respectively; the Venezuelan Gulf and Lake Maracaibo to the east; and the Magdalena River to the south, the area was known until the late 1960s as the Greater Magdalena. A bridge between the Caribbean and Andean basins, the Greater Magdalena and its contours corresponded to the colonial Gobernación de Santa Marta, the first area of Spanish exploration and settlement on the South American continent. With the pyramidal Sierra Nevada at the center, expeditionaries founded Santa Marta (1525) on the bay area near the western watershed; Riohacha (1545) on the long coast facing the sea and the peninsula and bordering the northern watershed; and Valledupar (1550) in the great valley between the Sierra Nevada and the Perijá cordillera, next to the southeastern watershed. Through trade with and war against native peoples, each settlement generated its area of influence along its respective watershed.[19] But because climatic and soil conditions, chronic labor scarcity, and demographic dispersion doomed large-scale agriculture in the Gobernación de Santa Marta, raising and trading cattle became the area's only viable economic activity. English, French, and Dutch merchants arrived regularly at various bays and inlets, especially in the upper Guajira peninsula, looking for livestock and hides to exchange for goods and African slaves. For centuries, the socioeconomic life of this "Caribbean without plantation" consisted of contraband commerce, cattle ranching, and an intimate connection with the maritime circuits of the Atlantic world.[20]

By the end of the nineteenth century, when what had been the Gobernación de Santa Marta became the Department of Magdalena—popularly known as Greater Magdalena to differentiate it from the smaller and contemporary department of the same name—a new export economy emerged in the Andean interior. The prosperity from several coffee booms allowed the existing Liberal and Conservative parties to consolidate. In the process, a new ideology of whiteness as *mestizaje* developed in Colombia.[21] Although the discourse of *mestizaje* celebrated cultural and racial mixture, it also inscribed racialized regional differences "in the spatial ordering" of the nation-state, placed whiteness at the top of the hierarchy, and justified the marginalization of territories and peoples that did not conform to this vision.[22] Building upon Enlightenment conceptions of the voluptuous nature of the New World and nineteenth-century European racial theories, poets, artists, intellectuals, lawyers, diplomats, and politicians imagined a temperate center of the nation located in the Andean region and inhabited by whites and *mestizos* as being the seat of civilization. In contrast, the darker races living in the periphery of tropical lowlands and agricultural frontiers were predestined to barbarism.[23] Although lowlands and frontiers were not excluded from the nation, their peoples did not exercise citizenship in meaningful ways or benefit from state resources.[24] In contrast to what happened in other Latin American countries, Colombia's coffee booms helped to both fragment the nation along racialized regional differences and exacerbate difficulties in economic, political, and cultural relations between the central state and the peripheries (both tropical lowlands and agricultural frontiers).[25]

Paradoxically, this long-term process of transforming the Greater Magdalena from a corner of the transnational Caribbean world into a frontier of the Colombian nation-state played in its favor during the first half of the twentieth century. The United States was increasingly interested in Colombia because of its strategic location at the gateway of South America and adjacent to the recently completed Panama Canal. This interest contributed to turning the tropical lowlands of the Greater Magdalena into a setting where national governments experimented with various approaches to agrarian modernization.[26] In search of raw materials—and enticed by Colombia's favorable policies for attracting foreign capital—Boston-based United Fruit Company began to invest financial and technological resources into its large-scale agriculture projects located in the most fertile areas of the Sierra Nevada's western watershed. During the following decades, US foreign aid and international development agencies joined the efforts to transform other sections around the mountain range in order to produce tropical crops. In a country that was centered in the Andean region and depended on coffee exports, these foreign interventions helped integrate the national territory, modernize the economy, and consolidate the state. The cultivation, commercialization, and export of coffee, bananas, cotton, and other commodities restructured natural and social landscapes, set up circuits of production and exchange, and created opportunities for Colombians to accumulate capital and become upwardly mobile. As a contact zone where "ideologies, technologies, capital flows, state forms, social identities and material cultures meet," twentieth-century Greater Magdalena was an important site for the encounter and mutual constitution of the "local" and the "global."[27]

The marijuana boom of the 1970s was a pit stop in this long history of formation and transformation of region and nation passing through world markets, particularly that of the United States. Indeed, the *bonanza marimbera* was an eruption of layers of socioeconomic contradictions—some of which had colonial origins—that twentieth-century modernizing reforms in pursuit of agrarian development and nation-state formation revitalized. The marijuana boom of the 1970s spurred a vertical integration of territories—from highlands and foothills to lowlands and littoral—and facilitated the formation of competing social groups and synergies among them—from local elites to peasants, settlers, and urban working and middle classes—all of which made commercial export agriculture feasible and profitable. Fulfilling the promises (albeit temporarily) that modernizing state reforms made but failed to deliver, the marijuana boom succeeded in boosting the region's agricultural productivity, entrepreneurial innovation, capital accumulation, urbanization, and cultural projection.

MARIJUANA AND COCAINE

Experts have failed to see the *bonanza marimbera* as a chapter in Colombia's history of agrarian modernization, nation-state formation, and integration with the United States. This failure is due to a combination of disciplinary methods with political urgencies marinating in the *mestizo* ideology of the coffee republic, which prevented these analysts from recognizing capitalist dynamism and historical agency in areas that nationalist discourses defined as premodern. When the study of the illicit drug trade consolidated as an academic field in the late 1980s, the marijuana boom had already occurred. Economists, political scientists, and sociologists—invariably white and *mestizo* men from the Andean interior—focused their research on the current war between cocaine drug lords and the state. These scholars typically analyzed either the role of the state or that of the cocaine elites—whose members were also white and *mestizo* men from the Andean interior. Scholars examined structural factors such as rural poverty and Colombia's geostrategic position in relation to consumption markets, or they analyzed the macroeconomic and foreign policy ramifications (in the latter case, especially with regard to the United States) of the new illicit business.[28] The *bonanza marimbera* fell through the cracks.

After Pablo Escobar was killed in late 1993, a revisionist scholarship emerged. Following the death of *El Patrón* (the Boss), the cocaine exportation and wholesale distribution monopolies underwent a reorganization that de-escalated the war between traffickers and governments, thereby eliminating the urgency to study the cartels. Understanding how the long-running conflict and the production and traffic of drugs interacted with each other became the most pressing need. Economic and social historians, international relations scholars, sociologists, and anthropologists examined the interactions between governments, traffickers, guerrillas, paramilitaries, and the rural and urban working classes that participated in the illicit economies. This literature concluded that the internal conflict contributed to the loss of the state's legitimacy and tenuous territorial presence, which led to a political culture that relied on weak control of individual behavior and high levels of competition and individualism.[29] The recession of the 1970s helped trigger the mutation of these old dynamics and traditions into a new, illicit economy, because it opened a vital social and moral space for private actors to develop alternatives to the economic slump (including drug trafficking).[30] In the process, illicit entrepreneurs displaced traditional elites, assumed state functions, built extensive social bases, and took over entire regions.[31] Despite their valuable contributions, scholars continued to focus on cocaine, the commodity that fueled the country's war.[32]

Anthropologists, cultural critics, educational scholars, and public intellectuals from the former marijuana region, or with personal connections to it, were the only ones looking back. By examining continuities among various cycles of contraband trade in general merchandise and agricultural commodities, these interdisciplinary studies demonstrated that the marijuana boom built upon these patterns, some of which had colonial origins dating back to the eighteenth century.[33] As contraband commerce depended on interethnic relations between smugglers from diverse racial and national origins and the Wayuu people of the upper Guajira peninsula, where the natural seaports are located, indigenous practices and norms became relevant cultural codes according to which smugglers organized procedures and established hierarchies.[34] This long history of contraband generated a value system that celebrated smuggling as a legitimate strategy for both individuals and groups to attain social recognition.[35] The *bonanza marimbera* was part of the evolution of contraband commerce, and it was also a crucial phase in the "Colombianization" of the Guajira, the region's integration into the nation.[36] However, this insightful literature did not call into question the underlying premise of the absence of the state, and more often than not, the marijuana boom got lost in either *longue-durée* perspectives or cultural analyses of identity that focused exclusively on the local and regional levels, leaving national and international causes and implications of the boom unexamined.

Building upon the revisionist scholarship and interdisciplinary literature, this book presents the *bonanza marimbera* as a history of nation-state formation and interstate relations in the Americas. But to frame Colombia's first drug boom in this way forces me "to bring the state back in," taking me into muddy waters.[37] Lamenting the weakness or absence of the state is an old tradition in Latin America.[38] In the case of Colombia, the debate on the absence of the state is even more relevant, given that integration into world markets through coffee exports intensified the fragility of the state by strengthening the two political parties through which "geographically fragmented, landed oligarchies maintained regional and local supremacy in the face of challenges from below."[39] In this "nation in spite of itself," sovereignty was increasingly fragmented into regions; thus the *patria chica*—understood as the regional world of commerce, politics, and culture—was a more powerful binder and source of meaning than the nation-state.[40] As a result, questions of hegemony are apropos of what I examine in this book. By observing how political projects "from above" entered into conflict with visions "from below," I understand the state as "a series of decentralized sites of struggles through which hegemony is both contested and reproduced"; in other words, I view the state not as a "centralized institution of sovereign authority" but as an arena of evolving social and cultural relations of power in which public life is regulated.[41] And acknowledging the centrality of regional dynamics, I widen the unit of analysis from the Guajira and Sierra Nevada de Santa Marta to the Greater Magdalena. By studying this broader region, I analyze the various and interlocking scales in which Colombia's first drug boom brought to completion a long-term process of mutual constitution of region and nation.[42]

In placing marijuana at center stage in the story, I discovered new avenues for linking the history of twentieth-century Colombia with the history of the US hemispheric project. The transient marijuana boom was a bridge that not only connected the coffee republic and the narcotics nation, in terms of political economy, but also ushered in the transition toward a new national culture and identity, which came to fruition when cocaine linked the destinies of Colombia and the United States in various social and cultural ways. By exploring this particular case, I aim to contribute to a new historiography that recognizes the centrality of values and culture in the process of integration between Latin America and the United States, and the role that apparently remote and isolated areas in Latin America and their peoples played in shaping this integration.[43]

Focusing the story of the origins of Colombia's drug trade business on marijuana also invites us to introduce a gender perspective in order to understand the critical role that masculinity played in the business. Women in

Latin America have participated in drug trafficking for generations and in many capacities. As carriers, or mules, women have used the ostensible weakness of their gender to deceive authorities; as business partners, they have resorted to their social capital and sexuality to advance their interests; as bosses, they have operationalized their maternal roles to build networks of relatives and subordinates in pursuit of profits; and as enforcers, they have relied on their fiercest instincts in imposing order through terror and violence.[44] This was not the case with the *bonanza marimbera*. Given the cultural codes of the contraband-smuggling business on which the marijuana boom was built, trafficking marijuana was an exclusively male activity anchored in relationships among men rather than between men and women. At a time when men were losing ground as money earners, being a marijuana trafficker came to be an important vehicle of masculine reconstitution. Showing how and why the political economy and culture of the marijuana business empowered men more than women is one of the contributions of this work.

HISTORY AND STORY

This work began as a personal quest to understand the country of my childhood. Because my father's hometown was one of the epicenters of the marijuana boom, my first visit to the region was a family event. In 1988 my younger brother and I came for the first time to stay with our grandmother Nina in San Juan del Cesar, Department of Guajira. Perched on the foothills of the southeastern watershed of the Sierra Nevada de Santa Marta, San Juan extends down to the Cesar riverbank. Because any traces of the *bonanza marimbera* were hidden from public display, to two kids born and raised in Medellín, a city drowning in blood and cocaine, the town looked like a Nativity scene. Surrounded by uncles, aunts, cousins, and neighbors, we found impossible to remember all of their names. Towns, villages, and hamlets dotted a vertical landscape connected by intricate social webs. Indigenous peoples came to San Juan from the mountains and the peninsula to sell their products and visit relatives and *compadres*. And Venezuelan cars, groceries, and TV shows marked the rhythm of daily life in such a natural manner that one forgot this was Colombia.

Sixteen years later, I returned to the Guajira ready to explore as an adult what had dazzled me as a child. By that time, the paramilitaries had taken over. After years of war against the guerrillas in the Sierra Nevada and between two enemy factions, the United Self-Defense Forces of Colombia (AUC) in the early 2000s expanded their reach along the corridor that connects the mountain range with the great valley of the Cesar and Ranchería Rivers, and accessed the natural seaports of the Guajira peninsula for their export-import operations in cocaine and arms.[45] Navigating webs of kinship and *compadrazgo* (relations among *compadres*, that is, parents and godparents) with the help of my family—particularly Uncle Arique, a renowned storyteller and civic leader—I began collecting testimonies on the marijuana boom for a master's thesis in anthropology.[46] Just a couple of months later, the paramilitary armies massacred the Wayuu people of Bahía Portete, in the upper peninsula, announcing their triumph on the Caribbean coast.[47] Over the following decade, as I returned every summer to conduct research for a PhD dissertation in history, the critical situation only worsened. Every time the national administration of Álvaro Uribe in Bogotá skirmished with the Bolivarian government of Hugo Chávez in Caracas, flows of legal and illegal goods were interrupted, including food, drinking water, and fuel. Malnutrition and starvation were prevalent in vast areas due to droughts and floods, strained relations with Venezuela, the violent displacement of entire towns after the paramilitary takeover, the environmental effects of the open-pit coal mine of El Cerrejón, the corruption that plagued municipal and departmental governments, and the central state's misguided policies. Meanwhile, attracted by the sharp contrast between the littoral and its beaches, the Sierra Nevada and its snow caps, and the peninsula and its desert, tourists continued to flock to the region.

This book is the product of my having sailed safely through these dangerous waters in search of vantage points from which to observe a neglected problem. Challenges presented themselves at several levels. First, how to research and write on a historical illicit activity whose protagonists used cash and resorted to violence in order to keep their affairs clandestine? Second, how to see through the heavy, gloomy flog of representations and cultural production about drug traffickers more generally without reproducing these "socially constructed archetypes," which historian Luis Astorga calls "the mythology of the narcotrafficker"?[48] Third, how were we to understand these traffickers in terms of national and global historical processes through which they emerged without reducing them to simplistic dynamics of national and global history?[49]

My solution was to combine methods from journalism, anthropology, and history—the three disciplines in which I am trained—in order to collect the most diverse array of evidence possible. By juxtaposing and triangulating these myriad sources in my analysis, I drew conclusions based on coincidences and divergences. From journalism, I used methods for locating participants and witnesses across the region, and for conducting unstructured and semi-structured thematic and life-story interviews. Drawing on anthropology, I conducted participant observation, which included listening to songs from the marijuana era in both social and private contexts, writing ethnographic descriptions and notes on various subjects, drawing maps, and personal journaling. And from history, I employed strategies to identify and examine published and unpublished sources from public archives, private family collections, US and Colombian printed media, and libraries and bookstores in various locations throughout Colombia and the United States. Thousands of cups of coffee, hundreds of digital pictures, and dozens of recordings and notebooks later, a vast assemblage of oral, visual, and documentary evidence emerged before me like a jigsaw puzzle. Details of the methods, sources, and protocols for the oral history portion of my research, which merits special attention, are provided in the appendix.

In putting the various pieces of this puzzle together, I have been guided by two powerful metaphors in clarifying the narrative arc of Colombia's marijuana boom. First, the hurricane, the meteorological phenomenon that has leveled human and natural landscapes in the Caribbean since time immemorial.[50] Like a cyclone system, the marijuana export economy formed in the maritime world of commerce and labor and moved inland with great centripetal force. As a uniquely explosive mixture of natural conditions and historical contradictions, this hurricane-like boom was the product of economic models, politics and policies, social reforms and struggles, and worldviews and identities.[51] And, like all hurricanes until 1979, this one also had a female name.[52] Although the scientific term for the plant that is the protagonist of this story is *cannabis,* the term I use is *marijuana*, a composite of two popular Spanish female monikers. Today medicinal and recreational producers, merchants, and consumers use *cannabis* and *marijuana* interchangeably; nevertheless, an increasing number of activists for drug policy reform have begun to question the latter for its racist connotations in favor of the former.[53] Although I recognize the power of words in shaping our political imagination, I use *marijuana* because it was the most common term used by the people who participated in or lived through the Colombian bonanza. Using *cannabis* in this book would be a theatrical posture in the name of political correctness. *Marimba* is the other term (hence *bonanza marimbera* and *marimberos,* two terms I also employ), which is a euphemism that refers to a musical instrument and is a derivation of *mariamba,* the name that people of African descent on the country's Caribbean coast use for hemp.[54]

The second metaphor that helps clarify the narrative arc is paradise, one of the oldest imaginaries of modernity in the Caribbean. As Europeans searched for a "new world" untouched by the ecological degradation already evident in the "old world," they accidentally arrived in the Caribbean. The appeal of the tropical paradise where civilization attempted to correct its fall from grace shaped the European imperial project in the Americas for centuries.[55] This "tropical gaze," or "imperial eye," was the culmination of centuries of European interaction with Caribbean environments.[56] The *bonanza marimbera,* itself a transient moment of abundance in the paradise of modernity, embodied the fallen Eden of Colombia, where the "forbidden plant" blossomed to challenge patterns of capital accumulation, establish new forms of social mobility, forge novel popular identities, and reconstitute interstate relations with the United States.[57]

This book is thus an effort to step into "paradise" and follow the wake of the hurricane that turned it upside down in three distinctive cycles of ascendance, peak, and decline. In the first part of this book, "Ascendance," I examine the Greater Magdalena from the early twentieth century until the late 1960s in order to understand how deeply rooted traditions of contraband smuggling and production of tropical export commodities intersected to create the basis for the new marijuana export sector. Here I focus on how various actors engaged in disputes with the state and its two political parties, and I assess what the consequences were of those alliances and conflicts for defining the Greater Magdalena as a region, its role in the country's modernization, and the course of such reforms more generally. I use the terms *Liberal* and *Conservative* (capitalized) to refer to the two main political parties and their members rather than abstract philosophies or political doctrines.[58] In chapter 1, "Wheels of Progress," I study each of the Greater Magdalena's three sections in relation to the tropical commodities that shaped their physical, socioeconomic, and political contours and underpinned the hectic and accelerated agrarian development of the whole region. This is a work of political history that weaves together local, regional, national, and international interests and struggles in pursuit of productivity, accumulation, and recognition. In chapter 2, "Coming from the Mountain," I address the beginning of the marijuana business in the late 1960s. Using social history approaches, I profile some of the most prominent smugglers from the rural popular classes who exported coffee to the United States outside state-sanctioned channels and without paying taxes. I show how they established circuits of routes and alliances that connected them with powerful merchants from the region's urban world, the Andean interior, and the United States, and I describe how they subsequently switched to smuggling marijuana, a new agricultural commodity about which at first they knew nothing.

In the second part of the book, "Peak," I explore the bountiful years between 1972 and 1978, when this inchoate traffic turned into a full-fledged export sector after the emergence of local crops grown exclusively for export. Here I grapple with the thin, often blurred line between the legal and the legitimate to shed light on how producers, intermediaries, and exporters understood their activities as socially sanctioned, therefore legitimate, practices despite being aware that such business practices contravened the law. In chapter 3, "Santa Marta Gold," I use political economy and labor history approaches to reconstruct the inner workings of marijuana cultivation, commercialization, and exportation, and shed light on who did what, when, and why. In chapter 4, "Party Animals," cultural history with a gender perspective on masculinities allows me to explain the rise of the *marimberos,* the emergent class of marijuana merchants who sought to cement their newly acquired economic status through social and cultural projection, achieved by imitating practices established earlier by a much older and more powerful class of agrarian entrepreneurs. In doing so, they opened space for themselves in regional society, though temporarily.

In the third part of the book, "Decline," I address the violent years between 1978 and the mid 1980s, when producers, intermediaries, exporters, and buyers became targets of criminalization, and the intermontane valleys of the Sierra Nevada, the desert plains of the Guajira, and villages, ports, and surrounding cities became militarized settings and, in the process, the marijuana export business collapsed. In chapter 5, "Two Peninsulas," I employ diplomatic history to illuminate the conflictive consensus making between several US and Colombian governments during the 1970s to define the state's response to the growing drug traffic between the two countries, and ultimately to transform the marijuana region into an experimental laboratory that featured new approaches to state control and repression. In chapter 6, "Reign of Terror," I resort to cultural analysis to deconstruct the series of tropes about violence and terror that emerged as a corollary of criminalization and militarization, eclipsing state violence and stereotyping the peoples and territories as savage peripheries of the nation. At the same time, I also reconstruct the multiple ways in which state-led militarized interventions aggravated existing tensions, intensified competition among traffickers, and made irrelevant the cultural codes of honorable masculinity that had once kept conflicts and violence in check. Following the book's three parts, a brief conclusion summarizes its central arguments and contributions. Finally, in a short appendix I address the methods and protocols used to conduct oral history for this book.

In search of my own roots, I turned away from my hometown of Medellín and its lethal affair with cocaine to cross to the other side of the mirror and discover that there was no "other." From that viewpoint, I offer this panoramic picture of the rise and fall of Colombia's first drug paradise. This is an exercise in historical inquiry and imagination that puts together fragments of evidence in order to understand the constellation of factors that produced a perfect storm, one that subverted life in a corner of the Caribbean and changed Colombia for decades to come.

PART ONE

Ascendance

ONE

Wheels of Progress

TROPICAL COMMODITIES AND REGIONAL
FORMATION

Those who are resistant to progress are crushed under its wheels.

GENERAL RAFAEL REYES,
president of Colombia (1904–1909)

TRANSFORMING THE FERTILE AREAS of the Greater Magdalena in order to produce tropical commodities destined for the markets of the industrialized world was a dream that came about with the birth of the Colombian nation. Actually, the first sacks of coffee that the country ever exported in the early nineteenth century were produced in the Sierra Nevada de Santa Marta.[1] But environmental constraints, labor scarcity, and a lack of infrastructure—all of which had hampered commercial agricultural production since colonial times—obstruct the success of these enterprises, as did the tumultuous political conflicts that characterized the earliest decades of the republic. Despite these obstacles, many entrepreneurs embarked on the enterprise of utilizing the different altitudes of the Sierra Nevada de Santa Marta for the production of tropical export commodities.

Irrigated by seven rivers and located near the port of Santa Marta, the western watershed became a focal point for all kinds of agricultural endeavors in the last decades of the nineteenth century.[2] Ciénaga, the largest town in the area, was the main destination for European and Middle Eastern immigrants, as well as settlers from other parts of the Colombian coast looking for business opportunities.[3] By the time the two principal political parties in the country, Liberal and Conservative, went to war at the end of the century and, after the War of a Thousand Days (1899–1902), the coffee republic was consolidated, producers in the Sierra Nevada's intermontane valleys, foothills, and surrounding lowlands near Santa Marta were exporting coffee, tobacco, cacao, and bananas to Europe and the United States in modest amounts.[4] While the perennial coffee bush grew in the highlands, tobacco, cacao, and

MAP 2. The Greater Magdalena. Map by Bill Nelson.

bananas grew on the foothills and lowlands. During the following decades, other cash crops made stellar appearances in transient bonanzas that left long-lasting consequences. The marijuana export economy of the 1970s was one of those episodes in a longer history of agrarian modernization in Colombia.

In this chapter, I examine the main periods in which the cultivation and exportation of agricultural products allowed local interest groups to take advantage of national necessities and international demands. I argue that the difficulties and opportunities presented by the unique vertical geography of the territory—from the great valley, the peninsula, and the coast, to the mountainous hinterlands in the Sierra Nevada de Santa Marta and Perijá—defined various patterns of economic development, while political competition and solidarity among landowners, commercial elites, and diverse popular sectors shaped the trajectory of each tropical commodity boom. In the process, a region emerged out of a disconnected territory whose physical and social fragmentation made it a dry-land archipelago. The circuits of production and exchange bonded the different sections of this part of the continental Caribbean by connecting its population to the social circles and political party structures of a Bogotá-centered nation. Moreover, these commodity booms integrated its geographies as peripheries and borderlands of the nation-state as well as distant satellites of the US hegemonic orbit in Latin America. The contradictions created by each of these historical periods erupted in the second half of the 1960s as localized feuds. This happened at a time when a new elite agreement between Liberals and Conservatives to put a stop to yet another civil war began to work toward agrarian reform to address the root causes of the mid-century conflict. This ideological opening at the top intensified the proliferation of responses at the bottom. All sectors with vested interests in the reform now had recourse to the law, making it difficult for the state to overlook their demands. The bonanzas of different tropical commodities not only failed to resolve but in fact exacerbated conflicts over land, labor, and markets, making the Greater Magdalena one of the most heated settings of modernization. In the following sections, I trace how these key moments contributed to the configuration of a region that served as a laboratory of agrarian development.

BANANAS AND MARKETS

On a certain day in the late nineteenth century, a Genoese young man born in a lineage of Freemasons arrived to the port of Santa Marta with chests of books in different European languages. His name was José De Andreis Blanchar. After fighting in Garibaldi's army in his native Italy, he decided to settle in Ciénaga, a thriving tropical town in Latin America. Over time, his personal library earned him a reputation as a wise man, and his anticlerical views labeled him an atheist. More important, he became one of the forefathers of a powerful Liberal party dynasty in Santa Marta. The many branches of the Vives family, descendants of De Andreis's daughter and the son of

Salvador Vives Ferrer—another young radical European who arrived from Catalonia, Spain, at roughly the same time as De Andreis—played central roles in deepening the contradictions that brought the regional economy to a breaking point in the late 1960s. At their arrival, however, neither De Andreis nor Vives had any advantage over anybody else; they, too, resorted to retail commerce to survive the ups and downs of their agricultural ventures.[5] As in other parts of Latin America, patterns of land tenure, precarious infrastructure, difficulties in labor mobilization and market organization, and the power of local elites in relation to the central state and other elites defined the success of investors in export crops.[6] In the case of Santa Marta and its area of influence, landowners, most of them descended from colonial nobility and authorities, mobilized their political clout to pressure the Conservative government in Bogotá to donate public lands to foreign and local investors.[7]

The War of a Thousand Days (1899–1902) between Liberals and Conservatives sealed the fate of men like De Andreis and Vives. The violent conflict battered the coffee haciendas in Santander and Cundinamarca, on the eastern side of the Andean interior, contributing to the displacement of the country's coffee belt to the west, in the departments of Antioquia and Caldas, where families of peasants colonized the slopes of the western and central cordilleras with their small coffee farms.[8] After the parties at war signed the Treaty of Neerlandia, a peace accord named after the banana farm near Ciénaga where the pact was negotiated, the cultivation of the fruit began to fulfill its promises.[9] With coffee growers in the Sierra Nevada highlands struggling with excessive rainfall, an absence of infrastructure, and low productivity, the new Conservative president, General Rafael Reyes (1904–9), focused his attention on the fertile lowlands along the western watershed.[10] In contrast to coffee, the production of bananas was not capital intensive as it required no mechanization or technology. Consequently, banana profits were high as markets expanded rapidly in Europe and the United States, thanks to the aggressive practices of the recently created United Fruit Company.[11] Since the fruit had clear advantages over coffee, the new president began to use state resources to finance this budding sector.[12] Perhaps because he felt indebted to the Greater Magdalena for his electoral victory, or simply because he found a golden opportunity of political clientelism to favor war veterans and allies, President Reyes used concessions of lands, subsidies, and tax exemptions for investors to support the formation of *la zona bananera* (the "banana district").[13]

The banana district was part of a larger design in which President Reyes inaugurated a new era in Colombian politics and economics.[14] Although his electoral victory was marked by fraud, his presidency had clear achievements. During the heated electoral campaign that followed the end of the war, one of Reyes's supporters, General Juanito Iguarán, a powerful indigenous authority of the Wayuu people of the Guajira peninsula, took advantage of the fact that the provincial capital of Riohacha voted without a formal assembly, and he filled out the electoral results with the number of ballots that Reyes needed to win.[15] Known as the Registro Padilla—named after the Greater Magdalena province for which Riohacha served as the capital—the fraud proclaimed Reyes president-elect. A military commander who professed that "those who are resistant to progress are crushed under its wheels," Reyes did not hesitate to speed up the locomotive of development.[16] He reorganized public finances, stabilized the exchange rate, dissolved any trace of federalism by converting states into less autonomous departments, and finally led Liberal and Conservative elites in reaching an ideological and programmatic consensus on economic development.[17] The political hegemony of bipartisan export-import interests consolidated during his administration.[18]

Much like other political leaders in Latin America, President Reyes viewed the United States as both a model to emulate and the source of capital to attract.[19] Relations with the United States were strained, however, because of Colombia's loss of the Panama territory in 1903, just one year after the end of the war and largely because of Washington's military and political involvement. Although anti-American sentiments simmered in many sectors, dominant elites in both parties unanimously professed that the economic future of the country was predicated upon stabilizing diplomatic, commercial, and financial relations with "the polar star." In time, *Respice Polum* (Look to the North) became Colombia's foreign policy doctrine.[20] The Greater Magdalena's banana district was thus an important setting in the effort to forge a more intimate relation with the Colossus of the North.

Along with the new *eje cafetero* (coffee axis) on the western side of the Andean interior, the *zona bananera* helped to bring Colombia into twentieth-century currents of development.[21] In both sectors, small growers dominated production while a few exporters at the top channeled the products to foreign markets.[22] The substantive difference was that the United Fruit Company was the sole buyer, exporter, and marketer of bananas in the Greater Magdalena, whereas in the Andean coffee region, a vast number of Colombian merchants bought and exported the bean.[23] Coffee offered significant new economic opportunities for Colombians in comparison to bananas: peasants and merchants received cash and capital from coffee production and commerce; entrepreneurs financed industries in the region's urban areas; politicians financed their clienteles; and peasant units of production sheltered the national economy against the fluctuations of the international markets.[24] Coffee merchants and financiers became powerful political actors and interlocutors of the state.

In contrast, the sweet banana was a bitter fruit of discord. Popularly known as *Yunai* (the phonetic translation of "United"), the United Fruit Company used state patronage in the form of land concessions, subsidies, and tax exemptions to sponsor its own expansion.[25] By buying lands and building infrastructure—a railway, a telegraph line, a dock, and irrigation canals—the company created a land market where none had previously existed.[26] The company also offered credit and rental leases to a banana-growing clientele comprising members of the local landed elite and certain sectors of the merchant class that depended on the company's monopolistic practices to market the fruit.[27] This tactic secured the support of the local elite when the company had to negotiate with or lobby the government, and by reaching out to families of enterprising merchants who took advantage of the company's credit to cultivate the fruit, the company financed the formation of a layer of brokers. The Vives de Andreis family was among these brokers, after its members managed to obtain small loans from the company beginning in 1921, when one of the sons, José Benito, better known as Pepe, came back to Santa Marta from New York City, where he had worked six years for a commercial firm.[28] Thanks to Pepe's international business experience, the Vives de Andreis family became *libres* (free growers), a category that meant they were not required to sell their harvests to United Fruit exclusively. However, vertical integration and dumping practices made the company the only outlet for "free" production, and thus *libres* like the Vives de Andreises became highly dependent on the company.[29] Hence, *libres* began to play key roles in buffering conflicts between management, large and small growers, departmental and national governments, and the labor force.[30]

In sum, coffee in the Andean interior sustained the rise of a new type of mercantile, industrial, and financial class that translated its economic and social capital into state power. In contrast, bananas in the Greater Magdalena gave birth to an absentee propertied class whose members lived in various locations in Europe and the United States, had no control over the terms of exchange, and were unsuccessful—and even uninterested—in vying for national political power.

However, the highly complex, class-based society that formed in the banana district was not barred from significant participation in national life.

Commerce, education, labor mobilization, radical activism, and party politics allowed competing sectors to come closer to the nation-state centered in Bogotá, and also to become protagonists in the country's history.[31] The role that peoples in the banana district played during the 1920s—a decade when labor movements effectively challenged the Conservative hegemony—provides the best example of *la zona bananera's* centrality to the construction of a modern nation. In 1922, Washington began making payments on the $25 million owed to Bogotá as indemnity for the loss of Panama, which coincided with an oil boom and a consequent relaxation of foreign banks' lending terms. The country acquired "the habit of thinking in millions."[32] But the mismanaged "dance of the millions" created inflation and did not trickle down to the masses as had been promised, triggering popular discontent and protest.[33] Social movements and radical activists of different stripes who congregated under the umbrella of the Liberal party's left wing and the new Socialist party planned an uprising to coincide with a work stoppage.[34] Meanwhile, harvesters and dock and railway workers in the banana district pushed forward a list of demands to the company; settlers fought land encroachments; small and medium growers protested against United Fruit's land and infrastructure monopoly; and agitators and activists from the Andean interior flocked to the region to support grassroots organizations.[35] On November 24, 1928, Thomas Bradshaw, United Fruit Company's local manager, met with a governmental commission accompanied by a group of representatives of the company's clientele led by Pepe Vives.[36] After the company refused to negotiate directly with the workers, General Carlos Cortés Vargas ordered troops to open fire on the masses during a rally on the morning of December 6, 1928, killing a still-debated number of people that ranges between 47 to 3,000.[37]

The banana district was now at center stage in national history. Nobel Prize–winner Gabriel García Márquez, born and raised one year earlier in one of the towns in the *zona bananera,* immortalized this tragic event in his most famous novel. But contrary to *One Hundred Years of Solitude,* in which the strike and massacre are obliterated from Macondo's memory, these were the most controversial topics of the time.[38] The magnitude and cruelty of "the massacre of the banana fields" demonstrated the incapacity of the Conservative party to deal with labor problems; together with the world economic depression, this episode contributed to the end of forty years of Conservative rule.[39] Furthermore, the bloody episode coincided with the end of the national tax exemption for banana producers that President Reyes had decreed decades prior.[40] The United Fruit Company began to disinvest from Colombia, turning its attention to Ecuador.[41] Large growers moved definitively to Europe to live off their "banana checks," unemployment in the district rose to 80 percent, and settler families occupied 10,000 hectares formerly controlled by the company.[42]

The Liberal party benefited from the Conservative political debacle. Although the return of the Liberals to power in the 1930 election marked the beginning of the end of the *zona bananera*'s golden age, the transformations unleashed during the heyday of this export economy had long-lasting repercussions. The *zona bananera* was a complex class-based society that resulted from the clash between US private interests, national modernizing plans, and local colonial legacies. The cultivation of the fruit allowed elite cattle barons with century-old land titles to become a banana-growing clientele directly connected to the US economy. The production of this tropical commodity also underpinned the emergence of a middle class composed of literate hacienda employees along with merchants and artisans who migrated from coastal towns, Caribbean islands, Europe, and the Middle East.[43] At the same time, a working class formed from waves of men and women immigrating from the Greater Caribbean and the rest of Colombia.[44] The system that United Fruit Company developed to manage diverse modes of production— from cultivation in the company's own plantations to subcontracting with small, medium, and large growers—existed in no other United Fruit Company district (except for Ecuador decades later).[45] The company depended on local planters to supply at least half of its total output. In turn, planters depended on the company's marketing system around the world, and both depended on multiple forms of state patronage, which in turn depended on the success of the banana district to advance the state's model of economic development.[46] These layers of interdependencies opened space for an accommodation of interest to prevail that prevented the United Fruit Company from becoming all-powerful.[47] This feature differentiated the Colombian case from other contemporary "banana republics" in Guatemala, Costa Rica, and Honduras, where the United Fruit Company owned and controlled every aspect of the trade and local life.[48]

From this point of view, the Greater Magdalena's *zona bananera* was not an enclave, in the sense of an economic zone created by foreign direct investment where capital, technology, management, and labor are introduced from the outside.[49] Although this was partially the case, the unique and intricate webs of interdependencies complicate using this term. As a "contact zone" where cultures and economies met in a context of asymmetrical relations of power, the *zona bananera* was outwardly oriented toward the Greater Caribbean, the United States, and Europe, and was also a protagonist in Colombia's development drama.[50] In economic terms, the banana export economy provided a model for integrating the country's lowlands into international markets. In political terms, its diverse labor movements fought to be interlocutors for national reformist elites leading the process of political centralization and economic integration. And in social and cultural terms, the banana district helped foster radical and nationalist popular consciousness, as well as modern urban identities.

DIVI-DIVI AND GEOPOLITICS

Whereas the advent of the Liberal Republic marked the beginning of the end of the banana district's golden age, it represented the integration of other areas of the Greater Magdalena to national and international circuits. The triumph of Liberal candidate Enrique Olaya Herrera in the 1930 presidential election was a watershed.[51] But despite the important labor and social rights he enacted into law, his coalition government frustrated the revolutionary dreams held by the left Liberals and social movements and radical activists who supported him. Their hopes now rested on the next Liberal candidate, Alfonso López Pumarejo, the mastermind behind the party's return to the presidency and its foremost leader. Despite belonging to an oligarchic family of coffee financiers, López Pumarejo proclaimed that the country's future depended on stabilizing relationships with the masses, that is, the "vast and miserable economic class that does not read, that does not write, that does not dress, that does not wear shoes, that barely eats, that remains ... on the margins of [national life]."[52] Taking inspiration from Roosevelt's New Deal, he put forth the "Revolution on the March," a plan of reform that offered an alternative to a potential social revolution from below led by Jorge Eliécer Gaitán, his competitor within the party.[53] Whether *Revolución en marcha* was the true end of an oligarchical democracy or the handbrake on a popular mobilization is beyond the scope of this book.[54] The point to make is that despite the important Law 200 of 1936, which created the conditions for an agrarian reform by establishing land occupancy as a legal basis for tenure, the Revolution on the March did not endanger the position of the landed elites or upper classes. Its greatest beneficiaries were coffee merchants and financiers, industrialists, landlords, and foreign investors.[55]

López Pumarejo's Revolution on the March showed its true colors in the Greater Magdalena. Having been orphaned at an early age, López Pumarejo did not remember his mother, Rosario Pumarejo Cotes, and he grew up with little connection to her family, which still owned the hacienda El Diluvio, in the great valley along Valledupar's area of influence. Trying to reconnect with his maternal family, the president traveled to Santa Marta along with three of his ministers in early March 1935. The entourage arrived in Riohacha on March 11 and was welcomed by a crowd of supporters and Wayuu leaders dressed in ethnic clothes. The president's cousin, the powerful smuggler Luis Cotes Gómez, hosted him at a feast including drinks and music.[56] On March 15 the president was welcomed in Valledupar by Dr. Ciro Pupo Martínez and more than two hundred cowboys on horseback. They marched him to the Plaza Mayor, decorated with red flags and filled with hundreds of peasants cheering "Viva el Partido Liberal!"[57] During the next few days, López Pumarejo learned "about the needs of a very seigniorial city full of traditions but with its back to progress."[58] Finally, he visited the house where the initials of his great grandfather were engraved on the front, and at the age of forty-nine he "experienced the unexplainable kind of emotion of a kid" when he entered the bedroom where his mother had been born, and openly wept.[59]

After this emotional trip, López Pumarejo transformed the physical and political landscape of the Greater Magdalena's lowlands. The substantial outlays that the banana district required for its formation in terms of land, labor, and infrastructure inhibited the development of other sections.[60] Revolution on the March aimed to fix this imbalance by promoting the areas of influence around Riohacha and Valledupar, which remained stuck in political economies with deep colonial origins—contraband in the case of Riohacha and the peninsula, and cattle ranching in the case of Valledupar and the great valley. The problem was that in carrying out this program, President López Pumarejo reactivated entrenched principles of nepotism and state patronage of elite sectors.[61] With no Conservatives in the cabinet for the first time in over half a century, López Pumarejo "governed in a frankly partisan fashion."[62] He displaced Santa Marta's Conservative families whose members had occupied the departmental government for generations as their birthright, and replaced them with his Liberal friends and relatives. First, one of his cousins in Santa Marta, a pioneer of the banana industry, Manuel Dávila Pumarejo was appointed governor.[63] Then, in April 1935, López Pumarejo resolved a quarrel in his cousin's administration by passing the torch to Valledupar.[64] He appointed Ciro Pupo Martínez, the doctor who had welcomed him during his visit, and months later replaced him with another of his hosts, Pedro Castro Monsalvo, a young politician who was the party's rising star in the Greater Magdalena.[65]

With Liberals in charge of the departmental government, López Pumarejo focused on the other important economic actor in the region, the United States. As part of a free trade agreement he signed with Washington in April 1935, López Pumarejo created the conditions for a stronger US presence in an area on the Caribbean continental coast with a geostrategically important location: the borderlands in the Guajira peninsula next to Venezuela's rising oil district. Despite his nationalist rhetoric, López Pumarejo "was a realist, especially on trade issues"; thus he considered the treaty to be vital in protecting Colombia's export markets.[66] The pact reduced tariffs on almost two hundred US products and excluded them from sales taxes in exchange for preferential treatment for coffee and bananas in the United States.[67] After the accord was signed, President López Pumarejo ordered the establishment of a new provincial capital, Uribia, in the Wayuu village he had visited with his cousins the Cotes brothers, in order to strengthen the presence of the Colombian state in the area and lessen the influence of Venezuela and its booming oil economy in indigenous territory. He consequently decreed the opening of a free port on the Colombian inlet closest to the border in order to legalize the importation of US goods and the exportation of native products, which in time came to be known as Puerto López in his honor. He authorized the construction of a paved road to connect this new port to Riohacha and Valledupar, a project that local elites had been requesting for decades, since it would "take to the sea, that is to say to the currents of world commerce, the produce of a bountiful region, and facilitate the import of machinery for industry and agriculture."[68] Finally, he approved various projects of urban infrastructure in both provincial capitals, including housing, government buildings, schools, hospitals, roads, and bridges.

These reforms were lifesavers to an economy "whose foundations rested on quicksand."[69] When López Pumarejo visited the region in early 1935, Riohacha and the Guajira was a fragmented society with three faces. There was Maicao, a contraband hub in the middle of the peninsula's steppe, in Wayuu territory, that was the commercial and economic supplier of US and European goods and native agricultural products for Venezuela's oil region. Second, Riohacha, the provincial capital, located on the coast, served as the political and cultural center. The third face was the upper peninsula, the historic Wayuu territory—the source of most native products and labor and the location of natural ports for importation and exportation. Smugglers connected the three pieces together in at least two ways. On one hand, *criollos*, nonindigenous men native to Riohacha, operated from there, trading locally harvested products with the Wayuu people for export to the North Atlantic markets passing through the Dutch islands, and importing goods to barter with their indigenous suppliers and for sale in the local market.[70] On the other hand, various groups of *turcos* (Middle Eastern immigrants) and *cachacos* (from Colombia's Andean interior) worked in Maicao importing goods to send to neighboring Venezuela and the Andean region of Colombia over the "Jerusalem Road," a web of trails with colonial origins that connected the Guajira with Lake Maracaibo and the Magdalena River, the artery to the Colombian interior.[71]

With the first skirmishes of a new war in Europe, and while the banana district battled a fungal plague, the Sigatoka disease, which caused premature ripening, Colombia inaugurated a new Liberal president. Eduardo Santos (1938–42) won the elections with an agenda diametrically opposed to López Pumarejo's.[72] The Santos administration, which came to be known as the Great Pause, neutralized the supporters of the Revolution on the March throughout the country. In the Greater Magdalena, Santos closed ranks with Santa Marta's Liberal cliques that were part of the United Fruit Company's clientele, beginning with Pepe Vives, whom the new president appointed governor on September 19, 1939, hoping he could deal with the Sigatoka plague.[73] But Vives's attempts to solve the banana district's crisis proved insufficient when the European conflict evolved into a world war and the United Fruit Company interrupted all of its operations.[74] At this point, the Guajira took center stage, particularly Riohacha, where international, national, and local interests clashed.

Because the Guajira was located in the northernmost section of South America's continental platform, where the pipelines that supplied oil to the Panama Canal ran from the Gulf of Venezuela, its control was indispensable to the Allied Powers. Its close proximity to the Dutch islands, which Roosevelt feared Germany might convert into bases for military aggression, complicated the situation even further.[75] Moreover, in addition to Colombian Conservatives, a small but influential community of Italians and Spaniards lived in Riohacha who were vocal about their Fascist and Falangist sympathies, giving the impression that the peninsula was an outpost of European totalitarianism.[76] On the eve of another world war, this geostrategic area,

FIGURE 1. Riohacha's old pier and divi-divi storage facility, circa 1950. Franco Estrella photographic archive, Riohacha, Guajira.

which was "little affected by the Good Neighbor policy," became a concern for Washington, which sought "to preserve regional economy and to vinculate [i.e., unite] it with the United States."[77]

In fact, Washington's strategy to bind this region to the United States unintentionally contributed to destroying its local economy. For years, relations between the United States and Germany, latecomers to the imperial game, had become strained over international trade as both rising powers sought to fill England's shoes in Latin America.[78] The loss of its colonies during World War I and the Great Depression severely affected Germany's access to raw materials and export markets. To compensate for this deficit, Germany aimed to boost its share of Latin American trade at the expense of the United States. After sending a delegation to tour the continent in 1934, the Nazi government established a new system of trade based on direct barter transactions in which a quantity of imports was exchanged for exports of equal value, without using scarce foreign currency.[79] "German conspiracies for the conquest of parts or of all of South America are by no means solely the outgrowth of Hitlerism," the Office of the Coordinator of Inter-American Affairs reported once the war heated up.[80] However, it was "Hitlerism" that added renewed vigor to this old plan by implementing a campaign of exclusive trade agreements, barter exchanges, export subsidies, and inflated prices for Latin American products.[81] And, at least from the US point of view, this rivalry played out in the Caribbean, where a well-equipped fleet expanded Germany's domain.[82]

Perhaps the compatibility between the Germans' barter system and the modus operandi of the *criollo* smugglers in Riohacha is what led the latter to welcome Wilhelm Eikhof and Herbert Muller when they arrived in 1935.[83] It is not clear how and where the two men met. In any case, together they opened Casa Muller in Riohacha and began working with Gratiniano Gómez, owner of the main commercial house in town, vice-consul of the Dutch West Indies, and local Conservative party chair.[84] In his multiple capacities, Gómez cooperated with Eikhof and Muller, helping them to buy native products as cheaply as possible, and the Germans advanced money, food, and merchandise to Gómez and his friends.[85] Even Luis Cotes Gómez, López Pumarejo's cousin, a smuggler known for his jealous control of what he considered his territory, "allowed them to use his lighterage facilities for bringing in their own contraband through his headquarters ranch in Santa Rosa."[86] This sustained trade made the Guajira's native products the most important Colombian exports to Germany. For example, the Colombian comptroller general reported in 1940 that the Colombian products the Third Reich most frequently bought were goat and sheep hides as well as divi-divi—a tree whose fruits were used to extract tannins and transform hides into leather, a tree that abounded only in the Guajira.[87] In other words, Eikhof, Muller, and Riohacha's *criollo* smugglers took advantage of Germany's militarization to create a market for Guajira's hides and divi-divi in a country that needed leather as it marshaled for war.[88] And the national government apparently welcomed Eikhof and Muller's businesses as much as local smugglers did. When Revolution on the March opened Puerto López, the Ministry of Public Works subcontracted the construction of the paved road and authorized the purchase of tools and other inputs at Casa Muller.[89]

Apparently, only Washington worried about their presence in the Guajira. Indeed, all of Colombia was on the US national security radar.[90] German migration to Colombia increased after the end of World War I.[91] Although the numbers of German immigrants were not as large as in Brazil, Argentina, and Mexico. Washington began to worry about German settlement in a country with such a strategic location. "Germans are generally well-liked," the FBI noted; "they came to the territory and worked hard, proved to be progressive colonists and honest businessmen . . . they lived moderately and unpretentiously, learned the language and married into the local families."[92] By the time the war began in Europe in 1939, Washington rated Colombia "of the first importance" to US security and so launched a diplomatic campaign to secure the country's cooperation.[93] Liberal president Eduardo Santos was thus caught between contradictory expectations; those of Washington, the Conservative opposition that considered the United States a more dangerous threat than Germany, and his own personal, antimilitarist beliefs. Conciliatory by nature, Santos determined that the country's "essential interest" was to support "American solidarity," since any interruption in intercontinental relations would be a blow to Colombia's economy and living standards.[94] Courted by the US government, the president approved a series of joint military missions beginning in January 1939, and then tasked the Colombian diplomatic service with promoting solidarity among the neighboring governments.[95] While Santos concentrated his efforts on high-level politics, US diplomats took care of an array of activities that wartime counterespionage entailed, but that also constituted a "state-building exercise" that ultimately laid the foundations for renewed US-Colombian relations in the postwar era.[96]

The battle for the Guajira, Colombia's most important corner in the delicate Caribbean theater of the war, evolved out of this tension between national sovereignty and continental solidarity. Leading the mission was Spruille Braden, the first US ambassador to Colombia, appointed in April 1937.[97] After handling his most urgent mission, the annihilation of the oldest airline in South America, SCADTA (the Colombian-German Air Transport Company), Braden moved on to his next task, monitoring the country's coasts facing the Panama Canal, where the US Department of State ordered him to open two vice-consulates: one in Riohacha, on the Caribbean, and the other in Buenaventura, on the Pacific.[98] From late 1940 to mid-1943, three US vice-consuls, under Braden's orders, waged commercial warfare against the *criollo* smugglers that supplied Nazi Germany with divi-divi and hides.

The first of them, Terry Sanders Jr., arrived in Riohacha on November 27, 1940, a town he found bursting with "anti–United States sentiments," and whose small elite posed insurmountable obstacles to his mission of opening an office and gathering intelligence on the smugglers trading with the Germans. He established residence in Barranquilla but traveled regularly to Riohacha.[99] After a few months' work, Sanders concluded that smugglers' sympathy for Germany was instrumental. The proof was that, "as far as domestic politics are concerned," they are "very strong for Dr. Alfonso López [Pumarejo]," which "may seem paradoxical" but was not. "As long as Germany on the one hand is their best customer and the Liberal Party on the other hand is willing to build them roads and piers," he observed, this support would continue.[100] A year later, on November 24, 1941, the second vice-consul, Lewis E. Leonard, arrived to replace Sanders and finally open an office in town. Twelve days of work were enough for him to grasp the basics of a "community of crooks," as he described this society of smugglers working in groups of friends and relatives and passionately competing against one another.[101] "The maneuvers that some of these Local Merchants go thru to try to convince me that all their competitors are bums keeps me in a good supply of humor," Leonard reported.[102] And, in late April 1942, the third and last vice-consul, Chadwick Braggiotti, arrived to find that the Proclaimed List—a mechanism to block people suspected of Nazi connections from doing business in the United States or with US companies—had turned into a weapon for settling disputes that had nothing to do with Washington's interests.[103] Additionally, Braggiotti became the liaison between the National Police Department of Investigations, the local army garrison, and US military attachés in multiple operations of surveillance of Guajira's coasts, as well as the arbiter in a series of disputes among smugglers over the valuables salvaged from the ships sunk by German U-boats, which included thousands of cans of Pabst Blue Ribbon beer, around twenty 55-gallon drums of oil, a well-equipped launch, and six moving pictures.[104] During these three years when the US government meddled directly in Riohacha's local affairs, intrigue, rumor, and jealousy proved to be more dangerous than the German submarines that operated in the Guajira's waters.[105]

With practically every smuggler blacklisted, their bank accounts frozen, and no new markets in sight, export commerce passing from Riohacha to transatlantic markets through the Dutch islands declined. The "degermanization" of the Guajira and the final defeat of Nazi Germany represented a dramatic economic downturn for Riohacha and the peninsula. Thanks to the kinship ties as well as the credit-and-debt relationships that *criollo* smugglers established with Wayuu clans, the trade in divi-divi and other native products expanded into wider networks, constituting an alternative to Maicao, where *turcos* and *cachacos* dominated. Some wealthy smugglers migrated to other parts of the Colombian coast, Venezuela, Panama, or the Dutch islands; indeed, Riohacha's population decreased from 14,450 in 1938 to 13,058 by 1951. People joked about "com[ing] to Riohacha before it is over."[106] The commercial warfare that US diplomats waged against *criollo* smugglers deepened a paradox that resulted from the clash of two different historical processes: long-term consolidation of the Guajira as a corner of the Atlantic trading system, and the region's short-term integration into the Colombian nation-state as an international border region. As a consequence of World War II and severance of the Guajira's ties with European markets crossing the Caribbean Sea, economic life in the peninsula became more dependent on the Andean-centered Colombia, its bipartisan system, its coffee economy, and its principal ally and market, the United States.

COTTON AND MODERNIZATION

Like the rest of the Greater Magdalena, Valledupar and its area of influence experienced the first half of the twentieth century as a clash of historical currents. Since colonial times, life in the great valley had revolved around cattle ranching. Neither the War of a Thousand Days (1899–1902) nor the Liberal Republic (1930–45) resolved the problems of infrastructure, technology, and labor that made cattle ranching the safest economic activity and the most secure path to political prominence and social status. World War II and La Violencia, two conflicts that unfolded sequentially in the 1940s and 1950s, had the effect of solving these problems while creating others.

The generation whose coming of age coincided with the two wars defined the direction of such change. Raised under the Liberal Republic, they were the first cohort of cattle ranchers to attend public school after López Pumarejo secularized education in a Liberal effort to use cultural politics to "generate the sense of a united, horizontal nation while at the same time legitimating their [Liberals'] position as this nation's rightful leaders."[107] Unlike their grandfathers and fathers, who had been sent to prestigious educational institutions in the Andean interior or abroad, this generation was educated in the *provincia*—as Valledupar's area of influence along the great valley was popularly known—sharing their daily lives with the children of the peasantry.[108] Pepe Castro Castro, nephew and grandson of governor Pedro Castro Monsalvo, told me during an interview on the patio of his house in Valledupar's central square that public school was "a horrible situation." He remembered "twenty-year-old kids sharing the classroom with five-year-old kids like me, and there was no hygiene—the bathroom was outdoors."[109] In addition to unhealthy facilities, students faced severe discipline that included corporal punishment.[110] Yet, although public education did not meet the standards of private Catholic institutions, and many children of ranchers attended only for short periods, the bitter experience led to an important realization. In classrooms filled with *"cimarrones"*—as Castro Castro called his peasant classmates, using a term that refers to both runaway slaves and people from the mountains—ranchers' children discovered that they were "exactly like them [*cimarrones*]."[111] This epiphany shaped their political imagination, preparing them for the opportunity that the national government in Bogotá, working in association with the US federal government and multilateral institutions, offered for agrarian modernization beginning in 1948.

Indeed, there was a lived experience that supported their *campesino* class consciousness. No matter how much land or cattle they owned or how well connected they were, ranchers also led rustic lives. Take Pepe Castro Castro, for example. A midwife assisted his birth at home in the 1920s.[112] After surviving the many sicknesses that afflicted him in infancy, he grew up to live in three different residences: a house in Valledupar, a ranch in the lowlands of the great valley, and in relatives' or friends' country houses in the intermontane valleys of the Sierra Nevada and Perijá. Like open-range herds and transhumant cowboys, ranchers and their families made vertical and cyclical use of the territory in order to avoid floods and droughts, and the many pests and epidemics that went along with them, such as malaria, anemia, parasites, and vitiligo.[113] They also moved up and down to renew their moral-economic pact with local residents, including indigenous peoples. Like peasants in the countryside, rancher families in municipal and county seats, including children, were drowning in chores such as milking cows, splitting wood, and carrying water from the rivers. They also lived surrounded by cows, pigs, chickens, and dogs; and they ate meals rich in proteins and starches prepared on wood stoves, such as fresh cheese with grilled plantains, rib stew with yucca and malanga, and milk curd and biscuits. They ate only fresh fruits and nuts when the indigenous Arhuaco people brought them from the Sierra Nevada. They either walked barefoot or wore *guaireñas* (sandals) made by indigenous people; wearing shoes was a luxury reserved for First Communion.[114] In the evening, after playing games with neighbors and relatives, they had dinner and accompanied adults to their *tertulias*—gatherings under a tree, on a patio, or on a sidewalk where they gossiped, "speculated about politics" and "naturally criticized left and right."[115] And at about nine o'clock, they hung their hammocks in rooms they shared with siblings, without distinction between sexes, and went to sleep.[116]

The mid-twentieth-century confluence of a national conflict and an international war broke this rural world apart. World War II did not affect

Valledupar and the *provincia* in the same way that it disrupted Riohacha and the Guajira, or Santa Marta and the banana district. The only disturbance involved a community of Germans living in the village of Pueblo Bello, in the highlands of the Sierra Nevada among the Arhuaco people. The Germans negotiated a deal with the national government in Bogotá whereby they could stay in town instead of migrating to the concentration camps that the Santos administration had constructed in the Andean interior.[117] In Bogotá, however, World War II upset the stability of the Liberal Republic. In 1942 Alfonso López Pumarejo was inaugurated president for a second term. A pugnacious Conservative party under the leadership of Laureano Gómez stoked the political fires. The owner and editor of *El Siglo,* Gómez used the newspaper's pages to accuse López Pumarejo, his brother, and his two sons of mishandling sequestered German assets. The corruption scandal boiled over in July 1945 when López Pumarejo resigned.[118] A year later, a divided Liberal party lost the presidential elections to Mariano Ospina Pérez, a Catholic Conservative born and raised in Medellín to a wealthy family of coffee exporters, who planned to recover his party's base in the coffee region.[119]

A new conflict between Liberals and Conservatives gathered momentum in the Andean interior after World War II, while a stagnant global economy paved the way for an economic crisis. Inflation worsened, and an extraordinary increase in the price of inputs and technology encouraged a flood of cheap imported goods.[120] The textile sector was particularly affected. Cotton production had always suffered serious deficiencies because of an insufficient labor force and inefficient pest control.[121] Since national cotton production lagged behind industrial demands, the country depended on imports.[122] Concentrated in Medellín—and to a lesser extent in Barranquilla—the textile bourgeoisie organized to demand the government's protection.[123] But their pleas were not met by Ospina Pérez, who believed that the monotony of working in factories would atrophy Colombians' initiative and intelligence.[124] However, as mounting violence between Liberals and Conservatives in the coffee region affected the national economy—violence that Ospina Pérez personally promoted—the president became more susceptible to lobbying by textile industrialists and their allies in the United States and multilateral organizations.[125] In 1948, while the country sank into an undeclared civil war following the assassination of presidential candidate and leftist Liberal leader Jorge Eliécer Gaitán, Ospina Pérez closed ranks with the industrial bourgeoisie and appointed Liberal Pedro Castro Monsalvo as minister of agriculture and cattle ranching.

Since his tenure as governor of the Greater Magdalena during the Liberal Republic, Castro Monsalvo had proved to be an efficient modernizer.[126] He was an "admirable speaker, measured, with ideas well defined and thought out," and had a charismatic personality.[127] He was appointed prefect of Valledupar province at the age of twenty-one; at twenty-four, defeated the traditional Liberal bosses in the elections to the departmental assembly; became manager of the Agrarian Bank in Valledupar at twenty-six; was appointed governor at thirty; and was elected House representative in Bogotá at thirty-one.[128] By the time he became minister at the age of forty-three, he was an expert in translating the abstract principle of progress into specific projects.

Although Castro Monsalvo resigned in 1949 along with five other Liberal ministers in protest against Ospina Pérez's aggressive strategy against their party, he produced a coherent set of policies to promote the formation of a cotton economy in his native land during the year he held the post.[129] He overhauled the coupling of private and public interests by turning the Institute for the Development of Cotton (IFA)—a private organization controlled by Medellín's textile entrepreneurs—into a public organization managed by Bogotá. He entrusted IFA with the responsibilities of conducting scientific research, as well as financing and managing the infrastructure for cleaning, processing, and classifying the fiber.[130] He changed IFA's by-laws to include cotton growers on the board of directors and created new exchange mechanisms for technical assistance between the IFA and the US Department of Agriculture. He authored and defended new legislation in the Colombian Congress that forced industrialists to buy Colombian-grown cotton and imposed customs duties on imported fibers, to the point they were effectively prohibited beginning in 1952.[131] In sum, saying that Pedro Castro Monsalvo championed state protectionism is an understatement. He enabled ranchers to transition to cotton, paving the way for the rise of this section of the Greater Magdalena as one of Colombia's bastions of commercial agriculture geared to import-substitution industrialization, an economic policy that advocated replacing foreign imports with domestic production in order to reduce countries' dependency on external forces.[132]

With the institutional and legislative framework that Castro Monsalvo helped set up, the generation educated under the Liberal Republic stepped into the political scene and, in the process, articulated a novel political discourse of modernization based on their collective identity as *campesinos*. They seized and created new opportunities for themselves on two interconnected fronts. On one hand, a small but influential batch of agronomists and engineers who had been trained in universities of the Andean interior and abroad (like Castro Monsalvo himself); and on the other, a larger group of young cattle ranchers who had not attended college but managed their families' interests. Agronomists and engineers clustered around José Vicente Lafaurie Acosta, the son of a rancher who worked for years conducting studies of soils and irrigation systems for an engineering firm in the United States, until he discovered that the temperature range, humidity, evaporation, sunlight, and rainfall in the town of Codazzi, where his family pastured herds, were ideal for cultivating cotton.[133] At the same time that Castro Monsalvo was leading the design of the cotton sector, Lafaurie Acosta was closing his office in Bogotá and buying lands in Codazzi. Appropriately called El Porvenir (The Future), Lafaurie Acosta's farm became the first site of commercial cotton production in the great valley, and its success soon attracted other agronomists and engineers.[134] Their prosperity enticed some of their relatives and friends to consider entering the cotton business. For example, Jorge Dangond Daza, grandson of the Frenchman who introduced coffee cultivation in the Perijá in the mid-nineteenth century, joined forces with a cousin and bought Convención, a small farm of twenty hectares. Just three years later, they owned two hundred hectares of cotton fields.[135] Because cotton was "more lucrative than coffee, and definitely better paid, than cattle ranching," Dangond Daza explained, a few harvests convinced other ranchers to take a chance and buy lands from peasants, some of whom are said to have died of sadness once they realized their mistake.[136]

Both young professionals and ranchers dreamed of shedding the colonial legacies that characterized the society in which they had grown up. According to Dangond Daza, they were a "brotherhood of dreamers ... that, with a bulldozer, scraped off the feudal scab of the old Valle de Upar [great valley], and turned its four centuries of oblivion into flourishing expectations, thanks to cotton."[137] However, as they gradually expanded into public or collectively owned lands, they pushed small farmers out of the most suitable areas and inadvertently reproduced the socioeconomic inequalities that characterized the "hierarchical, convent-like [society that] ... divided our towns into two classes: common people, that is, peasant workers, and upper-class people, fewer in number but dominant based on their status as owners of landholdings and cattle."[138]

Like many local elites in Colombia, cattle ranchers–cum–cotton growers vacillated between radical aspirations, reformist plans, and conservative values, unable and unwilling to shake off the Catholic "anti-modern spirit" that characterized political culture in many regions of the country.[139] Cotton growers' temporary success is partly explained by their being in sync with the paradoxical interests of the United States. While Washington sought to guide underdeveloped nations toward economic growth and democratization, it also feared losing them to either nationalism or communism.[140] US postwar modernization efforts thus had two, contradictory features: promoting industrialization as a solution to ending poverty and preventing revolution in the Third World; and creating obstacles for Latin America's industrial development because it would purportedly undermine US economic hegemony in the Western Hemisphere. As a result, US cooperation ended up fostering the growth of the primary sector—raw material production and agriculture—at the expense of the secondary sector—industry.[141] Ranchers-cum-growers benefited from these layers of conflicting interests and intentions.

Once again, the ongoing conflict in the Andean interior defined cotton growers' destinies. The war brought to power the military government of General Gustavo Rojas Pinilla (1953–57), with the acquiesce of certain Liberal and Conservative factions. As a military dictatorship, the new government took seriously the lesson the military class had learned in World War II: that the Guajira peninsula was a borderland where the national state exercised little sovereignty. Added to the fact that the family of Rojas Pinilla owned lands near Riohacha, this perspective prompted the dictatorship to focus on the Guajira.[142] With Decree 1824 of June 13, 1954, Rojas Pinilla severed the Greater Magdalena by separating Riohacha and the peninsula and creating the Intendencia de la Guajira, a new administrative unit under the national government's control. This new entity, with its capital in Riohacha, merged the Comisaría de la Guajira, the indigenous territory of the upper peninsula, and the Provincia Padilla, the southern part near Riohacha and one of the three sections of the Greater Magdalena.[143] Local elites rejected the decision because "the voice of many sons of those municipalities was silenced when we pointed out the disgraceful violation that dismembering us from the Department [of Magdalena] was."[144] The loss of Villanueva, San Juan del Cesar, Barrancas, and other towns "from the heart of the *provincia* to make them part of the Guajira" was felt as an "unjustified political recourse."[145] The mayor of San Juan del Cesar during Rojas Pinilla administration, Yim Daza Noguera, told me in an interview conducted on the sidewalk by his house that he did not like the Intendencia at the beginning; "but later I changed my mind as I noticed the transformations in the budgetary allocations, [and] the economic aspect improved for the people."[146]

FIGURE 2. Seasonal workers arriving for the cotton harvest, January 20, 1970. *El Espectador* photographic archive, Bogotá.

The creation of the Intendencia de la Guajira marked a pivotal point in the formation of the cotton belt, as it defined its geographical expansion. From 1948 to 1954, ranchers-cum–cotton growers expanded north from the initial epicenter in Codazzi into cultivated lands and pastures, thanks to the access to unsecured credit and subsidized prices that the national government, US agencies, and multilateral institutions offered them.[147] During this period, because of the high cost of machinery, growers relied on manual labor and hired local peasants—many of whom were the former owners of the lands they now worked—or seasonal labor from the Andean interior to clear land and plant between July and September and harvest from November to March.[148] And, after the creation of the Intendencia—from 1955 to the mid-1970s, with a peak in tons produced in 1964—cotton growers moved southward onto uncultivated lands and forests, from Codazzi to Aguachica.[149] During this second period, new bureaucracies created by the Colombian Ministry of Agriculture and the US Agency for International Development assisted the local IFA branch in implementing the recommendations of the International Bank for Reconstruction and Development, which in a 1957 mission report to Colombia advised the government to finance the spread of cotton fields onto "lands that are not used currently" in the Cesar River valley.[150] Under Green Revolution precepts, growers mechanized fields, introduced pesticides and fertilizers, and took advantage of the liberalization of credit to open the agricultural frontier. By 1958 the great valley contributed 60 percent of the cotton harvested on the Caribbean coast, at a time when the country's Caribbean region was the number-one producer. Colombia was a cotton exporter by 1959.[151]

Adoption of the Green Revolution made this section of the Greater Magdalena a workshop for a new understanding of development. Premising this novel paradigm was the idea that the path to industrialization passed through a phase of commercially and scientifically based agriculture, as in the United States in the late nineteenth and early twentieth centuries, because it would not require a large labor force and therefore was more compatible with an urban-based manufacturing economy.[152] Ultimately, however, the Green Revolution in the cotton belt not only damaged the environment but also contributed to land concentration and reactivated the "feudal scab" that young innovators such as Dangond Daza wanted to shed. Catherine LeGrand rightly questions the old argument about Colombian elites as irrational economic actors and demonstrates that land concentration was not the by-product of a feudal mentality but the solution to labor scarcity, environmental factors, and inflationary cycles.[153] Building on LeGrand's insightful observation, I argue that the new cotton sector did not offer clear alternatives to industrialization but rather abundant credit to large growers, whose surpluses were then not properly channeled to new markets or transformed into value-added chains. Land concentration and the reactivation of the cattle economy were thus the results of an overflow of cash going to people who were accustomed to living in a precarious economy and who were not properly trained in long-term agricultural planning, investment, and diversification.[154]

Because mechanization and reliance on chemical fertilizers and pesticides were prerequisites for access to loans, banks granted financial credit only to those who could afford these technologies. This policy favored growers who owned large fields. Jorge Dangond Daza remembered that "one had money all the time," as growers' accounts received regular infusions throughout the year.[155] His capacity to use cotton profits in commerce, other agricultural enterprises, and real state was exceptional.[156] In general, the Green Revolution's financial mechanisms nourished a culture of squandering and waste. Jacobo "El Pano" Mejía, once a prosperous cotton grower from San

Juan del Cesar, explained his rationale to me while sitting outside one of his daughters' homes, where he lived as a guest. Mejía spent his fortune because of "the facility I had, I did not have to work hard to earn it; it was given to me, thus I threw it away."[157] He dressed in fine linen clothes bought in Maracaibo, Venezuela's oil cosmopolis, and traveled in his many cars throughout the region, visiting lovers with whom he had twenty children. Most cotton growers were like Mejía, "like members of the mafia, good cars, tractors, women, *parrandas* [parties], trips, lots of trips."[158] Pepe Castro Castro, remembering the cotton years, concluded, "One of the consequences that modern life has brought us is the possibility that some have to change their economic conditions rapidly." Then he added, "This can be made possible thanks to the lottery or the agricultural exploitation of our lands."[159]

By the time the cotton sector reached its production peak in 1964, the continual deforestation transformed the great valley into a large field where cotton cultivation and cattle ranching took turns from one growing season to the next, depending on market fluctuations. Herds multiplied, as cotton growers invested in cattle, liquid assets that insured them against periods of low cotton prices or failed harvests.[160] Moreover, those who had cattle "took them to the cotton fields after harvest [to eat the residue and thereby clear the plots], and the animals got fat and gave lots of milk," which saved growers money during the final phase of production.[161] This practice became customary because of its low cost; however, the residue that remained in the fields after harvest promoted growth of fungi and pests that lowered cotton yields.[162] As cotton cultivation aided the growth of herds, it also helped ranchers concentrate land and wealth in fewer and fewer hands.

Perhaps the most radical and long-lasting transformation brought about by the cotton economy took place in the political sphere. Thanks to cotton, elites in Valledupar and the great valley became central players in national politics through the process of conception and creation of the new Department of Cesar, the aim of which was to give cotton growers economic and political autonomy from Santa Marta by establishing a direct connection with Bogotá. The idea began circulating publicly for the first time on June 23, 1958, when lawyer Jaime Dangond Ovalle introduced it during his show on Radio Valledupar as the solution to "the predicament of the Colombian economy," that is, its dependency on coffee exports.[163] It took several years to forge a consensus among the different factions of the cotton elite and produce a bill to present to Congress, which Alfonso Araújo Cotes did during the 1962–63 legislative session.[164] But a fellow congressman from Santa Marta had other plans for the disintegration of the Greater Magdalena and obstructed the initiative.[165] Despite this first failed attempt, cotton growers made important changes as they seized the opportunity that the state and its international allies offered them. They forged new channels of capitalist accumulation, revitalized local power networks, envisioned themselves as autonomous political actors in national politics, and presented Valledupar and the great valley as offering a future for Colombia brighter than coffee and civil war.

AGRARIAN REFORM AND CONFLICT

When Liberals and Conservatives inaugurated the National Front in 1958—a pact between the two parties to end the military dictatorship of General Rojas Pinilla and definitively stop what came to be known as La Violencia—the banana district was entering its final stage of decline, and the cotton belt was set to boom after the adoption of the Green Revolution model. Because the National Front was anchored in two principles—namely, alternation of the two parties in the presidency and parity in the distribution of state posts between their members—it eliminated competition between Liberals and Conservatives, but stimulated factionalism and rivalry within each in a way that exacerbated local disputes. Furthermore, the architects of the pact laid its foundations on a counterinsurgent ideology as both parties agreed that political challenges from below would pose a threat to the fragile status quo. Making Colombia a wall of contention against the spread of revolutionary movements was paramount. The National Front's first president, Liberal Alberto Lleras Camargo (1958–62), toured the continent to gather support for expelling Cuba from the Organization of American States (which he had served as its first secretary general) and then began turning Colombia into a showcase of modernization and anticommunism.[166] He believed that an agrarian reform law to redistribute fertile lands to the destitute rural classes was the most effective way to prevent a social revolution and another conflict. The president's cousin, Carlos Lleras Restrepo, masterminded the bill and became its champion in Congress. In the Greater Magdalena, this congruity of a counterinsurgent mindset with modernizing ideals worsened the socioeconomic and political dislocations created by the three moments previously analyzed, during which region and nation were mutually constituted through integration with world markets.

In many regions of the country, large growers of agricultural commodities were among the most determined enemies of land redistribution. In the

Cauca Valley's sugar belt, for example, landowners resisted the reform while using it to displace peasants and expand agribusiness.[167] In the Greater Magdalena, landed elites in the banana and cotton sectors also rejected the reform, fearing the loss of the state patronage that had enabled their rise and continued existence. Cotton growers in the middle of the Green Revolution–induced bonanza showed greater resistance. When Lleras Restrepo toured the Greater Magdalena in 1961 to meet local leaders and build support, banana and cotton growers affiliated with both parties put their differences aside and orchestrated a concerted response through the Santa Marta and Valledupar city councils and the departmental assembly. They called Lleras Restrepo's presence in the region a "provocation," accused him of "disorienting public opinion and exciting the people," and even declared him dead with flyers that announced his burial.[168]

Former governor and minister Pedro Castro Monsalvo voiced their collective discontent, though the initiative had been crafted by his own party.[169] As an agronomist, one of the architects of the cotton belt, and a cotton producer himself, congressman Castro Monsalvo spoke with great authority about the agrarian reform bill, which he considered a demagogic piece of legislation full of technical misconceptions. Colombia was not Cuba, Castro Monsalvo reminded Congress in 1961, just two years after Fidel Castro entered Havana triumphantly and a few months before the agrarian reform bill was enacted into law. Redistribution of lands was hardly indispensable to promoting economic growth, industrial development, and expansion of consumer markets in Castro Monsalvo's view, for "large landholdings never had more than one million hectares."[170] Issuing titles of ownership to peasants would not resolve agriculture's predicament, he argued, because the real obstacle was a combination of obsolete technologies and methods on one hand and a state incapable of absorbing surpluses and creating markets on the other. Instead, he proposed limiting the reform to *baldíos* (uncultivated public lands), promoting the colonization of agricultural frontiers, respecting property rights, and helping large landowners to introduce new technologies to increase productivity.[171] In contrast to the Cuban Revolution, which was "creating dangers very difficult to resolve in the continent," Castro Monsalvo observed, the cotton growers of his native land had "made a true agrarian revolution."[172]

In other words, Castro Monsalvo envisioned extending the patterns established in the cotton belt to the rest of the country. Years later, he published his speeches in congressional debates under the title *Un campesino previno al*

FIGURE 3. Liberal congressman Pedro Castro Monsalvo and Liberal president Carlos Lleras Restrepo (1966–1970) in 1967. *El Espectador* photographic archive, Bogotá.

país (A *campesino* warned the country). Passing as a peasant himself, Castro Monsalvo called for displacing poor or landless peasants to the agricultural frontiers, reflecting a belief held by Latin American "elites concerned with retaining their position of power in traditional agrarian socioeconomic structures."[173] Yet his insistence on adopting technologies to increase productivity and on strengthening the state's capacity to absorb surpluses and create new markets typifies the scientific thought that had characterized Latin American agronomists since the early twentieth century when US agricultural science and farming practices became the norm.[174] Fearing what was happening in Cuba—and had happened in Mexico a half-century before—Castro Monsalvo sought to shield landed elites from being forced to give up all control of land tenure patterns, agricultural modes of production, and agrarian social relations, all of which worked in their favor. His congressional debates were efforts to reconcile his traditional vested interests and his modernizing vision for the future.

But not all Liberals in the Greater Magdalena feared the agrarian reform. Some dreaded what could happen if the problems the bill aimed to address were left unresolved. Francisco Dávila, for example, a longtime business partner of Pepe Vives and a banana grower himself, described to US Embassy functionaries who traveled the region in 1961 the urgent "need for social reform and for the support of a strong non-Communist left." He added: "The wealthy of the country have got to stop acting like parasites and do things for the people or they will all be hanged . . . [and] when the hanging starts it will be done too quickly to distinguish between the parasites and non-parasites."[175] Other Liberals even looked forward to revolution. José Ignacio Vives (known as Nacho), one of Pepe Vives's nephews, viewed the bill as a historical opportunity, though he considered it mediocre in its ambitions. Unlike his uncle the former governor, who pursued politics through alliance making with the landed elite and the United Fruit Company, Nacho relied on shifting coalitions involving organized sectors of the urban and rural working class. Journalist Pedro de Andreis, one of Vives's cousins and collaborators, called his style "street corner politics."[176] Like other radical Liberals of his generation, Vives relied on his academic training to translate radical theories into a language for the masses, using metaphors, poetry, and popular lyrics to bring crowds in plazas, fields, and slums to ecstasy.[177] "Stillness was never his style," one of Vives's sons wrote in an obituary, "because he thought that turbulence was equivalent to force and opportunity in the face of [the challenges of] life."[178] In seizing opportunities in turbulent times, Vives fought for the approval of the agrarian reform bill alongside unions, cooperatives, and other organizations of the people.

In the end, these rifts among elites were indicative of the ideological breaches over the prospect of land redistribution that divided regional society at a time when modernization became the "language of contention."[179] Banana elites tried to survive the gradual withdrawal of the United Fruit Company by appropriating the irrigated lands that the company turned back to the national government over the years in preparation for its termination in 1965. They also returned to cattle ranching, since livestock was the safest investment in uncertain times.[180] These strategies produced clashes with peasants and settlers. For example, in Pueblo Viejo, in the heart of the banana district, peasants denounced the army for killing four members of their union—allegedly on the governor's orders—with the goal of "favoring the ambitions of *latifundista* Ana R. de Dávila Limitada."[181] In Sitionuevo, on the Ciénaga Grande (the large swamp extending south to Santa Marta), the police "obeying orders from landowners Renaldo Donado and Julio Ferrer, shot humble peasants that [had] been working peacefully on the island [of] Pennsylvania owned by the Nation."[182] In Taganga, a fishing village located in one of the inlets of Santa Marta Bay, the leaders of the indigenous reserve denounced invasions of plots along the beach by nonindigenous people.[183]

In the meantime, popular organizations occupied unproductive farms and irrigated lands formerly belonging to the United Fruit Company with the hope of resisting elite encroachment and procuring titles under the new agrarian reform law. Frequently supported by professional organizers and agitators, families of banana day laborers invaded haciendas that had shifted from bananas to cattle, where the common experience of having worked for the United Fruit Company made the collaboration of estate employees more likely.[184] The police arrested a group of twenty-six peasants in February 1960 near Ciénaga on charges of vandalism. Union leaders explained that "many times men commit crimes harrased by the hunger of their kids."[185] In Pivijay, the Riascos Vives family destroyed the huts and crops of around thirty settler families. In response to the state crackdown, the peasant union requested a special commission from Bogotá to examine land titles and denounce police complicity.[186]

In the cotton belt, unions and cooperatives were either absent or weak compared to the better-organized banana district, where collective action had an established history dating back to the 1920s. Invasions of estates were therefore less frequent because unproductive lands were fewer and far apart, and cotton growers acted as a more cohesive force through *combos,* shock troops sent out to defend property rights, undermining popular groups' capacity to articulate their resistance; hence, settlers' direct action usually took the form of crimes against property and vandalism.[187] In San Roque, a hamlet south of Valledupar, the chief of police affirmed that he "lived under the threat" of a family of cattle rustlers well known in the area for "attack[ing] cattle ranchers in this region."[188] In the villages of Manaure and San Diego in the highlands near Valledupar, authorities informed Bogotá of "bloody cases among numerous communities of families from [the Andean department of] Santander," and, without explaining what they meant, requested an immediate army response.[189] In La Jagua de Ibirico, authorities reported that cattle ranchers feared rustlers, who practically controlled the area.[190] Even in isolated areas of the agricultural frontier, settlers and indigenous communities fought each other for land and resources. In Carua, indigenous people complained of "abuses civilized people committed, destroying crops and killing cattle," and invoked their poverty and ignorance to mobilize sympathy for their cause.[191]

Elites appropriated anticommunist rhetoric as their most effective tool in portraying themselves as victims in order to get the state's attention. The mayor of Valledupar, Alfredo Araújo Noguera, for example, reported "alarming cases of cattle rustling and new invasions of farms led by notorious unions whose communist extraction is known by the Governor."[192] In Río de Oro, also in Valledupar's area of influence, the owners of a farm informed the minister of government in Bogotá about the "frequent and reckless invasions provoked by people interested in artificially creating material possessions of plots that belong to our farm," and complained that there was "no police protection for property," a lapse the owners considered "absurd and unconstitutional."[193] In San Sebastián—known as Nabusímake among the indigenous Arhuacos— located in one of the highest valleys of the Sierra Nevada facing Valledupar, the chief of the Liberal directorate denounced two men who had been "stirring up working people with authentically communist slogans, inciting them to vandalism and invasion of lands that belong to honest citizens."[194] Arhuaco students of the Capuchins' boarding school also deployed the "red scare" device against other indigenous people. They denounced Arhuaco leaders who were fighting against landowners as "communist agitators" who sought to take away their religion and deceive them with slogans.[195]

Thanks to the interconnections among these many conflicts, Nacho Vives rose to prominence. A fixture in Santa Marta's belts of misery, Vives began to climb the ladder of the regional structure of the Movimiento Revolucionario Liberal (MRL), the Liberal party's radical wing.[196] The MRL was led by Alfonso López Michelsen, one of former president Alfonso López Pumarejo's sons, and opposed the National Front's principles of presidency alternation and parity in the distribution of state posts between the two parties on the grounds that they betrayed "the trust of the people."[197] Although Colombian and US intelligence services were sure that the MRL was infiltrated by Cuban communists—and the MRL did recognize Cuba's right to self-determination—the movement "did not go after the same goal as communism" but rather called for a "left-Liberal revolution" that was essentially reformist.[198] As a member of the MRL, Nacho Vives created his own clique in order to win elections to several municipal councils and become a powerful political *cacique*.[199] Then, in 1960, he ran for Congress as the MRL representative from the Intendencia de la Guajira, and defeated the Liberal patriarchs, including his own uncle Pepe Vives and Pedro Castro Monsalvo.[200] He found that the time for a generational replacement had arrived. But his contemporaries in Valledupar aspired to cash in their cotton surpluses and profits in order to establish a direct connection with Bogotá, separating Valledupar and the cotton belt from Santa Marta and creating the new department of Cesar. Vives joined others who opposed the bill because it did not meet all constitutional requirements, and together they defeated it.[201] He then began to work toward his alternative vision, namely, to promote the Intendencia de la Guajira to the status of a department.[202]

The Guajira was in more urgent need to become a department, Vives argued. The peninsula's reserves of coal and natural gas held the potential to fuel the country's industrialization, but only if the Guajira substituted "the activity of contraband for another more important [one]" under a development plan designed by the state and carried out by the local professional class. The problem was that Guajira's "capable and suitable ruling class or elites," who were "people with an old cultural tradition and nobility [*señorío*], of great wealth, a group of humans with an inexhaustible capacity for work," found no opportunities in their "*patria chica*" [the region], and "[had] undertaken the exodus to other geographies."[203] The creation of the Department of Guajira would stop this brain drain and implement an ambitious plan of economic development. Vives also warned Congress about powerful Venezuela and its petro dollars, a country with which Colombia had an unresolved conflict over the peninsula's coastal waters.[204] Only departmental status, Vives insisted, would provide the Guajira with the instruments necessary to carry out all these needed reforms.

After two years of debate, Congress issued Law 19 of 1964, which created the Department of Guajira, with Riohacha as its capital. Appointed its first governor, Nacho Vives structured the new department during the few months he occupied the post—from July 1 to September 10, 1965, when he resigned to run in the next legislative elections. His personal assistant, Meña Melo, remembered with admiration that Nacho Vives would arrive at his office at 5 A.M. to work at his typewriter until 9 A.M., drafting the decrees and resolutions to create the departmental assembly, tribunals, courts, taxes, customs, and utilities offices.[205] Then, at 10, he would open the doors of his office and receive "all the people who wanted to talk to him."[206] When he resigned, Vives was no longer Santa Marta's black sheep; he was the Department of Guajira's forefather.

Meanwhile, cotton growers planned their comeback. Determined "to manage by ourselves that powerful economy, get a share of the highest governmental posts, administer the agrarian credit policy, in sum, fully incorporate us into the national life," cotton growers appointed Alfonso López Michelsen—Nacho Vives's boss in the MRL and López Pumarejo's son—as "Cesar's *ad honorem* attorney in Bogotá."[207] A cotton grower himself, López Michelsen viewed the Department of Cesar as having great potential for his own career and for the nation, and secured the sympathy of important national politicians, including recently elected Liberal president Carlos Lleras Restrepo (1966–70) and his most influential minister, Darío Echandía, who pledged to "give birth to this bill in a natural manner, or in C-section."[208] Approved on June 21, 1967, the process of creating the Department of Cesar glued back together a fractured Liberal party and enabled it to attenuate the model of development put forward by the agrarian reform law (which some of them had fought so fiercely for in 1961) and to protect its class interests. Six months later, on December 21, 1967, thousands of people gathered in Valledupar's Plaza Mayor (renamed Plaza Alfonso López, in honor of both father and son) to witness the reconciliation between official Liberalism and its self-styled "revolutionary" faction.[209] Despite the absence of the powerful leader Pedro Castro Monsalvo—whose tragic death in a car crash on March 3, 1967, shook the region—the crowd gathered to celebrate the new Department of Cesar, welcomed President Lleras Restrepo and his cabinet, and attended the inauguration of the department's first governor, Alfonso López Michelsen.[210] To paraphrase the title of the book by Dangond Ovalle, one of the initiative's architects, "Cesar was a love child" of the political affair between the competing factions that constituted the Liberal party during the National Front; that is, it was a product of a new elite pact among Liberals in pursuit of agrarian modernization less radical than initially intended.

Although Nacho Vives supported the bill creating the Department of Cesar, in time he became the only Liberal calling attention to the problematic abandonment of democratization's promises for the destitute masses. Dubbed by the press as the *Vives v. Fadul & Peñaloza* case, the congressional debate that brought this issue to public notice began on July 20, 1969, the first day of the legislative year, when Vives, as the first senator elected from the Department of Guajira, summoned President Lleras Restrepo's minister of agriculture, Enrique Peñaloza, to respond to corruption charges against Fadul & Peñaloza, a law firm that the latter-named partner had established with the director of the Institute of Industrial Promotion, Miguel Fadul. Vives accused the two men of using the National Institute of Agrarian Reform (Incora) in a scheme to illegally expropriate lands that belonged to dozens of peasant families in Tamalameque, one of Vives's strongholds in the Department of Magdalena.[211] For two months, Vives fought against his own party since most Liberals supported the Lleras Restrepo administration, including his own boss in the MRL, López Michelsen, who was now in the president's shadow. Alone in this new battle, Vives suddenly became the topic

FIGURE 4. Supporters of Nacho Vives at a protest in Plaza de Bolívar, Bogotá, December 18, 1969, after Vives's arrest. *El Espectador* photographic archive, Bogotá.

of debate when he was accused of bribery. On September 11, 1969, Congress voted to take away his parliamentary immunity, and his arrest the next day was a public spectacle.[212] For the following three months, the imprisoned Vives released "revolutionary pronouncements" that his supporters broadcast on national radio, putting forward the idea that this was a clash between elitist politicians and technocrats and "a humble man from the provinces," a contrived humility that won him the sympathy of the student movement and labor unions but alienated him from Bogotá's political circles.[213] When Vives was finally released in December and all charges were dropped, the corruption behind the agrarian reform was revealed and the Liberal party was discredited.

Once again, the Greater Magdalena was a critical site where all that hindered the future of Colombia's development came to the surface. The fact that the government of Lleras Restrepo, the man who masterminded the agrarian reform law, was also responsible for protecting the corruption that infested its implementation brought disgrace to the Liberal party and contributed to the counteroffensive that Conservatives mounted against land redistribution in the following years, during their turn in the presidency.[214] The Vives scandal, which began with denunciations from a group of peasants in a small town in the fractured Greater Magdalena, proved to the public that the two cornerstones of the National Front's modernization—agrarian reform and industrial promotion—were instruments of land and wealth concentration, a realization that damaged the credibility of state-sponsored solutions to the problem of development.

In more than one sense, the Greater Magdalena differed little from other places in Latin America where production and exportation of tropical commodities integrated regions into the nation via links to global markets.[215] The three periods during which region and nation mutually defined each other in dialogue and conflict with international interests—the banana, divi-divi, and cotton booms—did not resolve old problems of land, labor, infrastructure, or markets. The National Front's modernizing reforms, though intended to address those problems, only accentuated them, which benefited elites, marginalized popular sectors, underpinned land and wealth concentration, and intensified dependency on the United States. It was not a coincidence that during the National Front's first decade the Greater Magdalena became a pressure cooker, and finally did explode and disintegrate.

While the banana and cotton economies underwent drastic transitions and their capacity to employ workers shrank, popular classes comprising settlers from the Andean region and other parts of the coast, local peasants, seasonal workers, and proletariats were relegated to the agricultural frontiers and urban peripheries. Living in the social, political, and geographic margins, they refused to give up on the promises of upward mobility, urbanization, capital accumulation, and cultural representation that the discourse of modernization brought to the fore. Relying on long, unguarded coasts punctuated by many bays and natural ports, and on well-established traditions of contraband, these diverse popular classes mobilized in pursuit of their own interests. The most audacious of them joined forces with factions of the local elites also affected by the sea changes, and with intrepid US buyers to make the Santa Marta Bay area and the ports near Riohacha the epicenters of a novel business—smuggling coffee and marijuana. Following the example of banana producers, divi-divi merchants, and cotton growers, the emergent class of coffee and marijuana smugglers made the most of the socioeconomic chaos that characterized the late 1960s in the fracturing Greater Magdalena, and constituted themselves as the newest elite of agrarian entrepreneurs, albeit temporarily. The cultivation, commercialization, and exportation of both coffee and, subsequently, marijuana offered a provisional solution to myriad conflicts and brought a long-term process of agrarian modernization to a problematic and temporary close.

Coming from the Mountain

COFFEE CONTRABAND AND MARIJUANA SMUGGLING

I come from the mountain, / from there, the cordillera, / where I
left my *compañera* / along with my two little children.

MÁXIMO MÓVIL,
vallenato composer

ON THE INAUGURATION DAY OF LIBERAL president Carlos Lleras
Restrepo, August 7, 1966, an adolescent boy who was nicknamed Chemón
gunned down the legendary José Durán. As Durán stood at the door of a
pharmacy in San Juan del Cesar drinking a soda, Chemón came in to fill a
prescription. While the pharmacist prepared the order, the boy shot the man
who had excelled at using motorized vehicles in the contraband business.
Born and raised in Caracolí, a hamlet in the southeastern watershed of the
Sierra Nevada, in the municipality of San Juan del Cesar, José Durán reached
the height of his career during the decade prior to his murder, when new policies for exporting coffee created the ideal conditions for smuggling the bean.
Durán took advantage of infrastructure projects that national governments
financed to innovate by using trucks and establishing strategic alliances with
powerful men in the region and the Andean interior. In doing so, he consolidated his prominence as one of the most feared and admired *contrabandistas*
(smugglers) in a land where many could be found. Although his murder was
a private affair, since the motivation for the crime was intertwined with a
family vendetta, his death had social consequences.[1] It marked the arrival of
a new breed of smugglers who built upon practices established by Durán and
his cohort to pursue new business opportunities in marijuana.

In this chapter, I weave together the stories of these two generations to
demonstrate how coffee contraband paved the way for the marijuana business. I argue that smuggling coffee out of the country and through the
Guajira allowed *contrabandistas* to develop novel procedures and cultural

Legend:
- 🍌 Banana
- ☕ Coffee
- Divi-divi
- ⚘ Cotton
- 🐂 Cattle/dairy
- 🐐 Goats

CARIBBEAN SEA

Bahía Honda
Puerto Estrella
Puerto López
Bahía Portete
Manaure
Uribia
Riohacha
Rancheria
Maicao
GULF OF VENEZUELA
Santa Marta
Buritaca
Ciénaga
Palomino
Ancho
Barrancas
Frio
Sierra Nevada de Santa Marta
San Juan del Cesar
Maracaibo
Villanueva
Aracataca
Aracataca
Ciénaga Grande
Fundación
Fundación
Valledupar
Guatapuri
Codazzi
Cesar
Serranía del Perijá
LAKE MARACAIBO
VENEZUELA
Magdalena
Aguachica

0 10 20 30 40 50 mi
0 20 40 60 80 km

MAP 3. Tropical Commodities. Map by Bill Nelson.

codes to complete the vertical integration of this section of the Greater Magdalena, from highlands to lowlands, as well as the horizontal integration to the Andean interior and US markets. After years of smuggling coffee exclusively, *contrabandistas* began to include small quantities of marijuana in their coffee cargos. This activity was a response to the rise of marijuana smoking as part of countercultural movements in the United States that engaged in fierce battles over state power and imperialism, patriarchal and racial hierarchies, gender roles and mass-media representations. But unlike marijuana consumers in the United States, and their contemporaries in many places in Latin America, these suppliers of the intoxicant who came of age in the "long sixties" widened the intergenerational gap not in the political and ideological spheres but rather in the commercial and cultural realms.[2] Expanding the notion of the "political" to include economics, identity, gender, and everyday life, this chapter offers another angle with which to view the gradual disintegration of the Greater Magdalena in the 1960s.[3] It focuses particularly on the ways in which the region's breakdown opened legal and ethical interstices in which a new generation created business opportunities that contravened the law but gained them social legitimacy. By pioneering the marijuana trade, these young men became protagonists in the making of a new and unsanctioned economic identity for which gender, and generation were as relevant as class, party affiliation, and regional origin.[4] At a time when young people took their frustrations from the private to the public sphere and celebrated counterhegemonic conceptions of the world and the self, these young smugglers refurbished older commercial traditions and cultural codes in the hope of taking advantage of the rapid urbanization of the fractured Greater Magdalena and its integration into national and international markets. This chapter tells a story of youth discovering marijuana during "the global sixties," but from a vantage point other than consumption or dissent.[5]

CACHACO MIGRATION AND COFFEE CONTRABAND

While lowlands and foothills underwent dramatic transformations as a result of tropical commodity booms, the opening of the agricultural frontiers in the Greater Magdalena's highlands intensified with the arrival of peasant families and agricultural workers from the Andean interior who were escaping the bloodiest phase of La Violencia (1946–53) and its aftermath.[6] They headed to the cotton belt and the banana district in search of seasonal jobs and land. Popularly known as *cachacos,* Andean migrants represented both an opportunity and a threat. As a labor force, they constituted a valuable resource, though more so in the rising cotton belt than in the declining banana district.[7] In contrast, as settlers, *cachacos* represented a surplus. Landed elites expanded their farms onto lowlands, foothills, and even intermontane valleys, and feared the *cachacos* as competitors for land.[8] *Cachacos* provided cheap labor during cultivation and harvest seasons, but were harassed the rest of the time by private shock troops and local and police

FIGURE 5. A *cachaco* coffee grower during the harvest, Sierra Nevada de Santa Marta, November 1967. *El Espectador* photographic archive, Bogotá.

authorities working in favor of landowners. Despite their contested arrival, *cachacos* took advantage of their numbers as well as the knowledge they brought with them to colonize the agricultural frontiers and make peasant agriculture sustainable in the highlands. In temperate valleys that were similar to their places of origin in the Andean region, *cachacos* founded new hamlets, such as Cuesta Plata, Costa Rica, Marquetalia, Las Flores, Palmarito, Soplaviento, and San Pablo.[9] In doing so, they helped consolidate the coffee belt in the Greater Magdalena. According to the first national coffee census conducted in 1932, 682 coffee farms occupied 5,510 hectares in the region; by 1955, there were 2,088 farms over an expanse of 17,356 hectares.[10]

In the Sierra Nevada and Perijá, *cachacos* reproduced the patterns of agricultural colonization that their elders had established in the *eje cafetero* (the coffee-growing region on the western and central cordilleras of the Andean interior). They penetrated to the mountain ranges through mule trails, dirt roads, and rivers in order to find the *corte* (edge), that is, the boundary between cultivated areas and virgin forests.[11] They chose their sites and established pastures by slashing and burning. Around the house they planted corn, sugar cane, malanga, yucca, and *ñame*. In fields further out, they cultivated coffee among bananas, rice, and beans. In the interior gardens they sowed medicinal herbs, decorative plants, pumpkins, and fruits.[12] They consumed most of the starch crops, as these comprised the principal component of their diet.[13] They also kept some cattle for household milk and meat consumption and to obtain petty cash in local markets. Theirs was a modest economy of subsistence built on the efforts and sacrifice of the whole family unit. As *vallenato* composer Máximo Móvil explains with impeccable rhyme and rhythm:

> I come from the mountain,
> from there, the cordillera,
> where I left my *compañera* [partner, companion]
> along with my two little kids.
> I bring my little donkey well loaded,
> sell my load and get back.
> I plan to return very early [in the morning]
> because my woman is waiting for me,
> my poor companion who with much suffering,
> sorrows, and torments,
> accompanies me in those lands.[14]

The coffee bush takes five years to yield its first harvest. When *cachacos* began to produce at full capacity, the national government changed the rules governing the bean's circulation, which contributed to an unexpected transformation of the region's economic life for the following decade. Since the end of World War II, the National Federation of Coffee Growers, known as Fedecafé, had managed the country's share of the US coffee market as stipulated in the Inter-American Coffee Agreement of 1940.[15] Fedecafé's control created tensions between the government and the industrial bourgeoisie, whose interests diverged from those of the coffee sector. Hence, while Liberal and Conservative peasants killed each other in yet another civil war (La Violencia), coffee growers and industrialists aligned with the Liberals and Conservatives, respectively, thereby deepening party divisions, and fought for the right to define the country's macroeconomic policies.[16] A new trade agreement between Bogotá and Washington, signed in April 1951 by Conservative president Laureano Gómez (1950–53) and intended to supersede López Pumarejo's treaty of 1935, resolved the quarrel. It established new coffee quotas and stable US coffee prices, among other basic domestic protections to Colombian goods.[17] But the plundering of coffee crops on abandoned farms during La Violencia kept exports at high levels, skewing the country's balance of payments.[18] Thus, the national government prohibited the exportation of coffee outside Fedecafé's sanctioned channels, contributing to a surge of coffee contraband, which in turn spawned a flood of foreign currency into Colombia, aggravating its inflation. The root problem of this vicious circle was the structure of the coffee economy—the bulk of Colombia's coffee came from small farms that exported through an interminable chain of intermediaries who controlled the means of exchange and were willing to do anything to circumvent restrictions on the circulation of the bean and profit from exporting without paying taxes.[19]

The Greater Magdalena was one of the country's two most active areas for smuggling coffee out of the country.[20] The long tradition of contraband in the Guajira peninsula, its proximity to two of the main stopovers on the way to US markets (Maracaibo and Aruba), and the consolidation of a coffee belt in the Sierra Nevada and Perijá after the arrival of the *cachacos*, all contributed to the region's importance in the new smuggling business. Heretofore, coffee had never been part of the smugglers' portfolio in the Guajira, because Fedecafé controlled the commercialization of harvests and smuggling coffee was not yet a profitable activity.[21] Export contraband of agricultural commodities was limited to products that were either native to the peninsula steppe and harvested in Wayuu territory, such as divi-divi, or raised and produced in the great valley, such as cattle and hides. The deleterious effect of the "degermanization" of the Guajira during World War II, which disrupted the networks that controlled these exchanges, left smugglers empty-handed. A decade later, coffee contraband turned out to be the opportunity they had been waiting for.

Because coffee smuggling was largely a creation of the state's restrictions and prohibitions, the repressive measures the national government took to deter an activity that the same state unwittingly fostered were destined to fail.[22] As part of a wider effort to erase the legacies of the Liberal Republic and close ranks with the United States after the ratification of the new trade agreement, Conservative president Laureano Gómez sought to repress coffee contraband by increasing surveillance of Puerto López, the main port of the Guajira, which his adversary López Pumarejo had inaugurated in 1935.[23] But the only lasting effect of Gómez's orders was a song that is now part of the country's folkloric repertoire; it tells the story of what happened the night in 1953 when the crew of the *Almirante Padilla*, a frigate that fought in Korea alongside ships of the US Navy, received the order to disembark at Puerto

López and confiscate thousands of coffee sacks.[24] The song laments the fate of Silvestre "Tite" Socarrás, great grandchild of the Frenchman who introduced coffee in the Perijá in the mid-nineteenth century, and one of the smugglers who lost everything in the raid.[25] Back in his hometown of Villanueva, Socarrás drank to his misfortune with his friend Rafael Escalona, a young composer of vallenato songs who later immortalized the event:

> There, up in the Guajira,
> where contraband is born,
> Almirante Padilla
> arrived in Puerto López
> and left it in ruins. . . .
> Bandit pirate ship,
> Saint Thomas, be my witness,
> I promise you to throw a party
> when a submarine
> sinks it in Korea.[26]

But not all smugglers had a run of bad luck like "poor Tite, poor Tite, / poor Tite Socarrás," and during the rest of the 1950s and most of the 1960s, coffee contraband was a profitable and respected commercial activity in this section of the Greater Magdalena.[27] To a young rural man like José Durán, who reached adulthood when the cattle-ranching elite ventured into cotton production and the agrarian reform sparked fierce struggles over land as well as natural and state resources, smuggling coffee provided opportunities that were lacking in agriculture. Durán thus positioned himself along with his partners as "intermediaries of various social groups that would hardly have connected without them."[28] This generation of *contrabandistas* was aided by the new restrictions on coffee circulation, imposed by the military dictatorship of General Rojas Pinilla (1953–1957) to manipulate the value of the peso and address the problems of the currency market that the previous president could not resolve.[29] Smugglers like Durán were not the only ones using the new policies to their advantage. Coffee contraband became such a popular activity during the dictatorship that even Fedecafé was accused of participating in the smuggling endeavors.[30] Official statistics from 1956 estimate that around 100 million coffee sacks had been smuggled out of the country that year.[31]

With larger and more frequent coffee loads traversing the roads, mule trails, and rivers that crossed the Greater Magdalena to the Guajira, smugglers consolidated two routes.[32] According to Callo, a former coffee smuggler who welcomed me into his house in Riohacha to share memories of the past, one route extended along the coast. Drinking a cup of the dark, sweet coffee customary in the Guajira, he explained that he worked with roasting companies in Barranquilla that bought tons of coffee for domestic consumption but also sold a portion to smugglers for export. He transported the sacks in trucks through the Troncal del Caribe, the paved road that connected the towns along the coast, which at the time ended north of Santa Marta. Where the Troncal ended, they unloaded the cargo and transferred it to canoes to move it from river to river, thus avoiding the open sea, where the coastguard could easily catch them. When they finally reached the first town in the Guajira, they transferred the loads to trucks again and drove to warehouses in Riohacha, or to the natural seaports of the upper peninsula, to ship it to Aruba or the Panama Canal's free trade zone.

The second route followed the old "Jerusalem road" from the Magdalena River across the great valley to the natural seaports of the Guajira. The Troncal de Oriente, the paved road that connected the eastern cordillera with the great valley, was completed up to Valledupar, which smugglers therefore used as a transshipment point. Coffee was brought "easily from Santander and Medellín in caravans of 100 to 200 trucks," Callo remembered.[33] Yim Daza Noguera, mayor of San Juan del Cesar during Rojas Pinilla's dictatorship, explained to me that the local army garrison, "the [Rondón] Group [of Mechanized Cavalry,] pulled you over, and they gave you a voucher to continue to Aruba" if they found everything in place. If not, they seized your freight.[34] The existence of a coffee belt in the Sierra Nevada and Perijá helped smugglers to develop new procedures to trick authorities. For example, farmers claimed exportation permits from the Rondón Group offices to later sell them to smugglers, who used them to pass through checkpoints.[35] Bribes paid to customs agents and army commanders were also standard practice.

Along the two main routes, *contrabandistas* offered transportation from Santa Marta, Valledupar, and Barranquilla to storage points in Riohacha or Maicao, as well as to the natural ports of the upper peninsula and, for those who owned ships, Aruba. In both trucks and boats, they charged the exporter per sack. Raúl told me, while rocking in his chair in the living room of his house in Riohacha, that after years of working in land transportation he decided to buy a boat because "I got better profits." He recalled he had between six and eight trucks, but also managed his brothers' and partners', "like 20 trucks in total." He charged in dollars for each sack of coffee transported in the boat, and also for each sack transported in the trucks.[36] Silvio, a sailor who worked for José Durán and many others, remembered that he and his associates mostly smuggled coffee produced locally and commercialized "in the *provincia*: Barrancas, Papayal, Hato Nuevo, Fonseca, and we transported it over dirt roads" to the ports, and, "depending on where customs was, we moved to another port," he added.[37] Journalist Consuelo Araújo Noguera explained that coffee cargoes, "like marijuana decades later," were shipped by a single exporter "who was the boss of the business." But behind these exporters there were two or three powerful families of merchants from the Andean interior or the coast that provided the money and thereby made larger profits.[38]

Smugglers also purchased coffee with their earnings and added this supply to larger cargos, which they shipped to Aruba or Panama, where buyers paid them directly. "The coffee we bought for [the exporters] was transported by freight," Justiniano Mendoza, José Durán's *compadre* and partner, told me while drinking coffee on my grandmother Nina's patio in San Juan del Cesar. "When we bought our own coffee, we sent it directly to Aruba.... Thus we went up [to the upper Guajira] full, and went down full," Mendoza pointed out.[39] That is, they traveled to the ports loaded with coffee and came back down full of whiskey, cigarettes, and general merchandise, which they later transported to various destinations along the coast. Those who smuggled thousands of sacks "did not bring merchandise back but dollars, which they later sold in Barranquilla, Bogotá, or Medellín," Raúl explained, specifying that those who exported smaller cargos "were the ones who brought back whiskey and cigarettes."[40] Smuggling manufactured and luxury goods back into the country made the circuit more profitable for those who moved smaller quantities of coffee or worked on their own. Large exporters of coffee rarely imported contraband.

All these activities required cooperation among disparate socioeconomic actors spread across a vast geographic area. Smugglers thus occupied a middle position that earned them both profits and respect. Although rural people in the Greater Magdalena had experienced class differentiation before, the multiple changes that came about during the postwar period and La Violencia accelerated this process: the wave of migration of violently dispossessed *cachacos,* the colonization of the mountainous agricultural frontiers with coffee, and the consolidation of a coffee belt; the macroeconomic policies that resulted from new alliances between the coffee growers' guild and industrialists, Liberals and Conservatives, and the US government; infrastructure projects that created new physical and social landscapes; and the booming postwar markets in Europe and the United States, where working- and middle-class people relied on caffeine to maintain high levels of productivity.[41] Young rural men like José Durán turned coffee contraband into a maelstrom of dispersed groups pursuing similar interests.

Outlaws emerge when "the jaws of the dynamic modern world seize the static communities in order to destroy and transform them," Eric Hobsbawm once wrote.[42] In this case, however, one can hardly tell what was "static" and what was "dynamic," as old and new forms of social relations of commerce combined to define the course of change. For example, traditional bonds of kinship, including *compadrazgo* (relations among *compadres*, or parents and godparents), that customarily mediated social relations among competing actors in the smuggling business could not contain the changes unleashed by a greater integration of the region into national and international markets. However, kinship and *compadrazgo* continued to define alliances and discords. Take Durán and his peers as examples. They followed the century-old practice of interethnic marriages with women from wealthy Wayuu clans, because the Wayuu were an essential part of the smuggling business, providing guidance, surveillance, and labor in loading and unloading goods. Kinship relations offered smugglers "safe conduct" and a valuable "relational capital" with the extended families that controlled the natural seaports.[43] Simultaneously, smugglers cultivated friendships and *compadrazgos* with *criollo* men (nonindigenous native people) in Liberal and Conservative networks of clientelism in order to secure a host of strategically placed allies inland. Justiniano Mendoza boasted of a powerful cattle rancher, cotton grower, and Liberal party politician who used to praise him by saying: "You are a man who is worth a lot . . . there might be rich people here and so on, but somebody with more human relationships than Mendoza there is none."[44] Mendoza added: "I was friends with the *pueblacho* [the people], but my people were the *cocotudos* [the rich]."[45] According to Mendoza, Durán followed a similar pattern of forging alliances with both elites and indigenous peoples of the peninsula in order to guarantee his autonomy on the ground.

Another indispensable element to *contrabandistas'* sovereign control of business operations that shows how "old" and "new" social relations of commerce intertwined was an evolving knowledge of territories and their people. The infrastructure projects that Rojas Pinilla financed improved the old roads that the Liberal Republic had built two decades before, which made it possible for trucks to drive these routes for the first time.[46] But neither the Troncal del Caribe nor the Troncal de Oriente along the littoral and the great valley, respectively, reached all the way up to the peninsula. Without paved roads it was difficult to reach the natural seaports because of Guajira's characteristic cycles of rain and drought. Smugglers required a deep understanding of both the area's geography and its people in order to evade authorities, sandstorms, mud, quicksand, and lands that belonged to clans allied with competitors. Durán was one of the few *contrabandistas* "who could put the merchandise in the natural ports; nobody else could pass through, it was hard," my Uncle Arique assured me. "José went on evading guards, he played games, he wore costumes, he dressed as a soldier, he disguised his cars, he painted them like customs cars."[47] He even mobilized his social capital in pursuit of business. My uncle recalled that Durán paid cantina owners to play one of his favorite vallenato songs, "La perra" (The Bitch) as loud as possible as a signal that the roads were clear. Thus, when he heard the verses, "Here comes the bitch / that was biting me, / brave bitch / that bit her master," he knew he had a green light.[48]

With the creation of the Intendencia de la Guajira in 1954, Rojas Pinilla not only disgruntled the cotton elite and shaped the expansion of the cotton belt, but also created the territorial framework for the rise of a renewed cultural identity in which *contrabandistas* became aspirational figures.[49] When the Intendencia merged some of the *criollo* towns of the Greater Magdalena with the Wayuu territory in the upper peninsula, smugglers found their cultural mobility between the two worlds legally sanctioned, and they became active agents in the formation of a new, Guajira-based identity not exclusively indigenous. Their kinship relations with Wayuu clans and their knowledge of the peninsula's territories and ecologies informed their understanding of their unique skills in moving commodities. Borrowing from the Wayuu gender code—according to which ideal men are like Juya (the male god of rain, mobile and unique) and ideal women are like Pulowi (the female god of drought, fixed and manifold)—they unleashed a process of "counter-accultur-ation," involving nonindigenous people's adaptation of indigenous patterns, which served as basis for their new identities as *guajiros* and *contrabandistas*, and for the defense of an economic vocation that the Andean-centered nation-state considered illicit.[50]

One of Durán and Mendoza's deeds illustrates this point and suggests the ways in which this new ethos defined smugglers' understanding of their position within the Colombian nation-state. One night in 1963, customs agents pulled over Lobo Loco (Crazy Wolf), a red Ford pickup truck that was driven by an intrepid young man known by the same moniker. That night, Durán and Mendoza traveled together in a Toyota jeep named La Ley de Texas (the Law of Texas), which was working as *la mosca* (the fly), a smaller car with no cargo that was sent ahead to confirm that roads were free of authorities, or to bribe any officer encountered.[51] As per the routine, Durán and Mendoza were armed with grenades, an M1 semiautomatic, and their personal .45 revolvers. They came from Valledupar, where they picked up dozens of sacks of coffee and headed to Riohacha to deliver them to the exporter. Because the exporter told them that customs had already been bribed, they thought this was a mistake. They got off *la mosca* and asked for the commander of the check-point. "We need to talk to him, because we are *guajiros*, and you are in the Guajira, and in our land, contraband never gets lost," they told customs offic-ers before they offered them money. But they failed to persuade them, so Durán ordered the drivers to flee, while he and Mendoza defended their escape with gunfire. The shooting lasted an eternity, Mendoza remembered, until Durán threw grenades to create a smoke screen that allowed them all to scamper away on foot. Days later, the exporter in Riohacha used his con-nections to recuperate the confiscated coffee and truck, but neither the sacks nor Lobo Loco were returned. Meanwhile, Mendoza and Durán celebrated their exploit with a *parranda* (party) lasting several days, held in a Wayuu *ranchería* (village) where Durán had a wife.[52]

Now that the Intendencia's jurisdiction embraced both the northernmost part of the great valley and the indigenous territory of the peninsula, Durán and Mendoza presumed that they were ruled by a different set of norms, like the Wayuu. Anthropologist Giangina Orsini Aarón recorded a strikingly similar story in Maicao.[53] Although the outcome was different, the argu-ments and presumptions were the same. Smugglers felt excluded from the political body of the Colombian nation-state and therefore not accountable to its regulations and legislation. And because of their kinship with the Wayuu, who considered them clan members, their recourse to an exceptional sovereignty over the Guajira was genuine. They understood their activities as illegal vis-à-vis the Colombian state, but also as socially legitimate—a cus-tomary practice that deserved special consideration—and expected state agents to accept their bribes as personalized taxes. In fact, as anthropologist Diana Bocarejo concludes in her ethnography of mule drivers' ethics in the bonanzas of the Sierra Nevada's western watershed, "What is lawful and legal [to these drivers] is opportunistic, as the state apparatus mainly legalizes what is convenient only for those involved with or in close relation to state bureaucracies and politics."[54]

Fearless smugglers, Durán and Mendoza had no problem in resorting to violence to ensure their success. Eliminating competition and monopolizing routes made violence an indispensable instrument in the smugglers' toolkit. Violent disputes among them, and between them and state agents, were the visible manifestation of the constant struggle to control relations of exchange.[55] Nevertheless, violence was more than a practical device, as it was also another cultural pattern of social organization that they borrowed from the Wayuu, adapted to their specific needs and reproduced through the code of honor.[56] Anthropologist Anne Marie Losonczy argues that in Dibulla, a coastal town south of Riohacha, the use of violence among smugglers was an identity formation mechanism, as conflicts never involved people beyond the outer limits of extended kin.[57]

For Durán and Mendoza, violence had been part of their lives before they started working together. On June 12, 1954, Mendoza got into a machete fight with Crisóstomo Rodríguez in Hatico de los Indios, a hamlet in the Sierra Nevada, in the municipality of San Juan del Cesar.[58] After Mendoza murdered Rodríguez, the Rodríguez family needed to restore the wounded honor and the social balance between the two families, but each attempt to settle the dispute unleashed a spiral of pain, anger, and revenge. Uncle Arique, who was a friend of both families, did the arithmetic for me: at the end of the first year, "the fight was tied; Justiniano killed Crisóstomo, Damaso [Rodríguez] killed Arturo [Mendoza], Elías [Mendoza] killed Damaso, and Santos [Rodríguez] killed Pedro Segundo [Mendoza]."[59] The Rodríguezes got into another fight with other relatives, the Mejía family, to which José Durán's wife belonged. Then Durán fought with his Mendoza brothers-in-law after a failed business venture with a common *compadre* who smuggled *chirrinchi* (moonshine).[60] Rumors that one of the Mendoza brothers was having an affair with one of the Mejía sisters did not help.[61] By the time Durán and Mendoza began to work together in the early 1960s, five families were involved in a war. They managed to be partners for a few years, while killing others for honor and in revenge. On August 7, 1966, Chemón, a member of the Mendoza family, gunned down José Durán—the most feared man among those involved in the fight, he who was rumored to be the devil, capable of metamorphosing into a stack of plantains—and the conflict deescalated.[62]

Popularly known as vendettas, these wars among smuggler families were similar to the feuds that characterized medieval and early modern Mediterranean families, whence the term *vendetta* comes. Historian Edward Muir argues that the ideal of masculinity as "performative excellence," which required a "good man" to engage in a public display of physical risk and aggressiveness, was the norm in societies where laws were inconsistent at best and in most places absent.[63] Smugglers in the Guajira lived in that kind of society, but not because their social dynamics were archaic or feudal. On the contrary, the state of lawlessness in the mountainous Greater Magdalena was a by-product of the modernizing reforms that reconfigured the physical, social, and cultural landscapes but failed to offer alternatives to disparate social groups with which they could adapt to the increasingly interconnected economy. In their efforts to navigate these changes, men who sought to make a living in commerce rather than agriculture adopted the Wayuu code of honor for conflict resolution, eliminating the phases of negotiation and reparation that were central to indigenous people, and making "blood price" the first and only option.[64] The complexity of sexual relations and kinship ties among multiple families that lived in closed proximity often helped precipitate warfare. Once a war was set off, it evolved through specific attacks on selective targets rather than through combat between massed forces.[65] Men were the ones who killed and got killed. They were familiar with the use of weapons because generally they were part of the contraband, and because rural men learned to hunt when they were young; some, like Durán, even went through military conscription. Women set their men on enemies, decided who would perpetrate the next attack, and mourned the dead.[66]

The rumor about Durán as an evil creature with supernatural skills, and the importance of his death in the de-escalation of the vendetta, reflects the symbolic power of the *contrabandista* in the collective unconscious of a rural society going through rapid class differentiation, urbanization, and integration into the national and international markets. To be a *contrabandista,* a man had to display a complex and multifaceted set of attributes that the masculine figure of the devil represented. A "mix of agility, mobility, cleverness, vitality, tenacity, astuteness, prodigality, physical resistance, relational talent, and aggressive attitude" was expected of them, as Losonczy describes the ideal.[67] Anthropologist Michael Taussig found that in the sugar belt of the Cauca River valley, in southwestern Colombia, the devil was "intrinsic to the process of proletarianization of the peasant and to the commoditization of the peasant's world."[68] Similarly, the people of the new Guajira (first *intendencia,* then department) interpreted the enhanced economic and social capacities of smugglers in terms of their folk beliefs, rooted in traditions of sorcery, witchcraft, and *curanderismo* (healing rituals).[69] These popular ideas surrounding *contrabandistas* reflected efforts to make sense of new

FIGURE 6. "Here, life meets eternity." Entrance to the San Juan del Cesar cemetery, where all family vendettas ended. Photo by the author.

forms of creation and destruction, growth and stagnation, accumulation and destitution.

In waging war, smuggling goods, cultivating mythical public personas, and engaging in close relationships with various social groups, these young men breathed new life into exporting contraband agricultural products, an enterprise through which they participated in national circuits of capital accumulation and forged ties with powerful sectors in the Andean interior. Negotiating their position as *guajiros* within the nation, these smugglers assimilated indigenous cultural patterns of social organization (i.e., the Wayuu code of honor) in order to legitimize practices that were prohibited under Colombian law but were nonetheless socially accepted and respected.

The routes, procedures, identities, and ethos of coffee *contrabandistas* served as springboards to a more profitable business in marijuana, placing these men at the crest of international currents.

MARIJUANA CONSUMPTION AND DEMOGRAPHIC TRANSITION

Marijuana arrived in Colombia by sea. The habit and culture of smoking reflected a legacy of labor migration and circuits of commerce that connected the banana district and the ports of Santa Marta and Barranquilla with the Greater Caribbean.[70] Exclusively consumed by the initiated, marijuana in Colombia embodied "'globalizing forces' in the Atlantic economy."[71] As in Jamaica, whence the habit of cultivating and smoking marijuana spread to the insular and continental Caribbean after indentured servants from India introduced the practice, the plant in Colombia was not an export commodity but the intoxicant of choice of people living and working in undesirable conditions.[72] A man recognized in the town of Taganga in the Santa Marta Bay area for his prodigious memory and talent for storytelling, Pebo asked me for a pound of coffee and a pack of cigarettes in exchange for his time. While we drank the coffee and he smoked the cigarettes, he told me that when he was an adolescent in the 1930s, in "Ciénaga there was the best, the real deal in marijuana, and there I became a *fumón* [heavy user]." Candidly, he added, "Then came the prostitutes, the brothels, and we all fell for the illusion, we lived off the women, there was nobody who worked." Pebo affirmed that sailors who worked on the ships that transported refined sugar from Cuba to the banana district brought marijuana with them; along with Barranquilla merchants who also promoted marijuana seeds, this introduction stimulated the initial crops in the Sierra Nevada. Mocho Zenón was one of the first investors from Barranquilla to get involved in marijuana cultivation; he paid "César Sánchez, and his whole family, and they moved to the Sierra [Nevada], because they were workers there, and planted the seed."[73] Despite his old age, Pebo's recollections are consistent with what scholars have found in other localities in the area.[74]

Marijuana was initially produced for local consumption among men and women of the lowest status rather than for an international market. The habit was popular among the proletariat in the country's two poles of agrarian development—the Greater Magdalena's banana district, and the Andean

coffee region and sugar belt along the Cauca River valley, between the western and central cordilleras. In the Andean interior, crops grew in numerous
dispersed areas that were easily concealed among other cash crops and where
the urban and rural worlds battled to establish a border: Manizales got its
supplies from neighboring Villamaría; Medellín from nearby Bello; and Cali
from Buga.[75] In cities, marijuana users were also proletarians: factory and
street workers, artisans, musicians, pimps, prostitutes, and con artists.
Brothels, cantinas, *fritangas* (fried-food shops), theaters, and hotels sold marijuana in cigarettes that cost a few cents each.[76]

The artists and intellectuals who frequented these places, and were known
to smoke, played a key role in spreading the habit to other social classes and
elevating to poetic heights what mainstream society considered a harmful
vice. Porfirio Barba Jacob, one of Colombia's most celebrated authors, sym-
bolizes this generation of *marihuanos*, as regular consumers were known at
the time.[77] A journalist by profession and wanderer by vocation, Barba Jacob
traveled the continent: Barranquilla, Peru, New York, Cuba, Mexico, and
most Central American countries. He wrote for newspapers and magazines
and had a reputation for getting in trouble with authorities for his homosexu-
ality, anticlericalism, and radicalism.[78] Criticized for his late romanticism,
Barba Jacob's most important legacy is perhaps having introduced younger
readers to Latin America's cosmopolitan bohemia.[79] "The lady of the burning
hair," as he called marijuana in a poem by the same title, was part of his world
and a recurrent topic in his poetry.[80] He bragged about planting it everywhere he went, even in New York City's Central Park.[81] And with his verses,
Colombia's damned poet represented the type of user that characterized the
earliest domestic marijuana market: marginal members of the most dynamic
social sectors undergoing a rapid process of urbanization and connected to
international flows of people and cultural practices.

For decades, marijuana was just a minor domestic affair. The expansion of
the national market and the creation of a more robust legal framework for its
control formed two interconnected aspects of the country's postwar modernization. During the height of La Violencia in 1947, when Conservative
president Mariano Ospina Pérez created the Ministry of Agriculture and
appointed Pedro Castro Monsalvo to develop the legal and institutional
framework for the cotton belt, one of the measures was to import *cannabis
indica* seeds from India for the textile industry. Rumor has it that these seeds
spread outside industrial channels where they were used to produce textile
fibers, and contributed to the proliferation of marijuana crops in the Sierra

Nevada de Santa Marta and the Cauca River valley.[82] I found no evidence to prove or disprove this theory. However, the evidence is irrefutable that the state made a series of efforts to restrict the plant to industrial uses and thereby comply with the Geneva Conventions of 1925 and 1931 that regulated the manufacture, distribution, and use of drugs, which the country ratified in 1930 and 1933, respectively.[83] With Decree 896 in 1947, Ospina Pérez penalized the cultivation, distribution, and sale of coca and marijuana, and he ordered local sanitary authorities to destroy crops. With Decree 1858 in 1951, Gómez declared that "malefactors are those who cultivate, elaborate, commercialize or in any way make use or induce another to use marijuana."[84] With Decree 0014 in 1955, Rojas Pinilla increased the sentences for cultivation, trade, and use by two and seven years.[85] These laws contributed to a tenfold growth of the inmate population in the country, from 53 people incarcerated for marijuana-related crimes in 1956 to 597 in 1963.[86]

Some of these "malefactors" served sentences in isolated penal colonies. The archives of Araracuara, an agricultural prison located in the eastern lowlands, preserved more than a dozen cases of marijuana-related crimes that were prosecuted while these new decrees were enforced.[87] There were proceedings, for example, against José Manuel Vanegas Cardona and his accomplices, which took place from March to September of 1954. Out of the six people arrested for three pounds of dried marijuana stored in sacks in a farm in Calarcá in the coffee region, only three were charged: forty-six-year-old José Manuel Vanegas and brothers Israel, twenty-one, and Julio Ernesto Pérez, twenty-four. The judge decided to give Israel, the youngest, two years, as he proved during trial to be a "peasant-like, good-natured, naïve young boy"; the judge ruled that on his brother Julio Ernesto and partner José Manuel Vanegas "should fall the full force of the harsh law." Each got a sentence of five years because "the Machiavelli-like deeds of these two perverts" constituted "perhaps, the most harmful [crime] for society" as "its consequences are incalculable." Furthermore, the judge stated that "it is competence on the part of authorities [to cut] on time, from the root, . . . the plentiful ramification of countless evils."[88]

Enforcing the new laws gradually became more politicized. The National Front, fully committed to containing Cuba, set the tone for a new discourse about marijuana that merged anticommunism with Catholic moralism. According to historian Eduardo Sáenz Rovner, religious and civic leaders as well as coffee entrepreneurs in Caldas, the largest department in the coffee region, believed that Cuban penetration was turning the peasant Liberal armies that had fought La Violencia and had not demobilized in the amnesties of 1953 and 1958 into a guerrilla movement. In response to their outcry, the departmental government enforced the anti-marijuana laws.[89] *Bandoleros*—the term used for the remnants of the Liberal guerrillas—assumed bombastic aliases such as Tarzan, Sangrenegra (black blood), Chispas (spark), Venganza (vengeance), Desquite (retaliation), Veneno (poison), and Peligro (danger), and with their noms de guerre circulated stories of their activities and lifestyles, which included smoking marijuana.[90] These rumors helped cultivate an aura of fear and legend that was essential to their survival.[91] They also fed a media discourse that justified a series of police campaigns whereby local authorities pretended to impose the rule of law, as "a 'theater' or forum" intended as a form of state-sanctioned "pedagogic work."[92]

Between law enforcement and the shaping of public opinion, a discourse that linked the moral decadence of marijuana to the political degeneration of *bandolerismo* gradually took shape. In fact, *bandoleros* were weaker in those areas where there was an actual guerilla movement. Historians Gonzalo Sánchez and Donny Meertens argue that their strongholds were zones where peasant communities "suffered the effects of governmental state terrorism without being able to articulate their own forms of resistance."[93] During the war, peasant armies had been directly connected to the Liberal party and its local leaders. But once the Liberal elites reached an agreement with their Conservative enemies to support, first, the military Rojas Pinilla dictatorship and, second, the National Front, they delegitimized their peasant allies as political actors. Local merchants, landowners, and politicians pulled back their support, and state forces began persecuting them. Sánchez and Meertens contend that violence worsened in the 1960s after the institutionalization of the National Front, not because of Cuban penetration but because a new generation of fighters came of age who had been raised during the war and for whom "the only meaning of their actions was an exercise of retaliation and vengeance."[94] The destitute and traumatized peasant youth who made up *bandolero* armies allegedly smoked marijuana before committing crimes, an image used by the local media to create a "moral panic" that helped authorities publicize the values of a Catholic anticommunist state.[95]

"The full force of the harsh law," however, was not restricted to *bandoleros* or farmers in rural areas; dissatisfied urban youth were also targeted. In 1958, the same year that Liberals and Conservatives inaugurated the National Front, a group of young poets and writers from the country's largest cities announced the formation of Nadaísmo, an artistic and literary group inspired by *nada* (nothing) and whose aim was to break with the asphyxiating Catholicism and provincialism that they believed characterized Colombia.[96] Nadaísmo followed no ideology and dictated no artistic precepts; its followers were an agglomeration of "diverse discontents under one single aesthetic manifestation."[97] They professed free love, vagrancy, and smoking marijuana. When accused of imitating European vanguards, Gonzalo Arango, Nadaísmo's leader, responded with a lesson in history: they had, rather, originated in the aftermath of La Violencia, which Arango conceptualized as "a change of 'rhythm,' historical and violent, that unhinged the structures of society and spiritual values of the Colombian man."[98] In one of his most widely circulated poems, Arango highlighted the historical connection between *nadaístas* and *bandoleros*. "I, a poet, in the same circumstances of oppression, misery, fear, and persecution, would have been a *bandolero*," he wrote in *Elegía a Desquite*; "that's why I wrote this elegy to 'Desquite,' because with the same possibilities I had, he could have been called Gonzalo Arango."[99] From the late 1950s until the early 1970s, when various events (including Arango's death in a car crash) dispersed the movement, *nadaístas* sought to lay waste to every symbol that was held sacred.[100] Their belief that "in Colombia there was only mediocrity and crappiness" got them in trouble; while they "experimented with everything," *nadaísta* Elmo Valencia said, "the establishment fucked with us and put us in jail for any motive," marijuana smoking being the most frequent cause.[101]

On the *bandoleros'* and *nadaístas'* "lips of fire"—as Barba Jacob once wrote—marijuana represented a rejection of the political, class, gender, and religious hierarchies on which the National Front was predicated.[102] The criminalization of marijuana producers, traders, and consumers in rural and urban areas of the Andean interior was a means of controlling the population of young people who refused to be part of the Catholic anticommunist nation birthed by La Violencia, at a moment when Colombia was entering a demographic transition and urbanization was accelerating.[103] Imposing order is precisely what Berta Hernández de Ospina advocated when she complained in 1966 about news of a marijuana confiscation in Bogotá. One of the National Front's moral defenders, the former First Lady (wife of Mariano Ospina Pérez) feared that publicizing the market value of the pounds of intoxicant seized would entice "all our bums and idlers" to look for ways to make money with "a little plant that can be easily hidden, that grows anywhere, and that gives such good economic return."[104] Apart from her dramatic tone, Doña Berta (as she was known) had a point. The specter of easy money would more easily materialize in the pursuit of the promises of urbanization, upward mobility, and social recognition in an increasingly restrictive political and economic order in which these proved otherwise unobtainable. The rule of law was not enough, nor was any moral panic campaign stoked by the media, to prevent youth in search of a better future from responding to the demand for marijuana in the United States when conditions were ripe.

MARIJUANA SMUGGLING AND URBANIZATION

In 1969, just a couple of years into the boom in consumption of marijuana, the United States experienced "a marijuana famine."[105] It resulted from the combined effects of summer droughts in Mexico, the main US supplier, and the first chapter of the "war on drugs" along the US-Mexican border.[106] At this time, Colombia was not a significant source of the drug, even though smugglers in at least five regions of the country included small amounts of marijuana—and occasionally cocaine and barbiturates—in their regular cargos of agricultural products, mainly coffee, that were exported to the United States via Panama or Aruba; and tourists also smuggled drugs concealed in their luggage, even from Bogotá's international airport.[107] The Greater Magdalena was just one of the regions involved in this traffic, which authorities around the world attributed to the sharply upward climb in drug use among white middle-class North American youth.[108] In Mediterranean Europe, Southeast Asia, the Middle East, North Africa, and Mexico, authorities reported young US men buying and selling marijuana and hashish in small quantities, exchanging it for LSD, and smuggling it in "large bulk shipments of drugs include [sic] concealment in transshipped vehicles and renegade pilots who fly drugs in small aircraft."[109] Smugglers in the fracturing Greater Magdalena counted on a privileged geographic location in relation to consumption markets, a long history of contraband bolstered by governmental macroeconomic policies that stimulated coffee smuggling, and the discontent created by the National Front's model of agrarian development, and readily participated in the trade.

These smugglers worked from two focal points that ultimately became terminals for two different routes: Riohacha and nearby seaports, and Santa Marta and its bay area. The pioneers in Riohacha and surrounding ports came from two intertwined but different sectors of Guajira's *criollo* society.[110] Forest engineer Rodrigo Echeverri and his research team from the National

Institute of Natural Resources (Inderena) in the Sierra Nevada confirmed, in the most exhaustive study of the marijuana export sector produced during the boom: "The first group that began working with marijuana were smugglers of liquors, cigarettes, appliances, and coffee," because "they had the know-how, the paraphernalia, and the personnel to export any kind of product illegally from the country."[111] They took advantage of the physical isolation of the Guajira's coastline and natural seaports to turn the profitable smuggling business of coffee and general goods toward trafficking in marijuana. A cliff known as Los Muchachitos, located on the coast between Santa Marta and Riohacha, posed a natural barrier to extension of the Troncal del Caribe, the paved road that linked the towns along the littoral. Isolated natural seaports located north of the cliff and near Dibulla and Riohacha, such as La Punta and El Pájaro, became ideal sites for smuggling small quantities of marijuana in the coffee shipments destined for the insular Caribbean.[112]

Among these pioneers were Chijo and his *compadre* Lucky. After many failed attempts over the years to get an interview with Lucky, whom I met at Chijo's funeral in Riohacha, the information I collected on his career trajectory is limited to public knowledge and interviews I recorded with his brother and business partner, Mantequilla. Descendants of divi-divi smuggler Luis Cotes Gómez and his Wayuu wife, Lucila Barros, the brothers were members of Riohacha's *criollo* elite and one of the wealthiest Wayuu clans of the upper peninsula. The rumor is that Lucky got his nickname from the Lucky Strike brand because he got his start in contraband with cigarettes. Then there was Chijo, another young man of Wayuu ancestry but of rural origins who belonged to a more modest family of merchants who traded in cattle and gold jewelry from their base in the village of Carraipía.[113] "One day, when I least expected it, a *compadre* gave me the opportunity to buy coffee," Chijo said about his first deal as a *contrabandista,* recorded on one of the ten surviving tapes on which he narrated his life history.[114] During the last years of his life, Chijo made a tape-recorded journal in which he preserved some of his most cherished memories. According to Mantequilla, it was Lucky who gave Chijo a chance. The two met in school at Riohacha, where Chijo studied before moving to Santa Marta to attend the prestigious public high school of Liceo Celedón.[115]

Chijo provided no evidence in his recordings as to how the two translated their knowledge, experience, and wealth in the coffee business into smuggling marijuana. Likewise, Mantequilla adeptly avoided discussing many details about the marijuana business; whenever I asked about this, he either made jokes or changed the subject. One thing is known, however: when Nacho Vives ran for Congress for the first time in 1962, as the candidate of the Intendencia de la Guajira, the local government in Riohacha was swamped in corruption scandals because of a renewed alliance between politicians and smugglers who were then mutually benefiting from the coffee contraband bonanza.[116] Callo, the coffee smuggler from Riohacha, learned first of the marijuana business around 1966. Only a few years later one of the dynasties of Liberal politicians who were involved in the corruption scandals hired him to drive a load of marijuana from their lands in La Punta, south of Riohacha, to a nearby airstrip.[117] In other words, at some point in the late 1960s smuggling marijuana along with coffee became a regular practice for a select group of smugglers who managed to secure buyers.

Smugglers reproduced the exact same circuit for marijuana that they used for coffee. They either transported it to seaports for exporters from the Andean interior or other parts of the coast, or bought small quantities locally in the banana district or in the black markets of Barranquilla and Santa Marta for their own ventures. In the former case, when the marijuana came from the Andean interior, they picked it up along with coffee freights in either Santa Marta or Valledupar, where the Troncal del Caribe and Troncal de Oriente ended, respectively.[118] Meco, a driver from San Juan del Cesar, assured me that during "the marijuana boom, we used the same trails, the same roads, the same paths [as with coffee]; there were also people who *mosqueaba* [drove "the fly"], the same law [enforcement]."[119] Journalist Enrique Herrera Barros from Riohacha recalled that during these early years "almost all the people who came from somewhere else had nicknames, nobody knew who was who, nobody knew their full names; it was said that they brought marijuana from Corinto [in the Department of Cauca, south of the sugar belt], because the marijuana from the Sierra Nevada was not known until years later."[120] And, as with coffee contraband, marijuana smugglers were the final link in a long chain of intermediaries. In Callo's disdainful words, "*Guajiros* were nothing, they were errand boys of the big shots [who] earned a commission, and thanks to this they got strong, and then they could send their own little cargos."[121] By the late 1960s existing smuggling networks of coffee were engaged in some way in the modest smuggling of marijuana.

Further south, *turreros*, smugglers of products from merchant ships into Santa Marta and the bay area, changed the direction of the commercial flows outward to supply the young US buyers who arrived in the port as tourists or sailors searching for marijuana for personal consumption.[122] Like *contrabandistas* in the Guajira, US consumers-cum-smugglers followed their own commercial traditions, which went back to the United Fruit Company's golden age, when the company's Great White Fleet passenger service regularly brought US tourists to Santa Marta attracted by the "mythmaking central to tourist industry publicity," promising results from modest investment.[123] And like US marijuana smugglers operating along the Mexican border, those who arrived in Santa Marta and the bay area refrained from moving large quantities, and learned through observation and from others' mistakes.[124] They were also quintessential hippies—predominantly white, "male, young, single."[125]

Juan "Ios" Vieira, an environmental activist from the coffee region who moved to the bay area in the late 1960s, told me at a café in downtown Santa Marta that when he arrived in the region, "there was *marimba* [marijuana], but there was no business." Having just come back from the United States after graduating from college there, he decided to settle in Taganga, a small fishing town north of Santa Marta, when "out of the blue, suspicious boats began to arrive; they brought LSD to exchange." Whenever local marijuana crops in the former banana district or supplies in Santa Marta's black market were insufficient in quantity or quality, visitors would travel to the Andean interior, and sometimes return to the bay area with the few pounds they had obtained and export them in their own sailboats. They "all looked like hippies, they were not big businessmen; they did not look for large quantities, but they were many, many," Vieira affirmed.[126] And with their arrival en masse, opportunities for marijuana connections multiplied. Backpackers, dropouts, and runaways, the young US men who engaged in this trafficking during the late 1960s were regular smokers who embarked on the adventure of supplying themselves and friends in order to finance their itinerant lifestyles.[127] Smuggling was the flip side of the new habit of smoking marijuana, a distinct aspect of a new youth culture that valued irreverence, risk taking, self-sufficiency, and independence.

The Colombian rural and urban youth who supplied US buyers were not that different. Most young men in the disintegrated Greater Magdalena lived in limbo between the countryside and the city, where they received low-quality public education and were unemployed, participated in petty commerce, or worked menial jobs. The expansion of the educational system that started with the Liberal Republic in the 1930s did not keep up with the country's rapid urbanization and demographic transition during the 1950s and 1960s.[128] Despite successfully implementing the French model of *liceos* (public high schools), the Colombian educational system had great deficiencies.[129] And in the Greater Magdalena, these inadequacies proved stubborn to those who wished to address them. Congressman Nacho Vives reported in 1965, while defending the bill to upgrade the Intendencia de la Guajira to a department, that "the Guajira does not have educational services sufficient to offer the young population job training [to] prepare them in the near future to perform profitable labor."[130] Public schools were substandard, and for those who did not have relatives in town, living conditions in dormitories or *pensiones* (private boardinghouses) were deplorable or expensive. Vallenato composer Rafael Escalona complained about the pitiful situation he faced in Santa Marta's Liceo Celedón (which Chijo would attend decades later) in the song "El hambre del liceo" (High School's Hunger):

> With that news they went to my mom,
> that as thin as I was, I looked like a noodle,
> and it is the hunger experienced in the *liceo*
> that prevents me from gaining weight.[131]

To poor young men accustomed to working on farms and in fields or to living on the streets since childhood, school represented a kind of miserable confinement that required obedience. Martín López, an educational scholar, told me at his house in Riohacha that those who dropped out of school and "devoted themselves from an early age to work and other things, the so-called slackers," were the ones who made money with marijuana.[132] "They studied in the 'school of life,'" López elaborated in his master's thesis in social psychology; "they learned early how to drive, were exceptional at billiards, skillful in trades, and the first to jump with no fear from the bridge to the river or from the pier to the sea."[133] Chijo recalled his own ups and downs in life, which he attributed to the fact that he "was a mischievous kid," one who "liked to ride animals, go to the river to catch fish, catch wild cattle without permission, fall in love and get home late."[134] The youth who got involved in smuggling marijuana were the children of the "educational breach" in the 1950s and 1960s that separated the generation trained in their family's craft from the one formally—albeit poorly—educated by public institutions and in the "school of life."[135]

Being poor and precariously educated proved advantageous for the new business. Young rural and urban men's wandering and hustling, their inclination to physical work rather than intellectual labor, their audacity and bravado, yielded good results in the new circumstances. The career of Lucho

Barranquilla, a pioneer of the marijuana business in Santa Marta, illustrates how improvisation, innovation, and irreverence were tools necessary to surviving the fracturing of the agrarian world in which this generation had been born and the rapid urbanization that followed.[136] Named Luis Pérez Quesada, Barranquilla was from a town not far from the city where he got his nickname.[137] According to Silvio, a childhood friend of Barranquilla who became a sailor for coffee and marijuana smugglers, Barranquilla was a *gamín* (street kid) who after wandering around Riohacha and Maicao performing menial jobs, settled in Santa Marta.[138] Years passed and Silvio never saw him until he heard rumors of his sudden wealth and visited him in Santa Marta. Barranquilla told Silvio that he was in the *turreros* market on 11th Street when a group of sailors from Puerto Rico asked him where they could get five hundred pounds of marijuana. "Because all his life he had been shrewd, he got them that marijuana," Silvio said. Satisfied with how Barranquilla handled the deal, the sailors sent their contacts directly to him, "and more people, and more people, and suddenly Barranquilla had many clients."[139] Years later, Barranquilla confessed to a journalist that he used captains and crews of the Flota Mercante Grancolombiana—the fleet that transported Fedecafé's coffee to the world—to send marijuana to the United States concealed in coffee sacks. Barranquilla was tall and robust, and functionally illiterate. He was an aggressive merchant but "kind in the extreme, charitable, with a big heart," a patron of the destitute classes. When a competitor killed him in January 1976, the press reported that he was mourned by the "dispossessed who received help from his hands, the policemen who received his bribes because their salaries were insufficient, and the kids from the neighborhood of Las Delicias who played every afternoon in the park he built as a *criollo* Robin Hood."[140] Writer Eduardo Galeano recounts in his poetic fictionalized chronicle of twentieth-century Latin America, *Century of the Wind,* how Barranquilla's murderers "sent to the funeral a floral wreath in the form of a heart and took up a collection to erect a statute of the departed in the main plaza."[141]

Whether Silvio's testimony is a truthful rendition of their conversation, or even whether that conversation actually happened, is irrelevant for my purposes here. The story is meaningful because of its powerful tropes about the uncertain origins of the marijuana trade's pioneers.[142] The rags-to-riches narrative of Barranquilla's life—his humble upbringing, uprooted childhood, vagrant life, menial jobs, followed by a stroke of luck leading to rapid success, a penchant for generosity, and, ultimately, a tragic death—circulates as folklore and explains why so many young men seized the opportunity to work in the marijuana business.

Chijo's trajectory contains some of the same tropes but in more nuanced ways, revealing an epistemological and heuristic problem in the scholarly study of smugglers and illegal commerce. Thanks to his higher level of education, Chijo gained a certain degree of control over his life's narrative when he decided to record his memoirs in the hope of publishing a book. One of his nephews told me in a cafeteria in Riohacha that the purpose of Chijo's project was to celebrate relatives and *compadres* rather than to produce an autobiography.[143] After weeks of living with Chijo's voice in my head as I transcribed the tapes, I learned that his project was even more complex and ambitious than his nephew knew. Although Chijo was undoubtedly trying to show his love for his homeland and the people who gave meaning to his existence, he was also seeking to set the record straight and reveal the most intimate truths about his life's ups and downs. One of Chijo's sisters, who helped me obtain the tapes and the family's permission to transcribe them and use their content, thought that one of the broken cassettes contained his memories of the marijuana years. In any case, in the surviving recordings Chijo never addressed in detail the period of his fame and fortune, which is curious, to say the least.

Lacking any evidence to explain this omission, I can confirm that Chijo's story is one of a daring young man engaged in a protracted struggle to assert himself. He told us that "trying to broaden my horizons," he dropped out of Liceo Celedón in Santa Marta and traveled to Barranquilla to join the Junior soccer club. Nicknamed El Burro (the Donkey) for the strength of his legs, Chijo was nevertheless rejected from the club. Frustrated, he spent his monthly allowance on a trip to Medellín, where he went to the Atlético Nacional soccer club. He got the attention of the coaches, and after several practices he signed a contract for the junior leagues. When he learned that one of his uncles had died, Chijo returned home and asked his father for forgiveness for having dropped out of the *liceo*, and joined the family in the funerary rites. Soon thereafter, one of his brothers was hurt in a fight and Chijo embarked on a mission to restore his family's honor. Again estranged from his father and other relatives, Chijo saw "years [pass,] and the most horrible thing happened: papa was killed, and everything was over." Chijo did not explain the cause or context of the homicide. Clearly, however, from this point he became "a different man; it began the endless swings of my life, full of restlessness, sadness, and pain."[144]

Although the first swing in Chijo's life came with joy. Thanks to Lucky, one of his friends from school in Riohacha, Chijo got involved in coffee con-traband. By then, he had run into an old friend in Maicao, stayed at his house, fell in love with one of his sisters, married her, and straightened him-self up. For his first coffee deal, he recalled, he went to Caracolí, Urumita, and Codazzi, three towns in the foothills of the Sierra Nevada, Perijá, and the great valley, respectively, to buy harvests with the money his *compadre* advanced him. After paying Lucky back, he continued buying coffee for his partner to export to Aruba. He became familiar with cultivation sites, Fedecafé's agencies, and smuggling practices, and he quickly amassed a small fortune.[145] By trading in coffee, Chijo forged ties with Lucky and Riohacha's contraband elite and began a new life as a successful merchant.

The peripatetic lives of Chijo and Barranquilla demonstrate how impor-tant personal autonomy, self-sufficiency, and risk taking were for the young men who embraced the new opportunity. Building on routes, procedures, values, and codes established by a slightly older generation that thrived with the coffee contraband, the earliest marijuana traffickers combined both activities. Germán Rojas, a journalist from Riohacha who worked as a cor-respondent for national and regional newspapers during the marijuana boom, told me on the sidewalk by his office in Riohacha while we watched the sun set that "it had not been told, it had not been discovered that there was a great number of people transporting, selling marijuana; they worked in secrecy."[146] During this initial stage, disparate networks responded sporadi-cally to the demand of specific buyers with manageable supplies of marijuana. In a region where the smuggling of the valuable coffee bean and general mer-chandise was frequent, profitable, and voluminous, and where there were no *bandolero* or *nadaísta* movements to fear and suppress, authorities did not bother to enforce the anti-marijuana laws as they did in the Andean interior. Young men involved with these counterhegemonic economic practices had open space in which to innovate, improvise, and experiment with old pat-terns of commerce while establishing the foundations of a completely new export sector. Between indifference on the part of local authorities and acceptance of smuggling on the part of society, marijuana traffic rooted.

While the Lleras Restrepo administration (1966–70) gradually abandoned the agrarian reform and its promises of redistribution and development in order to close ranks with regional elites and protect their socioeconomic interests and the National Front's status quo, smugglers responded with a series of counterhegemonic commercial practices to protect their livelihoods. The "juridical pluralism" of the Guajira (a result of its demographic diversity and juxtaposition of various ethical and judicial systems), its open doors vis-à-vis Caribbean islands, and the direct connection between Santa Marta bay and the United States (after decades of banana exportation and tourism) created apertures in which coffee and marijuana smuggling thrived as socially sanctioned practices.[147] In a regional economy transitioning from bananas to cotton, where land and wealth concentrated at the top of society, the cultivation and smuggling of coffee and marijuana became outlets that released the pressure of accumulated social conflicts in the agricultural frontiers and growing urban peripheries. Young men from the elite and lower classes in Riohacha and the Guajira, and in Santa Marta and the bay area, joined the new business in different capacities. The synergy between these sellers and the US buyers infused the new activity with a characteristic dynamism. "Youth was the carrier of sociocultural modernization *and* its discontents," historian Valeria Manzano reminds us in the case of 1960 Argentina.[148] But in contrast to the case Manzano studies, and many others in Latin America, in which dissatisfaction was expressed through cultural rebellion and political radicalization, in the former Greater Magdalena, discontent manifested as a reactivation of the old in pursuit of the new as younger smugglers revitalized the connections, knowledge, and wealth acquired through smuggling coffee and general merchandise in order to participate in a novel business that would shake the region to its core. In a matter of years, by the early 1970s, the rising demand for marijuana in the United States prompted rapid growth in the volume and frequency of this trade in the former Greater Magdalena. Marijuana smugglers from both sides of the supply-and-demand equation set forth audaciously to transform an incipient contraband business into a robust agricultural export sector, one that reproduced many of the production and commercial patterns established in previous booms in a region where people were used to experimenting with tropical commodities for export in pursuit of agrarian development.

PART TWO

Peak

THREE

Santa Marta Gold

TECHNOLOGICAL ADAPTATIONS AND BOOM

[In] the very name of Santa Marta lay both mystery and prestige
[where] the gold of the Taironas sparkled ... where there were,
or should be, fabulous riches to be had in the continent which
lay at the city's back.

GERMÁN ARCINIEGAS,
historian and novelist

AFTER MONTHS OF LIVING AMONG MARIJUANA cultivators without
engaging in business with them, William Partridge still found it hard to
convince them that he was not "a wealthy buyer who intended to transport
tons of cannabis to the United States."[1] It did not make sense that a *gringo*
spent so much time in the Sierra Nevada without trying to get rich in the
green gold rush. Partridge arrived in late 1972 to do fieldwork on marijuana
consumption for a doctoral dissertation in anthropology. He conducted participant observation in Majagua, a town that extended from the Ciénaga
Grande (a swamp located south of Santa Marta) to the intermontane valleys
of the Sierra Nevada, in the former banana district. He examined a wide
range of activities in the area's different altitudes and ecological niches.
Partridge purchased a horse, secured housing with a family, and hired a cook,
a laundress, and guides. In the course of his research, he expanded his initial
focus to include not only consumption but production and commerce as
well. From January 1973, when he obtained his "first concrete information
regarding cannabis," until October, when he left town, Partridge studied
both exchange relations and the social implications of marijuana as a cash
crop, export commodity, and intoxicant. His dissertation offers a glimpse of
how marijuana smuggling evolved into an export sector.

This chapter examines this turning point, when a series of technological
adaptations prompted the spread of export varieties of marijuana along the
Sierra Nevada's three watersheds, launching the boom's second cycle—its

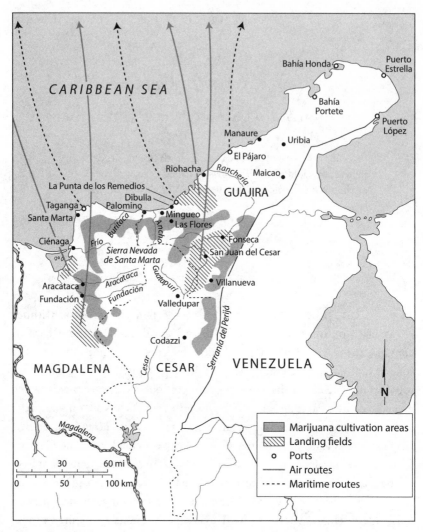

MAP 4. The Marijuana Belt. Map by Bill Nelson.

peak. This stage took place from approximately 1972 to 1978, climaxing in 1976 when two harvests coincided for the first and last time.[2] At some point in the late 1960s, the pioneers of the marijuana-smuggling business began to finance crops for export in order to meet the flourishing international demand. The boom involved the rapid ascension of marijuana as the most important cash crop of the peasant economy of the intermontane valleys, as well as a proliferation of intermediaries devoted to circulating the commodity from the cultivation areas in the highlands to the natural seaports and landing fields in the lowlands. These intermediaries connected *cachacos* (Andean settlers), local peasants, and seasonal agricultural workers with the region's urban middle classes, along with landed and political elites who invested in marijuana and, ultimately, US buyers. The dynamics that prompted this peak and that unfolded for the rest of the decade enabled *cachacos* initially and local peasants later to extend the agricultural frontier and settle in. The marijuana boom also provided young men from towns and villages in the new departments of Guajira, Magdalena, and—to a much lesser extent—Cesar the opportunity to participate in the commercial economy and urban society.

The irruption of popular sectors as central economic actors temporarily broke down old patterns of development in the region. The boom also marked the rise of Colombia as principal supplier of marijuana to the United States, the world's largest market at the time.[3] By examining both the synergies and conflicting interests among those involved, I show how marijuana briefly ameliorated the strained relationships between these sectors by helping to defuse the blossoming social tensions in the countryside and growing urban world.[4] Marijuana cultivation, commercialization, and export trade became solutions to problems of access to land and markets, credit, employment, and wealth while also fulfilling the promises of capital accumulation, urbanization, and social recognition that modernization put forward but failed to advance to the majority.

CULTIVATION AND THE FORMATION OF A MARIJUANA BELT

Marketed as "Santa Marta Gold" (or Golden) in the United States, the marijuana produced in the former Greater Magdalena could not have had a better name. "Gold" alluded to its yellow color and filigree-like texture, which was similar to Acapulco Gold, a Mexican strain famous in the United States. "Santa Marta" might as well refer to the fact that the territory originally named as such—which roughly corresponded to the Greater Magdalena—was the initial locus of El Dorado, the myth of an Indian kingdom of gold and precious stones for which thousands of men sacrificed their lives and souls over centuries. In "the very name of Santa Marta lay both mystery and prestige" for Spanish expeditions at the dawn of the sixteenth century, writer Germán Arciniegas observes.[5] The entrepreneurs of conquest, Arciniegas writes, described Santa Marta as a land where "the gold of the Taironas sparkled, where there were pearls to be had for the fishing, and where there were, or should be, fabulous riches to be had in the continent which lay at the city's back, and which was still to be explored."[6] When conquerors finally penetrated that continent and arrived at the high plateau where they later established Bogotá, they found the Muisca *zipa* (chief) covered in gold dust and submerging himself in Lake Guatavita. They believed that they had finally found El Dorado. Ironically, Santa Marta Gold seemed to realize these old fantasies.

Local lore and academic research concur on one point: during the golden years of the United Fruit Company, incipient marijuana crops emerged in the intermontane valleys of the Sierra Nevada's western watershed, up from the banana district, and along the basins of the tributaries of the Ciénaga Grande swamp. As chapter 2 discusses, sailors and seasonal workers from the Greater Caribbean, as well as merchants from Barranquilla, contributed to this development. According to Partridge, these meager crops did not sustain the million-dollar export commerce to the United States in the 1970s. He found instead two separate cultivation and distribution systems. On one hand, marijuana was a subsistence crop and a means of exchange for families of day laborers who were native to the region and other parts of the coast. They planted it for the male members of the family or work unit to consume, and sold or bartered it in the course of agricultural and cattle-ranching activities.[7] On the other hand, marijuana was a cash crop for *cachacos* in higher valleys of the Sierra Nevada who, acting on instructions from intermediaries with whom they had verbal contracts, planted it in areas no larger than ten hectares each.[8] Urban-dwelling men from different towns and cities across the region exported to US buyers the marijuana that *cachacos* cultivated. Partridge described these men as "physicians, teachers, agronomists, landowners, managers of rice and cattle estates, and government employees at the municipal, departmental, and national levels," people who had lived comfortably until the decline of the banana district.[9] Local peasants—for whom cultivating and selling the plant was a tradition and a part-time specialty— did not reap the fruits of the new export business, at least not initially. The "market-induced system"—involving *cachacos* in the Sierra Nevada's highlands and urban buyers and their intermediaries, and oriented toward the United States—"may be considered deviant and marginal to normal social relationships in the community," Partridge concluded.[10] In other words, commercial marijuana for exportation was an abnormality in the evolution of the domestic market.

How did this abnormality come into existence? The origins of Santa Marta Gold are as mysterious and elusive as El Dorado itself. Because smugglers purposely avoided leaving any evidence of their business operations, and agreements between cultivators and intermediaries were always verbal, oral history is the best way to shed some light on conflicting narratives.[11] Hernando Ruiz and Rodrigo Echeverri, two engineers who wrote the earliest studies on the marijuana boom, told me in separate interviews that if anyone had the answers to my questions, that person was agronomist Ariel Martínez.[12] Martínez had worked with Echeverri for the Santa Marta branch of the National Institute of Natural Resources (Inderena) in the early 1970s, and in that capacity he became an expert on the Sierra Nevada. However, Ruiz and Echeverri did not know how to find him, and I searched unsuccessfully for his name in phone books and online. A year passed, and one sunny morning, I was introducing myself to a colleague at the Universidad del Magdalena in Santa Marta when he advised me to talk to his friend Ariel Martínez. By a sheer stroke of luck, I then found him drinking coffee among a group of friends in a supermarket food court in downtown Santa Marta.

Martínez's hypothesis is that a higher-quality marijuana variety evolved as an endogenous species in one of the Sierra Nevada's microclimates. He found it in "only two places: in Quebrada Seca, around Tucurinca [in the banana district], and on the Tapias River [near Dibulla]."[13] Its color was gold and its flavor subtle, but its intoxicating effect was acute. The problem, Martínez explained, was that this strain was available only in small quantities. It required at least two flowers to make one joint, whereas commercial varieties produced flowers big enough to roll up to three joints. He contended that cultivators experimented with combining the native variety with other strains from Hawaii and Sonora, Mexico, a project that US buyers facilitated.[14] The new crossbreed preserved the delicate flavor, the golden color, and the velvety texture of the native strain, and was resistant to plagues and had high yields. According to Martínez, this was Santa Marta Gold.

Martínez's hypothesis resonates with other sources. Apparently, the new, export variety was first produced in Tucurinca and later in Pénjamo, two areas in the Sierra Nevada's western and northern watersheds, respectively, where the driest microclimates in the mountain range offered ideal environments for a strain that grew best in plentiful sunlight and low humidity.[15] The marijuana fields in which Pebo, the old storyteller from Taganga, worked when he was young were located along the Frío River in the Tucurinca area.[16] Sociologist Alfredo Molano and the research team he led on an ambitious

FIGURE 7. Río Ancho, a village of *cachacos* displaced by La Violencia, and an entry point into the Pénjamo area in the Guajira's side of the Sierra Nevada de Santa Marta, 1965. Abby Wasserman personal collection.

oral history project focusing on the colonization of the Sierra Nevada found that by 1966 the marijuana cultivated along the Frío River was considered the highest-quality variety, though it was produced on a small scale.[17] Cultivators told Molano and his team that the seed had been imported from Mexico.[18] Raúl, a *contrabandista* of coffee from Riohacha who smuggled marijuana during the business's ascendance, assured me that it all "started near Santa Marta, and then came over here, to the foothills of the Sierra Nevada, to Pénjamo, towns that belonged to the municipality of Riohacha."[19] Carlos, a marijuana intermediary, affirmed that "there was no marijuana here [the Guajira], and that was the town from where it expanded to the rest; it was the Sierra's exit to the sea;" that was around 1969.[20] Carlos was referring to his hometown, Las Flores, a village in the Pénjamo area. Josefina, also from Las Flores, recalls that the new cash crop arrived in the late 1960s with *cachacos* who went uphill, cleared a patch of *baldío* (public land), and planted it.[21]

Although the Frío River valley and the area known as Tucurinca had a history of marijuana cultivation that dated back to the United Fruit Company's era, the zone popularly known as Pénjamo was new to this business. The cliff Los Muchachitos prevented construction of the Troncal del Caribe from Riohacha to Santa Marta, isolating Pénjamo from the rest of the mountain range. The only access to this area was through the Guajira or by sea. And although the villages located in Pénjamo formed one of Riohacha's breadbaskets, they had never participated in previous export booms. Its rugged terrain, remote location, and lack of roads complicated colonization when *cachacos* arrived in the agricultural hinterlands and settled in with coffee cultivation. Later, however, in the 1970s, when marijuana intermediaries presented a new way of making money to those seeking to escape the socioeconomic and political conflicts that beset the banana district and the cotton belt, Pénjamo became the new frontier.

With a market at their disposal, cultivators viewed marijuana as their best chance at gaining control over both the means of production and their own labor.[22] As a crossbreed, Santa Marta Gold was also a mixture of different technologies and historical temporalities, just as the coffee and banana economies had been, in which an agricultural commodity that flowed through capitalist circuits of exchange was produced within a labor system that continued to operate under noncapitalist modalities.[23] Small farmers and settlers produced marijuana for exportation to international markets by combining techniques of commercial and subsistence agriculture, including exploiting their own labor in order to finance themselves. And as with coffee, the marijuana economy was a product of a global moment in time: when technology transfer, and the "panoply of other technical and social changes" that made the transfer possible—from instruments, tools, and materials to know-how, abilities, and social values—brought about the spread of new methods of plant breeding and high-yielding plants.[24]

A question remains: Who had the vision to identify the potential of the Sierra Nevada for such technological adaptation? Again, mystery, myth, and rumor blend to form a theory that US buyers were the agents of innovation. The first versions of this theory emerged as the political rhetoric of President Alfonso López Michelsen (1974–78), who sought to resolve a diplomatic impasse with the administrations of Gerald Ford and Jimmy Carter—a topic I address in chapter 5. In this context, Colombia's most prestigious think tank, the National Association of Financial Institutions (ANIF), organized a conference in Bogotá to propose legalizing marijuana. Based on fieldwork conducted by Rodrigo Echeverri, Ariel Martínez, and other Inderena experts, ANIF contended that US buyers "stimulated the cultivation of marijuana while at the same time [creating] the mechanisms that would make possible its exportation to the United States."[25] Because ANIF sought to convince the US diplomatic corps to support establishing a commission to study legalization, blaming US buyers for the marijuana boom was a strategic political move. Echeverri found the claim to be inconsistent with the evidence that Inderena collected on the marijuana export economy's origins.[26] In 1980 journalist José Cervantes Angulo published *La noche de las luciérnagas* (The Night of the Fireflies), a collection of his newspaper articles on the workings of the marijuana belt. Basing his claims on unnamed sources, Cervantes Angulo affirmed that "a couple of gringo hippies ventured into the foothills of the Sierra Nevada de Santa Marta to confirm the quality of the *cannabis sativa* that the Indians cultivated," returned to the United States with a big stash, contacted "wholesale distributors in Miami, Los Angeles, Las Vegas, Chicago and New York," and got smugglers Billy Santoro and Jimmy Chagra interested, and soon thereafter, "a group of botanists, agronomists, and technicians in tropical crops" formally launched the marijuana connection.[27] A few years later, this theory became fact in the public mind when former ambassador to the United States Víctor Mosquera Chaux blamed Peace Corps volunteers (PCVs) for inaugurating the marijuana and cocaine businesses.[28] For the rest of the 1980s, politicians wielded this "truth" as a powerful discursive weapon in public battles in which nationalist rhetoric helped further their careers. Even reputable scholars repeated it as a mantra, without providing readers with concrete references or sources of information.[29] Even today this rumor mill continues to spin, shaping national historical imagination and imagery. For example, one of the most celebrated Colombian-made movies of recent years, *Birds of Passage,* which was on the short list for Best Foreign Language Film in the 2019 Oscars, features three PCVs who establish a connection in the Guajira for exporting marijuana.[30]

A cross-check of sources reveals a drop of truth in a sea of imprecise information. On one hand, it is true that US buyers triggered growth in the supply of marijuana when they arrived in Santa Marta's tourist district and bay area in search of small quantities for themselves and friends, and they were instrumental in the experimentation with and adaptation and expansion of local crops. But they did not inaugurate the business, nor were they the main agents of innovation. Agronomist Ariel Martínez, who claimed to have coordinated the PCVs assigned to Inderena in the Sierra Nevada in the early 1970s, argues that those volunteers who had technical training contributed to improving the native variety that was marketed as Santa Marta Gold. But he does not go so far as to affirm that they pioneered cultivation. By the time Martínez worked with the Peace Corps program, marijuana was already a valuable export commodity. Because the US economy was in an economic recession, Martínez surmised, PCVs smuggled exotic birds, butterflies, decorative fish, and marijuana as a way of saving money for their return trip to the United States. "The only dumbass that did not know anything about it was me," he joked.[31]

On the other hand, memories and testimonies of those who were actually in the region at this time do not support the claim of a PCV-sparked boom. Journalist Abby Wasserman, for example, was a PCV in Dibulla from 1964 to 1965. In an email to me, she called "sheer nonsense" anthropologist Anne-Marie Losonczy's undocumented claim (made in an influential essay on Dibulla) that "local memory remembered three young Peace Corps volunteers in the 1960s, marijuana consumers, who introduced the seed." According to Wasserman, the only PCVs in Dibulla were herself and Howard Converse, who "was as straight an arrow as I was." Wasserman and Converse were replaced by Dan and Nana Ellison, who served as volunteers until 1966, when the program in the Guajira was discontinued.[32] During their two years in the Peace Corps, Wasserman and Converse worked with the Junta de Acción Comunal (Community Action Council) and regularly visited Dibulla's hamlets and villages in the Pénjamo area. "I never heard about drugs in my time," Wasserman affirmed emphatically during a phone interview. What she heard were stories of vendettas among families of smugglers "who had a long-standing feud that made them not to want to work together."[33] "Did Dibulleros really conflate me and Dan and Nana, who lived in town and established relationships and worked with local juntas, with stoned hippies on the beach? It is depressing to think about," Wasserman said.[34] Her friend and former PCV in Colombia Maureen Orth, now a well-known investigative journalist, spent days trying to identify, for an op-ed on the movie *Birds of Passage,* the volunteers who worked in the Sierra Nevada with Ariel Martínez.[35] She located only one, an archaeologist who had recently died.[36] Another similar inconsistency exists regarding the participation of US smuggler Jimmy Chagra, whom journalist Cervantes Angulo reported as having been responsible for hiring agronomists and experts on tropical crops. Chagra disclosed to journalists that his first transaction involving Colombian marijuana was in the summer of 1975 when he orchestrated a shipment of more than fifty thousand pounds of marijuana from Colombia to Massachusetts.[37] By that year, marijuana crops for export were the main commodity of the Sierra Nevada economy, which was about to reach its peak.

In sum, little evidence supports the theory that US buyers, and Peace Corps volunteers in particular, pioneered the marijuana connection. The

FIGURE 8. Peace Corps volunteers *(left to right)* Howard Converse, Abby Wasserman, and Arleen Cheston attend a meeting in Mingueo with the Junta de Acción Comunal (Community Action Council), Sierra Nevada de Santa Marta, 1965. Abby Wasserman personal collection.

evidence that I found demonstrates, instead, that several interlocking social sectors worked together in ad-hoc alliances to experiment with local crops, introduce foreign strains, create crossbreeds, spread seeds, and share technical knowledge. Anthropologist William Partridge was unequivocal in asserting that urban elites and middle classes from the banana district and Santa Marta bay area played a crucial role in the emergence of a "market-induced system." Partridge witnessed professionals, state functionaries, hacienda employees, landowners, and politicians alike investing in the promotion of crops in order to grow the business from one of petty commerce to a large export-driven sector. And this was as much the case in Pénjamo as in Tucurinca, where an elite subset of smugglers, landowners, and politicians from Riohacha and other towns in the Department of Guajira responded to the rising demand for marijuana by slowly replacing coffee contraband with marijuana smuggling. Callo, a *contrabandista* from Riohacha, told me that his first experience with marijuana smuggling was around 1969 when a family of Liberal politicians hired him to transport a cargo. He arrived at their hacienda on La Punta, near Dibulla early in the morning, ate a big meal of pork and chicken, and waited for hours for the arrival of a train of mules bringing marijuana sacks from somewhere in Pénjamo. He drove the cargo to a land-ing field built years earlier for aerial fumigation of cotton and banana crops—landing fields were built in many areas after the Green Revolution mandated the use of agrochemicals—and observed the loading operation of the small fumigation plane with around three hundred pounds of marijuana.[38]

Although US buyers and urban elites and middle classes were important in the transition from smuggling to cultivation, the source of the marijuana export economy's dynamism lay with popular sectors available and willing to adapt such a novel business to their own productive and commercial tradi-tions. *Cachacos* pioneered cultivation for export when US buyers and "their Colombian partners—the smugglers—campaigned among cultivators and organized transportation of the weed."[39] Anthropologist Margarita Serje, who was part of the team that uncovered the Taironas's Ciudad Perdida in the early 1970s, a lost indigenous city located in one of the highest intermontane valleys of the Sierra Nevada's northern watershed, remembers that when the scientists arrived, *guaqueros* (tomb raiders) searching for archeological treasures were the vanguard of a massive colonization wave, for right behind them were *cachacos,* settling in to cultivate marijuana.[40] Ismael, an electrician from Santa Marta who grew marijuana with a group of friends in this area, confirmed that most cultivators were from the Andean interior—"they came from everywhere."[41] Josefina, from Las Flores, remembered Negro Kilo, a man from the Andean interior, distributing the seed. "People did not know about marijuana, and he was the first; he arrived with some *antioqueños* [from the coffee region] and started it all; it was a disaster," she lamented. By the early 1970s, Josefina told me, there were two areas near Las Flores where *cachacos* and local peasants grew marijuana, La Tremenda (the Tremendous One) and El Paraíso (the Paradise)—the latter named for the high quality of its product.[42] Even in indigenous lands in the Sierra Nevada, Colombian and US smugglers pro-moted the seed. Irma, one of the founding members of the hippie-kogis—a hippie commune of young men and women from Bogotá who lived among the Kogi people—told me, "We saw the gringos giving seeds to peasants; they offered them to us, they told us that if we planted so many quintals they would pay us so much money."[43] Parménides Salazar, secretary of treasury and finances of the Department of Cesar, reported in January 1973 to the Minister of Government in Bogotá that in Arauca, an area in the Sierra Nevada not far from Valledupar, there were "unscrupulous people disguised as hippies, scien-tists, and hikers promoting the cultivation of marijuana, which they subse-quently traded with Indians."[44] Salazar did not identify these people by nationality, but Arhuaco authority Bienvenido Arroyo remembered both foreigners and Colombians arriving as tourists to Pueblo Bello, located in the same area of the Sierra Nevada, and handing out marijuana seeds for free.[45] Santa Marta Gold and lesser-quality varieties spread across the three watersheds, replacing coffee as the main cash crop in the highlands. In places such as San Pedro and Palmor, where the bean had been a stable and profitable cash crop for decades, "the coffee economy succumbed."[46] The famous orchestra Los Melódicos moved their fans to dance to the rhythm of this story:

> I used to have my coffee plantation,
> it was a generous land, . . .
> until a fat, well-dressed guy came,
> did not want to identify himself, . . .
> the fat guy convinced me
> to plant in my coffee land
> a seed that will make me rich without watering it.[47]

Persuasion, seduction, and conversion were required to interweave the various threads of this technological adaptation. Modernization, Michael Latham writes, entailed a "cognitive framework" according to which the United States would "transform a world [it] perceived as both materially and culturally deficient." President John F. Kennedy's Alliance for Progress was modernization's highest expression, an integrated platform that sought to transmit US values and mindsets to the developing world by addressing simultaneously these countries' economic, social, political, and cultural issues, Latham argues.[48] In light of this cognitive framework, the unsubstantiated rumor that the Peace Corps volunteers were responsible for the onset of the marijuana bonanza makes more sense. The Peace Corps program was pivotal in bringing the Alliance for Progress to fruition in that it combined US national interests in the context of Cold War militarism with idealism and humanitarian internationalism.[49] Delivering on his campaign promise to create a "new frontier," Kennedy founded the Peace Corps in 1961 to offer young people the opportunity to play key roles in the "wild west" of the developing world.[50] The intimate relationship between Washington and the National Front contributed to making Colombia the program's pilot country in Latin America.[51] Through the global humanitarian organization CARE, young men and women arrived in impoverished rural areas to work on intensive farming techniques and to build housing, roads, and infrastructure.[52] This new approach, focused on local needs, seemed to contradict modernization's grandiloquent mentality of industrialization, bureaucratization, and centralization. But "thinking small," as Daniel Immerwahr wittily puts it, actually complemented the larger development project by opening a crucial path to it through small-scale solidarities. [53] And a commitment to the community was what led many Peace Corps volunteers to develop strong affinities with and loyalties to local people. As Wasserman reminded me, most PCVs had never engaged in political activities abroad, and they now find the idea of their having been pawns of US geopolitics to be quite cynical.[54] Regardless of their personal motivations, "they became enmeshed in a transnational web of overlapping and conflicting interests," Jasamin Rostam-Kolayi argues, which served a goal of Washington's political agenda: to contain burgeoning grassroots social revolutions around the world.[55] The Peace Corps volunteers' "heroic development work," Molly Geidel shows, required "seduction" whereby they presented themselves and the rich and powerful United States as part of an "enchanting vision" and "charm[ed] people into reimagining themselves and their nations."[56] No wonder that when PCVs brought this seductive baggage of intangible goods to the program's pilot Latin American country, their presence sparked fascination and apprehension, leading to rumors that they seeded one of the most intriguing moments in Colombia's history, the rise of the drug business.

In any case, many Colombians were persuaded and seduced by the allure of growing marijuana as a cash crop. To do so successfully, they relied on both the plant's natural qualities and their own labor and agricultural traditions. Marijuana's short growing cycle of five to nine months between planting and harvesting, its natural capacity to prepare virgin soils for cultivating more stable crops, and its high market prices made it ideal for the colonization of the rocky agricultural frontiers, particularly on Pénjamo, the virgin section of the Sierra Nevada. The first and most obvious result of this expansion of marijuana crops was accelerated population growth.[57] The hamlet of Perico Aguado, for example, swelled from sixty families in the 1950s to two hundred in the early 1970s. By the mid-1970s, the village of Mingueo, not far from there, went from slaughtering one cow every Sunday to provide the whole town with meat for a week, to sacrificing twenty cows for the same period.[58] The second and longest-lasting consequence was a rapid process of deforestation. Fundación ProSierra Nevada de Santa Marta, the most reputable environmental NGO in the region, estimated that 100,000 hectares of primary forests were cut down to plant marijuana, reducing forest cover by 82 percent and affecting the water supply even until today.[59]

While different social sectors took advantage of the novel economy, political developments in two neighboring countries contributed to this marijuana bonanza. The second-most important marijuana supplier to US markets after Mexico during the 1960s and early 1970s was Jamaica, where, in 1973, Prime Minister Michael Manley agreed to cooperate with the Nixon administration on "Operation Buccaneer," a campaign to "search and destroy" marijuana fields on the island.[60] A year later, newly elected Venezuelan president Carlos Andrés Pérez launched a militarized deportation campaign to stop immigration of undocumented Colombians seeking jobs in the latest oil boom.[61] The National Police of the Department of Guajira reported in 1975 that of those who were deported through Paraguachón, on the border near Maicao, only 30 percent came back to Venezuela, 10 percent returned to their places of origins in the Andean interior of Colombia, and 60 percent stayed in the region.[62] Seeking opportunities in their own country after failing to find economic stability in Venezuela, many deportees traveled to the marijuana belt in the Sierra Nevada looking for seasonal jobs or a patch of *baldío* (public land) where they could start anew. The crackdown on marijuana production in Jamaica, along with similar campaigns in Mexico, increased US demand for Colombian-grown marijuana, while the social and demographic effects of the Venezuelan deportation policy added to the labor force available to supply this demand.

As with bananas, coffee, and cotton in previous decades, a confluence of regional and international trends made marijuana cultivation the fastest-growing activity in the former Greater Magdalena. Since local inhabitants considered the crop an agricultural commodity like any other, its cultivation encountered no moral barriers and it spread rapidly along the slopes below 1,600 meters above sea level, at which altitude a different ecological niche posed a natural blockade.[63] "Marijuana was like food," said Meco, a contraband transporter from San Juan del Cesar who planted the crop. "The seed had to be bought, because whoever planted it classified it," Meco explained; "he selected the most seasoned seed, the one that produced best, like corn; sometimes, if they were friends, they gave it to you for free."[64] With the seeds, cultivators also acquired the technical knowledge necessary to produce a successful harvest. Such knowledge was passed down either by word of mouth among cultivators, Meco explained, or by intermediaries and even US buyers. According to Callo, "they came from there [United States] in their own boats, and stayed here for months, as tourists, walking around in shorts and going up and down there [Sierra Nevada] to instruct how to plant it, how to cultivate it, how to water it."[65] Journalist Cervantes Angulo reported seeing a free booklet on the ABCs of marijuana cultivation that was written in Spanish, edited in Florida, and distributed among farmers.[66]

At the rapid pace of its expansion, marijuana soon reached the neighboring mountain range of Perijá. The Administrative Department of Security (DAS) in Riohacha reported to the National Security Council in Bogotá that in 1975 the Ancho River valley and Las Flores—both located in the Pénjamo area—were the two largest marijuana producers in the Department of Guajira, followed by San Juan del Cesar, in the southeastern watershed of the Sierra Nevada, and Fonseca and Villanueva, on the Perijá.[67] José Agustín Llaguna, a storyteller and peasant from Conejo, a hamlet in the foothills of the Perijá, in the municipality of Fonseca, told me that a man whom everybody thought was from the United States was the initiator. "He was *mono* [white], old, big, gray-haired; he called meetings, he was the one who brought the seed here," Llaguna recalled. "He said, for example, one quintal of malanga costs 10 pesos, the quintal of this costs 100,000 [pesos]; and that is how it all began, he convinced all the peasants."[68] After surveying twenty marijuana farms, economists Betty Solórzano and Frida de Dangond concluded that "crops of marijuana appeared as long as there was a little bit of sun, water, and wind."[69] Basically, marijuana grew anywhere in a region where its economy and ecology combined perfectly to offer prime conditions for a "deviant and marginal" export economy, in anthropologist William Partridge's words, to become the norm.

Once the peak occurred in 1976, when two harvests coincided, new mechanisms emerged to mediate competition for lands in a transformed landscape. The completion of the Troncal del Caribe in 1975, between Santa Marta and Riohacha, finally connected all the towns along the littoral and thus expedited the colonization of the Pénjamo area, which had previously been isolated from the rest of the coast by the cliff of Los Muchachitos. Following patterns established in the coffee region, cultivators developed new arrangements for mediating the social relations of production and facilitating negotiations among themselves for land and labor.[70] In one arrangement, growers paid as much as 12 percent of the final product in rent to the landowner. In another, *amediería,* or sharecropping, growers provided the inputs and labor in exchange for the right to cultivate without paying rent, but they were required to share profits equally with the proprietor.[71] In time, cultivation also spread to conservation lands in protected areas when cultivators took out loans from other growers, intermediaries, friends, or relatives.[72]

FIGURE 9. A family of marijuana cultivators and their crop, Sierra Nevada de Santa Marta. *Time* Magazine, January 29, 1979. Center for Creative Photography, University of Arizona: David Kennerly Archive © CCP, Arizona Board of Regents.

Whatever the agreement with the landowner, all cultivators worked under the same set of restrictions and procedures. They all depended on external sources of financing. They all planted in areas no larger than a peasant farm—up to ten hectares, but with an average size of three hectares. They all followed the same eight basic stages of marijuana production.[73] They provided the labor, which usually meant employing family members or neighbors during cultivation, and relying on workers from other commercial crops such as coffee, cotton, or bananas—or on the "floating population of waged workers from around the country" including deportees from Venezuela—during harvest.[74] And most important, they all depended on intermediaries to commercialize their product. If, during the earliest years of the marijuana boom's peak in the early 1970s, producers worked at the behest of specific buyers who hired them through intermediaries, as Partridge attested, by the height of the bonanza's peak in the mid-1970s, around 60 percent of them planted "without having a buyer, and practically none [sold] the harvest directly to foreigners."[75]

This reliance on intermediaries represented a valuable opportunity to the growing mass of rural and urban young men who were native to the region and wished to make a living in commerce rather than agriculture. Like coffee *contrabandistas* in the 1960s, marijuana intermediaries in the 1970s assumed the profitable and essential task of connecting disparate social sectors, from growers in the intermontane valleys to exporters and buyers in the lowlands, creating novel patterns of wealth, power, and prestige in the process.

INTERMEDIATION AND THE FORMATION
OF AN EXPORT ECONOMY

In more than one sense, the marijuana belt's boom reproduced patterns of the coffee frontier's heyday. Marijuana was an agricultural export commodity, without value added, whose profits were the exclusive result of its circulation along chains of intermediaries who benefited from a growing international market. These intermediaries were young men from the countryside, towns, villages, and urban peripheries. If cultivators considered marijuana to be "like food," and thus held no moral prejudices against its adoption, intermediaries approached their work as an extension of contraband smuggling. They believed they were practicing a legitimate and profitable—albeit illegal—activity that fulfilled an indispensable function in the regional economy. Popularly known as *marimberos,* these intermediaries coordinated all the parties and activities involved in putting a cargo at the exporters' and buyers' disposal. They secured harvests from cultivators through their ability to extend credit and power to set prices. They based their pricing on quality and quantity, as well as the proximity of the farm to the exportation outlet, their own position in the intermediation chain, the type of payment required—cash, kind, or credit— and the degree of trust or kinship between themselves and the cultivators.[76] They acted like sommeliers by reconciling taste preferences with budget restrictions, and they saw to other logistics such as coordinating the strenuous tasks of packing and transporting loads from highlands to lowlands.

Their classification system consisted of five criteria: color, smell, cleanliness, humidity, and maturity. The best marijuana was yellow, dry like tobacco, clean, aromatic, and mature, and it cost twice as much as the lowest quality. Within this category, "gold" was the superior variety that not only met the five aforementioned criteria but also contained "only flowers, no leaves."[77] Other categories, from greatest to least quality, were *concha de coco* (coco shell), *mango biche* (green mango), *rayada* (striped), *negra* (black), and *cafuche* (residue); all were exported.[78] These varieties resulted not from species differentiation or genetic modification but from environmental conditions and cultivation methods that manipulated growth and watering during maturation.[79]

Much as with coffee, the widening of the marijuana frontier did not require large investments in labor, because cultivators exploited their own and relatives' labor, but its commercialization and transport did require financing.[80] This investment came from exporters. With a few exceptions (Lucho Barranquilla being one), exporters were male urban elites who relied on their "connections"—the term used for US buyers—and worked in closed networks of relatives, friends, and *compadres*; hence, outsiders who aspired to become intermediaries had to resort to kinship ties or friendships to gain access to exporters' cliques. For example, Carlos's brother-in-law introduced him to an exporter and vouched for his credibility. Native to Las Flores, Carlos learned about marijuana in the late 1960s, when as a teenager he witnessed the town's bosses negotiating over loads with Lucky and his people. "'No, no, this is not for kids,'" Carlos recalled the elders saying when he and his friends pried into loading operations. "We always approached [when they loaded], and they gave us something [money] so we would clear out, or we carried a sack on our shoulders, because I carried it without knowing what it was," Carlos remembered. "When Lucky's people arrived to buy, those responsible were the bosses of the town," he said.[81] Years later, the activity had grown so much that he did not hesitate to get involved in it. "I brought a sample [from cultivators]," Carlos told me during one of our several conversations on a bench at Simón Bolívar Park in Riohacha. "I was afraid; I did not have a penny, I was broke, thinking that I was going to be rejected [but] he liked it."[82] Through his brother-in-law, Carlos won the trust of the exporter, and thanks to his judicious work, he became part of a "hierarchy [in which] you advanced by being skillful and not fearing the business, not fearing to invest," Carlos explained. "Not mixing work with money, because that is how you made money, [by] working without thinking about what you will earn."[83]

The troubled agrarian modernization and urbanization of the region, and the related waves of migration from the Andean interior, created a large pool of unskilled labor that found employment in packing, transportation, surveillance, and loading. Intermediaries connected these workers with exporters in order to amass the tons that were necessary to complete a shipment. These intermediaries usually worked for only one exporter at a time, who procured their labor by giving some cash in advance and the remainder after the US buyers paid.[84] The smallest operations required at least two intermediaries, one to deal directly with cultivators, the other to coordinate directly with exporters.[85]

Intermediaries fulfilled two needs. One was practical, related to the logistics of marijuana exportation; the other was cultural, concerning the economic values of a society with a historically limited market of goods and money. Given that the supply came from thousands of small producers, intermediaries mushroomed to connect both ends. The *tienda,* a type of grocery store that *cachacos* introduced in the Sierra Nevada during the coffee colonization of the agricultural frontiers, provides the best example of a form of market circulation that defined marijuana intermediaries' work. As William Partridge explained, the *tienda* operated on a "simple market mechanism of dividing a given item into smaller units so that each unit accrues value through exchange."[86] Notwithstanding its exorbitant profits, the marijuana economy replicated the values of this economic culture of scarcity, as intermediaries were also obliged to work with small "units" and their earnings were the exclusive result of exchange. They bought harvests from myriad peasant producers, then sold them to next-level intermediaries at a higher price, and so on until the whole chain managed to put together the amount the exporter required. "We paid a sum to the peasant, and then we doubled that sum to the wholesaler, and he did the same with the connection; thus, the one who imported it was the one who made the most," Carlos explained.[87] This system created numerous opportunities for credit and money making for the largest group of people possible.

I address the intermediaries' cultural values and social codes in the following chapter, but it is worth noting here the apparent contradiction in the profitable marijuana economy adopting a feature from a system of scarcity. In spite of the marijuana business's bountifulness, there was a shortage of connections (buyers). Finding buyers and developing enough stable business with them to produce a shipment posed the greatest challenges. Simply put, its illegal nature and complete reliance on US buyers to reach consumer markets contributed to the marijuana export economy's taking on a pyramidal structure, with large numbers of producers at the bottom and a few exporters at the top. In 1978, ANIF estimated that there were seventy air exporters and twelve maritime exporters in the former Greater Magdalena.[88] This small number of exporters channeled the fruits of the work of "more than 150,000 [people], including producers, intermediaries, and employees more or less permanent and their relatives."[89] Despite the democratizing effect that cultivation had in the region by offering a source of income to masses of cultivators, and a golden opportunity to young men from popular sectors to become merchants, the economy as a whole was narrow and meager. This paradox of abundance and scarcity also manifested in other economic sectors as food crop shortages and labor scarcity. Merchants in local markets bought and transported corn, beans, potatoes, and other vegetables from the Andean interior because such produce was no longer grown locally, which increased prices. And managers of cotton, banana, and other plantation crops could not compete for seasonal workers against marijuana's higher wages.[90]

The business was as exclusive during its peak as it was during its ascendance, and exporters were the ones who benefited most from this paradox of abundance and scarcity. Their work started when they established a connection with a US buyer, and continued when they centralized investments from different sources to buy harvests and advanced money to intermediaries. They also coordinated with intermediaries and buyers on both the times and the places where the pick-ups or transshipments would occur. Mantequilla, Lucky's brother, explained that they "ordered to pack it, then ships came from abroad, and we loaded, and paid for the loading."[91] They negotiated with those landowners whose properties were suitable for building improvised airstrips, and with families that controlled natural seaports and the labor of the younger members. The Department of Guajira's National Police reported to Bogotá in 1975 that "there are true capitalists" paying local people to use their farms and lands for marijuana cultivation or exportation.[92] Exporters also bribed authorities, personally or through intermediaries.[93] Finally, they distributed profits according to each investor's percentage of participation once the operation concluded and everybody else was paid.

Exporters also created new procedures for dealing effectively with the business's meteoric growth, and with their innovations they widened its social reach. While crops extended along the intermontane valleys, larger shipments became the new standard. "The lowest weight you could have in order to make a [maritime] marijuana shipment profitable [was] around three hundred quintals [approximately thirty-three tons]," Carlos recalled. Putting together a cargo of this size required weeks if not months of work on the part of at least two intermediaries, especially if the buyer demanded the marijuana during the off-season—between harvests, when supplies were lowest. Such an operation involved nearly forty people in transport and loading alone.[94] Engineer Manuel Lineros, head of Incora (the institute that managed the agrarian reform) in the Department of Magdalena in the early 1980s, remembered that with larger and heavier freights, costs of putting a cargo together increased exorbitantly, forcing exporters to implement new methods to collect investment money. Exporters invented the strategy they called *apúnteme* (sign me in) or *va a salir el bus* (the bus is leaving), Lineros explained, which consisted of pools of investors who shared the cost of shipments according to percentages of the total exported, like selling tickets for seats in a bus.[95] Banana and cotton growers, merchants, cattle ranchers, politicians, professionals, and employees in the public and private sectors became increasingly more involved in the business.[96] "Here, in 1977 and 1978, everybody was somehow involved in the *marimba* [marijuana business]," journalist Edgar Ferrucho Padilla told me over a snack in Riohacha's downtown. "If you knew a peasant with a patch of land, you financed him, and whatever he produced you split it in half; there were a lot of people with a peasant cultivating for them," he said.[97]

In addition to involving more members of the urban elites and middle classes, the boom also incorporated the youngest Wayuu men at the lowest levels of the commercialization chain, and enriched smugglers of general merchandise. Germán Aguilar Epieyú, a Wayuu authority and *pütchipü* (or *palabrero*; conflict negotiator), explained that young Wayuu men got involved in the business during the peak of the boom as low-paid unskilled labor. Because most seaports are located in ancestral indigenous territory, Aguilar Epieyú observed, exporters and intermediaries relied on families in the area to rent the caravans of canoes needed to load the ships—vessels with heavier freights could not tie up at the shore because they would run aground. To navigate the shallow waters, they hired young men for loading and surveillance during the operation. That is why "the most negative impact of the marijuana boom took place among the youngest Wayuu generations, because they deserted [their clans]" to pursue a mirage, Aguilar Epieyú concluded.[98]

On the other hand, smugglers of general merchandise concentrated in Maicao benefited even though they invested little in the business. "There was a tacit agreement between *contrabandistas* and the people who traded in marijuana not to export marijuana there to avoid problems," journalist Enrique Herrera Barros said in reference to the natural ports of the upper Guajira. "The people who worked with contraband did everything humanly possible not to get involved," Herrera Barros assured me. Marijuana was thus exported "from the middle Guajira [i.e., Riohacha-Maicao] to the south, and from the middle Guajira to the north was the traditional contraband," Herrera Barros pointed out.[99] The natural seaports located near Riohacha, such as La Punta, Camarones, and El Pájaro, were their domains.[100] Smugglers of general merchandise and luxury goods nevertheless benefited, because for the first time ever, there was a local market for their commodities. In 1975 the National Police reported that since 1969, the number of stores in Maicao had increased by 100 percent, of taxis by 600 percent, of privately owned vehicles by 60 percent, of trucks by 40 percent, of street vendors by 800 percent, and construction of residential and commercial housing by 60 percent.[101] Part of this growth was attributable to the short bonanza that Venezuela experienced after the 1973 oil crisis. Most of it, however, was a reverberation of the marijuana boom.

But these side effects also came with headaches. Journalist Ferrucho Padilla, who was appointed mayor of Maicao during the boom years, declared: "I never found marijuana to be a problem; the problems were the usual—lack of water, electricity, there were no teachers, there was a health care center but [it] was not in service."[102] Ferrucho Padilla emphasized that deportees from Venezuela who stayed in the Guajira were the ones who shook Maicao to the core. They occupied vacant lots, built shantytowns, clashed with both the police and the merchant class who owned most of the urban property, and challenged the municipal government regarding public administration, public health, and public order. These same problems occurred in most of the other departmental capitals.[103]

Unlike the destitute classes that scrambled for both land and jobs, rural or urban, wealthy Colombians from the Andean interior arrived in more auspicious conditions to capitalize on the green gold rush. The Department of Magdalena National Police reported that "a true, and each time larger and better organized, mafia is devoting its efforts and money to this crime [marijuana traffic]."[104] The testimony of Chucho, a former enforcer for the Medellín cartel whom I met in a maximum security prison in Bolivia while I was reporting on another case, complements these police reports. Drinking espresso in La Paz shortly after his release from jail, Chucho told me that he arrived to Calabacito, in the Pénjamo area, around 1977, having been sent by his boss. Chucho worked for an experienced *contrabandista* of general merchandise from Medellín who became part of a pool of investors in marijuana. Searching for growing sites, they "found this [one], because marijuana grew faster and better."[105] At age seventeen, Chucho guarded their marijuana plantation along with at least forty other poor young men from Medellín under the supervision on an older man from the same city. It was like an estate, Chucho said, "around 80 to 100 hectares; it looked like a tapestry, very beautiful." Most of the plantation employees—around six hundred men—were from the Andean interior, along with a few *guajiros.* "It was a huge compound, like an army," as he described it. "We all lived in bunk beds of three levels, with fans in the ceiling, without walls, and a chest with a lock for each, because they stole each other's money and belongings."[106] At the peak of the bonanza, the Sierra Nevada, its Guajira side particularly, became Colombia's new frontier of development, where adventurous men pursued their dreams of capital accumulation and social recognition.[107]

And like Colombians, US buyers also found in the marijuana belt of the Sierra Nevada and Perijá a horizon of possibility. Larger shipments prompted them to adapt their procedures as well, by introducing changes that had immediate implications for the social relations of exchange. First, US buyers trained Colombians on how to use the hydraulic press. Elber, a tractor operator in the cotton fields who became a hydraulic press mechanic for marijuana exporters, recalled that a Cuban exile from Florida taught him how to press, pack, and waterproof loads either for maritime transportation or for dropping bales from airplanes into swamps, rivers, or the high seas. They used boxes of Marlboro cigarettes and waxed paper from sugar sacks—both products smuggled in and out of the Guajira—to pack up to seventy pounds of marijuana in small, tight loafs called *panelas.*[108] Elber went inside his house and came back with the wooden mold he used to make *panelas,* which he had kept as a memento of his prosperous days. "[When] it was sent in sacks, you carried a ton," José Luis, a driver from San Juan del Cesar, explained, "but when they started to press it, they loaded up to three tons in the truck, and cars were so heavy that tires exploded."[109]

The introduction of the hydraulic press forced exporters and intermediaries to create another technological innovation, *caletas.* A nautical term that refers to the smallest inlet on a coast and the most hermetic bunker in a ship, *caleta* alluded to the storage facility improvised near natural seaports or landing fields where intermediaries pressed, packed, and stockpiled marijuana in preparation for export. Silvio, a sailor who worked in transportation and loading, said that "*caletas* came late," meaning after the peak; "there we pressed, and aired [it], because sometimes marijuana was brought in humid, and we had to dry it or it would rot," Silvio recalled. "And then we poured *aguapanela* [sugarcane juice] and rum on it, because that helped to preserve it."[110] Although *caletas* facilitated the transport of tons of marijuana from farms to seaports and airstrips, they also complicated logistics. For one thing, long storage periods in hot weather increased humidity, which contributed to the growth of a fungus that spoiled marijuana irremediably.[111] For another, *caletas* were expensive for exporters because they needed to hire more people for surveillance and security in order to prevent seizures from authorities, attacks from competitors, and robberies from workers.[112] Chucho, along with other young men brought from Medellín to the Guajira to guard the plantation, also safeguarded the *caletas.* They were heavily armed. "I used machine guns, Inga, 9 millimeters of twenty-eight rounds, Mini Uzi, and pistols," Chucho recalled with delight.[113]

After the hydraulic press and *caletas*, the third change in procedures that affected the social relations of exchange occurred when US buyers altered the means of transportation in order to import larger and heavier shipments. During the period of ascendance, maritime transport was the main form of exportation, whether it took place in *guajiros*' boats setting sail from the natural seaports near Riohacha, or in the hands of sailors working in merchant ships and arriving at and departing from Santa Marta, or in sailing boats navigated by US tourists–cum–petty smugglers. As the business expanded, transporters were obliged to change routes and procedures. Instead of the traditional destinations of Aruba, Curaçao, and (to a lesser extent) the Panama Canal, smugglers of marijuana had to go farther north. Silvio, who worked on the ships that carried cargos to pick-up points on the high seas, explained that "the route was all north, to St. Martin, near Puerto Rico, the Bahamas, another place near Mexico, Santo Domingo—we never headed to Florida because of the surveillance, we could go anywhere but there." The US buyer coordinated the boats and yachts for the transshipment into US territory. Once the operation was over, Silvio recalled, "the boss who came from there in a motor launch with bodyguards gave us tips, a hundred or two hundred dollars to each one, because the *gringo* used to pay tips." Once the ship was empty, the captain anchored on the open sea, and sailors cleaned the ships' decks and storage facilities to eliminate odors and stains. Then they headed back to the Guajira, but "never through the same route," and exporters "never worked with the same captain twice, for security," Silvio pointed out.[114]

Soon, transporting large shipments of marijuana shifted from the seas to the air. Airplanes had clear advantages over ships as they took less time to arrive at their destination, they simplified logistics for the exporter, and provided the US buyer more independence and autonomy. Initially, US buyers used small fumigation airplanes or recreational aircraft like the Piper Cherokee and Beechcraft planes. But with larger and heavier shipments, US buyers began to use refurbished military aircraft, such as DC-3s, DC-6s, and DC-9s. The availability of former US military personnel who were trained to

fly such aircraft lay the perfect groundwork for the blossoming of this entrepreneurial idea. Ex-pilots from the US wars in Vietnam, Laos, and Cambodia
played a significant role in the temporary success of the US-Colombian marijuana connection. So far, much of what we know about US soldiers, drugs,
and wars is limited to consumption and addiction.[115] However, US military
exploits in the Third World also produced important legacies in the form of
bold commercial adventures such as drug smuggling. Reconnecting with a
powerful metaphor in their own country's historical imagination—namely,
the sky as the new frontier—these former US military pilots revived a historical pattern of US hegemony in the Caribbean region by making the airplane
a potent tool for the generation of profits, and by joining the Colombian
marijuana bonanza to attain economic mobility and opportunities.[116]

After the creation of Santa Marta Gold, air transportation constituted the
most important technological innovation contributing to the peak of the
boom. Old airplanes were easy to refurbish or rent in the United States, landing fields were quickly constructed in the windswept desert plains of the
Guajira and the great valley, the duration of the trip was short enough that
fuel was affordable, and airplanes smuggling marijuana cargo could fly unde-
tected thanks to the intense air traffic of private jets carrying vacationers in
the Caribbean. K. "Hawkeye" Gross was a veteran from Colorado who
aspired to work for Pan Am after his return from Vietnam, only to find the
United States heading toward an economic recession. When a friend proposed entering the risky marijuana business, Gross had an epiphany. "It hit
me like a smack in the mouth," Gross writes in his memoirs: "smuggling was
what I'd been trained to do . . . the jet training, the survival schools teaching
me crash survival and torture resistance, the battle experience in Vietnam,
the flying in and out of dirt roads in Cambodia, the ragtag charter flying for
Exec Air" all had prepared him to become a marijuana smuggler.[117] Along
with his friend Mike Buff, who had received a dishonorable discharge from
the Air Force, Gross spent months searching for the right aircraft and making preliminary trips to the Sierra Nevada. For the actual operation, they
took the longest route—through Haiti instead of Cuba—and on their
return, they paid the captain of a fishing boat to pick up the loads they
dropped into the sea, as well as operators of several motorboats that transported the bales to US territory. Gross and Buff conducted these smuggling
operations for years until they were caught and sent to jail.

On their end, exporters and intermediaries learned how to improvise
airstrips, assist pilots during landing and takeoff, and provide them with

what they needed for their return. Composer Hernando Marín commemorates this adaptation in "El gavilán mayor" (The Big Sparrow Hawk), a vallenato song that pays homage to a marijuana intermediary known by this nickname, and whose hometown of La Palma, near Riohacha, was perfect for use as a landing field:

> Among the birds I am the greatest flyer,
> because in my wings I have more power,
> because I carry my beak with intention
> for those who want to betray me,
> and with my claws I know how to defend myself.
> I am the Big Sparrow Hawk
> in the air, I am king.[118]

Dozens of songs like this one voiced the sense of personal importance and social relevance that intermediaries cultivated as part of their membership in the marijuana merchant class. Marijuana traffickers, whether they were Colombian exporters and intermediaries or US buyers, worked with friends, relatives and *compadres,* and through their closed networks they set all the cogs in the machine in motion and kept them moving. Their work constituted the only stage in the marijuana export economy that produced value; therefore, constantly adapting to the imbalances between supply and demand was crucial to their staying in business, generating opportunities for mobility within the pyramidal structure, realizing economic and social gains, and reconciling the illegal character of their activity with its social legitimacy.

If we understand technology to be a collection of instruments, materials, knowledge, know-how, and social values that resolve challenges through adaptation, then Santa Marta Gold and other export varieties were the most revolutionizing technology for the problem of modernization in the former Greater Magdalena. Adopting marijuana as a cash crop spurred the emergence of a new export economy centered on tropical commodities, and created a class of intermediaries and exporters that temporarily became a powerful regional elite. US buyers played a crucial role in the technological transfer that made this possible. Like pollinators, their demand for marijuana facilitated the expansion of cultivation and commerce, as did their widespread presence in the region. However, it was the local population that made the success of this novel business possible; these people opportunistically forged business alliances with their US counterparts, willingly switched to a new crop, and tenaciously experimented with cultivation and commercialization practices and methods. Colombia's marijuana boom is not a case of a developed country transferring technology to a developing one, but one of intricate circuitries in which ideas, methods, and tools became tangled and untangled in all directions.

However, as creative as these innovations were, they were limited in terms of producing long-lasting change. The accelerated pace at which the marijuana export economy expanded and its pyramidal socioeconomic structure limited its protagonists' ability to create conditions conducive to their reproduction as a new class in the long term. Although a series of technological adaptations assisted cultivators in opening the agricultural frontier and establishing farms, provided rural and urban young men the opportunity to participate in the commercial economy and urban society, and ameliorated social tensions between all these sectors, the marijuana business was as narrow at the top as other tropical commodity booms before it, concentrating social gains and economic profits in fewer and fewer hands. In this context, previous patterns of production and exchange—defined by the *contrabandista* code of honor, including honorable masculinity, personal relationships among friends and *compadres,* and credit and debt—continued to offer useful solutions to the structural problems that the technological innovations did not alter completely. These old social relations of production and exchange made it extremely difficult for those at the bottom of the marijuana export economy's pyramidal structure to articulate an ideology of class antagonism and exploitation.[119] In any case, the masses of intermediaries situated in a central position in the overall structure—as motors driving the circulation of the commodity and the creation of value—attempted a consolidation as an emergent class. They articulated a grandiloquent sense of their socioeconomic role through a discourse of masculine honor and plebeian virtues that projected onto the regional public sphere. In the process, these traffickers, popularly known as *marimberos,* revitalized the most problematic legacies of previous agrarian booms, and paved the way for their own demise.

FOUR

———

Party Animals

VALLENATO MUSIC AND CULTURAL NEGOTIATION

What the hell! I don't care if people say that I am a degenerate drunk. I just want them to keep in mind that I work and don't beg. So what if I am a party animal, who cares?

LENÍN BUENO SUÁREZ,
vallenato composer

IT ALL BEGAN in "a great *parranda* [party] in the patio of my house," Chijo recalled in one of his recordings, "when a humble but affectionate and charismatic boy called Diomedes Díaz arrived, and he went crazy because he was meeting the man he dreamed of meeting, Chijo." One of the most famous marijuana traffickers in the Guajira, Chijo cultivated a reputation as a *folclorista* (musical folklore fan). Díaz was just a young man who was trying to make it in the vallenato music scene after making a few albums that went unnoticed. A mutual acquaintance introduced them with the hope of getting patronage for the young musician's career and enriching Chijo's social life with a fresh new talent. Admiration and affection were instantaneous and reciprocal. At the *parranda,* Chijo agreed to pay for Díaz's personal expenses while he recorded a new album. When the album was finally released, Díaz brought a copy to Chijo saying: "Here you go, *papá*—because he called me dad—I brought you this tape so you can listen to your son."[1] With this album, Díaz became a sensation. He proved to be an innovative singer and a prolific composer whose high-pitched voice, expressive performance style, and narrative lyrics touched Colombians' souls. In time, Díaz became vallenato's all-time superstar, and a controversial figure whose eccentric life was well documented in the news and on a telenovela that garnered the highest ratings of the year.[2] Chijo, meanwhile, went bankrupt and for decades lived off the good will of relatives and *compadres.* Not coincidentally, both men died in their late fifties of multiple health complications associated with their lifestyles.

Whether Chijo's rendition of Díaz's rise to stardom is factually correct or not is irrelevant. Regardless of its accuracy, the story he recorded in his audio-memoirs illustrates an essential aspect of the peak of the marijuana boom: vallenato music and the *parranda* were important components of the cultural realm where complex hierarchies of masculine exchanges and relations were negotiated within the social sphere of the new export economy, and where regional and national popular culture were reshaped. A musical genre that emerged in the cattle range out of the encounter between the improvised verses cowboys sang while pasturing herds and the accordions that smugglers imported from the Caribbean islands, vallenato became an arena of hegemonic struggles during the cotton boom of the 1950s and 1960s.[3] At the time, cattle ranchers–cum–cotton growers used vallenato as an instrument to negotiate political and social gains with elites in Bogotá, and to project an idealized image of themselves onto the national public sphere as the vanguard of modernization. Popularly known as *marimberos,* marijuana traffickers followed cotton growers' example and used the vallenato *parranda* as a mechanism of social projection. Understood as "a group of numerous friends . . . hav[ing] fun to the rhythm of folkloric music mixed with other folkloric gems such as jokes, anecdotes, tales," a ritual that follows a strict protocol "without a single written word," the *parranda* became *marimberos'* stage on which they could perform as the new generation of agrarian entrepreneurs in the region.[4]

This chapter reconstructs and examines these processes of cultural negotiation and class formation. Here, I argue that during the peak of the boom, vallenato *parrandas* marked the rhythm of marijuana's cycles of production and trade by serving as transitions between one operation and the next, as showcases for abundant wealth, and as occasions for creating and disseminating rumors, jokes, tales, and songs that represented *marimberos'* attributes as manifestations of the male regional identity, defined by masculine honor and plebeian virtue. The music and the celebratory ritual around it helped in various ways to form the emergent, transient class of marijuana intermediaries and exporters. With vallenato and in *parrandas, marimberos* made sense of the ambiguity of the new export economy—socially legitimate yet illegal, abundant yet scarce, central to regional life yet underground for national and hemispheric life. The set of gendered values, cultural practices, and discourses that vallenato and *parrandas* helped *marimberos* to articulate presented this paradoxical economy as a social order structured by reciprocity and solidarity, instead of disparity and competition.[5] At the crux of these paradoxes, vallenato music and *parrandas* constituted the arenas in which *marimberos* organized their social lives and forged a class consciousness for themselves as agrarian entrepreneurs, which eclipsed the intrinsic inequalities of the marijuana boom, masked their own precarious position in it, and ultimately contributed to their demise.

HARMONIES AND COTTON POLITICS

Popular music in Colombia, as in the rest of Latin America, has played a key role in struggles over hegemony, socioeconomic mobility, and nation-state formation, and it mediated urbanization processes unleashed by modernization projects during the twentieth century.[6] But if in Latin America's other large countries, such as Brazil, Argentina, and Mexico, populist governments used the state to appropriate and transform folk music as a marker of national identity, in Colombia the state played a minimal role; hence this process was more decentralized and privatized. Anthropologist Peter Wade finds this decentralized model of musical production and dissemination to be the main reason for the multiplicity of actors pursuing varied and conflicting agendas in the commoditization of popular musical genres.[7] Colombia's exceptionalism here was due in part to the marked and unresolved tension between populism and elitism that characterized twentieth-century Colombian Liberalism, especially on the Caribbean coast.[8] This tension introduced an "ambivalent sliding" in the public discourse of the nation and limited cohesion of the modernizing state, which could not resolve a paradox between claims to *mestizaje* as the unifying essence of the nation and "the maintenance of hierarchies of class and culture—and their frequent corollaries, region and race—that is wanted by those who are located in the higher echelons of those hierarchies."[9]

Scholarly literature on the evolution of vallenato music traces its origins to this tension between popular and elite Liberalism during the two key moments of reform and agrarian modernization in the Greater Magdalena— namely, the consolidation of the banana district near Santa Marta during the 1910s and 1920s and the rise of the cotton belt around Valledupar during the 1940s and 1950s.[10] In these contexts, popular artists voiced their sympathies for the Liberal party and its leaders in compositions that were either recorded by professional musicians or circulated by word of mouth.[11] This direct link between popular Liberals in the Greater Magdalena and elite Liberals in Bogotá created an opening for the diffusion of musical expressions from the region to the nation. Similarly, massive numbers of migrating workers from all over Colombia got to know and enjoy these sounds that were initially foreign to them. In the process, the Andean-centered part of Colombia discovered the music of the Greater Magdalena. The lyrics of the classic song "Compae Chipuco," composed by José 'Chema' Gómez in 1938, could not be more explicit about these dialogues:

> They called me Compae Chipuco,
> and I lived on Cesar River's shore.
> I am *vallenato* through and through,
> I have stained legs,
> a wide-brimmed hat,
> and to cap it all I like rum. . . .
> I am *vallenato* through and through,
> I don't believe in lies, don't believe in anything,
> only in Pedro Castro [Monsalvo], Alfonso López [Pumarejo], and nobody else.[12]

Although the transnational recording industry and the Andean-centered mass media responded to the popularization of the Greater Magdalena's music by promoting and commercializing it in stylized formats, local elites enacted both tacit and explicit bans on the music in their private spaces and in the local public sphere.[13] Upper classes especially despised accordion music for its lowbrow social origins—this was, after all, the musical instrument that accompanied the recreational activities of the peasantry, the agricultural working class, and the urban underworld.[14] Composer Gustavo Gutiérrez Cabello—one of the first stars to emerge from Valledupar's elite, and whose music marks a watershed in vallenato's transition from its folkloric roots to a modern sound—told me in an interview that "in respectable houses . . . along the coast, people danced with orchestras, and the accordion was looked down on; the Valledupar Club's norms prohibited it."[15] The low regard for this musical tradition extended to the countryside. For example, the legendary *vieja* Sara, matron of the Grammy Award–winning Zuleta clan of vallenato musicians, who lived in a remote hamlet in the mountains and was an unparalleled improviser of *décimas* (ten-line stanzas), used to scold her grandchildren by saying that accordion music was for "slackers, drunks, and lazy bums."[16] Training in classical music was an integral component of the education of local elites.[17] "There was a grand piano in every three houses, and there were performers of all ages," journalist Enrique Herrera Barros recalled about his hometown, Riohacha.[18] Even smugglers of general merchandise and agricultural commodities who celebrated successful export operations in *parrandas* animated them with sounds other than accordion music, and when they played regional folklore, it was on guitars and during the earliest stages of the *parranda*, rarely at prime time.[19]

The elites' preferences for classical music, pianos, and guitars defined the contours of regional mass culture, particularly on the radio. As everywhere else in Latin America, radio broadcasting in Colombia shaped people's tastes and imagination by popularizing certain sounds. In the case of the Caribbean, historian Alejandra Bronfman argues, "wires and sound waves" created sonic spaces that redefined the region's politics and language of contention.[20] Composer Gutiérrez Cabello recalled that during his childhood in the 1940s, accordion music was a rarity that they could only enjoy live because Mexican and Cuban genres dominated the airwaves. "When an accordionist arrived [in town], it was an event," Gutiérrez Cabello affirmed; "vallenato is recent."[21] Radio host Édison Hernández Pimienta, popularly known as the "father of radio broadcasting in the Guajira," remembered that when Ondas de Riohacha, the peninsula's first radio station, was founded in 1956, accordion music was not included in its repertoire.[22] Every day at noon he broadcast classical music from European composers "for spiritual relaxation," followed by Argentinean, Mexican, Cuban, and Dominican music, as well as Colombian folklore from the Andean region. The only music from the Colombian Caribbean that Ondas de Riohacha broadcast consisted of the stylized songs recorded by the transnational industry and played by big-band orchestras based in Barranquilla and Cartagena, such as Lucho Bermudez's, or by white-*mestizo* musicians from the Andean interior with a mixed lineup of stringed instruments, such as Bovea y sus Vallenatos, the most internationally recognized band of this style.[23]

As with many other aspects of regional life, La Violencia marked a watershed in the role popular music played in the modernizing reforms that the state undertook to pacify the country. Once the war was officially over and the Conservative and Liberal parties signed the National Front pact, political and social elites began to pay closer attention to the Caribbean coast in an effort to distance themselves, at least discursively, from the Andean interior, where the civil war had been waged.[24] Representations of the country as an Andean nation that danced with slow and melancholic rhythms such as bambuco and guabina yielded to images of a tropical nation that moved to the faster and more sensual sounds of Caribbean cumbia, porro, and vallenato.[25] The generation that came of age during and in the aftermath of La Violencia embodied this sea change and rode its wave. Educated under the Liberal Republic of the 1930s and early 1940s in schools where they shared classrooms and daily lives with the peasant children, they ignored the strict upper-class prohibitions that separated elite tastes and spaces from those of the people, bridged mass-media codes with local traditions, rescued subordinate masculinities from the shadows of popular culture and put them at the forefront of regional life.[26]

The open borders with the greater Caribbean afforded by contraband of general merchandise and agricultural commodities, and by the banana district, made the emergence of counterhegemonic masculinities expressed in musical cultures more evident in the coastal areas of Riohacha and the Guajira and of Santa Marta and the bay area. In Riohacha, Cuban and Puerto Rican musical genres such as mambo, guaracha, and guaguancó became popular among all classes during the 1950s and early 1960s, when the town experienced a renaissance thanks to coffee contraband and an influx of state resources following the creation of the Intendencia de la Guajira. With these rhythms, a new youth culture, known as *bacanería* ("hanging loose"), which celebrated rebelliousness, Caribbeanness, and cosmopolitanism, reached this section of the region and took root among certain sectors of the population.[27] One of its most famous figures and role models was Puerto Rican superstar and publicly recognized marijuana smoker Daniel Santos, also known as El Jefe (the Boss). Smuggler Callo, for example, remembered that poor young men who worked on contraband merchant ships came back to Riohacha from the islands "wearing funny clothes, flowered patterns, and smoking [marijuana], and they supposedly saw things [hallucinated] and walked suavely, and so on." But, Callo explained, local elites and mainstream society disdained these imported fashion and behavior trends, and those who followed them were few and "isolated because here [smoking marijuana] was not acceptable—they were not invited to anybody's house or parties."[28] Meanwhile, in Santa Marta and Ciénaga, banana laborers and other working-class people enjoyed a diversity of musical styles from all over the Caribbean, and even brothels disguised their sexual commerce behind musical activities.[29]

But the subordinate masculinities expressed through accordion music were not part of the cultural repertoire of *bacanería*. It was the cohort born and raised away from the coast, in the hinterlands of Valledupar and the great valley, that led the transition to cotton, the generation that claimed for themselves these marginalized popular understandings of being male and made them hegemonic. Ironically, it was a woman who theorized this historical change. Consuelo Araújo Noguera, a prominent figure of this generation, explained that she and her group of friends made public a practice that their fathers and grandfathers had cultivated in private. Under the name *colitas* (tails), ranchers used to hold parties in their workers' living quarters after upper-class social events.[30] In this way they extended "the entertainment of the rich [to] the realm of the people and briefly mixed with these others."[31] In the context of these *parrandas,* local elites accepted and celebrated the accordion and found a socially legitimate opportunity to engage in social and sexual relations with their servants.[32] When Araújo Noguera's generation of cattle ranchers came of age and migrated to the Andean interior in search of higher education, they took accordion music to the new, urban setting as an instrument with which to mediate their social relations and open space for themselves in the Andean world. As musicologist and vallenato artist Julio Oñate Martínez argues, the role played by agronomists, engineers, doctors, dentists, lawyers, and other professionals from Valledupar and the towns along the great valley in introducing Greater Magdalena's accordion music to the upper classes of the Andean interior cannot be underestimated.[33] Known in Bogotá as the Magdalenos, these men—and a few women—cultivated personal relationships with their Andean peers through *parrandas.* This diaspora built a cultural scene in Bogotá that nurtured rising stars such as writer Gabriel García Márquez, a native of the banana district, and politician Alfonso López Michelsen, son of the great Liberal reformer Alfonso López Pumarejo and heir to lands in the great valley.[34] These bohemians lived in Bogotá but "traveled every month to Valledupar to drink, and lasted even three and four days *parrandeando* [partying]," Gutiérrez Cabello recalled.[35] Thanks to these artists, Araújo Noguera explained, accordion music "made a grand entrance into Bogotá's intellectual high society."[36] And once it was accepted in Bogotá's cultural circles as a legitimate expression of a tropical regional ethos in the country, "through a phenomenon more akin to snobbism than appreciation," older members of the local elites accepted it in their private and public spaces.[37]

And with the cotton boom, the region's musical folklore became a powerful cultural device in the political negotiations between elites in Valledupar and the great valley and their Andean counterparts. With the unconditional support of Alfonso López Michelsen, now head of the Revolutionary Liberal Movement (MRL), the Liberal party's radical wing, the cattle rancher–cum–cotton growers lobbied politicians at the highest levels in Bogotá to create the Department of Cesar. With vallenato *parrandas,* they promoted the idea that the new department would be an oasis of racial democracy and capitalist productivity where the local peasantry would merge with the dispossessed laborers who had been wandering the countryside since La Violencia in order to build a future for the country beyond coffee and civil war.[38] Together, cotton growers and politicians manufactured a new image of this part of the Greater Magdalena as the quintessential paradise of "tropical *mestizaje*" in Colombia.[39] "It is no secret that we got the approval [of Congress] in large measure through *caja* beats and accordion keys," boasted Araújo Noguera.[40] Their lobbying efforts paid off in 1967 when the Liberal administration of Carlos Lleras Restrepo mobilized its ranks within Congress to sanction the law that created the Department of Cesar, with its capital in Valledupar, and López Michelsen as its first appointed governor.

Months later, on April 27, 1968, Governor López Michelsen, composer Rafael Escalona, and writer Araújo Noguera led Valledupar's most respected families in launching the Vallenato Legend Festival. According to Gutiérrez Cabello, one of the founding members, the festival involved "inviting the mass media, TV, and so on, bringing [in] important figures, the press, and showing them the music, and supporting rising talents, and making contacts to internationalize them." Asked about the name Vallenato Legend, the composer said, "it suddenly took the name of vallenato, and in the festival achieved a category."[41] He meant that the festival adopted the term "vallenato"—which up to this point had been a derogatory reference to peasants from the great valley—and used it to designate various musical genres played with the accordion.[42] The name Vallenato Legend also honored a colonial-era narrative according to which a small group of Spaniards aided by the blessed intervention of Our Lady of the Rosary conquered the hinterlands along the great valley by killing a much larger group of indigenous Chimila people. In Gutiérrez Cabello's telling, the organizers picked this legend because although "many people dislike it because it is racist—I do not like it—López [Michelsen] said that we need to have myths . . . people need to be deceived with legends, well, not deceived, but people have legends and they are important because they are imaginary facts."[43] With their grand event honoring a colonial legend, the white-*mestizo* cotton elite linked the commemoration of the violent defeat of the natives to the derogatory term "vallenato", converting both into celebratory acts that invoked belonging to the great valley around Valledupar and embracing its mixed-race peasant traditions.

The Vallenato Legend Festival spanned four days, during which poor men from surrounding towns, hamlets, and villages competed with one another for awards as Vallenato Kings and, years later, for the single crown of King of

FIGURE 10. Governor Alfonso López Michelsen dances vallenato with the pageant queen at a *parranda* during the first Vallenato Legend Festival in Valledupar, April 29, 1968. *El Espectador* photographic archive, Bogotá.

Kings, titles given to the most remarkable musicians who performed their own original music and sang their own *décimas*. Musicians also battled one another for media attention, patronage from record labels, and the honor of being asked to play at *parrandas*. According to the rules of the festival, musicians could perform only four *aires,* or genres (*son, paseo, merengue,* and *pulla*), accompanied by an accordion, a *caja* (drum), and a *guacharaca* (a scratching instrument native to the Sierra Nevada de Santa Marta). By establishing four genres and a basic instrumentation, the festival set the parameters for validating the authenticity of this popular tradition. By claiming that *décimas* and the accordion represented the European heritage, the *caja* the African heritage, and the *guacharaca* the Indian heritage, the cotton elite presented vallenato as the harmonic fusion of Colombia's racial diversity and made it a powerful mechanism of homogenization within a *mestizo* national identity and culture.

With the festival, a tight web of families connected through politics, business, and marriage appropriated a popular musical expression as their own and used it in their efforts to facilitate and shape the region's integration into the nation. Pulling the strings of the social imaginaries created in popular culture, the cotton elite redefined old concepts, set the canon for regional popular music in terms of basic rhythms and instruments, and asserted the historical continuity of their own right to rule. In 1973, five years after the festival's inauguration, Araújo Noguera published *Vallenatología*, considered the bible of the genre.[44] Her book includes a prologue by Alfonso López Michelsen, whose tenure as the first governor of Cesar served as the springboard to his successful bid for the presidency in 1974, after a campaign that moved to the rhythms of vallenato.[45] Both Araújo Noguera and López Michelsen asserted that vallenato music symbolized the fusion of the aristocratic and popular elements of local society in spite of racial and class differences.[46] Not surprisingly, the most frequent metaphors were sexual in nature, with some religious overtones of Catholic mysticism, such as the claim that "region and men are attracted to each other . . . and merged like lovers," giving birth to a "Holy Trinity . . . in one true vallenato."[47] As literary critic Jacques Gilard and ethnomusicologist Ana María Ochoa Gautier argue in their respective works, both the festival and the literary contributions on vallenato by writers such as Araújo Noguera, Gabriel García Márquez, and others helped invent a tradition.[48] And with this alchemic act, the cotton elite appointed themselves the leaders of a region they would now govern in concert—and occasionally in conflict—with Bogotá. They defined the terms for the Andean-centered nation's appreciation of the music, set a standard for the recording industry, and made vallenato a rich topic of research and writing.[49] These processes ushered in a golden age of accordion music.

With the Vallenato Legend Festival and the political lobby and literary production associated with it, the cotton elite used a popular musical expression as part of their own cultural repertoire, projecting an image as progressive, modern, thoughtful leaders of a region with something authentic and traditional to offer the nation.[50] Through the festival's carnivalesque subversion of hierarchies, they validated in the public sphere the class, racial, and gender hierarchies and dynamics of colonial origin that their families reproduced in the private sphere of the cattle hacienda. The affirmation of patriarchy as a cultural norm was particularly visible in the male fraternity that the festival's version of vallenato embodied, which constituted the core of the new Department of Cesar's political body. Using vallenato music as their backdrop, the cotton elite successfully navigated between region and nation, as well as between the Caribbean region and the Andean center of the country.

Yet, while the cotton elite became fearless and confident actors in Colombian politics and culture, the cotton economy's internal contradictions grew more pronounced. By the early 1970s, the negative environmental, financial, and social effects of the Green Revolution model of development (addressed in chapter 1) had compounded, initiating the decline of the cotton sector. Musicologist and composer Julio Oñate Martínez registered the crisis in the song "La profecía" (The Prophecy), in which he imagines the desert of the upper Guajira as a cautionary tale for the cotton belt, where the overuse of agrochemicals and mechanization was producing droughts and failed harvests:

> Alert, alert, *Vallenato*,
> look, there comes La Guajira.
> Pedro Castro commented,
> Pedro Castro commented
> that the great desert is approaching . . .
> And so,
> the green grass in your region
> will be changed by *tuna* and *cardón* [cactus],
> and the intense green of your cotton
> will not be seen there in Valledupar (bis) . . .
> They destroyed irresponsibly
> the divi-divi forests, the natural barrier,
> and they knocked down the coffee plantations.[51]

The rise of the *marimberos* took place in the region precisely at this time, at the beginning of the end of the cotton belt, in the early 1970s. Although it was in part a consequence of the socioeconomic failure of the modernization that made the cotton economy possible, *marimberos*' ephemeral reign was not experienced as a failure. On the contrary, as a result of their meteoric rise to economic prominence, *marimberos* imitated the cattle ranchers–cum–cotton growers in celebrating themselves for their apparent social and cultural achievements. With the *parranda*, *marimberos* adopted vallenato as their own sound in a highly organic way, since most of them were countrymen from hamlets, villages, and farms located in riverine hinterlands, foothills, or intermontane valleys. With their newfound wealth, *marimberos* did not intend to dispute the cotton elite's political, cultural, or social authority. Rather, they followed their example, using vallenato as a way to forge public personas; to imagine communities out of extended families and relations among *compadres*; to map what they considered their territories; and to reproduce the gendered values on which capital accumulation in the region was contingent.

But unlike the cotton elite, *marimberos* did not pretend to make vallenato music an instrument with which to carve out a political space within the national sphere. Their desire to be celebrated in vallenato songs was an end in itself. These different motivations were products of the disparity in origins and access to resources between cotton growers and marijuana traffickers as two factions of the same agro-entrepreneurial class.[52] Most cotton growers were descendants of either noble castes with colonial titles or high-ranking veterans of the War of Thousand Days, while some of them belonged to the emergent middle classes that had access to higher education. These three sectors of regional society had previously invested their wealth and prestige in cattle, coffee, land, and politics. In contrast, the vast majority of *marimberos* were members of the rural and urban proletariat who were poorly educated and had nothing to invest other than their own labor. And whereas cotton growers were central to the national economy for more than two decades, when they supplied the nation's textile industry with cotton and contributed to industrialization, *marimberos* provided foreign markets with an illegal commodity for just a few years, and the central state soon came to see the illegality of their business as a threat to Colombia's national well-being. These different trajectories were apparent in the nation's public sphere, in which cotton growers were well represented but *marimberos* were not. Thus, while the former mobilized their political and intellectual resources to legitimize, socialize, and project their discourse of regional hegemony and class and racial harmony, the latter relied only on the orality of vallenato music and the encoded ways its artists celebrated their deeds and personas.

DISSONANCES AND *MARIMBERO* CULTURE

When the marijuana export economy reached its peak in the mid-1970s, many sectors of the population amassed small fortunes, an achievement that modernizing reforms had failed to provide them.[53] Many of the young men from rural communities who found employment and wealth in the growing marijuana export business as intermediaries between cultivators and exporters had previously migrated to the region's urban centers in search of education or jobs. Called *mitios, corronchos, cáncamos,* or *pata-pintá,* country people did not typically feel welcome in towns and cities. This urban inhospitality eventually contributed to the *marimberos'* desire to turn fortune into respect, recognition, and status. Carlos, an intermediary from Las Flores, one of the hamlets in the Sierra Nevada de Santa Marta where marijuana was first planted for exportation, recalled that when he moved to Riohacha to enroll in public school, he and his neighbors "suffered discrimination, they called us names, they shouted at us on the streets, '*mitios, mitios,*' everywhere." Years later, when he made his first marijuana deal, Carlos remembered, "I went crazy, it transformed my life immediately; I was in a bad situation, and then I bought a watch, I bought this and that."[54] Hugo Rocha Molina, head of the Administrative Department of Security in Valledupar, remarked that part of the reason that illegality flourished in the region was that dominant social codes normalized the "underestimation of persons in relation to their scant economic potential and not belonging to predetermined social classes."[55] Education scholar Martín López concluded that those who "had never had social recognition were the ones who accumulated tons of money out of the blue, and with the money tried to prove that they were useful for something."[56]

Insecurity, pride, and resentment accompanied *marimberos'* efforts to conquer towns and cities with the profits of the illegal business.[57] The very term *marimbero*—marijuana was euphemistically called *marimba* (see the introduction)—refers to the efforts that dispossessed rural young men made to reinvent themselves as successful urban merchants. According to Callo, who never used the term for himself or his partners: "Some liked to be called *marimberos* to have fame—those from the *monte* [mountains or countryside], the *cáncamos,* they loved it; but the others [from the city] did not like it because it ruined their reputation."[58] Sociologist José Guillermo Daza Sierra, who produced the first academic analysis of marijuana intermediaries in the late 1980s, constructed a typology for the *marimberos* based on socio-ethnic extraction. He included exporters, intermediaries, cultivators, guards and bodyguards, loaders and unloaders, and anybody involved in the illegal business whose public behavior was characterized by extravagance and flamboyance.[59] In this book, the term *marimbero* applies only to those who were devoted to the commercialization of marijuana, whether at the intermediation or exportation level. Cultivators and people performing menial work did not share the circumstances and fate of the merchant class and, therefore, did not engage in the cultural negotiation that the new commercial bourgeoisie used to consolidate their ascendance at local and regional levels.

The *marimberos'* search for status and prestige was a distinctive characteristic of their emergence as a faction within the region's merchant and agro-entrepreneurial class. Former marijuana trafficker Carlos said, "We looked up to [Riohacha's upper class] when we did not have money, but as soon as I made money, I dared to fall in love and date one of their girls. . . . I dropped by her home early in the morning and then I turned on the car stereo for [her father] to know. Because I had money in my pocket, I arrived like a macho man."[60] Chijo noted, quoting a neighbor, that "he who has money does not fear, and if he does it is because the money is not his."[61] *Marimberos* would light cigarettes with bills; decorate Christmas trees with dollars instead of crystal balls; shower with Roger & Gallet Jean Marie Farina cologne; wear Ray-Ban sunglasses, designer clothes, Italian shoes, and gold jewelry; race their Ford pickup trucks in chase games that ended with the cars' destruction; carry guns in the back of their waistbands and walk around defiantly, for which habit they were nicknamed *culo-pullú* (thorny asses) because the guns protruded from their backsides like stingers; and place large bets at cockfights with sacks of pesos or dollars that were weighed rather than counted.[62]

Emergent classes begin their ascent to prominence with transgressions, sociologist Pierre Bourdieu argues. Flouting "the sacred frontier which makes legitimate culture a separate universe," and stylizing life in ways that favor the primacy of form over function, Bourdieu contends, are the first steps in the process of class formation.[63] In their search for distinction, *marimberos* adorned themselves and their intimate spaces with luxury goods and services. "Rather than building a house, they built parking lots with monumental kiosks in the middle, unreal," said Wilfredo Deluque, former chair of the Guajira Society of Architects and Engineers. Those who invested in housing, Deluque observed, "built masses of concrete, luxurious houses that not even they could afford later, houses that invited not imitation but envy."[64] They popularized marble and other imported stone—even gold—as construction materials, as well as expensive devices and appliances such as electric doors, large television sets, and sound systems. Chijo, for example, built a massive house of three levels with a large backyard on the outskirts of San Juan del Cesar, which today still looks out of place in a neighborhood full of houses made of stucco, clay, and palm tree roofs. A well-known *marimbero* in Santa

FIGURE 11. Uncle Arique visits Chijo's mansion in San Juan del Cesar, 2018. Today the building is a day care facility. Photo by the author.

Marta bought a small, rocky island in the bay area and built a mansion with two swimming pools filling one with freshwater for people and the other with sea saltwater for a shark. Rumor has it that he used the animal to threaten young women who refused to have sex with him.[65] The fictional Cacique Miranda, the main character in *La mala hierba,* a novel written by journalist Juan Gossaín based on interviews with *marimberos,* "did not know what to do with so much money" and decided to "buy imported marble from Italy, a refrigeration system, Persian rugs to cover the floors, Philippine gold dust to paint the walls, and three Mercedes Benz, two of them sport models, bringing his collection up to four."[66] The famous Lucho Barranquilla paved the streets of the neighborhood where he lived in Santa Marta, and built fifty houses and an office building just for his family.[67]

But among all the signs of social and economic mobility that marijuana traffickers flamboyantly exhibited, hosting a vallenato *parranda* with one's *compadres* was the most visible symbol of one's success.[68] As Germán Rojas, a correspondent for newspapers in Bogotá and Barranquilla during the boom, explained, "When the youth got involved in the business is when it

became loud." He added, "When they sent their loads successfully, they celebrated with whistles and in *parrandas* with good *vallenato* bands, and everybody noticed that they had *coronado* ["crowned," successfully made] a
shipment."[69] Like cattle ranchers in their transition to growing cotton, the
marijuana traffickers regularly hosted parties that allowed them to forge a
gendered discourse of upward mobility around their outsized personalities.
In the *parranda, marimberos'* and vallenato artists' divergent trajectories and
interests intersected. These parties provided both groups the opportunity for
cementing friendships and *compadrazgos* and for exhibiting the two groups'
talents—in the case of the former, to unite economic and social resources in
smuggling networks and, in the case of the latter, to entertain and create
original forms of expression.

Among all vallenato artists, *marimberos* particularly valued the work of
talented composers. During *parrandas,* these musicians would compete with
one another following the format of *piqueria*—the equivalent of a cockfight
in which they attempted to discredit one another with their improvised
verses.[70] As composer Sergio Moya Molina explained to me at the Departmental
Library in Valledupar, most of the songs in honor of *marimberos* emerged
from these rounds of improvisation. A surviving member of the so-called *trío
de oro* (golden trio), a group of composers famous for their *piqueria,* Moya
Molina described how, after a round of improvisation, hosts and guests would
decide which songs should be recorded, suggested the accordion player and the
singer, and discussed which record label would be the best fit. Often with their
aid, the artists signed agreements to record these songs, produced albums, and
booked concert tours to popularize the new music. At the end of the party,
artists got paid for their services in kind or in cash, "sometimes in dollars,
when [the *marimberos*] did not have time to exchange [currencies]," Moya
Molina recalled.[71] Once the album was in stores, *marimberos* bought great
quantities of LPs and tapes to give to relatives and friends. With these three
mechanisms—financial patronage, payments for services, and purchases—
marimberos created a market for composers that had barely existed before, and
they broadened the existing market for vallenato musicians. "They raised our
prices, and record companies had to begin to pay us better," Moya Molina
concluded.[72]

More important, *parrandeando* (partying) vallenato composers and musicians found inspiration for their art in the *marimberos'* personalities and
lifestyles. Dozens of vallenato songs recorded in the 1970s and 1980s celebrated marijuana traffickers.[73] Composer, producer, and radio host Lenín

Bueno Suárez affirmed that this form of sponsorship emerged during the peak of the marijuana boom in the mid-1970s, when artists would call out the names of traffickers in the middle of choruses in exchange for their contributions to recording and other expenses.[74] Although vallenato singers had inserted comments and phrases during the instrumental sections of songs since the 1940s, most of these original shout-outs were phrases that characterized each singer, such as "*ay, hombre,*" and "*gózalo*"; they rarely mentioned the name of a particular person or celebrated his public persona.[75] This changed during the cotton boom, when the names of growers, politicians, and their relatives were introduced for the first time in stanzas and choruses. Institutionalized in radio jargon with the English word *payola,* payments in cash or kind were made by *marimberos* to composers, musicians, and radio hosts to write, sing, and promote songs in their honor. It is important to note that although payola was an essential component of the relationship between *marimberos* and vallenato artists, greetings and homages were often sincere expressions of admiration and respect, and the outcomes of specific friendships and *compadrazgos.* In "Soy parrandero y qué" (So What If I Am a Party Animal?), for example, Bueno Suárez highlights the idiosyncrasies of Lucky, one of his childhood friends and the most renowned marijuana trafficker of the day:

What the hell!
I don't care if people say
that I am a degenerate drunk,
I just want them to keep in mind
that I work and don't beg.
So what if I am a party animal [*parrandero*],
who cares?,
I am Lucky . . . listen to me,
who cares?
If I party it is because
life is very short.[76]

According to Bueno Suárez, the celebrated trafficker never paid him and would not have had to, because "the person deserved [the honor for being] a friend, a relative, somebody always involved in vallenato music, a great host of vallenato bands, a *folclorista* [musical folklore fan] to the end, a great person."[77] The song "Soy parrandero y qué" became one of the biggest hits of Bueno Suárez's career. Even today, it is intoned at *parrandas* with the passion of an anthem.

Songs written in honor of *marimberos* were not very different from other vallenato songs and thus do not form a musical subgenre.[78] Unlike Mexico's *narcocorridos* (ballads that celebrate drug lords), *marimberos'* vallenato music was not a counterdiscourse against regional elites or state-controlled media representations of those involved in illegal activities. Nor was it the commodity of a clandestine subculture and industry residing in a liminal space beyond the nation-state, as is the case of US-Mexican *corridos prohibidos* (forbidden *corridos*), which constitute a more explicit version of *narcocorridos*.[79] On the contrary, songs written in honor of *marimberos* adhered to the existing lyrical and technical formats that gave vallenato its characteristic elasticity as a cultural expression of celebration, entertainment, criticism, and protest.[80] Songs that paid homage to *marimberos* were also about love and heartbreak, machismo and patriarchy, fortune and poverty, ignorance and wisdom, *compadrazgo* and rivalry, *parrandas* and festivity, customs and traditions, and the region's landscape and natural riches.[81] For example, another member of the *trío de oro,* composer Hernando Marín, honored el Gavilán Mayor (the Big Sparrow Hawk), a *marimbero* who controlled landing fields near Riohacha, with a song that described him as bird of prey (see chapter 3). Here Marín celebrates his friend's personality while observing the vallenato custom of using animal metaphors. Puerto Rican superstar Daniel Santos provided another example when he sang "El marimbero," a song Romualdo Brito composed about a trafficker known as Pocholo, whose personality and career are associated with social traditions of self-reliance and autonomy from the central state. The song meets the criteria of social critique and protest in vallenato music:

> Today you call me *marimbero*
> because I tried to change my situation,
> without knowing that before
> I was a *gamín* [street kid] and *pordiosero* [beggar]
> without any education.
> Today, because I have money,
> the government persecutes me
> seeking to know who I am. . . .
> Nothing to be ashamed of,
> you can happily call me
> *marimbero* and filthy rich.[82]

In sum, the marijuana export economy magnified the social relevance of vallenato music, but it did so without affecting vallenato's "integral aesthetic function."[83] With vallenato music and the *parranda, marimberos* not only marked the beginning and end of the marijuana circuit but, more important, forged an arena for the public display of the masculine values that character-ized the new agrarian economy and society, such as resourcefulness, audacity, and flamboyance. In *parrandas, marimberos* found a legitimate space in which to exercise generosity, solidarity, and reciprocity among *compadres*—three essential principles for the accumulation of social and economic capital from the bottom up. *Parrandas* were the glue that held together the collective vision of modern progress that led to upward social mobility. Like the cotton grow-ers, *marimberos* used vallenato music to project an idealized self-image at local and regional levels while using their success in capitalist enterprise to nourish noncapitalist social dynamics according to principles of prestige, *compadrazgo*, and reciprocity rather than productivity, competition, and profitability.

As a result, *marimberos* hastened vallenato's commodification with their economic, social, and cultural resources, which contributed to another golden age, one characterized by more urban-inflected lyrics and more dance-able accordion routines.[84] Composer Bueno Suarez said that he "stopped seeing vallenato as cowboy music, from its rural profile, because it was com-ing to the city to animate the serenade."[85] Ethnomusicologist and vallenato musician Roger Bermúdez explained that the generation of musicians who came of age in the 1970s during the marijuana boom used "the standard melodies that gave identity to vallenato music," which had been produced in the cattle pastures and used during the earliest stages of commodification in the 1940s and 1950s, to "extend the introductions, the preludes, the inter-ludes, the codas, and the phrases." With these alterations, he argued, "val-lenato songs became longer, and exploited more the sound of the accordion, its pitch; they became more rhythmic."[86] Record labels established in Barranquilla and Medellín began to rapidly produce more technically sophis-ticated and commercial vallenato recordings that included electric and bass guitars, drums, and chorus voices.[87] As vallenato became more festive, a new form of mass entertainment emerged: the *caseta* (meaning "shack"), or itiner-ant stage. "[You] just have to bury some beams and put corrugated iron walls around, [add] a sound system, and there you make the show," explained jour-nalist Enrique Herrera Barros. "Once the night is over you disassemble eve-rything, load it in a truck, and head to the next town."[88] With the mobility of *caseta*, vallenato gained a broader audience because people no longer had to depend on either buying the albums, listening to the radio, or attending private *parrandas* to hear the newest hits.

Although the *marimberos'* stimulation of this urban, more commercial vallenato could have been at odds with the folkloric tone of the Vallenato Legend Festival, their activities never entered into conflict with the cotton growers' agenda. As members of an agricultural and merchant class—albeit an illegal faction within it—*marimberos* considered the festival and its high-profile *parrandas* as part of the social universe and cultural territory to which they pledged allegiance. Mantequilla excitedly recalled his adventures at the festival: "'There's festival in Valledupar!' and we traveled to Valledupar with Chijo, and composers, and *folcloristas,* and we drank with them for three or four more days, and that was the *farándula* [scene], as we called it."[89] As a news correspondent reported in 1978, "The Vallenato Legend Festival is for ranchers to sell their cattle, record labels to promote their sales, politicians to take their share, and *mafiosos* [drug traffickers] to exchange shout-outs."[90] Moreover, in the Vallenato Legend Festival, *marimberos* cultivated relationships with cotton growers while scouting new talent. Composer Moya Molina related that his first *parranda* with the marijuana traffickers took place after his first appearance at the festival, at the age of twenty, when a cotton grower from a reputable family from Valledupar invited him to participate in a *parranda* at Chijo's house in San Juan del Cesar.[91]

Whereas *marimberos* cultivated social ties with vallenato artists as part of the construction of their public personas, aspiring musicians, singers, and composers found a stepping stone in friendship and *compadrazgo* with *marimberos* toward locating themselves at the center of an ongoing cultural revolution. Those vallenato musicians who managed to become professional artists embodied the dreams and aspirations of the growing population of young people who left their hamlets and towns behind to look for a future in the city. Psychologist and education scholar Marina Quintero, host of one of the oldest and most respected radio shows on vallenato in Colombia, recalled that the old accordion music that she and her friends in the Universidad de Antioquia in Medellín (all migrant students from different towns along the Caribbean coast) had known forever was being played in the mid-1970s by young people like themselves. "It was not old people's music . . . with their old voices, but young men with their beautiful voices . . . and I was going to faint, it was adoration, it was respect, it was veneration."[92]

The cohort of professional musicians, composers, and producers whom *marimberos* helped to develop gave voice to the illusions and frustrations of immigration and urbanization. Originally inspired by agricultural work, seasonal weather, pastoral love affairs, and parochial goings-on, vallenato artists were now also singing and composing about city adventures, student affairs, professionalization, travels, and conspicuous consumption. Quintero sang a stanza of a famous song: "I left worried / for the big city, / I had come from my town / bringing in my chest / those memories that will never return." Then she explained, "These verses had a great historical significance. Only those who lived that, arriving in the big city from a little town, could understand the depersonalization, going from face-to-face relationships to 'I do not exist'; that was what those songs were all about."[93] The appeal and passion their works produced in the public's mind stemmed from the connection they created between personal life trajectories and collective experiences.

And as vallenato was the medium and the message of a cultural transformation, it also became the vehicle of profound individual reinvention. Colombia's three most established recording companies for vallenato were in Medellín, where professional musicians embraced their newly acquired stardom. Quintero, who through her radio show befriended all the rising stars who traveled regularly to Medellín, recalled that "musicians did not arrive with a humble attitude,... because they carried the most weight," and record companies understood that "they offered an extraordinary possibility of growth for the company, so they treated them well." In the studio, musicians worked for weeks in exhausting recording sessions. The analogue system required that each instrument be recorded separately, which "took a long time, and they ended up drinking in order to get emotional and reached the exact pitch," Quintero said. Animated by food and alcohol, and accompanied by friends, devotees, and protégés, musicians transformed their recording sessions into *parrandas*. "They were like a different way of living a *parranda*," Quintero concluded. Outside the studio, attention from fans and privileges continued. As Quintero recounted, the more famous these musicians became, the more petulant was their behavior, especially as the numbers of adoring young female fans began to grow. "Most [female fans] were from the Caribbean coast and worked in domestic service," Quintero recalled, "and had arrived in the city seeking a better life, and these bands were their dream come true."[94]

With national and regional elites promoting vallenato music as if it was their own, with the recording industry willing to do anything to persuade them to sign contracts, with legions of fans adoring them, and with the profits of the marijuana export economy at their disposal, vallenato musicians were no longer viewed as slackers, drunks, and bums. They were ambitious young men with high hopes and strong opinions of themselves. Superstar Diomedes Díaz, who was a *mitio* through and through, born in a mountain hamlet in the Sierra Nevada in the jurisdiction of San Juan del Cesar, voiced this newly acquired status in his song "El profesional" (The Professional):

> I am proud of my art,
> my beautiful profession nowadays.
> I perform as a composer,
> something very beautiful on my part,
> and I am a singer. . . .
> Because I could not afford to study,
> my education was impossible.
> But there are beautiful things in the world,
> like natural intelligence,
> and any man can succeed,
> and then share it with pride.
> My studies were incomplete,
> but I am a good professional.[95]

The professionalization of vallenato musicians, which began with the commodification of this folk music from the 1930s to the 1950s, consolidated in the 1970s with the boost that the marijuana economy gave to artists. Although in the national sphere, Valledupar's festival and the record companies were the places musicians wished to conquer, in their localities, *marimberos* offered the necessary access to the first step toward professionalization and stardom. Aspiring musicians, singers, and composers looked for *marimberos'* friendship and *compadrazgo* in their path toward fame and fortune. As the personal relationships between composer Sergio Moya Molina, singer Diomedes Díaz, and marijuana trafficker Chijo illustrate, *vallenato* became an arena in which different factions of the same generation balanced their disparate interests. In an old photograph that Chijo's neighbors in San Juan del Cesar showed me, I could see an example of the emotional connection beneath this improvised community of successful young men. Chijo, big and heavy, hugs Díaz, skinny and wearing sunglasses, with his left arm; both men are squatting so Díaz can hug one of Chijo's little daughters, who leans on him on the other side. The two men and the girl in close proximity, looking at the camera, form a single central figure within the frame. Chijo smiles with restraint, and Díaz grins showing a gap that he later replaced with a

FIGURE 12. Diomedes Díaz (with accordionist Juancho Rois) at the peak of his fame, performing at Barranquilla's Carnival, 1994. *El Espectador* photographic archive, Bogotá.

diamond-encrusted implant.[96] Bright sunlight fills the picture illuminating the joy and pride all three exude.[97]

Joy and pride were precisely the emotions that *marimberos* sought to express in vallenato. Enjoying pleasures that had been denied to people like them, *marimberos* celebrated their newly acquired economic power immodestly. And since respect for one another's networks and zones of influence guaranteed peaceful relations in the marijuana business, *marimberos* exhibited physical and social strength in the form of pride and cultivated friendships and *compadrazgos* in order to ameliorate the state of rivalry in which they lived. *Parrandas* facilitated these contradictory behaviors. During these festive occasions *marimberos* showcased their abilities to marshal economic and social resources into a cultural display; *parrandas* also temporarily diverted competition away from the commercial sphere (where confrontations could be deadly) into the sociocultural realm, where tensions dissolved amidst the music and alcohol. With his sharp sense of humor, Mantequilla joked that "during the boom I suffered symptoms of cirrhosis because I drank one day, and the next fourteen too."[98] Physician and essayist Guillermo Velandia attended many *marimberos' parrandas* as a friend and doctor of a trafficker who died at an early age of complications from diabetes and obesity. "In a parranda," Dr. Velandia noted, "the bottle of Chivas 21 or [Johnny Walker] Blue Label was for Lucky, while the Chivas 12 or the Old Parr [cheaper brands] were for the rest; in the *parranda* you knew who was who, by the jewelry they wore, the cars they drove." While slowly drinking a liter of Coca-Cola in the living room of his house in Riohacha, Dr. Velandia elaborated: "There was collegiality and collaboration, and as long as there were no family wars [vendettas] they looked after one another, talked to one another, negotiated with one another."[99] The *parranda* was a safe zone free of animosity where rivalry was expressed in festive ways, an ideal setting for weaving the social fabric of the export business. At *parrandas, marimberos* were kind and amicable, composer Moya Molina asserts, "as if they could give their lives for each other, [but] we knew that they shoot each other for anything, that is why we feared failing them."[100] *Parrandas* united several links in the commercial chain to affirm the hierarchy of status on which their work depended. In a relaxed atmosphere, they renewed the terms of the moral pact of loyalty, kinship, and devotion to the code of masculine honor that ruled their activities.

Marimberos acted out their code of masculinity in at least two ways during vallenato parrandas. First, they demonstrated their physical capacity to drink and eat to excess over an extended period of time, since only the strongest, most determined, and most committed to the ideal of brotherly love could endure to the end of a *parranda.*[101] Composer Bueno Suárez captured this idea well in one of his famous compositions: "The *parranda* is for staying up all night / And he who falls asleep, we will cut his hair."[102] Mantequilla remembered that Chijo "began to gain weight when he began to make money; when I met him he was skinny, and then he was as wide as a table."[103] With *sentimiento vallenato* (vallenato sentiment), or a man's incessant yearning and "spiritual surrender to the stimulus of all the beautiful things in life and nature," the *marimberos* constructed a public image of themselves as insatiable eaters, drinkers, womanizers, and friends who were loyal until death.[104] Appealing to *sentimiento vallenato,* a man displayed his tenderest emotions, such as appreciation for his *compadres,* love for his women, and nostalgia for his hometown, without judgment or criticism from anyone else, and contributed to the collective construction of a modern regional identity.[105] As Chijo stated in one of his recordings, "A man from the countryside does not adopt city manners, but sticks to the customs of his hometown and cultivates them."[106] In the internationally acclaimed song "La celosa" (The Jealous One), composer Moya Molina captures this stereotypical behavior:

> When I go out and am delayed,
> do not worry, Juanita.
> Because you know very well
> that I like the *parranda,*
> and I have lots of friends.
> And if I do not come back later,
> I will be back next morning.[107]

The second way that *marimberos* acted out their code of masculinity was to hire or summon high-profile guests and artists to attend their *parrandas.* Only the best-connected *marimberos* could organize unforgettable parties, like the one that took place sometime around 1978 in El Pájaro, one of the primary natural seaports for marijuana exportation. A few marijuana exporters organized it and agreed that each of them would hire a band. Because every trafficker wanted to outdo his peers, some of the most expensive and famous orchestras on the continent came to perform. Journalist and former student leader Edgar Ferrucho Padilla, who was a childhood friend of several of these men, described the occasion: "In [this] one-street town, there was a band in each house . . . one did not know which one to go to because there were so many great bands."[108] Smuggler Callo, who also attended, remembered: "There were ten houses there at most, no more, and in ten shacks you found the Zuletas, Diomedes, the Chicas del Can, the Sonora Matancera, the Billo's Caracas Boys, and so on." Callo continued: "They took a truck full of whiskey, and another truck full of cans of Heineken beer, and they brought those there, where there were no eggs, no salt, no rice."[109]

Just as they were intrinsically bound up with each other, *parrandas* and marijuana trafficking collapsed simultaneously. With the implementation of a military campaign against marijuana cultivation and commerce that started in November 1978, the vallenato *parranda* ceased to be a place where *marimberos* could gather and mediate tensions, de-escalate conflicts, and discourage violence. "After being successful merchants," composer Moya Molina said, "*marimberos* became fugitives and they had to lower their profile," and so they partied much less often.[110] And when they did party, the atmosphere was tense. Journalist Ferrucho Padilla recalled that by the late 1970s "aggressiveness was a very evident feature [in their behavior], in the way they drove their cars, to treat other people; they became intolerant."[111] When the number of antinarcotics agents multiplied, the space for the free circulation of goods and people was reduced considerably. In this new, more restrictive climate, some *marimberos* abandoned the business forever, many others lost their lives or went bankrupt—including Chijo—and a handful of them either transitioned to trafficking cocaine in alliance with associates from the Andean interior or turned to electoral politics for protection and impunity.

Likewise, their contributions to regional popular culture vanished from memory. Despite the manifold ways that *marimberos* helped to make vallenato the most popular commercial musical genre in Colombia, vallenato is today presented as a pristine patrimony of the modern nation, removed from its complexities and contradictions.[112] Today, even those musicians who directly benefited from their relationships with *marimberos* minimize the role that the marijuana economy played in the process of commodifying and popularizing vallenato music. Bueno Suárez, for example, claims that "public figures who helped to position vallenato in Bogotá, the great Colombian metropolis, had a more important impact than marijuana profits ... marijuana was just a stepping-stone."[113] This may be because the discourse on vallenato as a tradition that the annual Vallenato Legend Festival circulates is so pervasive, or because association with the drug-trafficking business would jeopardize musicians' accomplishments. In any case, to the Andean-centered Colombia that knew *marimberos* as fugitives of the "war on drugs," these outlaws did not represent the "rebelliousness" that, according to what the Vallenato Legend Festival had institutionalized as this music's ethos, takes "expression in the spirit and the mind rather than in a real insubordination against the establishment."[114] Although the mainstream media and political discourse portrayed *marimberos* as violent and dangerous men whom the Colombian military forces, in association with the United States, hunted down as enemies of the state, for years they were affluent, extravagant, audacious, respected, and admired social figures in the region. Like the indigenous people of the colonial-era legend that Valledupar's festival commemorates annually, *marimberos,* along with their contributions, vanished from national memory as a defeated and anonymous mass of people subject to forces not of their own making.

From a distance, Chijo's funeral looked like a parade. A crowd of people walked along Riohacha's waterfront toward the cemetery followed by musicians who serenaded Chijo's body with vallenato songs. That night, at the novena, people gossiped that the walls between vaults had to be knocked down in order to accommodate his oversized coffin, donated by his *compadre* Lucky, who had also helped him to get started in marijuana trafficking when they were young. The gossip referred to one of Chijo's most memorable *parrandas* in San Juan del Cesar, in the middle of which he promised to buy the house next door and ordered that the fences that separated them be demolished.[115] His rationale was simple: more room was needed to accommodate all his guests. But, as unexpectedly as money, status, and fame came to his life, they melted into thin air. "Life! What a beautiful opportunity, it vanishes like hurricane winds," Chijo lamented on one of the audiotapes he recorded to document his life story.[116]

Indeed, hurricane winds turned the former Greater Magdalena upside down during the boom in marijuana traffic to the United States in the 1970s. This decade also bracketed the years when vallenato music became the best-selling musical genre in Colombia.[117] *Marimberos,* who incarnated the failed promises of modernizing reforms in the former Greater Magdalena, invented themselves in part by investing in vallenato music financially and emotionally. They expressed their new class identity with designer clothes, colognes, watches and jewelry, guns, pickup trucks, and, first and foremost, vallenato songs and *parrandas.* These objects and status markers were more than symbols of wealth. They sustained the mirage that these men had a real chance of becoming constitutive members of the regional elite. Music and festivity were thus about masculine reconstitution in a double sense: celebrating the new role of money earners for their households and local communities, and seeking approval and respect from other men, both elite and plebeian.[118] But the older, more powerful—and legal—sector of cotton growers had already seized vallenato as their own and established its leadership in both the region and the nation. Their agenda and discourse eventually overshadowed the role of the *marimberos,* who represented the illegal faction of the regional agro-entrepreneurial class.

Although any serious collector or fan is aware of the relationship between *marimberos* and vallenato musicians, in the scholarly literature and in public discourse this connection has been minimized or ignored altogether. However, a close examination of both the protagonists of the marijuana boom and the voices and songs that narrate their values, views, and aspirations reveals that *marimberos* participated in shaping national culture by promoting vallenato music on the local stage, helping to modernize its sound and lyrical content, and hastening its national popularity. In this sense, the *marimberos,* the first regional class of Colombian drug traffickers, were important, if problematic, agents of cultural modernization. Although both politicians and the media contend that the marijuana business in Colombia was orchestrated by foreign actors—a topic I mention in the previous chapter and address in the following one—the evidence left by these pioneers of the trade disprove this theory. *Marimberos* remained anchored to their localities while they sought to insert themselves in regional society by using the very same cultural practices employed by the most successful faction of the regional elites in their previous rise to national notoriety. In this sense, these outlaws were quite traditional. They were also genuine. There was nothing imported from abroad in *marimberos'* cultural practices. Perhaps this authenticity in their engagement with regional culture in terms of financial, social, and emotional support of vallenato musicians and the *parranda* is what infused the songs of the 1970s with the originality and ardor that struck a chord with the popular classes all over the country and contributed to making this music and form of festivity a key element of late-twentieth-century Colombian culture.

PART THREE

———

Decline

FIVE

Two Peninsulas

NARCOTICS DIPLOMACY AND THE WAR ON DRUGS

The Two Peninsulas campaign has been a success and will
continue to be one; there is no need to get bitter about the traffickers' excesses; it is possible to eradicate this problem from
Colombia.

DIEGO ASENCIO,
US Ambassador to Bogotá (1977–1980)

ON JANUARY 29, 1979, *Time* Magazine put Colombia on its cover for the
first time. Under the title "The Colombian Connection: Billions in Pot and
Coke," the magazine with the world's largest circulation explained why the
US government was spending millions of dollars to collaborate with the
South American country. Although journalist Donald Neff mentioned
cocaine in the article, he conducted most of his fieldwork in the Guajira and
Sierra Nevada de Santa Marta's marijuana belt. In a direct reference to the
"French connection" of heroin, a topic that had fascinated the US public in
the 1950s, *Time* described the "Colombian connection" as networks of "nov-
ices and small-time entrepreneurs" controlling thousands of "farmers, smugglers, brokers and fixers" and operating "an armada of ships and planes" and
"an army of bush pilots, seamen, electronics experts, roustabouts and cut-
throats," providing "roughly two-thirds of all the pot smoked in the US" at
a time when smoking marijuana was the "most widely accepted illegal indul-
gence since drinking during Prohibition." Neff elaborated that "those who
enjoy smoking the weed may regard the traffic as essentially harmless," but
anywhere the "Colombian connection" spread, "violence and corruption"
ruled, which had turned one of the most stable democracies in the hemisphere into "a trafficker's paradise."[1]

The remarkable size of the marijuana and cocaine businesses was the *Time*
article's hook; however, what the magazine also uncovered was a more dramatic but less flashy truth: a rapid evolution in the state's response to the

growing drug-trafficking business. This chapter addresses this transformation in order to illustrate how the third and final cycle of the marijuana bonanza, its decline, was triggered by a succession of diplomatic impasses between Colombia and the United States and political crises within each country that culminated in a militarized campaign of crop eradication and traffic interdiction. Known as the Two Peninsulas campaign, the initiative was launched on November 1978 in the Guajira and Sierra Nevada de Santa Marta as a provisional response to the challenges created by these interconnected battles.

The cascading crises of the 1970s that precipitated a major change in US foreign policy and diplomacy began in the political realm with the Watergate scandal, continued with the US defeat in Vietnam, and ended with the collapse of détente after the Soviet invasion of Afghanistan. All of these developments took place against the backdrop of oil shocks, high energy prices, a falling dollar, rising Third World nationalism, and political dissent. The Nixon, Ford, and Carter administrations were confounded by the dilemmas they faced, and "flailed between competing imperatives."[2] Conservative factions within both US political parties offered the most cohesive solution to this crisis by reinstating a "fundamental conception of America and the world," one that explained "domestic failure in terms of foreign causes and so found it at first necessary and ultimately desirable to save the world in order to save [the United States] itself."[3] But given that US citizens were increasingly averse to becoming involved in any conflict that even remotely resembled the war in Vietnam, policymakers and diplomats revamped early–Cold War formulations of US drug control and, to varying degrees, resorted to the "illegal drugs portfolio" as a more palatable mechanism for reallocating government functions, forging diplomatic alliances, and enhancing and legitimizing state power.[4] Countries that supplied drugs became places where the US federal government could claim it was fixing a whole host of social, political, and economic problems by marrying counterinsurgency efforts and modernization-informed policies with antidrug missions.[5] The first Latin American country where the United States initiated this new approach was Mexico. In the process, the Mexican federal government tackled layers of domestic problems that had put its stability at risk.[6]

In this chapter, I untangle how and why Colombia, like Mexico, adopted and adapted the "war on drugs" to facilitate the physical and discursive demarcation of a geography of illegality, in which the US and Colombian governments established a novel approach to statecraft at a moment when their authority and legitimacy were called into question. By criminalizing cultivators and intermediaries in the Guajira and the Sierra Nevada, and by militarizing drug control, the Colombian and US governments opened new channels of interstate cooperation, established novel patterns of collaboration between counterinsurgency and antinarcotics agencies, overhauled state bureaucracies, created and expanded budgetary allocations, supported a policymaking community of experts, and constructed a new kind of internal enemy. These developments unfolded in a global context of revived militarism and Cold War containment.[7] Elevating the "war on drugs" to the forefront of US-Colombian relations during the 1970s and enacting state policies to carry out its agenda contributed to the reinstatement of US hegemony in Latin America and the Caribbean and prepared the ground for the offensive that the two countries waged against the cocaine cartels beginning in the mid-1980s, which made Colombia one of the world's most important theaters for the global drug wars even until today.

FROM COOPERATION TO DIPLOMACY

While it is true that the US Department of State and intelligence agencies pressured Colombia to modernize its law enforcement apparatus in order to better fight drug trafficking, the Colombian government was already motivated to follow Washington's designs.[8] As I show in chapter 2, normative ideas regarding drugs have old roots in Colombia's Catholic moralism.[9] During the decades when antinarcotics rhetoric, laws, and enforcement became part of the Colombian public sphere, however, these were not so much essential tools of state formation as devices with which to occasionally negotiate the level of state investment and involvement in local markets, regional politics, and private lives.

When President Richard Nixon launched the "war on drugs," the demonizing discourse against drugs was well established among Colombian authorities and in public opinion, particularly in the Andean interior. Born out of a campaign promise made in September 1968 in Anaheim, California, the "spawning ground for grassroots political conservatism" and the home of Nixon's "silent majority," the "war on drugs" was one side of his foreign policy.[10] The other pillar was détente, which Nixon announced during his inaugural speech on January 20, 1969, as central to "an era of negotiations" with the Soviet Union after a "period of confrontation."[11] During his first year in office, Nixon moved toward implementing both goals. He first established the Special Presidential Task Force Relating to Narcotics, Marijuana, and Dangerous Drugs, including twenty-two representatives from ten different federal agencies, to be supervised by Attorney General John Mitchell and tasked with assessing the situation and producing a report.[12] In the meantime, National Security Adviser Henry Kissinger coordinated a meeting with Soviet prime minister Leonid Brezhnev as the first phase of negotiating the Strategic Arms Limitation Treaty (SALT), whose goals were to freeze both countries' stockpile of nuclear weapons at current levels and to establish a foundation for future agreements on commercial relations and political cooperation with the communist world.[13]

Although seemingly contradictory, the "war on drugs" and détente were in many ways complementary. These policies had been in the making since the 1960s as Cold War conflicts evolved in different places. The increasing prosperity of North Atlantic Treaty Organization (NATO) member countries influenced Western Europeans' desire to improve relations with the Eastern bloc. Fearful of the prospect of being left behind by competitors, US business groups demanded that their country's government do more to improve the climate between East and West. Concurrently, the nuclear arms race reached a point of "mutual assured destruction," in the words of Secretary of Defense Robert McNamara, making the threat of using nuclear weapons to achieve ordinary political aims less credible.[14] Meanwhile, in the developing world, President Lyndon Johnson addressed the contradictions and failures of Kennedy's Alliance for Progress by using coercive and aggressive measures, recognizing military coups against left-leaning governments as legitimate, and even invading the Dominican Republic in order to prevent a "second Cuba" at whatever cost necessary.[15] Moreover, the escalation of the Vietnam war yielded its most problematic by-product in the domestic realm. Heroin abuse among US soldiers and veterans skyrocketed, and the youth who opposed the war burnt bridges with the status quo one marijuana joint at a time. This proved to the general public that drug use and addiction were mainstream problems rather than being exclusively inner-city phenomena.[16] In approaching this wide range of challenges, Nixon simultaneously ameliorated tensions with the communist bloc but exacerbated them with the Third World. Détente and the "war on drugs" were thus two sides of a single effort to demonstrate a renewed determination to defend US interests at home and abroad.

Mexico became the first laboratory for Nixon's "all-out offensive."[17] The report that the task force on drugs released on June 6, 1969, singled out

Mexico as "the primary source of nearly all of the high potency marihuana seized in the United States" and noted that "a significant percentage of the heroin consumed by addicts in the United States is produced surreptitiously in Mexico," while European heroin and South American cocaine were smuggled into the United States via the Mexican border. The report recommended that the Mexican government "should be urged" to establish a bureau "solely for the enforcement of narcotic laws" and "encouraged" to carry out other permanent measures.[18] But all that Nixon received from Mexican president Gustavo Díaz Ordaz was a series of cordial but noncommittal responses. To force Mexico into compliance, Nixon launched a surprise attack on the border in September 1969 called Operation Intercept, what FBI agent G. Gordon Liddy later called "an exercise in international extortion, pure, simple, and effective, designed to bend Mexico to our will."[19] The poppy and marijuana eradication and traffic interdiction campaigns that ensued in the Pacific tristate area along the northwestern section of the Sierra Madre made Mexico one of Washington's antidrug showcases (the other was Turkey, a main supplier of opiates for the pharmaceutical industry).[20]

Because the underlying premise of the "war on drugs" was that drug control can work only if it starts "at the source," the definition of the "drug problem" changed from a domestic issue to a foreign policy and diplomatic challenge.[21] Following the example of Harry Anslinger—the decade-long director of the Federal Bureau of Narcotics and leading force behind the most punitive antidrug legislation in the United States—Nixon used his clout at the United Nations. During the twenty-fourth session of the UN Commission of Narcotic Drugs, held in Geneva, Switzerland, in September and October 1971, US representatives explained during a meeting that the Nixon administration intended to find "realistic concepts to fight the illicit supply and demand for drugs, and break illicit traffic." The US representatives highlighted Mexico's effective actions in deterring drug traffic, and stressed the value of close cooperation between the two governments.[22] The session also offered an ideal opportunity to create new bureaucratic positions, including Senior Advisor for International Narcotics Matters, commissioned to "bring narcotics control considerations to bear systematically on the development of foreign policy," and Narcotics Coordinator, a senior diplomatic post in key embassies charged with bringing together the work of several departments and agencies—the US Customs Service; the Agency for International Development (USAID); the Departments of Agriculture and Defense and the latter's office of legal affairs; the Central Intelligence Agency

(CIA); and the International Communications Agency—in order to "gain the commitment of the host government to take action against illegal drug cultivation and trafficking."[23] With these strategic moves in the international arena, Nixon transformed drug policy from an instrument of state intervention in the domestic sphere into a tool of foreign policy.

By the time of this meeting, the marijuana belt in the Sierra Nevada had begun to spread from the Pénjamo and Tucurinca areas to the rest of the mountain range and even to the Perijá; however, Colombia attended the session as a mere observer. Both the US and the UN representatives contended that Colombia's minor role in the global narcotics trade had remained stable for decades; the country was thus considered just one of many transshipment points for opiates from Europe and a stopover for cocaine from Peru on its way to US markets.[24] According to the report that the US delegation prepared for the session, "the illicit drugs from outside sources which are of critical importance to the United States continue to be heroin and cocaine," but Colombia was not listed as a source.[25] Before the meeting, the US Department of State reported that the International Criminal Police Organization (Interpol) had found that "cannabis trafficking [is] now worldwide"; but again Colombia was not on Interpol's list, which included Mexico, the European shore of the Mediterranean, Lebanon, Morocco, Afghanistan, Pakistan, Nepal, and Central African countries that produced hashish. Colombian marijuana was not discussed, even though it was public knowledge that during Operation Intercept, Florida authorities had seized a two-ton shipment of marijuana from Colombia at an airport.[26]

This state of affairs changed dramatically in 1973 when Cold War politics produced a series of unintended effects in Colombia at a moment when Nixon's "war on drugs" became more systematized. The Nixon administration–backed coup against Salvador Allende in Chile began with joint maneuvers between Chilean and US military forces on the morning of September 11, 1973, in the Pacific port of Valparaíso.[27] The coup and the terror that proceeded it dispersed what historian Paul Gootenberg calls "the Andean connection"—transnational networks of traffickers who shipped cocaine to New York from several ports in the Southern Cone (Valparaíso being one of the most important ports), passing through the Panama Canal and by Cuba. These trafficking routes had existed since at least the end of World War II, and their dispersal created a window of opportunity for Colombians, some of whom began to participate more actively in this smuggling enterprise.[28] Aware of the altered situation, the new narcotics coordinator stationed at the US embassy in Bogotá worked closely with agents of the Drug Enforcement Administration (DEA), an agency that Nixon created on July 6, 1973, to unify all federal antinarcotics efforts.[29] The mandate of the narcotics coordinator and the DEA was to confront drug trafficking as a threat to "the very existence of any nation because if they [nations] permit trafficking in narcotics it builds a sort of shadow government that can bring down any government because the traffic is large, the money that's involved is large," generating "inflation and a wrecking of government's economic plans."[30] Alongside the DEA and the narcotics coordinator, the US Information Service held a series of seminars for professionals working on drug abuse in order to spread the message that "the narcotics problem is international and that the US is a leader in seeking solutions to it."[31] These newly created bureaucracies and programs found in Colombia a clean slate on which to delineate the specific threat that would help them generate specific fields of action, and thus prove their worth within the state apparatus.

More important, Nixon's novel approach to the "drug problem" forced a major change in the way Washington engaged with Colombia. To its long-term agenda of economic development and counterinsurgency, the Nixon administration added a short-term plan to reduce drug production and traffic. This shift prompted the government of Conservative president Misael Pastrana (1970–74) to launch several legal and administrative reforms to upgrade the country's capacity to participate in the "war on drugs." Notwithstanding the changes in legislation and state administration, both governments failed to adequately identify and address Colombia's potential role in the transnational drug business. This oversight was not due to a lack of information, as official reports indicate that the Colombian government was aware of both the size and the scope of the traffic in cocaine and marijuana to the United States. In "General Diagnostic of Public Order, 1967–1972," the National Police warned Pastrana that "delinquent activities have grown throughout the country" and cited in particular crimes against property and illegal narcotics production and export trade.[32] Submitted to the president on January 23, 1973, the report labeled 1972 "the narcotics commerce year," when drug traffic had spiked. The report noted, "Colombia is the producer of the best marijuana in the world, according to technicians and scientists, in addition to being a platform for cocaine export." It also identified five regions involved in marijuana cultivation: the eastern lowlands; the Urabá Gulf in northwest Antioquia, on the southernmost part of the Caribbean; the Sierra Nevada de Santa Marta and neighboring Guajira;

FIGURE 13. A National Police detective exhibits more than thirty kilos of confiscated marijuana, April 19, 1972. Larger seizures alerted authorities to a growing traffic. *El Espectador* photographic archive, Bogotá.

the coffee region, from the Department of Caldas to the Department of Huila; and the border with Venezuela, in the Departments of Santander, Boyacá, and Arauca. Coca leaf for cocaine processing did not grow anywhere within the country. All the product that Colombians exported was refined from coca paste smuggled in from Peru and Bolivia.

Two aspects of this report clarify what Colombian authorities believed about the problem at hand. First, the National Police distinguished between the marijuana and cocaine businesses using statistics on seizures and arrests as well as intelligence information. Whereas marijuana was cultivated and commercialized in at least five different regions (and exported primarily from the Caribbean coast, both the Urabá Gulf and the Guajira peninsula), cocaine was produced in its basic form abroad and only refined in Colombia for export to the United States. This meant that the marijuana business involved more segments of the population (from cultivators to intermediaries and exporters), and was geographically more widespread, than the cocaine business, which was concentrated in a few hands and limited to processing and exportation. The report therefore recommended the use of intelligence, technology, and international cooperation, particularly with the United States, to address the situation. The National Police also called for both making eradication of marijuana crops a state policy and stationing antinarcotics squads on international borders. And due to the problem posed by foreigners involved in the traffic, the National Police urged the signing of extradition treaties.

The report's second aspect clarifying how Colombian authorities began to define the "drug problem" was the distinction the National Police made between consumption as a public health issue, and production and trade as matters of public order. It concluded that drug use and addiction were not major social problems, despite the increasing prevalence of marijuana smoking among middle- and upper-middle-class youth. Cocaine was not widely consumed, and opiates were used only for medical purposes. In its recommendations, the National Police encouraged the continuation of educational campaigns in high schools and universities to publicize the dangers of drug use and persuade young people to cooperate with authorities as informants. It also suggested reforming existing legislation to permit authorities to coerce addicts into rehabilitation.

After the report was released, Pastrana launched reforms that replicated the administrative, medical, and legal frameworks that President Lyndon Johnson had outlined in the United States a few years earlier, which preserved the divide between issues of public order and public health. Pastrana created the National Narcotics Council within the Ministry of Justice, whose purpose was to serve as a consultation board made up of scientists and law enforcement agents tasked with coordinating domestic programs.[33] In June 1974, as Pastrana prepared to leave office, he signed Decree 1188, known as the National Narcotics Statute, which the US Department of State celebrated as a step in the right direction.[34] This decree synthesized existing laws dealing with health and drugs, and categorized responsibility for addressing possession and use of "drugs or substances that create physical dependency" as an exclusive function of the Ministry of Health; whereas production, sales, possession, and advertising outside the Ministry of Health's domain were criminal offenses prosecutable under the penal code of 1971, which the Pastrana administration also reformed in order to increase minimum sentences. In addition, Pastrana restructured the National Security Council (created in 1968) and expanded its reach and functions to serve as a consulting board on public order and to include representatives from the Ministries of Justice, Foreign Relations, and Defense; the Administrative Department of Security (DAS); the National Police; and the Civil Defense.[35] Using the National Narcotics Statute as a guideline, the two new councils began to work in tandem to define the "drug problem." While the Security Council focused on drug production and trafficking as public order issues, the Narcotics Council addressed drug use and abuse as public health matters.

As a whole, Pastrana's antinarcotics measures modernized the state apparatus and enabled the US governmental and law enforcement agencies to systematically transfer knowledge, technology, equipment, and training to Colombia.[36] The transfer of knowledge went as far as attempting to shape public opinion with a TV show called *El enemigo oculto* (The Hidden Enemy). Produced and hosted by journalist María Isabel de Lince, the show was sponsored by the US State Department's Narcotics Control Assistance Program and provided the general public with "information and education" on the dangers of illegal drugs.[37] The use of antinarcotics propaganda, the reliance on technology, and the indispensability of interstate cooperation constituted the principles of Colombia's incipient antinarcotics apparatus.

When Pastrana's tenure ended and a new Colombian president was inaugurated, on August 7, 1974, Nixon's political career was hanging by a thread. Two days later, Nixon resigned. Although his resignation brought disrepute to his doctrine, the "war on drugs" continued operating through several bilateral programs around the world.[38] Paradoxically, Nixon's resignation marked the moment when Colombia became an important interlocutor in narcotics diplomacy. In October 1974 Secretary of State Henry Kissinger wrote to the US embassy in Bogotá, "The rapid growing importance of Colombia in the traffic signals the need for fast and effective reaction on the part of USG [US government]."[39] But Colombia, the embassy answered, "is not Canada, Germany or France, and unless we successfully 'upgrade the GOC [government of Colombia] narcotics interdiction effort,' we have no base on which to rest our coordination efforts."[40] The newly inaugurated administration was thus expected to facilitate such an upgrade in order to translate Pastrana's reforms into actual agencies and programs with which bilateral cooperation could be operationalized.

Building upon the groundwork laid by his predecessor, newly minted president Alfonso López Michelsen (1974–78) struggled to find a balance between contradictory political necessities. Leader of the Revolutionary Liberal Movement, the left wing of the Liberal party, one of the creators of the prosperous Department of Cesar and its first governor, a founder of the famous Vallenato Legend Festival, and a son of former president Alfonso López Pumarejo, the most popular reformer of the twentieth century, López Michelsen made a career of walking a thin line between offering an alternative to the status quo and serving as a leading figure.[41] After his election as president, he applied his political skills to playing a delicate game with Washington. Based on the foreign policy principle he designed while he was minister of foreign relations under President Carlos Lleras Restrepo (1966–70)—a policy characterized as *respice similia* (looking at the similar ones), in contrast to *respice polum* (looking at the polar star)—López Michelsen walked a tightrope between anti-imperialist nationalist rhetoric and deference to and cooperation with Washington.[42] In following this two-pronged strategy during his presidential tenure, López Michelsen made the drug trade a topic of public debate that extended beyond the realm of experts and law enforcement agents, and transformed the way the Colombian state understood and implemented antinarcotics initiatives.

Once in office, López Michelsen aligned himself closely with General José Joaquín Matallana, a military officer whom Pastrana appointed head of the DAS in 1973 and whose anticommunist credentials brought the sympathy and goodwill López Michelsen needed from Washington's hardliners. Educated in the South Command and the Inter-American Defense College, General Matallana perceived antinarcotics activities as indispensable tools for achieving national security goals. According to a November 1974 team report on DAS's performance produced by the Cabinet Committee on International Narcotics Control, López Michelsen "told Ambassador that DAS would be his chosen agent to deal with the narcotics problem" because "he has confidence in DAS under General Matallana and wishes it to assume a major role in the drug battle."[43] Matallana's vast experience in pacifying the Liberal guerrillas during and after La Violencia, and his leadership in the first aerial offensive against them in 1964, not only satisfied the US Embassy in Bogotá but also made López Michelsen appear diligent in addressing a series

of corruption scandals that he inherited from Pastrana involving public officials deemed complicit in the drug business.[44] With López Michelsen's support, Matallana continued the purge of compromised officials. He also set
out to modernize the agency under his leadership in order to remedy the fact
that "DAS has not yet developed an active campaign towards narcotics suppression, and its efforts are lagging far behind both the National Police, and
Customs," as USAID put it.[45]

Matallana's plan to fight drug producers and traffickers used a counterinsurgency approach and comprised seven initiatives. These ranged from broad-
ening existing definitions of "antisocial behavior" to include more offenses,
to enacting harsher sentences, reforming the penal code to simplify judicial
procedures, reopening several agrarian penal colonies to accommodate a
growing prison population, and increasing the frequency and length of military occupations of zones where conflicts threatened public order. Like any
well-educated Cold Warrior who understood that national security was an
ideological and cultural endeavor as much as it was a military and political
one, Matallana highlighted the need to produce propaganda on national
security issues in order to complement the other six points of his reform plan
"with a psychological intervention upon the totality of the Colombian population without divulging the state's involvement, not even minimally."[46]
With this plan, López Michelsen made a carom. First, he concentrated antinarcotics efforts in the national executive—DAS reported directly to the
president—thereby avoiding delays involved in congressional debates and
fulfilling Washington's demand for faster action.[47] Second, he gave the green
light to cross-fertilization between antinarcotics goals and counterinsurgency strategies and techniques.

Indeed, counterinsurgency theory and praxis gave substance and historical
depth to antinarcotics programs, a new type of state effort in which Colombia
was a novice. Since the end of World War II, and particularly since Liberals
and Conservatives instituted the National Front in 1958 and made Colombia
a wall of contention against Cuba's influence in Latin America, the doctrine
of national security had become foundational to the Colombian state. As in
Argentina and Brazil, two pioneers of this doctrine, in Colombia, Liberal and
Conservative governments alike adopted the new principles according to
which social problems engendered subversion and therefore the maintenance
of the status quo was the safest choice for preserving national and international security.[48] The emergence of several guerrilla groups over the course
of a decade confirmed the relevance of this approach. First, after the 1964

offensive against the remnants of the Liberal guerrillas of La Violencia—whose aerial component Matallana led—this sedentary self-defense militia became a mobile force that allied itself with the Colombian Communist party to form the Revolutionary Armed Forces of Colombia (FARC) in 1966. Second, a group of young middle-class people, graduates of universities in Colombia and exchange programs in Cuba and followers of Che Guevara's *foco* theory, joined forces with Liberal guerrillas and some sectors of the Oil Workers' Union to form the National Liberation Army (ELN) in 1965. Third, following the Sino-Soviet split, a group of Maoists who belonged to several agrarian organizations came together with former Liberal guerrillas and founded the Popular Liberation Army (EPL) in 1967. Finally, in 1974, dissidents of the FARC and members of the party that former dictator Gustavo Rojas Pinilla created to challenge the National Front launched the 19th of April Movement (M19), an urban guerrilla organization whose name commemorated the allegedly fraudulent presidential elections of 1970, in which Rojas Pinilla was denied a victory. Following the example of the Southern Cone guerrilla organizations the Montoneros and the Tupamaros, M19 recruited its members from city slums and universities.[49]

Matallana's comprehensive plan to tackle drug-trafficking networks built upon the longer-running fights against these guerrilla movements and used the doctrine of national security as its theoretical foundation for a renewed state praxis. The problem, however, lay precisely in praxis. Such plans seem easier to accomplish in theory than in practice, especially when they are disconnected from social contingencies. Thus far, the conversation between Bogotá and Washington regarding the Guajira and Sierra Nevada had focused on the prospect of a bonanza very different from the marijuana boom. Since the "second youth of coal" in the mid-1960s, when the largest US hydrocarbon companies invested in this fossil fuel as an alternative to oil, Exxon had fixed its attention on what promised to be the largest open-pit coal mine in the world: El Cerrejón, a hill located in the great valley between Riohacha and Valledupar in the Department of Guajira.[50] Most members of the Colombian ruling class and intelligentsia were elated at the prospect of the exorbitant currency reserves this project promised, while others were critical of its implications for national sovereignty and economic dependence on transnational capital.[51] Apparently, nobody in a position of authority at the national level seemed to have other interests or concerns about the region. In late 1974 the unresolved consequences of the incomplete agrarian reform of the 1960s erupted in a violent but localized social conflict that overwhelmed the capacity of departmental authorities to respond, which gave General Matallana the opportunity to visit the Guajira and to make the case for a more systematic approach to combatting the drug trade business as a serious threat to national security.

Two years earlier, in 1972, in the midst of a diplomatic dispute over the border between Colombia and Venezuela, the Venezuelan National Guard arrived at a village in the Perijá, in what inhabitants thought was the Department of Guajira, and forced 160 families to abandon their houses, crops, and animals. Although these families possessed titles to their property granted by Incora, the institute that managed the agrarian reform, the Venezuelan National Guard carried out the operation because those lands were in fact located in Venezuelan territory. The 935 dispossessed persons arrived at Fonseca, a town located in the great valley between Riohacha and Valledupar, where they lived with assistance from public charity. The Colombian government admitted that Incora had made a mistake by giving titles to lands in Venezuela and promised solutions; however, two years later, nothing had changed. In 1974 the majority of these displaced families moved to Mingueo, in the heart of the marijuana belt, on the other side of the Sierra Nevada. Upon arrival, they decided against following most settlers to higher elevations. Instead, they occupied Aguadulce, an uncultivated estate located in the foothills of the mountain range and owned by a dynasty of the Liberal party, a family that had pioneered marijuana exportation.[52] The National Police responded by repeatedly forcing the families to move from estate to estate in an endless cycle of occupation and expulsion.[53]

Despite receiving support from the National Peasant Association (ANUC), the most powerful of Colombia's agrarian organizations that had coordinated land invasions all over the country since 1971, the displaced families did not succeed in their effort to settle again. ANUC had a strong presence in the former banana district and, to a lesser extent, in the cotton belt, but had no similar stronghold in the marijuana region.[54] Access to land in the intermontane valleys was not yet a problem and, thanks to marijuana, living conditions were not an issue either. Moreover, in 1973, when the Conservative Pastrana administration joined forces with its party's members in Congress and with landlords in different parts of the country to orchestrate an agrarian counterreform and retaliate against peasants and their movement—an initiative known as the Pact of Chicoral—ANUC split into two wings, a radical one that prioritized direct action, and a moderate one that aimed to de-escalate conflict and reduce direct action.[55] As the latter wing was dominant in the former Greater Magdalena, the number of land occupations decreased, which added to the detrimental impact of marijuana cultivation on ANUC's appeal; as a consequence, the organizational capacity of the peasant movement waned. By the time the families displaced from Perijá arrived at Mingueo in early 1974 and decided to stay in the lowlands instead of colonizing the agricultural frontiers in the intermontane valleys, ANUC's strength had already dropped to its lowest.[56]

The solidarity of the student movement was the only force keeping the fight for land in the lowlands going.[57] Journalist Edgar Ferrucho Padilla, a native of Riohacha, was one of the leaders on the Caribbean coast of the youth organizations associated with the Revolutionary Independent Labor Movement (MOIR), the most important Maoist party in the country. He explained to me why students considered this alliance with ANUC a historic revolutionary undertaking. "There was a small working class here, but [a large] peasantry, especially in the Mingueo area"; therefore MOIR's efforts focused on this section of the mountain range in order to transform it into "a red zone, tremendously red, thanks to the symbiosis that we achieved with the peasant movement."[58] When the families displaced from the border arrived in Mingueo, MOIR and ANUC representatives coordinated activities, including a takeover of the departmental government building in Riohacha in the hope of staging a *paro cívico* (a citizens' strike). But local authorities repelled them violently, and the clashes produced dozens of wounded people and a few deaths.[59] In the meantime, some of Ferrucho Padilla's friends, *compadres,* and relatives got more enmeshed in the marijuana traffic, closing ranks with landowners to use their uncultivated estates as airstrips, gaining access to nearby seaports for export operations, and making social life in the low-lands more chaotic and dangerous.[60] Once again, the region's male youth was divided between students and merchants, each group trying to realize their aspirations on opposite sides of history, the former seeking a chance to trigger a revolution, the latter trying to preserve the status quo and profit from it.

These layers of synergies between different sectors in conflict are what concerned General Matallana when his commission visited Mingueo in late 1974, after rumors of a budding guerrilla front reached Bogotá. In his memorandum on the visit, the general reminded national authorities that the area was a "marijuana belt in which Colombians and foreigners participated."[61] He also wrote that the business was "practically managed from North America, in Florida and Texas, specifically, and the Italian and the Jewish mafias used their incalculable economic resources in order to keep it."[62]

FIGURE 14. General José Joaquín Matallana (seated, in uniform), director of the Administrative Department of Security (DAS), at a press conference, September 20, 1974. *El Espectador* photographic archive, Bogotá.

Matallana reiterated that although there was "no guerrilla activity in this sector, the psychological conditions and human capacities to form a subversive base in the future exist."[63] Currently, the only armed sector constituted a counterinsurgent force, Matallana explained. Landowners with marijuana connections were the ones who "spread the rumor of the existence of a communist guerilla [front]," since they were willing to repress any kind of insurgency or radicalism in order to defend their territories. Among his recommendations, Matallana proposed "to carry out a well-planned and well-executed operation by the Army, the National Police, and DAS to destroy marijuana crops in the Sierra Nevada, and arrest all foreigners involved in it."[64]

Two salient features of Matallana's report help us understand the marijuana boom's peak and decline through the lens of national security. First, despite the fact that the marijuana business provided temporary relief to the old problem of access to land, markets, and resources, these pertinacious issues persisted. The popular sectors that sought a state solution to these social problems were incapable of articulating a cohesive response. As they continued to fragment, marijuana exporters used their economic and social capital to finance private security forces in order to defend their interests. Second, Colombia's marijuana exporters were not autonomous. Instead, they occupied a precarious and dependent position as brokers in longer chains of traffickers, which made them vulnerable to attacks from above (i.e., the state) and below (i.e., popular sectors).

President López Michelsen, by profession a lawyer educated in elite universities in Colombia, Belgium, Chile, and the United States, was adept at translating complex political situations into comprehensible theories. He used these skills to rephrase Matallana's ideas and present them in his negotiations with Washington. Under the rubric "mafia wars," López Michelsen explained to the public that the drug trade had risen in the country because foreign syndicates had infiltrated Colombia's most vulnerable territories. Asked in September 1975 about his position on the narcotics trade during a press conference in Bogotá a day before his departure for Washington, D.C., for his first official visit, López Michelsen explained that "Colombia is the victim of its privileged geographic location, which permits American citizens, with American capital investment, flying airplanes with American registration numbers that take off from American airports, to turn us into a platform for the drug trade." He assured the public that the drug trade's continuance reflected "not the inability of the Colombian government to control its people," but rather "the American impotence to deter its criminals."[65] However, as soon as he landed in Washington, he qualified his statement. Asked at a press conference about cooperation with the United States on antinarcotics programs, López Michelsen affirmed that "if the mafias that traffic with drugs are organized at the multinational level, obviously, we have to fight them at the multinational level."[66] With the bombastic term "mafia wars," López Michelsen turned the drug trade, a topic that increasingly defined the relationship with the United States but that had been addressed only through confidential and diplomatic channels, into a catchy headline. This new term and the vision of the drug trade that it encompassed prompted public debates in which López Michelsen slyly alternated between nationalist rhetoric and flexible cooperation, depending on the audience.

This approach, which ultimately accomplished little, fit with the Colombian and US administrations' limited capacities to confront the multifaceted problem at hand. López Michelsen's official visit to Washington coincided with the release of the *White Paper on Drug Abuse,* a report to President Gerald Ford that recommended a considerable reduction in the antinarcotics budget, particularly for campaigns "at the source."[67] In this context, Secretary of State Henry Kissinger advised the US Embassies in Bogotá, Caracas, and Mexico City not to interpret López Michelsen's declaration "as a deliberate provocation," and reminded them that "we agree certainly that an important cause of the drug traffic in Colombia is the difficulty in combating it in the US."[68] Months later, in his "Special Message to the Congress on Drug Abuse" (April 27, 1976), Ford added López Michelsen to the list of cooperative heads of state in the fight against narcotics trafficking, along with President Luis Echeverría of Mexico and Prime Minister Süleyman Demirel of Turkey.[69] Thus, when López Michelsen was in Colombia, he publicly emphasized anti-imperialism to satisfy nationalist values, and when he was in Washington, he feigned political compliance with the United States. Similarly, Ford appeared uncompromising in the global fight against illicit drugs, but in practice his policies reflected budgetary realism. In this diplomatic game of mirrors, both administrations' public diligence masked their political limitations in terms of having either resources or a concrete plan of action.

By echoing General Matallana's ideas and framing the drug trade in Colombia as an invasion of foreign mafias, President López Michelsen made official a self-exonerating narrative that both countries shared. Historian Douglas Clark Kinder explains that in the United States the idea of drug consumption as a major social problem evolved from "deep nativist undercurrents in the nation's tradition" that presented drug use as something immigrants imported.[70] This premise was foundational to the new diplomacy that the "war on drugs" institutionalized, since the only way to protect "old stock" society from drugs was to eradicate drugs "at the source." Likewise, Kinder asserts, "Latin Americans could use nativism equally well" to rationalize US "hysteria over drugs" as none of their business.[71] Thanks to Ford's "new realism," which reflected a commitment to cutting federal spending, López Michelsen could afford to be "nativist."[72] And although the "war on drugs" remained part of the national discourse, in practice it was put on hold as Ford and López Michelsen turned their attention to hemispheric defense, which entailed practicing how the two countries would conduct a joint response with submarines, tankers, destroyers, warships, container ships, and planes in case of an attack on the Caribbean coast of a country located in such close proximity to the Panama Canal.[73] Ironically, the enemy that finally prompted Colombia and the United States to engage in a militarized bilateral campaign did not come from overseas, but from within.

FROM DIPLOMACY TO WAR

Elected on a platform of human rights and nonintervention, during his first two years in office Jimmy Carter struggled over how to deal with friendly governments whose antidemocratic practices undermined public institutions. This was the case with López Michelsen, whose administration lurched from crisis to crisis. Despite his landslide victory in the 1974 elections, after a campaign that moved at the rhythm of vallenato music and won the support of trade unions, the organized left, and social movements, López Michelsen was unpopular. Not only did he close ranks with the bipartisan establishment and abandon promises to his constituencies on the left; but he also came up short in handling several corruption scandals involving high- and low-ranking government military officers and civilian functionaries.[74] The leftist press labeled his administration a "corruptocracy."[75] At the height of these scandals, the Carter administration learned that complicity at the highest levels of the Colombian government was contributing directly to the drug trade. These concerns, along with the steady growth in marijuana and cocaine traffic, posed a new set of problems for which Carter's agenda on decriminalization and harm reduction was ill-suited.

First Lady Rosalynn Carter was the designated national representative responsible for addressing the predicament.[76] She arrived in Bogotá in June 1977 on her Latin American tour. After a meeting with López Michelsen during which she addressed six topics of mutual concern, she confronted him with CIA evidence of drug-related corruption in his administration, and the two "negotiated a follow-up action plan." The First Lady then convened a meeting with US foreign service officials and Assistant Secretary of State for Western Hemisphere Affairs Terence A. Todman (López Michelsen was not present).[77] Together, they addressed what they called "the narcotics situation."[78] The conversation revolved around the bone of contention: three helicopters that Ford had promised to López Michelsen but failed to deliver.[79] "Jimmy thinks President Lopez is turning his head to the corruption and we shouldn't give him the helicopters until he demonstrates he is willing to do something," Rosalynn Carter stated. Although opinions varied, the consensus was that Carter was right but that failing to deliver the equipment would "destroy what already [had] been accomplished" in terms of interstate cooperation.[80]

It was the DEA representative who made the strongest case for delivering the helicopters. After the agency's creation in 1973, the number of DEA agents stationed in Colombia had grown from zero to three hundred in just two years; by 1976 there were about five hundred.[81] Such growth occurred as a result of a heated rivalry between the DEA and other US agencies, particularly the CIA. Reports to the White House warned Carter that "our own efforts in Colombia have been hampered by an ongoing conflict between CIA and DEA over the collection of intelligence data."[82] Special Agent David Burnett, DEA's director in Colombia, took the opportunity afforded by Rosalyn Carter's visit to Bogotá to insist that because "all the drug rings use planes," Burnett said, "enforcement actions are impossible without them." Burnett reminded the First Lady that the DEA was ready to open its first offices outside Bogotá, starting in Barranquilla, near the marijuana belt on the Caribbean coast. The country was "worth a gamble," he concluded.[83]

The First Lady's trip to Colombia was a prelude to the arrival of Carter's drug czars. Peter Bourne, special assistant to the president for health issues and director of the Office of Drug Abuse Policy, and Mathea Falco, assistant secretary of state for international narcotics and law enforcement affairs, traveled in late June to Bogotá to ensure that López Michelsen removed corrupt officials from his administration. According to Deputy Secretary of State Warren Christopher, Bourne and Falco were also charged with responsibility "to appraise the serious cocaine problem there."[84] Advised by Assistant Secretary of State Vance Vaky "to withhold delivery of helicopters pending the outcome of [the] Bourne/Falco visit," Carter waited.[85] The meeting began with Bourne and Falco emphasizing that "drug trafficking between the US and Colombia is a joint problem" and that therefore "it makes no sense for one country to be blaming the other." They explored the idea of establishing a joint commission headed by the Colombian foreign minister to work on antinarcotics issues. Finally, when Bourne expressed Carter's concern about corruption in Colombia involving "many people in high positions benefiting from the drug traffic," and conveyed Carter's offer to provide

FIGURE 15. A US congressional commission visits President Alfonso López Michelsen, August 10, 1977. *El Espectador* photographic archive, Bogotá.

López Michelsen with a confidential briefing on the subject, the Colombian president accepted, making "no move to demand large amounts of money, as [the US officials] thought he might."[86] Ultimately, López Michelsen convinced Bourne and Falco to support delivery of the helicopters so they could patrol the national territory during a period of sociopolitical conflict.

At the time of Bourne and Falco's visit, the Carter administration considered the cocaine coming from Colombia to be much more troubling than marijuana.[87] In line with Carter's harm reduction goals of raising prices on the streets and discouraging consumption, Bourne framed international drug smuggling as an economic problem of supply and demand rather than a moral or social evil.[88] "The pharmacological distinctions among heroin, cocaine, and marijuana are irrelevant," Bourne wrote; "the critical factor is the economic value of the drug in the illicit distribution network."[89] While coca planting, trading, and chewing were indigenous practices in Peru and Bolivia—cultural traits that "make crop eradication or crop substitution, in our estimation, completely unfeasible at the present time"—only a few indigenous minorities in Colombia, a *mestizo* nation with no mainstream coca culture, cultivated the leaf used in the processing of cocaine.[90] No commercial coca crops were grown in Colombia yet for processing into cocaine. Because of this feature of the country's social makeup and identity, the Carter administration worried that the country could become the cocaine labora-tory of the Americas given the fact that coca in Colombia was not a sacred plant but all about adding value by refining it into cocaine.[91]

Regardless of this focus on cocaine, national and hemispheric security concerns eventually pushed the Carter administration in a different direc-tion. The discovery of a large marijuana plantation in the Guajira section of the Sierra Nevada triggered several alarm bells in Washington, DC. First, the plantation's large labor force and sophisticated irrigation systems indicated "the commercial and highly professional aspect of the marijuana business in Colombia." Second, because the discovery had "generated a spate of news articles in Colombia calling for tighter narcotics control," the Colombian armed forces were "apparently becoming involved in anti-marijuana opera-tions in the area" in a way that was "similar in design to the Mexican mili-tary's 'Operation Condor.'" Third, "the narcotics situation in Colombia could become a minor campaign issue in next year's presidential elections," a prediction that pushed Carter to reiterate his agenda of drug decriminaliza-tion and harm reduction, which in turn created an opportunity for Colombians to point out the "inconsistency between the US domestic policy of decriminalization of marijuana, and US efforts to convince foreign pro-ducers that marijuana is a dangerous drug."[92] Four, in contrast to the cocaine traffic, which in Colombia was limited in size and scope and had yet to gener-ate commercial coca crops, marijuana was at the center of a regional export economy. While various operations targeted cocaine networks in different parts of the Andean interior—including Operation Kitchen, carried out between October 1975 and March 1976 against laboratories, and Operation Funnel, between April and December 1976 against the smuggling of coca paste from Peru and Bolivia—tackling marijuana crops and chains of com-mercialization operating within a vast geography would require greater financial and political investment.[93]

Politicians were thus wary of making such expenditures until dire circum-stances forced drastic solutions. As the López Michelsen administration marked the official end of the National Front, the ability of patronage and clientelism to control and co-opt the popular sectors and middle classes con-tinued to approach exhaustion.[94] A serious crisis of authority and legitimacy manifested itself in various ways. Members of the president's own Liberal party in Congress did not support his policies, Conservatives and economic guilds blocked his initiatives, and labor, student, and peasant organizations mobilized on the streets against his mandate. To govern a country submerged in a general atmosphere of civil disobedience, crime, and political protest, López Michelsen declared a state of emergency throughout Colombia. Although the measure succeeded in suppressing social protest, it did not rebuild his authority. One thing seemed to go well, however: the US-Colombian relationship improved with the delivery of three helicopters, and López Michelsen's diplomatic efforts facilitated negotiations between Carter and the Panamanian government of General Omar Torrijos over the turnover of the canal. Hence, López Michelsen allied with Carter against drug trafficking as a reasonable measure by which to demonstrate commitment and dedication to the country's well-being.

According to López Michelsen, at his request, Carter sent a commission to Colombia to calculate the size of marijuana crops and provide technical support in light of "the experiences of Mexico and Turkey in eradicating illicit crops, providing us with new methods in order to make operations faster and cheaper."[95] Forest engineer Rodrigo Echeverri, then working for the National Institute of Natural Resources (Inderena) in the Sierra Nevada, was one of the hosts. He and other representatives of the Colombian Army and National Police and the DEA flew over the mountain range in the helicopters that Carter had provided López Michelsen. "We used to take them to good restaurants for lunch, we bought bottles of wine and whiskey, anything, we spent a lot of money on them to get the data"—that is, satellite information on crops and airstrips—Echeverri recalled about his work with DEA agents. Then, using this satellite information, Inderena extrapolated the total tonnage of marijuana exported annually and found it to be "extraordinarily lower than what the [Colombian] attorney general and the [US] Embassy claimed." Although Echeverri warned his supervisors about the discrepancies, he surmised "they were aware that they had inflated data in order to inflate the [size of the] problem," he told me.[96] As Echeverri understood, science and technology served political necessity.

Ideology and political interests also prevailed in the US House of Representatives, where a Democratic representative from New York found in the "war on drugs" his own opportunity to shine. Lester Wolff, a World War II veteran elected to Congress by a wealthy, predominantly Jewish constituency on Long Island, chaired the House Select Committee on Narcotics Abuse and Control, created in 1976. After a trip to Europe with Peter Bensinger, head of the DEA, during which they visited Pope Paul VI, Wolff was convinced that drug addiction was one of the most serious problems facing modern societies.[97] He professed that all efforts "must begin at the source; once the raw product leaves the farm there is no way known to man to follow it in its processed form to its ultimate destination."[98] Lacking jurisdiction over international issues, Wolff exercised his power domestically. In June 1977, when Rosalyn Carter visited López Michelsen, the committee he chaired began an inquiry into the extent and nature of drug trafficking in south Florida, the main port of entry for illegal narcotics into the United States. The committee determined that the whole economy in the peninsula revolved around the marijuana and cocaine businesses. The drug trade's predominance there emboldened traffickers, who "have begun to assume the aura of folk heroes," and "disrespect for the law" was eroding "the moral fiber of the community."[99] The House committee called on the White House to implement an interdiction campaign. Because the "overwhelming amount of drug trafficking in marijuana and cocaine" came from Colombia, and most of the total gross value came from marijuana sales, the solution seemed clear. First, the US general public had to reject the "[social] acceptance of marijuana as a recreational drug," because social relaxation made it "more difficult to secure convictions."[100] Then, the report recommended, the Carter administration had to abandon its "mistaken policy of overlooking the smuggling of large quantities of marijuana" and respond "in the manner it would if a natural disaster or other grave emergency had struck the area." Specifically, the White House should order special law enforcement task forces, coordinate with the Department of Justice in reducing the disparity in sentencing for drug-related offenses, and mobilize military assistance after a revision of posse comitatus laws, which limit the powers of the federal government to use the military for law enforcement. Finally, the report urged Carter to increase international cooperation with Colombia.

In the middle of these policy battles within the Democratic party, and between Congress and the White House, the institutional crisis in Colombia deepened. Labor unions declared a national strike on September 14, 1977, paralyzing the economy and convincing the military that the guerrillas had infiltrated social movements.[101] Kidnappings of wealthy entrepreneurs in Cali, Barranquilla, and Medellín multiplied; corruption scandals persisted and consequent conflicts between the president and the armed forces escalated to the point that politicians and the press talked about "the fragility of the state of law."[102] The Carter administration worried about losing Colombia to a coup, as had occurred in many other South American countries. But Colombia's military was also engulfed in the crisis, and it was overwhelmed by additional functions: political and criminal policing, administration of justice, and antinarcotics efforts, in addition to rampant corruption within their own ranks. High-ranking officers expressed their dissatisfaction, and a few signed a public document criticizing what they considered to be López Michelsen's erroneous policies and asking for emergency measures to prevent subversion.[103] In response, López Michelsen discharged some of the officers and transferred others.[104] As part of the restructuring, the president removed General Matallana from DAS and appointed him head of the Joint Chiefs of Staff.[105] Waiting to be promoted to commander of the armed forces—the logical post given his seniority—Matallana was asked instead to assume leadership of a new antinarcotics program. During a press conference, López Michelsen declared: "I even showed him a letter from President Jimmy Carter in which he outlined a great plan against drug trafficking, which will be launched next year, but General Matallana said that he would prefer to be discharged."[106] With Matallana's refusal of the offer in protest over López Michelsen's disregard for the line of succession in the military hierarchy, his career ended.[107]

A few months later, in January 1978, the crisis hit rock bottom after the French newspaper *Le Monde Diplomatique* published extracts from a memorandum to the US Senate in which the DEA and other agencies denounced the criminal activities of the Colombian minister of defense, General Abraham Varón Valencia, and other officials, including the head of DAS in the Guajira.[108] Colombia was in the middle of a campaign to elect the first president after the official end of the National Front; hence, the news came as a blow to the Liberal party. Hitherto, the front runner had been López Michelsen's closest collaborator and former ambassador to Washington, Julio Cesar Turbay Ayala, the man who led the National Front's diplomatic offensive against Cuba during the Lleras Camargo administration in the early 1960s.[109] But after April 1978, when CBS's *60 Minutes* leaked Peter Bourne's report to Carter following his visit to Bogotá, which named Turbay as one of the politicians involved in the drug trade, his lead diminished. Although Turbay was not a popular leader capable of galvanizing the masses, he was a savvy politician with extensive knowledge of how the party machinery and clientelist networks operated. Thus, when CBS aired what the Colombian press dubbed the "Bourne Memorandum," López Michelsen and the Liberal establishment discredited the news as "an infamous campaign" to undermine Colombia's efforts to halt a problem that had roots in the United States, and they accused Bourne and the international press of trying to stain Colombia's image in the world.[110] To save his campaign, candidate Turbay promised a counteroffensive to restore the rule of law in a country that seemed to be spinning out of control. As historian James D. Henderson argues, the scandal pushed Turbay toward a more severe response to the country's problems than he had initially intended.[111]

The leaked memorandum not only persuaded Liberal Colombians to move to the right but also contributed to pushing Carter's progressive drug decriminalization agenda off the cliff. According to Peter Bourne, the producer of *60 Minutes* contacted him in advance to corroborate the story, which included a dramatic argument between Rosalynn Carter and López Michelsen. "I told him his version was totally untrue," Bourne wrote in an email in response to a set of questions I sent him. But the TV producer said, "Quite frankly, doctor, that would not be much of a story."[112] According to Bourne, "the evidence against him [Turbay] was from a variety of intelligence sources but relied heavily on wire taps" from the CIA and the DEA.[113] In his email to me, Bourne speculated that the scoop to the press came from "[Zbigniew] Brzezinski [the national security advisor,] with whom I had a very competitive relationship," and who probably resorted to "someone at DEA who did not wish me or Carter well" to leak the report to the press and compromise Bourne's status.[114]

Whether or not Bourne is right about Brzezinski, midway through Carter's second year in office "the apparent incompatibility between our support for human rights and our concern for national security" fractured his administration from within.[115] An outsider who had minimal support within the Democratic party, and who did not command the kind of respect that Congress had accorded his predecessors, Carter put together an inner circle that resembled a patchwork of opposing ideological currents.[116] On one hand, there were those like Bourne who supported his drug decriminalization and Cold War détente agenda; on the other were those like Brzezinski who favored the "war on drugs" and containment. Likewise, the social forces behind his campaign were equally fractured, even within the left wing. For example, the directorate of the National Organization for the Reform of Marijuana Laws (NORML), an organization that was crucial in getting Carter elected, bitterly and regularly confronted members of the staff, even Peter Bourne, for not being radical enough.[117] And so, when the counterrebellion frequently referred to as the Parent Movement launched its crusade against drug use, the Carter administration was caught off guard. The president's personal friend and most vociferous drug toleration spokesperson, Peter Bourne, a "soft, uncertain man, a political amateur" in a pool of "battle-hardened veterans of the political wars," turned out to be the advisor most vulnerable to attacks from both left and right.[118] In late July 1978, more than a month after Turbay was elected president in Colombia, journalists who were sympathetic to the Parent Movement published a story based on information provided by a vengeful Keith Stroup, the director of NORML, claiming that Bourne had signed a prescription for quaaludes to a White House colleague under a false name and had used cocaine at a party given by NORML.[119] Bourne's ensuing resignation changed the balance of forces within the Carter administration, and by the fall of 1978 the White House stopped pressuring Congress to legislate marijuana decriminalization and harm reduction.

Similar to what had transpired in Colombia months earlier, the crisis in the United States only continued to deepen, forcing Carter to transition to a doctrine of militarization of foreign relations, including drug control.[120] The Soviet advance in central Asia was the most worrisome new development because it unleashed a "resurgence of Soviet-US competition in the Third World."[121] In this context, the decolonizing Caribbean—a strategic "backyard" for the United States—became sensitive terrain.[122] In the eventuality of a return to containment, several factors made the Caribbean an area for the United States to control: massive flows of immigrants from many of its islands to the United States, Cuba's military power compared to that of neighboring countries, ongoing negotiations with Panama to end US control of the canal dating to 1903, and civil wars in Central America, particularly in Nicaragua where the powerful Sandinista guerrillas were effectively challenging Somoza's dictatorship.[123] "The movement of marijuana in bulk, primarily by ship and light aircraft, from the north coast of Colombia to the eastern US" crossed the Caribbean, while traffickers used the section of the Colombia-Venezuela border near the oil-rich gulf to import automatic and semiautomatic weapons.[124] The discovery of natural gas in Guajira's waters, which required further exploration to assess its magnitude, along with coal deposits in El Cerrejón, called for a greater state presence in the peninsula.[125]

The expedient way to achieve closer cooperation was to break with multilateralism in favor of bilateral programs of assistance to "single out [our friends in the region] for favored treatment."[126] The new discourse about drugs and criminality that the Liberal party espoused in reaction to the Bourne Memorandum prepared the ground for such bilateral cooperation. "The contaminating wave of social decomposition and immorality that knocks on the doors of the majority of countries," new president Julio Cesar Turbay Ayala (1978–82) announced in his inaugural speech, "forced all nations to take care of the important problem of restoring ethical values, and security in cities and countryside, as my government will do."[127] In part because of personal conviction, and in part out of political necessity, national security became Turbay's mantra. During his first month in office, the president issued three decrees, known collectively as the Security Statute, that laid the groundwork for his regime. The first and third decrees targeted rural and urban insurgents; the second one, drug producers and traffickers, providing the legal foundation for implementing the plan that Carter had prepared a year before—the one Matallana refused to spearhead.[128] "Lately, organized crime has intensified in some regions of the national territory due to the wrongful use of airports, airplanes, maritime and river ships, terrestrial transportation vehicles of national and international origins," the decree stated, all of "which [has] generated other conduct such as bribery . . . and deterioration of the fundamental mission of the state, which constitutes one more factor disrupting public order."[129]

The Two Peninsulas campaign, as the initiative came to be known in governmental and diplomatic circles, was thus the result of a long-term, complex unfolding of forces in both countries under the umbrella of the "war on drugs." Launched on November 1, 1978, the campaign targeted both the Guajira and the Florida peninsulas, the starting and ending points of the drug circuit between Colombia and the United States. Although "the proximity of South Florida to South America, coupled with thousands of miles of shoreline and marshlands, created the ideal situation for establishing a base for large-scale cocaine and marihuana importation," most of the campaign's emphasis was "at the source," in the Guajira and neighboring Sierra Nevada.[130] With an initial budget including $31 million from Washington and $10 million from Bogotá, the Two Peninsulas deployed 6,500 soldiers in the region and more than 100 undercover personnel, including DEA agents.[131] In late November, Carter congratulated Turbay on "the firm measures being taken against narcotics trafficking in Colombia" and promised that Turbay could "count on me and my Administration for the cooperation and coordination that are essential if our mutual efforts are to succeed."[132] To gain Colombia's full alignment with the "war on drugs," he was willing to overlook the denunciations against Turbay for violation of human rights in enforcing the Security Statute. With the Two Peninsulas, Carter resolved the foreign policy predicament in favor of national security.

In Colombia, the armed forces were in charge of carrying out the Two Peninsulas campaign strategy, as if drug producers and traffickers were an invading army that warranted immediate military mobilization to defend the country's integrity and sovereignty. Administered by Battalion Number 2, headquartered in Barranquilla and supervised by the Ministry of Defense in Bogotá, the campaign ordered the air space to be closed and authorized the army to shoot down any airplanes detected. Troops were stationed along the Troncal del Caribe, the paved road that connected the peninsula with the rest of the littoral. The Colombian government also established checkpoints where police and customs agents monitored and controlled the movement of people and materials; deployed soldiers both to guard mule trails in the Sierra Nevada's three watersheds and to eradicate marijuana crops; transferred the administration of criminal justice to the executive branch and replaced civilian authorities with military personnel; and launched aerial fumigations of marijuana crops with paraquat, the same herbicide used in Mexico, where it sparked controversy for its toxic effects on food crops, sources of water, animals, and people.[133]

These measures were intended to make trafficking activities riskier and more expensive, though chaos and bloodshed were the immediate results. But given the impressive statistics of arrests and seizures, the two governments ignored its problematic social costs.[134] Not every member of the Colombian establishment remained silent, though. The military, in particular, became increasingly vocal about its involvement in law enforcement, "a kind of work that nobody in the Army wants to do" and that it believed distorted the armed forces' mission, threatened their legitimacy, and created opportunities for corruption.[135] The US State Department acknowledged that "opposition also exists within the Colombian military which is uncomfortable with its expanded role policing illegal drug activities."[136] Even General Matallana, now retired, declared his displeasure. Having studied the problem since leaving the DAS, he said, he found that the government now had only two alternatives. It could launch "an extraordinarily strong response to this traffic," as it had done. The downside, Matallana reasoned, was that "tomorrow lawsuits against the Nation for destruction of legal crops, irreparable damages to animals, lands, etc., would be successful." Alternatively, "the state takes control of the production, and the sale of these products to the countries that want them." This last recourse was "more courageous" in that "it targeted both the national and the international mafia and took the business away from them."[137] From a staunch proponent of antinarcotics operations, Matallana thus turned toward advocating state regulation of and intervention in the business itself.

FIGURE 16. Ernesto Samper Pizano, director of the National Association of Financial Institutions, delivers a keynote speech at ANIF's conference on legalization of marijuana, March 16, 1979. *El Espectador* photographic archive, Bogotá.

Like Matallana, a group of young technocrats made legalization of marijuana a topic of political debate. On March 15 and 16, 1979, the National Association of Financial Institutions (ANIF), Colombia's most respected think tank, held a conference in Bogotá attended by Colombian and US government officials, diplomats, scientists, and the press.[138] During his keynote speech, US ambassador Diego Asencio stated firmly that legalizing marijuana unilaterally would turn the country into "a pirate nation." He then praised President Turbay for "his bold stance," and assured the audience that "the Two Peninsulas campaign has been a success and will continue to be one; there is no need to get bitter because of the traffickers' excesses; it is possible to eradicate this problem from Colombia."[139] Finally, using the field-work conducted by engineer Rodrigo Echeverri's Inderena team, along with DEA satellite information, ANIF bombarded the public with statistics.[140] According to Hernando Ruiz, ANIF's lead researcher, the annual value of marijuana exports were equal to 83 percent of Colombia's coffee exports and constituted 39 percent of the country's total exports. The Caribbean coast produced 60 percent of the total, and traffickers exported 85 percent of Colombia's marijuana through the natural ports and desert plains of the Guajira.[141] Also at the ANIF conference was its chair, Ernesto Samper Pizano. A twenty-nine-year-old lawyer and economist from a reputed family, he would later become president (1994–98) amidst the greatest scandal in the country's history due to the cocaine cartels' financial patronage of a political campaign. At the 1979 conference, Samper Pizano delivered one of its most controversial addresses, arguing that the social and political costs of repressing marijuana "at the source" was producing costly economic side-effects that could be converted into gains if the state regulated production and commercialization. Samper Pizano asked governments to create a bilateral commission to study production in Colombia and consumption in the United States in order to provide recommendations on how to proceed with legalization in both countries simultaneously.[142]

The ANIF chair's proposal was unorthodox in many ways, but one feature stands out in particular. The exclusive focus on marijuana overlooked cocaine entirely, despite the fact that the latter was the drug coming from Colombia that most concerned the Carter administration. Hernando Ruiz explained to me in his office in Bogotá that ANIF disregarded cocaine because they considered marijuana to be "the vehicle for the gestation of macrosocial, macroeconomic, and macropolitical dynamics." In other words, "marijuana was very suitable to our [Colombia's] productive idiosyncrasy because we are not used to producing value added."[143] Building upon tradition, marijuana cultivators and merchants established linkages between Colombia and the United States that produced unprecedented profits. To ANIF's economists, this represented as dramatic a turning point in Colombia's history as the shift that had taken place in the late nineteenth and early twentieth centuries with coffee.[144] The marijuana export business was the philosophers' stone that ANIF's technocrats had been looking for: a product that took advantage of economic patterns of raw materials production without value added and that would overcome Colombia' s dependency on coffee exports and usher in a new phase of development—but only if the commodity were legal.

ANIF's report generated widespread controversy in both countries. Its boldness "caused an absolutely spectacular commotion," Ruiz remembered. Articles and op-eds on the subject proliferated—*Time* Magazine's "The Colombian Connection" was the most notable of them, published on the eve of the conference. "A parade of politicians from both parties" crowded ANIF's offices in Bogotá "to persuade us to give up the proposal," Ruiz recalled.[145] While the Liberal and Conservative parties rejected ANIF's idea, CEOs of the industrial and business guild associations, retired military officers, representatives from many branches of government, and newspaper and magazine editors all agreed that marijuana suppression would mean economic losses and bloodshed.[146] Even the president of the Senate, Héctor Echeverri Correa, an important figure in the Liberal party and brother of the president of the National Association of Industrialists, one of the country's most powerful lobbies, was intrigued by the idea. After the conference, he convened a congressional debate on the subject and gave interviews to several national newspapers.[147]

The greatest opposition to the proposal to legalize marijuana, however, came from two antagonistic sectors: Colombian marijuana traffickers and US diplomats and policymakers. Traffickers feared that once the business was legal and in the hands of the state, the country's oligarchic elite would seize it and close off all channels for popular access.[148] Meanwhile, US politicians warned that legalization would turn Colombia into a pariah. While it is hard to know for sure if the predictions of the former were accurate, it is evident that the warnings of the latter were on point. ANIF's proposal was inopportune and far too late: by early 1979, when the conference took place in Bogotá, Carter's marijuana decriminalization agenda was dead and about to be buried.

Congressman Lester Wolff took care of highlighting this fact when he arrived in Colombia a month later to review the Two Peninsulas campaign. His purpose was to answer questions that Colombians had about "the results obtained in the US portion of the Two Peninsulas campaign, and the prospects for additional funding."[149] At the time, Wolff was not only chair of the House Select Committee on Narcotics Abuse and Control, which had called for the campaign in south Florida, but also a member of the House Foreign Affairs Committee, which had approved a legislative amendment that would increase funding for Colombia.[150] After meeting with Turbay and top government officials, Wolff made sure to rule out the possibility of legalization. He visited the Guajira by helicopter and held a press conference in Bogotá in which he stated bluntly that "it would be a tragedy if Colombia legalized marijuana when the government of the United States is not willing to do it."[151] Finally, he announced that the House had approved an increase of $16 million in antinarcotics aid to the country, and he was hopeful that the Senate would do so too. With his visit and declarations, Wolff made clear that the idea of decriminalization that Carter had put on the table at the beginning of his administration was defeated.

A year later, the host of complications that plagued the Two Peninsulas campaign only intensified. In addition to military officers' initial reluctance to get involved in this low-intensity warfare, and antinarcotics officials' use of inflated statistics to obtain budgetary allocations, a judicial and humanitarian crisis arising from the growing number of US and Colombian traffickers sent to jail generated new tensions between the two governments. In 1975 the US Embassy in Bogotá created the Prisoners' Welfare Committee to respond to a number of congressional inquiries into the matter.[152] The embassy found that "with the Guajira interdiction campaign [the number of US prisoners] has begun to rise again."[153]

Seeking solutions to these problems, Turbay revamped Colombia's antinarcotics apparatus. Between 1979 and 1981, he signed the first Extradition Agreement and Mutual Assistance Treaty with Washington in order to address the problem of US traffickers arrested for narcotics-related crimes. He also created a new special unit, which would be under "military discipline but will not be part of the Armed Forces" and thus would address "high-rank military officers' reasoning concerning the need to separate the rank and file of the armed forces from these [antinarcotics] activities that go against their nature."[154] As he took these measures, he waged a war of statistics in the public sphere, since the size of US aid depended on quantifiable results.[155]

By early 1980, the other "internal enemy," namely, the guerrillas, burst onto the scene and forced the government to redirect its efforts toward more urgent matters. On February 27, 1980, sixteen members of M19 stormed into the Dominican Republic embassy in Bogotá during the official celebration of that Caribbean country's Independence Day, barricaded themselves inside the building, and took all guests hostage, including US ambassador Diego Asencio.[156] For the Turbay administration, the M19 operation was a major setback in that it showed the public that the Security Statute had not weakened the guerrillas and that the social cost and human rights violations

FIGURE 17. US pilots arrested on charges of marijuana trafficking walk shoeless to jail. *Time,* January 29, 1979. Center for Creative Photography, University of Arizona: David Kennerly Archive © CCP, Arizona Board of Regents.

resulting from it were pointless. For the White House, which was already dealing with another hostage situation in its embassy in Teheran, the captivity of Asencio and fifteen other ambassadors from all over the world demonstrated that antinarcotics interventions were not going to resolve the crisis in Colombia. For sixty-one days, all eyes were on the Dominican embassy. During that time, in March 1980, the Colombian armed forces announced that they were abandoning their US-assisted efforts to curb marijuana shipments from the Guajira.[157] More important challenges lay ahead for them. The news flew under the world's radar.

Although the Turbay administration revoked the state of siege immediately, the violence and social chaos the Two Peninsulas campaign had unleashed did not cease. Marijuana growing and trafficking declined and never peaked again. What did grow and expand were the policies and guidelines that the campaign helped to institute: the combination of crop eradication with traffic interdiction, the battle over data and statistics, the dynamic between interagency rivalry and cooperation, the extradition treaty, and the creation of special squads, all marked the beginning of a new phase in Colombian and US antinarcotics collaboration, providing the framework in which the subsequent war between the state and the cocaine cartels would take place in coming decades.

International relations scholar Bruce Bagley, a pioneer in the study of the "war on drugs" in Colombia, argues that "the Colombian experience with militarization in the Guajira" provides important insights into the functioning of the drug business. Bagley concludes that the campaign "put a serious dent in the marijuana trade in the region, even though it did not halt it altogether," because it only displaced cultivation and traffic to other areas, and once the military withdrew, traffickers quickly reestablished their activities.[158] I agree that the Two Peninsulas campaign revealed important lessons, but I disagree with Bagley's reasoning. The displacement of marijuana crops to other parts of the country did not create another regional boom, nor did traffickers in the Guajira and Sierra Nevada manage to reestablish activities once the campaign ended. The enduring lessons from the campaign exist at the level of interstate politics, policymaking, and diplomacy. As anthropologist Winifred Tate argues, the situations defined as problems and targeted by drug policy "are produced in part through the actions of the state to rein in, regulate, and control illegal economies and the reconfiguration of political power." In this sense, Tate explains, drug policies "are also central sites in which the future is deployed in the present, haunted not only by the past but also by the fears of possible things to come."[159]

Over the course of the 1970s, the Pastrana, López Michelsen, and Turbay administrations in Colombia, and the Nixon, Ford, and Carter administrations in the United States, worked together through agreements, alliances, and conflicts to define and tackle the problems posed by the drug trade, haunted by their own past failures and by future scenarios about the business's destabilizing potential. In the process, hardliners in both countries presented the most coherent interpretation of the challenge at hand—namely, that drug production and trafficking were major threats to national security that warranted nothing less than the full-scale mobilization of the political and repressive apparatus of the state.[160] This happened at a time when global Cold War politics swung back toward militarism and containment; therefore, these "nonspecific threats" offered expanded roles for military bureaucracies beyond the already-important task of counterinsurgency.[161] The Two Peninsulas campaign was the result of a long-term process of interstate reaccommodation to a new style of diplomacy and a novel type of foreign policy that allowed governments to use drug-related activities as justifications for delimiting geographies of illegality in which they could perform rituals of rule and state power during moments of crisis.

SIX

Reign of Terror

CRIMINALIZATION AND VIOLENCE

Terror reigns in Barranquilla . . . a city that used to be an oasis of peace and tranquility . . . is today a scared city, one that has lost its innocence.

JOSÉ CERVANTES ANGULO,
journalist

ON AUGUST 5, 1978, Lisímaco Peralta finalized the details of what promised to be his greatest marijuana export operation. News that elected president Julio Cesar Turbay was going to launch an antinarcotics campaign in the region had Peralta worried, so he rescheduled the transaction for a date before the presidential inauguration on August 7. But first he stopped at his family's house in Las Flores, in the Guajira's side of the Sierra Nevada de Santa Marta, where he learned that vallenato artist Diomedes Díaz was going to be at a *parranda* that night performing songs from his latest album, which included the radio hit "Lluvia de verano" (Summer Rain). The song was inspired by Peralta's trajectory from scarcity to abundance and included a shout-out using his full name. Having never heard it live, Peralta stayed despite the inconvenience. The first two times Díaz sang the song, the whole town joined Peralta in singing the chorus in tears. That is, everyone but Juanito Guerra, a young neighbor who whispered in Peralta's ear: "I'm going to kill you tonight." Peralta could not think of any motive behind such a threat, so he laughed and dismissed him. Past midnight, when Díaz intoned for the third time, "I sing, I laugh, I dream, I live happily," and Guerra said again, "I'm going to kill you tonight," a drunk Peralta did not laugh. "Do you think you are more of a man than anybody else?" he responded, grabbing the gun at his waist. Guerra, who was younger and faster, shot Peralta twice. A wounded Peralta shot back. One of Guerra's friends emptied his gun firing at Peralta's back before Peralta's *compadres* shot him down. The final account: four dead, four wounded, and a whole town terrified.[1]

Peralta's last *parranda* illustrates how envy trumped solidarity in this context of competition heightened by the criminalization of marijuana activities and the militarization of the Guajira and Sierra Nevada de Santa Marta under the Two Peninsulas campaign. Trapped in a paradox between the individualistic exigencies of the business and the social requirements of the smuggler's code of masculine honor, marijuana traffickers struggled with incompatible demands. They had to perform acts of virility and compete to overshadow others and preserve their tenuous business connections and their precarious position in the commercialization chain, while basing their operations on principles of honorable masculinity as members of extended families and communities. As they walked a high wire between camaraderie and ruthless competition, they strove to find an equilibrium between being generous and projecting credible danger. The state of emergency imposed over the region between 1978 and 1980 tipped the balance in favor of the latter.

This chapter addresses this shift, when the law of silence and the ethics of reciprocity that accounted for the peak of the boom disintegrated into gossip, violence, and greed, ushering in the decline of the marijuana boom. Here, I argue that the Two Peninsulas campaign marked a turning point at the levels of interstate governance and diplomacy, as well as on the ground. The campaign rendered meaningless the customary codes and norms for controlling smuggling activities, exacerbated tensions across the board, and made the intentional use of force an essential instrument for survival.[2]

For decades, scholars agreed that illicit drug markets were more prone to violence than markets in the legal economy. Without access to the protections of civil and criminal law, illicit merchants relied on coercion and brute force to prosecute grievances, punish those who made mistakes or were perceived as impediments, and deter those who might otherwise interfere. In the particular case of Colombia, this theory gained traction among economists and political scientists during the 1990s. Analyzing high rates of homicide and finding no correlation with political conflicts—the guerrillas, for example, were responsible for less than 1 percent of all violent deaths in 1993— scholars agreed that "violence and criminality are almost synonyms in the contemporary history, especially in the last years."[3] Recently, historian James D. Henderson made a strong case for this interpretation. He argues that after the establishment of the National Front in 1958, Colombia enjoyed a decade of peace and modernization that progressed at "break neck speed" until "the powerful external force of illegal drug money" that flooded the country during the marijuana boom planted the seeds for what later would become a "narcotics nightmare" under the cocaine cartels.[4] In Henderson's analysis, the drug business constitutes "the real source" of Colombia's violence and never-ending war.[5]

In the past decade, however, the connection between violence and drug trafficking has been revaluated as new perspectives that consider "the role of historical legacies in shaping contemporary patterns of violence in illicit markets" have gained relevance among social scientists.[6] In case after case, scholars proved that illegality was insufficient to explain high levels of violence. Rather, drug wars were often the result of a combination of three factors: internal conflicts within organizations (related to leadership succession and new management imposing discipline on the rank and file); conflicts between organizations (related to territorial or transactional struggles among competitors); and conflicts between traffickers and the state (as a result of intensified enforcement that produced turnovers in the highest ranks of traffickers, as well as the dismissal of corrupt officials, creating uncertainty and forcing traffickers to search for novel forms of protection).[7] This chapter shows how the last-described scenario was the case in the Guajira and Sierra Nevada, where criminalization and militarization triggered a bloody dynamic of survival after nearly a decade when the use of violence had been the exception.[8] Rather than awakening dormant violence intrinsic to the illicit business, the campaign eroded the moral economy that allowed marijuana exporters and intermediaries to prevent simmering conflicts from spinning into a violent spiral.

GEOGRAPHIC DISPERSAL AND THE CONQUEST OF THE CITY

Criminalization and militarization coincided with the coming of age of a cohort of young smugglers who had grown up during the peak of the boom and expected to exceed their predecessors' levels of wealth, power, and status. Historian Alan Knight points out, based on his examination of revolutionary Mexico, that the disproportionate involvement of young men in violence throughout human history "cannot simply be explained away by the logic of, say, state-building, warfare, and military conscription," but rather is an evolutionary disposition. Therefore, he concludes, "it is not surprising" that drug traffickers, among others, "drew disproportionately on young—and often unmarried—men." This biological argument, he warns, has explanatory power only when combined with social, economic, and political factors.⁹ In the case of Colombia's marijuana boom, what explains young men's proclivity to violence was a clash between their expectations of upward mobility and capital accumulation and the new, repressive circumstances forced upon them by the state. Schooled in the code of masculine honor that valued commercial shrewdness, physical and sexual assertiveness, territorial and economic mobility, and flamboyant social projection, seasoned and aspiring traffickers responded to new challenges by engaging in apparently senseless acts of violence.

Greater risks implied greater profits and greater tensions. All those involved in marijuana production and commercialization began to charge higher prices for their work once the Two Peninsulas campaign was set in motion. With more at stake, interactions and procedures became more belligerent, and competition more hostile. José Luis, a driver who transported marijuana to seaports and landing fields for twelve years, testified to this shift: "At the end was not like at the beginning, when you traveled to work and there were no problems; at the end you could be shot, you could get killed, trips were now and then, and at a higher risk."¹⁰ Silvio, a sailor who transported coffee and marijuana, described how antinarcotics operations made jealousy and envy deadly: "That was when the slaughter began, because I have my connection, and you have yours, but yours was more powerful than mine, and I did everything to take it away from you."¹¹ Raúl, a smuggler of coffee and general merchandise, analyzed the causes behind the bloodshed: "We [*guajiros*] have a great flaw—vanity, it kills us. And when they [*marimberos*] felt proud, they wanted to be noticed without reservation, and then any authority realized who was who, and who did what, and found out more."¹² The search for prestige and reputation, elements essential to *marimberos*' self-construction as a new agricultural merchant class, went against their capacity to survive under the new repressive conditions. Expressed through ostentation and flamboyance, *marimberos*' quest for respect and status made them easy targets for both the authorities and their enemies, and proved to be a deadly paradox inasmuch as those same values that took them to their peak now accelerated their decline.

Nonetheless, violence was not their first recourse. In the crosshairs of Bogotá and Washington's antinarcotics showpiece campaign, old and young cohorts of marijuana traffickers initially tried out different mechanisms of adaptation. In 1975, a year before the peak, the national government completed the Troncal del Caribe on its last segment between Santa Marta and

FIGURE 18. Colombian troops search civilians at a checkpoint on the Troncal del Caribe, the paved road along the coast. *Time,* January 29, 1979. Center for Creative Photography, University of Arizona: David Kennerly Archive © CCP, Arizona Board of Regents.

Riohacha, crossing the cliff of Los Muchachitos, thus allowing easier circulation of people and goods from the peninsula and the Pénjamo area of the Sierra Nevada to the rest of the littoral. That same year police departments reported to Bogotá headquarters a spike in crimes against life and property in Santa Marta, Valledupar, Barranquilla, and Cartagena under the label of the "Guajira influence," suggesting these crimes were by-products of the migration of marijuana traffickers from the peninsula. "There is a great quantity of crimes of other kinds that have their genesis in this traffic [of marijuana]," the police in Santa Marta asserted, citing killings, injuries, bribes, armed clashes, corruption, and weapons trafficking.[13] When the Two Peninsulas campaign was launched three years later, the Troncal del Caribe became the most expedient route for marijuana traffickers to widen their radius of operation, create room to maneuver, and decrease tension.

The emphasis on interdiction that targeted the peninsula more specifically was a push factor for this migration, whereas departmental and national governments' negligence to properly regulate urban planning was a pull factor. As in most other Latin American cities, urban growth in the former Greater Magdalena was a spontaneous process left to market forces, a historical trend that benefited marijuana intermediaries when they arrived with their money.[14] Wilfredo Deluque, former chair of Guajira's Society of Architects and Engineers, explained that "*marimberos* did not distance themselves from the city to build recreational houses in the countryside, as in Bogotá, Medellín, and Cali," where affluent people, including drug traffickers, invested in haciendas and country houses beyond the bursting urban world; instead, Deluque told me, "they concentrated in the city so much that they broke the mold."[15]

Guided by a mixture of ambition and necessity, *marimberos* intuited one of the fundamental principles of capitalist societies: urban space is produced through power struggles as an interlinkage of geography, environment, symbols, and routines, and is bought and sold in the market like any other commodity.[16] Classes or fractions of classes, philosopher Henri Lefebvre argues, "cannot constitute themselves, or recognize one another, as 'subjects' unless they generate (or produce) a space."[17] Marijuana traffickers had been using their profits to construct their own identity as "subjects" since the peak of the boom in the mid-1970s, but their efforts intensified with the launch of the antinarcotics campaign at the end of the decade. Historian Jorge Orlando Melo argues that beginning in 1975, drug traffickers' attempts to convert large quantities of dollars into pesos generated an unofficial and parallel dollar exchange rate, particularly after 1976 when the Bank of the Republic closed the so-called *ventanilla siniestra* (rear teller), where anybody could exchange dollars for pesos without declaring the dollars' origins. To compensate for the lack of outlets in which smugglers could launder money, Melo explained, drug traffickers artificially inflated the real estate market.[18] They were able to double property prices in Santa Marta, Barranquilla, and Cartagena, and in the process, they demarcated exclusive areas within these cities. In so doing, they engaged in a "production of space" that shook urban economies to the core and defined cities' landscapes for decades to come.

The local consequences of the *marimberos'* geographical dispersal and urbanization affected the national banking and financial systems. The Colombian Chamber of Construction (Camacol) denounced "intermediaries with unlimited economic resources of unclear origins" for creating a "parallel real estate market" in the country's major cities, which would "cause a social trauma of great proportions" when combined with a worsening economic recession and rising unemployment.[19] Ernesto Samper Pizano, director of the National Association of Financial Institutions, the think tank that was calling for the legalization of marijuana, explained that UPAC—a financial unit of exchange for controlling mortgage values and measuring capital investments in real estate—did not reflect the real market, but rather the influx of marijuana and cocaine money. Fixed-term deposits and other long-term financial products were not affected in the same way, Samper Pizano contended, because real estate was the main "port of entry" in which traffickers could invest their profits from illegal drugs in the legal economy. To the extent that traffickers needed "a type of investment that allowed them to retrieve their money from the market when they suspected a meltdown," owning real estate was not only an indisputable sign of upward mobility.[20] It was also the financially safest way to invest and launder money when conditions did not allow traffickers to continue with their usual commercial activities.

Although marijuana intermediaries and exporters migrated to different urban centers along the country's Caribbean coast, Barranquilla was the city that most attracted them. Their conquest of Barranquilla, a symbol of tropical modernity due to its early industrial development and mass culture, represented irrefutable proof of their socioeconomic mobility.[21] With their arrival en masse, an ever-increasing number of people engaged in ostentatious conspicuous consumption, which caused inflationary cycles that deepened inequality and raised the cost of living for all.[22] The big city's anonymity provided fertile soil for the most disruptive form of opulence, the "demonstration" or "bandwagon effect," reflecting a need to imitate trendsetters who have seemingly mastered the urban lifestyle of developed societies.[23] Silvio, who followed his boss to this city in the late 1970s, laments that "Barranquilla corrupted many." When I asked him to elaborate, Silvio replied, "I saw them [fellow *marimberos*] doing things that I don't [accept], like killing somebody just because they felt like it, because they had money, because they had fame, because they were drugged out, lots of cocaine; they were *marimberos* and all, but the thing was cocaine."[24] As lavish spending became commonplace among *marimberos,* they developed more outrageous and expensive ways to distinguish themselves from the rest, and in the process, they expressed their most obscure desires and resentments. Many marijuana traffickers felt compelled to flaunt their newfound but fleeting wealth in the playground of the city's effervescent nightlife.

Paradoxically, one of the "bandwagon" patterns of ostentation that they developed in Barranquilla involved cocaine, which also contributed to violent dynamics. Local authorities agreed that the spike in crime in Caribbean cities was directly associated with marijuana trafficking, but many of the men responsible for these crimes were not under its influence. Sociologist Sonia Sánchez, who analyzed police statistics from the coast's main cities during the late 1970s, including Barranquilla, concluded that "a drug that is in fact increasing the amount of bloody crimes, that is to say, crimes that are committed under the effect of the drug, is cocaine"—a substance "affordable only to people of economic means before the boom of marijuana commerce, and to the new socioeconomic group of exporters."[25] The product became increasingly available thanks to the growth of cocaine trafficking networks from the Andean interior and their advance onto the coast. Carlos, an intermediary from Las Flores who lived in Barranquilla in the late 1970s, confessed, "It seems untrue, but I did not like to negotiate with it [cocaine], but I fell for it, I became an addict."[26] I address the expansion of the cocaine business in the second half of this chapter, but here point out that cocaine's use and abuse among marijuana traffickers living in the big city was an effort to solve a crisis of masculinity among socially dislocated men who lacked the skills and social networks to enter the legal workforce.[27]

Cocaine consumption was also a new form of exhibitionism, much as it was in the United States among yuppies (young urban professionals), members of the growing financial, real estate, and entertainment class.[28] Facing slow job mobility caused by heightened competition in a declining illicit economy, marijuana traffickers rewarded their efforts to survive with consumer goods, cocaine included.[29] Where whiskey had been the main status marker and preferred recreational intoxicant during the boom's rise and peak—a luxurious commodity that had always been part of the inventory of smuggled goods that circulated from the Guajira to the rest of the country and Venezuela—cocaine was the expensive drug of choice for the individualistic, dog-eat-dog struggle that characterized life in the big city, especially when work conditions deteriorated after the state launched the Two Peninsulas campaign. Cocaine was also compatible with *marimberos'* code of masculine honor. The drug's effects on the mind and body allowed men who had precarious hold of their futures and worked under unsafe circumstances to perform virility, understood as physical strength and fearlessness in the face of danger.[30]

Removed from their communities of origin, many experiencing urban life for the first time, marijuana traffickers were uprooted in Barranquilla. As communications scholar Jesús Martín Barbero has theorized, "When one does not recognize oneself from that place, one feels insecure, and insecurity makes even the most pacifist people aggressive."[31] In need of a sense of belonging, in a city whose doors they kicked down by means of money and intimidation, they resorted to living among themselves through precarious grouping, which resulted in a form of tribalism.[32] Callo, a coffee smuggler who worked transporting marijuana and visited Barranquilla regularly as a professional cock fighter, noted that "when *guajiros* moved to Barranquilla they partied a lot there, then gossip came, and there was a lot of killing because of it, over gossip, and that was how *marimberos* came to an end." In a recriminating tone, Callo complained, "We finished ourselves off, we did not have a cool head to keep all that money, we wasted it on weapons, and that turned into a slaughter among *guajiros*."[33] Close relations among male peers defined not only personal identities but also each man's position in the commercialization chain. When the tribalism they re-created in the big city multiplied opportunities for business and interpersonal tensions, particularly in an environment of abundant alcohol and cocaine, unequivocal, blunt reactions seemed indispensable to settling disputes and setting precedents.[34] Much as in Mexico City between the Porfiriato and the Revolution, a period that historian Pablo Piccato has studied in depth, violence became the "legitimate way to solve disputes about honor" in an urban context of increasing gossip and gun proliferation.[35] Away from their networks of kinship and dispersed in small family units—those in the lowest echelons were generally living with other single men—these men had no protocol for mediation of disputes, and violence erupted.

The famous vendetta between the Cárdenas and the Valdeblánquez families illustrates how marijuana profits, migration to urban centers, a younger cohort's coming of age, and the antinarcotics campaign combined to contribute to both a restructuring of the code of masculine honor and a violent breakdown in old dynamics of conflict resolution. It all started on August 16,

1970, when José Antonio Cárdenas killed Hilario Valdeblánquez over a sexual affront to one of his female relatives. The fight initially unfolded like any other family war among *contrabandistas,* such as those addressed in chapter 2. But soon, marijuana money contributed to its metamorphosis into a new type of conflict. Novelist Laura Restrepo, who fictionalized the vendetta in *Leopardo al sol,* reimagines the conflict's origins as a war among the Wayuu people in the upper Guajira. In Restrepo's novel, one of the indigenous elders "revealed [to the murderer] the code of honor, the laws transmitted from generation to generation, the rules of war that must be respected." Named Barraganes and Monsalves, Restrepo's characters follow by heart the old man's sentence, and "abandon the land where they were born and raised, where their ancestors are buried" to migrate, one to the city, the other to the port. Restrepo's fictional old Wayuu man also predicts that "the fight will be man against man" and will happen only during "the zetas," meaning the ninth day after a new murder, or a month afterward, or on the anniversary of the original killing—in any case, at a time when the enemy will be waiting for the attack, so no one will be caught unprepared.[36]

Outside the pages of fiction, those involved in the confrontation soon lost sight of ancestral rules and customary codes. Impulsivity, improvisation, and escalation became the rules as marijuana profits gave them the illusion of being able to afford an endless conflict, so they abandoned the phases of negotiation and reparation, which are fundamental steps of the Wayuu justice system, and declared open war. Political scientists Nicolás Cárdenas and Simón Uribe argue that this was a *mestizo* conflict; in other words, the causes of the war were deeply rooted in the historical and cultural specificities of the Guajira's *mestizaje* with the Wayuu people, and not principally in the internal dynamics of the marijuana business.[37] While Cárdenas and Uribe make a crucial point about the importance of Wayuu ancestry, the evolution of the vendetta responded to the urgencies specific to the decline of the marijuana export economy.

Cárdenas and Valdeblánquez were natives of Dibulla, a coastal town located south of Riohacha that had operated as a meeting point between the Sierra Nevada and the peninsula since precolonial times. With the advent of the marijuana business, some of its inlets became important seaports for exportation.[38] At the moment of the conflict, the families were linked by blood and symbolic kinship ties. They were recognized in town as members of the "proletarian mob," that is, the intermediaries of "the oligarchic mob," or the exporters hailing from traditional elites of landlords, *contrabandistas,* and politicians.[39] Thanks to their business relationships with reputed families and powerful men who held sway over the state apparatus at municipal and departmental levels, Cárdenas and Valdeblánquez enjoyed impunity. Furthermore, marijuana profits allowed them to live in different places, which contributed to the rapid geographic dispersal of the conflict over a vast territory that included Riohacha, Santa Marta, Barranquilla, and Cartagena, in addition to a dozen other towns. The more distant the target from the initial conflict the better, since innocent blood would inflict more pain on the enemy. Women, minors, and old people, who were traditionally excluded from vendettas, were considered fair game. And as younger members of the extended kin became money earners thanks to their marijuana businesses, they displaced elders from all decision making and introduced cinematographic technologies of death such as car bombs and shootouts in broad daylight. Injury or death was not enough; violence had to be performed effectively to achieve a wide range of goals, from the "practical" purpose of eliminating the enemy to the "expressive" end of dramatizing revenge.[40] The accelerated pace of the marijuana boom days also contributed to the ancestral laws' loss of relevance. "We lived so fast [that we thought] nobody is going to remember anything, nobody is going to notice what is going on," a witness of this war explained; "all that was part of the code of honor could be violated, devastated, because it is going to be forgotten."[41] Implementation of the antinarcotics campaign in late 1978 accentuated the inapplicability of the code of honor by making negotiations or rendition even less likely than before. Civil, police, and military authorities were more concerned about producing visible results in the fight against marijuana, or making money through corruption, than they were about enforcing the law or administrating justice, which diminished any possibility for mediation or state intervention.

Although the war between Cárdenas and Valdeblánquez was unique, in that it took place in a confined social space limited to the boundaries of the two extended families, it sheds light on a reality that triumphalist official declarations masked. During the antinarcotics campaign, death loomed large over the region. In just the first six months, which accounted for the first phase of the campaign, settlers killed four indigenous Arhuaco people in the highlands of the Sierra Nevada to gain access to their lands for marijuana cultivation; a total of twenty people were killed in less than forty-eight hours solely in the Guajira in different episodes related to illicit businesses; aka Maracas, a well-known marijuana trafficker from Riohacha, was shot to death in the living room of his best friend's house in Santa Marta; soldiers and traffickers killed each other in a shooting at a seaport in the upper Guajira; combined army and navy forces killed five traffickers while trying to conduct an arrest; a navy officer was shot in the head after boarding a suspicious ship to investigate; a judge, a municipal comptroller, a director of tax revenue, and a director of customs were killed by *sicarios* (contract killers) on the streets of Barranquilla in the middle of rush hour; a wedding turned deadly with six people assassinated, all of them recognized traffickers, in what used to be a quiet neighborhood in Santa Marta; an undetermined number of US pilots fell from the sky in planes engulfed in fire after Wayuu men pretended to help them land but instead shot down their planes to rob them; and at least half a dozen other US pilots died when their airplanes crashed while looking for poorly demarcated landing fields.[42] Incinerated bodies, bullet-punctured bodies, dismembered bodies, stabbed bodies, all kinds of dead bodies awaited their murderers to dispose of them or waited for authorities to identify, classify, and exhibit them as trophies of war. In this context, the casualties of the Cárdenas and Valdeblánquez vendetta were mere statistics lost in a wilderness of social anomie and state complicity.[43]

To state agents and functionaries responsible for implementing the Two Peninsulas campaign on the ground, governance and administration of justice were their last concerns. The mobilization of the military apparatus under the legal mechanism of a state of emergency was a governance practice developed during La Violencia that the National Front perpetuated in order to control territories and communities perceived as threats to public order.[44] Following this pattern, the Two Peninsulas campaign created "an emptiness of law" as it suspended civil rights, replaced civil authorities with military officers, and facilitated the expansion of the executive at the expense of other branches of the government.[45] With this state-sanctioned lawlessness, violence became one of the few options by which to stay in business, which justified further state violence "while appearing to do so in defense of democracy and political stability."[46] Inefficiency and state corruption, combined with *marimberos'* treachery and aggressiveness, produced a "survival imperative": a symbiotic relationship between traffickers and law enforcers in which neither side eliminated the other because doing so would also destroy their own raison d'être.[47]

Corruption, understood as the use of a public post for private benefit, oiled the "survival imperative." Since the peak of the marijuana boom in the mid-1970s, corruption had been the most effective means of interaction between state agents and traffickers.[48] In the midst of criminalization and militarization, it was even more essential in preventing violent outcomes and securing the completion of export operations. And the more widespread corruption became, the more costly it was for individuals not to engage in it.[49] Carlos, the *marimbero* from Las Flores, assured me that he "never was in jail, never was arrested; I had the luck of talking to the law, and the law understood me."[50] He explained how the gears of corruption worked: "You know, the law [enforcers] always worked under recommendations; if you are the new antinarcotics boss here, two days before the old one leaves he tells you the special names." Then, Carlos added, "I had that with a lieutenant in Barranquilla—he recommended me to another lieutenant here in Riohacha... and I tested him, I put him to work from 2 P.M. to 5 A.M. guarding a road, and the guy delivered."[51] Most did not possess Carlos's charm. Some anonymously complained to the press that "[Turbay's] Security Statute had worked to increase the taxes that we always have paid to the authorities."[52] Considered a legitimate, if informal, tax, bribes and payoffs allowed traffickers to continue their activities in a context of repression without exercising all-out violence as their first recourse. Talking to state agents in the commercial language they used, in verbal, face-to-face transactions, marijuana traffickers tried to bend the power of the state to their own advantage. Informing on associates and rivals became another way to appease authorities or settle disputes in an environment of intensifying antagonism. Carlos affirmed that "a plague of snitches was unleashed with the arrival of the antinarcotics, and every time the law [enforcers] appeared, you had to pay them 500 thousand pesos, one million."[53]

Corruption also divided state agents and functionaries. Those involved in the dozen cases of high-level corruption in the Departments of Guajira and Magdalena that attracted press attention during the first six months of the campaign were on one side; those genuinely trying to impose order seemed to be on the other.[54] The governor of the Department of Guajira, Rafael Iguarán Mendoza, for example, complained about the lack of justice in the region at a press conference on April 21, 1979. "It is inexplicable to me," he said, "that there have been 187 homicides, not to mention minor crimes, and not even 10% of the criminals have been arrested."[55] Months earlier, during his first assessment of Turbay's "plan of emergency" for the Guajira, Iguarán Mendoza affirmed that the "big fish are still loose," meaning that most arrests had been of minor players, including US buyers who did not belong to any clientele network that offered them protection.[56] Between Iguarán Mendoza's first declaration in January and his second one in April, Colombia's father of psychiatry, Dr. José Francisco Socarrás, a native of Valledupar, published in

FIGURE 19. Wreck of a Douglas DC-3 on an improvised airstrip in the Guajira desert plains. *Time,* January 29, 1979. Center for Creative Photography, University of Arizona: David Kennerly Archive © CCP, Arizona Board of Regents.

his weekly op-ed in *El Tiempo* an analysis of the problems of justice under Turbay's Security Statute. He concluded that "85% of Colombian justice is devoted to persecuting 'muggers' and street fighters, while the true criminals walk unconcerned waiting for their cases to expire."[57]

Located at the northernmost section of the national territory, the Guajira was like the tip of an iceberg of a political order characterized by state repression without justice, a reign of impunity that extended throughout the country and involved the state as an active participant. As historian Mary Roldán conceptualizes the problem, in societies where violence "may be due as much to the tacit complicity of the state or its agents in promoting it, as it is to the incapacity of the state to rein in it," widespread violence cannot be considered an indication of the state's weakness.[58] Sociologist Álvaro Camacho Guizado spells it out even more clearly: "The deterioration of the conditions of legitimate social domination in Colombia, seriously associated with the production and commercialization of drugs, has heightened the role of the military in taking over of the judicial power and [their] growing access to state functions."[59] In other words, the militarization of the state's response to marijuana trafficking not only set the tone of violence and corruption but also constituted a desperate and erratic effort on the part of the incumbent

Liberal party to confront and resolve the crisis of its own modernization project once it hit rock bottom in the mid-1970s.

And since reconstitution of state power is also about winning hearts and minds, the mass media were crucial in shaping public opinion about these repressive measures. The mainstream and yellow press covered the Two Peninsulas campaign with morbid fascination, shaping the collective understandings of the chaos that such violence unleashed and constructing a discourse of memory.[60] In "I am the Indian," composer Romualdo Brito voiced the sense of injustice and despair that many in the region felt over what seemed a concerted attack by the state and the press. Vallenato superstar Diomedes Díaz recorded and released it in 1979:

> So, what's the deal?
> What's happening with our people?
> The government doesn't give us anything
> and censors us for what we do,
> instead all it gives us is a bad reputation
> through its trickster newspapers[61]

If anthropologist Michael Taussig is correct in arguing that "terror thrives on the production of epistemic murk," the Colombian press was essential in stirring the muddy waters, "flattening contradiction and systematizing chaos."[62] One of the catchiest tropes the press used, in various iterations, to synthesize complex situations was "reign of terror." Journalist José Cervantes Angulo, the on-the-ground reporter who covered the marijuana boom most consistently, unpacked the term a couple of weeks before he received death threats for his work. "Terror reign in Barranquilla," read the headline of the article in which he explained that in a city that used to be "an oasis of peace and tranquility, on the margins of the political violence that the country's interior lived just four lustrums ago, the contraband and drug trafficking mafias settled in," and turned it into a "scared city, one that has lost its innocence."[63] By the time Cervantes Angulo received his first death threat, the *New York Times* was reporting that in Barranquilla, "the big operators [of the marijuana business] are well known, but there have been no arrests or other measures taken against them," because whoever dared to interfere "is exposed to gangland killing" at the hands of traffickers who "have brought the violent habits of the Guajira badlands into this previously peaceful city."[64] Months later, when the first phase of the Two Peninsulas campaign was about to conclude, *El Tiempo* validated this interpretation with an editorial simply entitled "Why Are Guajiros Violent?" Echoing Dr. José Francisco Socarrás's scientific explanations, the country's most influential daily newspaper explained that "Guajiro violence is born out of ancestral norms that rule over social relations and the environmental circumstances in which its inhabitants' lives evolved." Nelson Amaya, former governor of the Guajira, was also cited for the theory that "the genetic aggressiveness, the harsh environment of the desert, and a culture with a primitive overtone of leaving people to their own fate . . . created a racial group that is used to resolving its differences violently." *El Tiempo* concluded that this "seed of violence," original to the Wayuu people, sprouted with the marijuana boom because of its intrinsic struggles for power and against the state.[65] By representing the spike in the number of crimes against life and property as a cultural problem that originated with the peninsula's indigenous people, the Andean-centered Colombian and US media reproduced regional prejudices and spread them to the rest of the nation. These racialized explanations blurred the differences between Wayuu and non-Wayuu *guajiros,* and reified the idea that brute force was a natural tendency inherited by all of them as a result of the cultural contagion of timeless practices that had now expanded to the rest of the coast at the pace of marijuana traffickers' migration, thus threatening the nation.

In a country that experienced two of the bloodiest civil wars in Latin America in the twentieth century—the War of a Thousand Days and La Violencia—the trope "reign of terror" in its many versions was humorlessly ironic. Although the term built upon previous narratives of violence that had become common during the National Front, it also pioneered a novel set of discourses about the emergent sectors that the state targeted as public enemies.[66] Historian Robert Karl asserts that in the late 1950s and early 1960s, the *país nacional* (the country of the majority), the *país letrado* (the country of the intellectuals), and the *país político* (the country of the politicians) came together to explore the diversity of terror that the country had faced during its mid-century civil war and, in the process, produced "La Violencia" (the violence), in uppercase letters, as a historical period. These narratives thus became essential elements of the peace-building efforts that ensued during the National Front's first decade.[67] Much as in other parts of Latin America, the generation of intellectuals, politicians, and military officers that interpreted what had happened were influenced by environmentalist and culturalist theories about how the social and natural milieu interacted with genetic dispositions to shape violent tendencies in individuals and collectivities.[68] These terms of debate and this corpus of knowledge, Karl argues, were picked up by a new generation of scholars in the mid-1980s. Later known as *los vio-lentólogos* (the violentologists), they revisited La Violencia in order to make sense of the cocaine wars, guerrilla warfare, and paramilitary reaction that had taken over the country and, in the process, they articulated a new concept, "las violencias" (the violences), lowercase and plural, as a state endemic to the national character and its variegated forms of expression. In this way, "past and present blended together" and continuities and discontinuities became undistinguishable.[69]

A "reign of terror," as idea and practice, coalesced in an epistemological and sociopolitical limbo at the juncture of "La Violencia" and "las violencias." The trope encapsulated a set of narratives that presented marijuana traffickers' strategies of adaptation to criminalization and militarization as senseless, depoliticized acts that constituted the polar opposite of what had taken place in the country's Andean interior decades earlier. As a social practice, "reign of terror" signaled a unique moment in Colombia's history, that is, the first time that the state violently confronted an illicit class in the process of consolidation, a group that responded with all the might that its profits could buy and heralded the cocaine cartels' wars of the second half of the 1980s and the early 1990s. As an idea, "reign of terror" emerged in the realm of the press, not in academia, and thus preceded the violentologists and their scientific rigor, while it provided the mass media with an opportunity to turn itself "into a part of the basic fabric of urbanity" by making fear a fundamental component of modern processes of communication.[70] Much as La Violencia, as a concept, had effected a discursive maneuver decades prior, "reign of terror" made room for a discussion about death and destruction "without assigning responsibilities, and, of course, without having to explain it."[71] In other words, it obliterated the state's responsibility from the picture, and depoliticized violence, when, actually, this was the language in which politics was conducted, serving as a tool for reconfiguring territories, power, wealth, and identities.[72] Ultimately, marijuana traffickers responded to the antinarcotics campaign in ways that differed little from the way Liberals and Conservatives (coffee peasants, landlords, merchants, and politicians) attacked one another in the Andean interior at mid-century. This assertion is not meant to imply that the so-called "reign of terror" did not represent a unique moment. In fact, the coast experienced no sustained cycle of violence of a regional magnitude until the Two Peninsulas campaign. However, this was not the antipode of La Violencia. The brutal decline of the marijuana business was indeed a novelty inscribed in previous patterns of violence, a culmination of the integration of the Caribbean coast into the geography of fear that defined twentieth-century Colombia.

COMPETITION AND THE EXPANSION OF COCAINE

If violence in Colombia was the language of politics, a modality of conducting business, and an instrument of territorial and identity construction, there was no better proof that this was the case than the state of affairs in rural areas, where the "reign of terror" had its corollary and where the heirs of La Violencia continued to arrive in search of business opportunities and a livelihood. By the time the Turbay administration launched the Security Statute and traffickers sought to conquer the city, the cotton economy's crisis had deepened. Minister of Agriculture Germán Bula Hoyos officially declared an emergency during a visit to Riohacha and Valledupar to study "the grave economic depression" in those departments. After three consecutive failed harvests of this fiber staple, Bula Hoyos explained, "the attraction of the cultivation of marijuana is going to result in a massive displacement of people who want to work honestly but are led astray to illegal crops."[73] As usual, the government caught up with the problem a little too late. What Bula Hoyos identified as a potential outcome was already a reality. A week earlier, after a trip to the Sierra Nevada looking for "the sea of marijuana" authorities reported, journalist José Cervantes Angulo had affirmed that former cotton workers composed most of its labor force. He assured readers that the workers were following the lead of "their former cotton grower bosses [who had become] prosperous *marimberos*" during the sustained cotton sector crisis.[74]

But marijuana did not offer the only hope for cotton workers. The rapid growth of cocaine processing and trafficking in various parts of the Andean interior, which concentrated in the industrial cities of Medellín and Cali, apparently offered them much-needed opportunity. Although the coca plant had from time immemorial been cultivated by the indigenous peoples of the Sierra Nevada for traditional practices, these crops did not produce the quality or quantities needed as raw material for the refinement of cocaine, nor was there any entrepreneurial initiative to make the plants more productive. Some of the cocaine business's pioneers worked with coca leaf from the Colombian Amazonian region, but most of them used coca paste imported from Peru or Bolivia, which they processed in improvised laboratories near urban centers along the western and central cordilleras, in the departments of Antioquia, Caldas, Quindío, Risaralda, and Valle.[75] Although what they did was highly profitable, their social reach was limited.[76] That is, until 1976, when the marijuana economy reached its peak, and when a series of arrests, failed businesses, and killings produced a crisis within one of the most powerful cocaine cliques—the one organized under the leadership of Alfredo Gómez López, also known as El Padrino (the Godfather), a smuggler of general merchandise from Medellín who operated between the Urabá Gulf, in the southernmost section of the Caribbean coast, and the Panama Canal.[77] "After almost a decade's reign of that initial cartel," lawyer and economist Mario Arango explains, "the peace that surrounded the business" ended, and a younger cohort from a lower social stratum came of age with a bolder entrepreneurial vision.[78] Pablo Escobar would become the most notorious representative of this new generation.

Similar to their peers in the marijuana business, these younger cocaine traffickers aimed to surpass the achievements of their predecessors. The ambition was to take over the wholesale distribution in the United States, where the biggest profits were made. Displacing their Cuban and US associates, they caused a war in south Florida and fueled accelerated growth of the cocaine business within Colombia.[79] Cocaine entrepreneurs expanded their activities from the western side of the Andean interior—where they initially operated, and where the Colombian and US governments conducted surgical operations against their laboratories and other facilities—to the foothills of the eastern cordillera and Amazonian basin, where they distributed coca seeds for free among settlers to promote commercial crops and reduce their dependency on Peruvian and Bolivian paste.[80] Some of them ventured into the marijuana belt in the Sierra Nevada and the Guajira, where logistical conditions for exportation were unbeatable. Official reports on commercial coca and cocaine laboratories suggest that the promotion of crops for the processing of the alkaloid was not part of their initial efforts—the first fields and refineries emerged in the Sierra Nevada in the mid-1980s.[81] Apparently, the hope in the late 1970s was to take over the seaports for the more profitable exportation of cocaine, not to develop a coca belt in the mountain range.

The Two Peninsulas campaign represented an opening for cocaine traffickers, as the small group of marijuana exporters at the top of the pyramidal structure sought to survive the government's frontal attack by making alliances with cocaine entrepreneurs, who were more powerful financially and better connected socially and politically. In his best-selling book *Los jinetes de la cocaína*, journalist Fabio Castillo listed a dozen families from Riohacha,

Santa Marta, Barranquilla, and Valledupar who transitioned to cocaine in the late 1970s. Some of them were members of the Liberal and Conservative party elites, which had also pioneered the marijuana business in the late 1960s. Without revealing his sources, Castillo traced connections between them and the new generation of cocaine entrepreneurs who would later compose the Medellín and Cali cartels.[82] Regrettably, I could collect little information to corroborate or expand on Castillo's findings. Given the paramilitary takeover of the region during my years of fieldwork, I decided not to conduct research with those who had transitioned from marijuana to cocaine; I thereby avoided attracting the attention of the paramilitaries that controlled the alkaloid's processing in the Sierra Nevada and its exportation through the Guajira (see appendix).

What I managed to learn and verify is that the majority of those involved in the trafficking of marijuana—that is, the mass of intermediaries who worked for a few exporters at the top—felt alienated and puzzled by cocaine trafficking and found it hard to accommodate to the new business. Meco, a transporter of marijuana who also cultivated it, said, "Cocaine arrived after marijuana, it was known here, but to a lesser extent because it did not have the same demand; then came cocaine, and marijuana declined."[83] Silvio, who helped his boss to export cocaine for the first time around 1977, told me that he traveled with others to Pereira, the capital of the Department of Risaralda, in the coffee region, to pick up the product. "I have never been in the [country's] interior," he recalled; "at the hotel, I wondered how does this work? You don't see anybody, what is this?" Silvio was flustered by the codes of the cocaine business, which were based on greater compartmentalization and individualism than was common with the exportation of marijuana, which depended on face-to-face transactions and personal relationships among male peers. He followed instructions, drove the car that his boss's associates provided him to Barranquilla, unloaded the cocaine hidden in the vehicle, and participated in the export operation using a merchant vessel.[84]

The newcomers were known as *paisas* because most of them came from Antioquia and the *eje cafetero* (coffee belt), where people are known by this moniker. Sometimes the term differentiated them from participants in the previous wave of migration, in the 1950s and 1960s, who were called *cachacos* and came from Tolima and Santander, departments located on the other side of the Andean region, to the south and east, respectively. Other times, the terms *paisas* and *cachacos* were interchangeable, erasing differences of regional origins and moments of migration. Carlos, referring to what he called an "invasion of *paisas,*" traced the differences and the ethics they reflected. "The dirty *paisa* was the one who arrived with no money, to hustle in the mountains," Carlos explained; "he planted marijuana, recruited ten *paisas* and at the end, to avoid paying them, he cheated them or killed them. Then [you had] the civilized, the rich *paisa,* whom you could talk to and make business with."[85] Carlos assured me that "the wars due to dirty business began with the invasion of the *paisas* . . . around 1978, '79, '80; thousands of people died because they came in groups of five or six, and the shrewd ones killed the fools, and at the end only one or two remained and took the money that all of them had worked for."[86] Whether they were identified as *paisas* or *cachacos,* their capacity to exercise violence in a more individualistic way is what gave Andean men an edge over local cultivators and intermediaries.

Working in either marijuana or cocaine, and facing state repression and increased competition, migrants from the Andean interior, who did not belong to any community that obliged them to follow customary codes, established and enforced hierarchies and rules through violent means, first among themselves and then toward *guajiros.* In May 1979, for example, when the first phase of the Two Peninsulas was winding down, *El Tiempo* reported on a "pitched battle" between a group of *guajiros* and another of *paisas* for a *caleta* (stash place) that each side considered theirs. The fight occurred in several episodes, including the funeral of the first batch of victims, and produced fifteen killings in twenty-four hours.[87] According to journalist José Cervantes Angulo, this battle was one of many, as "the displacement of *guajiros* at the hands of *cachacos* has generated rivalry between the two races." He concluded that "in general terms, it has been established that *cachacos* are the ones who control the areas of cultivation and dominate the transactions," which relegated *guajiros* to minor activities such as guarding stash places, acting as guides over mule trails, and clearing forests and fields.[88]

Violently displaced, local marijuana cultivators and intermediaries avoided getting involved with the newcomers, especially those who worked with cocaine. Journalist Enrique Herrera Barros affirmed that "*guajiros* feared very much [the cocaine business] because of retaliation; every time a cocaine cargo got lost there was a trail of killings."[89] Physician and essayist Guillermo Velandia, personal doctor of a renowned marijuana trafficker and head of the Guajira's Department of Forensics during the years of the boom's decline and beyond, explained that "*guajiros* worked freely with marijuana but panicked about cocaine, and only a few families got involved in it when marijuana was over." Dr. Velandia assured me that "all the *marimberos*

I knew feared cocaine—they did not want to have anything to do with the mafias from [the Departments of] Antioquia and Valle."[90] Carlos swore that he "never earned a cent with cocaine; cocaine threatened your life." Despite the artisanal character of its processing, cocaine required a set of skills that marijuana intermediaries lacked, such as the confidence to supervise and commercialize a commodity that required a degree of industrialization, and to enforce unwritten rules not through face-to-face mechanisms of persuasion but through individualistic competition and compartmentalization.

Furthermore, this aversion to cocaine trafficking and the Andean men who controlled it came as a response to a fundamental incompatibility with masculine honor codes. In the *guajiro* view, ideal men were heads of extended families who enjoyed a reputation for keeping their word and providing for and defending their clan's members. Even though the heightened competition that resulted from criminalization and militarization weakened this code, this was still the ideal, the operating principle behind marijuana traffickers' language of violence and conflict management. Ideal men from *paisa* or *cachaco* perspective, on the other hand, were solitary individuals with the physical, psychological, and economic ability to defend their autonomy and possessions, with their lives if necessary.[91] Chucho, a *paisa* enforcer on a marijuana plantation, recalled that in the camp, "there was no friendship between *paisas* and *guajiros*; they did not like us; *paisas* were murderers, so they were apart. *Guajiros* are tough when they attack in groups of three or four, but when they saw a *paisa* with a dagger or a knife, they got scared."[92] Dr. Guillermo Velandia explained the rationale behind these oppositional codes: "Using a knife in the Guajira is degrading for the attacker; the knife is for goats, to cut meat, but not to kill another man, it is not masculine; that should be done with a revolver." As he put it, this was "very different, for example, from what happened in Antioquia, where machismo is rooted in the duel of honor with daggers and machetes, it was a duel of manliness, of chivalry."[93]

The different code of masculinity and the business ethos that *paisas* brought with them to the marijuana belt were cultural legacies of various moments of economic development on the western side of the Andean interior. From colonial times, gold mining allowed a miner-merchant class to emerge in Antioquia, a class whose power was anchored not on land tenure but on "capital fluidity" through finance and commerce, including contraband.[94] Following independence, gold production continued to be the focus of the regional economy, giving Greater Antioquia—all the departments that later formed the *eje cafetero*—an unparalleled economic power within the new republic. This boom was also an opportunity for merchants to forge a discourse about *la raza antioqueña* as a separate ethnic group within the country, one defined by whiteness, business acumen, and respectability.[95] Gold profits, historian Frank Safford argues, not only allowed *antioqueños* to finance the earliest efforts toward nation-building, which granted them great political sway, but also "taught people the virtue of working in businesses."[96] When coffee experienced a worldwide boom in the late nineteenth century, gold miners and merchants financed the colonization of the central and western cordilleras for the cultivation of the bean, a process of frontier expansion that established a dynamic of cutthroat competition for scarce resources. According to historian Charles Bergquist, this fierce contest for lands, natural resources, social connections, and political ties among peasant families and individuals laid the cornerstone of the small, independent coffee holding system that characterized twentieth-century Colombia's economy and society, as well as one of the preconditions for La Violencia.[97] The industrialization ushered in by coffee's economic gains during the first half of the twentieth century spurred rural migration from the agricultural frontiers to the city, a process that spread these social values and ethical principles from the rural to the urban world. Anchored in Medellín, the new industrial economy of light manufacturing—with textiles as the most important sector—produced a peculiar society within the national context. Historian Ann Farnsworth-Alvear has characterized it as having a fervent allegiance to *la moral,* a form of Catholic corporatism and paternalism that buttressed relations between the working, middle, and upper classes and prevented independent labor action.[98] Meanwhile, as the coffee frontiers to the south reached their limits, settlers shifted the direction of colonization toward distant western and eastern areas of the tropical lowlands that were historically perceived as racially and culturally inferior. Soon, historian Mary Roldán asserts, these territories became the most economically dynamic and valuable and, during La Violencia, also the bloodiest theaters of war, where departmental and national governments tried to forcibly impose partisan hegemony and *antioqueñidad.*[99]

When the global economic recession of the 1970s hit the manufacturing sector and the coffee economy simultaneously, the business ethos characterized by commercial shrewdness and ruthless competition came in handy. The economic policies enacted by the National Front to respond to the crisis sent Antioquia's regional economy into tailspin. High interest rates and unemployment favored a shift in investment from industry to finance, which favored the merchant class. Based on the vertical ties of patronage and obedience that characterized coffee colonization and Medellín's industrial development, smugglers of general merchandise—historically, an important faction of the merchant class—innovated with marijuana and cocaine to create alternatives for "thousands of people who did not have any, or very few, possibilities of finding a profitable economic activity in legal markets."[100] They sharpened their proverbial *antioqueño* business acumen to take over the Urabá Gulf, the Caribbean periphery of Antioquia. When the United Fruit Company moved out of the former Greater Magdalena in 1965 and established its new banana district in Urabá, these smugglers used merchant ships that transported the fruit to the United States for the exportation of small quantities of marijuana and cocaine. But when the marijuana belt emerged in the Sierra Nevada de Santa Marta, these earliest drug traffickers concentrated their efforts on cocaine, which was more manageable in terms of volume and offered greater returns.[101] Historian Forrest Hylton explains that because they "could tap into a pool of skilled and semiskilled labor in a city with industrial rhythm, and infrastructure," cocaine proved a better fit with local ways.[102] Like their counterparts in the marijuana business, they worked in secrecy for years until 1976, when the clique led by Alfredo Gómez López, also known as El Padrino, collapsed, prompting a generational takeover at the leadership level, and a national and international expansion of the whole cocaine business.

The invasion of *paisas,* in the words of Carlos from Las Flores, was a moment in the unfolding of the crisis for Antioquia's industrial and business development model. Illegal entrepreneurs, merchants, and workers from Antioquia and the broader coffee region ventured into different lowlands around the country, from the Amazonian basin to the Sierra Nevada and the Guajira, in search of horizons where they could start anew. The criminalization of marijuana cultivators and intermediaries, and the militarization of the mountain range and the peninsula, evolved in sync with the *paisas'* en masse arrival, bringing with them their gender codes, ideas about the superiority of *la raza antioqueña,* and business ethos. Together, all these factors contributed to the disarticulation of the customary codes that structured marijuana activities during its cycles of ascendance and peak. Trapped between violent competitors and state agents, marijuana traffickers became aggressive merchants and passive rent seekers. Investing in real estate, finding protection from corrupt officials and functionaries, venturing into cocaine trafficking alongside entrepreneurs from the Andean interior, and even participating in

FIGURE 20. Colombian military troops burn tons of confiscated marijuana, October 1978. *El Espectador* photographic archive, Bogotá.

electoral politics were some of the opportunities that those at the highest levels of the marijuana pyramid could seize. Cheating, bribing, stealing, killing, or quitting were the mechanisms left to the layer of intermediaries and cultivators, which comprised the majority of the workforce.

Just as the cultivation, intermediation, and exportation of marijuana became an expensive and deadly activity, crops steadily decreased in size. By 1981, harvests were running short. In addition to manual eradication, which began with the Two Peninsulas campaign back in 1978, the government reintroduced aerial fumigations with *paraquat.* "It was the terrible year for marijuana, bad harvests, bad shipments," Carlos recalled of 1981.[103] A few years later, US official statistics estimated that the Sierra Nevada still produced between 4,100 and 7,500 cubic meters of marijuana in 1984; a year later, the official number dropped to only 1,300–1,800.[104] Also in 1985, Colombian economists' estimates showed that the country supplied only 22 percent of the US marijuana market, down from 70 percent during the peak of the boom.[105] Although in 1986 police and military authorities still burned confiscated cargos in public rituals of state power where the press was in the front row, the marijuana export business was marginal.[106] In the region's cities, surviving *marimberos* formed *combos* (gangs) to profit from other types of criminality, such as kidnapping and carjacking. In rural areas, two contradictory forces fought to impose their power in the intermontane valleys of the Sierra Nevada and Perijá. On one hand, representatives of guerrilla organizations such as the FARC and EPL organized peasants to wage armed struggle; on the other, cocaine traffickers financed them to plant commercial coca crops for the processing of cocaine.[107] By the following year, in 1987, cocaine trafficking dominated Colombia's illicit economy and the political debate, especially after Carlos Ledher, the cocaine kingpin who facilitated air transportation of cocaine from Colombia to the US East Coast through the Caribbean, became the first drug lord to be extradited to the United States, where he was sentenced to life in prison plus 135 years.[108] After his arrest, a simmering battle between the cocaine cartels and the Colombian and US governments reached its boiling point. In subsequent years, a breakdown between the Medellín and Cali syndicates would add another layer of conflict to the ongoing slaughter. By the end of the decade, the overlapping cocaine wars had dwarfed the marijuana export economy's "reign of terror" as much in media reports as in the country's memory.

One of the oldest debates in history centers on the role of violence in moments of change. From Karl Marx's characterization of violence as "the midwife" of every old society that is pregnant with a new one, to Hannah Arendt's postulation that "the greater the breakdown of sovereign power," the greater the scope for a rule of pure violence, brute force and bloodshed have been conceptualized as unavoidable concomitants of historical change.[109] And while violence has been deemed inexorable—almost an act of defense—terror has been theorized as assertive and incendiary, an instrument chosen to deal with circumstances perceived as endangering the survival of a fledgling change. In this sense, *reign of terror* was the accurate label with which to describe the marijuana traffickers' response to the Two Peninsulas campaign, since the aggregate result of their diverse strategies of accommodation and survival manifested as aggressive and provocative maneuvers. Terror was intended to navigate a general situation of change and indeterminacy, drawn from weakness and fright rather than strength and self-confidence, leaving a residue of latent fear that became an essential principle of everyday life.[110] But as historian Arno Meyer reminds us, any discussion of the escalation of violence and terror needs to examine the balance and interconnection between bottom-up and top-down initiatives and reactions.[111] The low-intensity war that the Colombian and US governments launched with the Two Peninsulas campaign was the trigger and the framework for this bloody interplay between state violence and traffickers' terror.

Although the war reached every corner of the region, its dynamics were displayed most starkly in urban centers and marijuana cultivation areas. The inauguration of the Troncal del Caribe's last stretch, between Santa Marta and Riohacha, in 1975 allowed a more fluid circulation of people and goods. The paved road gave marijuana intermediaries and exporters easier access to the apparently limitless possibilities that cities offered, so they took the last step in what was considered the supreme marker of upward mobility: urbanization. But the migration was a two-way phenomenon that included the arrival of a new wave of Andean migrants, the *paisas*, from various parts of the coffee region in search of business opportunities or jobs in either marijuana cultivation or cocaine trafficking. These migratory waves added to the arrival of contingents of state agents and military forces, many of whom found in the campaign an opportunity for promotion or private enrichment, resulting in a hectic movement of people and goods that heightened competition. Thus, the main achievement of the antinarcotics campaign was not curbing marijuana production and exportation per se, as policymakers had hoped, but weakening the "particular regulatory scale" on which the marijuana commodity was produced and circulated. That is, from a social regulatory authority defined by the participants in the business—and according to which marijuana activities and the commodity itself were legitimate, albeit illegal—to the political regulatory authority of the state and its web of controls and prohibitions—according to which this activity was not only illegal but criminal.[112]

By introducing state violence into the equation, the Colombian and US governments debilitated the customary codes that kept coercion and brute force in check. The spike in the number and severity of crimes against life and property, vendettas among traffickers, and extended corruption signaled the end of the law of silence and the ethics of reciprocity that were essential for the reproduction of the code of masculine honor on which the marijuana export economy had thrived. These juxtaposed and interlocking conflicts created a crust over the old and unresolved problems and struggles that had punctuated the history of agrarian development in the region. Criminalization and militarization not only helped bring about the demise of Colombia's first drug boom protagonists. More importantly, they induced and justified a sense of urgency in both the state and society that ultimately postponed addressing and resolving long-term disputes, and eclipsed political struggles and actors in pursuit of alternative futures.

Conclusions

A REMEMBERED HISTORY

ON THE PAVED ROAD that connects Valledupar and Riohacha, there is a traffic circle and a small park. In the middle of the circle, there is a giant accordion and a life-size statue of vallenato superstar Diomedes Díaz forged in bronze. Seated on a bench, Díaz sports a wide smile and open arms, inviting fans to hug him for selfies. Not far from this statue, a rusty Douglas DC-6, an airplane confiscated decades ago along with a cargo of marijuana, decorates a playground. With no stairs or ramps to facilitate access, the old aircraft lies on the dirt like the skeleton of a prehistoric creature with a coat of paint. The contrast between the two sites conveys the polarity of the collective memory about the region's recent history. While vallenato is honored with a monument, remnants of the marijuana boom are relegated to a corner, too large to be hidden, too unattractive to be explored. Without crosswalks or streetlights for pedestrians, walking from one place to another is risky. Writing this book has been like dodging traffic to bridge the enduring legacies of these two histories.

But instead of deconstructing the mechanisms of historical memory, my primary focus in this book has been to illuminate the available fragmentary evidence in order to decipher the causes of the marijuana boom's rise and fall, its protagonists' motivations, and the political, social, and cultural consequences of the boom that still reverberate with us today.

In these pages I propose that Colombia's first drug boom was a key moment in a long-term process of agrarian modernization and nation-state formation that encompassed deeper integration with US markets and a greater synchronicity with the US hegemonic project in the hemisphere. Since the early twentieth century, state interventions in the region had taken place in permanent dialogue with US public and private interests and with

FIGURE 21. A confiscated Douglas DC-6, once used for exporting marijuana, adorns a playground in a park in Valledupar, 2018. Photo by the author.

multilateral development institutions. These modernizing reforms galvanized a conflictive articulation of elite, middle-class, and popular sectors in pursuit of their own definitions of the terms, meanings, and beneficiaries of such reforms. This process exacerbated tension and friction among these groups, while a common language of contention emerged that allowed diverse actors with competing agendas to clarify intentions and goals, cement alliances, confront opposition, advance interests, and vie for economic, political, and technological resources.

Out of this gradual and mutual constitution of region and nation, new arenas of resistance and adaptation to the various changes emerged in the form of commercial initiatives and business ventures. Although upper classes and US buyers were crucial participants in the advent of a marijuana export economy, I argue that it was the irruption of the popular masses at the levels of production and commercialization that propelled the boom. Whereas in the beginning the cultivation of the plant was often a family endeavor that included wives and daughters, men were the principal participants, beneficiaries, and later, targets of the state's repression. The meteoric spread of crops, the need to satisfy mushrooming demand, the emergence of larger plantations, and ultimately the state's efforts to criminalize marijuana production and smuggling, all contributed to the masculinization of the whole export economy. Building upon century-old traditions of contraband smuggling and a shorter history of production of tropical commodities for export, those involved in trafficking marijuana made the commercialization and exportation of this agricultural good an exclusively male activity. Geographic and social mobility, skill at adapting to foreign influences and exigencies, loyalty as a friend or *compadre,* and devotion as a generous patron of vallenato music were cultural codes indispensable for achieving rank within the business. These practices also defined the unwritten procedural and ethical rules for establishing productive and commercial chains for marijuana trafficking.

The marijuana boom was thus a key moment of masculine reconstitution that unfolded in three cycles. During the first moment, the ascendance (approximately the mid-1960s to 1972), smugglers transformed deeply rooted traditions of contraband commerce and the production of tropical commodities for international markets into the basis for a new regional economy. During this stage, the marijuana business was geographically confined to the natural seaports near Riohacha and Santa Marta, and socially restricted to closed networks of *contrabandistas,* particularly those who exported coffee to the United States through Aruba and Curaçao without paying taxes. Coffee smuggling allowed the region's marginal social classes to participate in the national economy in alliance with powerful merchants from the Andean interior. These coffee smugglers established a circuitry of routes, procedures, and connections that they later repurposed for new commercial opportunities with marijuana. During these years, the trafficking was a modest, secretive practice that was part of the traditional contraband in agricultural products, and as such it produced neither significant trouble nor profits for those involved.

During the second moment, the peak (from approximately 1972 to 1978), local crops destined exclusively for export emerged in the intermontane valleys of the Sierra Nevada, turning the inchoate microtraffic into a full-fledged export sector. The accumulated contradictions of national modernizing reforms prepared the ground for this shift, but it was an international event—the "war on drugs" in Mexico, beginning in 1969—that triggered the shift. Facing a marijuana shortage, US consumers traveled the world looking for new sources of supply. Through ad hoc alliances with smugglers in the former Greater Magdalena, US buyers and their local partners assisted families of settlers in the Sierra Nevada in adopting and adapting marijuana as their main cash crop. Meanwhile, a new generation of rural and urban young men found employment and economic opportunities by working as intermediaries between farmers in the mountain range and smugglers in seaports and on improvised airplane landing fields. Whereas cultivation helped peasants to survive the hardships of settlement, commercialization allowed destitute young men to migrate from the countryside to the city and create space for themselves in the regional economy. These interlocking connections produced a peak in 1976, which convinced many that cultivating and commercializing marijuana offered a viable livelihood.

The third and final phase of the cycle, the decline, began in 1978 when producers and traffickers became targets of criminalization, and the territories where they conducted activities became the setting of militarization. As a global era of détente ended and a renewed militarism gradually took over world politics, a series of domestic crises within the United States and Colombia pushed governments to favor the most aggressive solution to the growing drug problem between the two countries. The new approach was based on a notion of illegality that excluded alternative forms of capital accumulation, as well as social and political recognition, and thus subjected producers and traffickers to the legitimate violence of the state. The crop eradication and trafficking interdiction campaign launched between November 1978 and March 1980 constituted the first chapter of the "war on drugs" in South America. It pushed farmers and traffickers to find more individualistic ways to maneuver and survive, rendering irrelevant the cultural codes they used to keep violence in check. Rumor, envy, fierce competition, and terror unraveled from within the circuits of production and commercialization, which contributed to the gradual decay of the whole marijuana export sector.

Throughout the course of these three moments, the marijuana boom linked fractured geographies, disconnected ecological niches, divergent histories, competing socioeconomic interests, and disparate cultures. Within this capacity to unite what used to be fragmented lay the roots of the marijuana boom's dynamism. From Riohacha and the Guajira peninsula, the marijuana export business refurbished old traditions of contraband smuggling based on interethnic and cosmopolitan connections. Because economic life in this section of the region had depended for centuries on the ebb and flow of international markets, boom-and-bust dynamics prevailed, making wealth ephemeral and spurring the construction of an ethos that praised innovation and adaptability as supreme attributes of competent men. The use of credit and the establishment of kinship ties to source labor were two operating values that marijuana intermediaries and exporters borrowed from traditional *contrabandistas*. In this way, they created patron-client bonds with farmers and among themselves in order to minimize risks and increase profits. Marijuana intermediaries and exporters advanced payments in kind or cash to achieve a degree of control over inputs and outputs so that they could complete multiple tasks during periods of insufficient liquid assets.

From Valledupar and the great valley the marijuana business adopted some of the socioeconomic dynamics and cultural practices that characterized cattle ranching, and later assisted the transition to a cotton agro-industry. Similar to the cattle economy, which worked through integrated chains of breeders, raisers, fatteners, and merchants, the marijuana boom worked through networks of growers, drivers, guards, intermediaries, exporters, and US buyers. Loyalty, respect for hierarchy, and one's word of honor became indispensable devices for mediating interdependency, while prestige, status, and reciprocity were three essential principles for accumulating economic capital from the bottom up. Thus, following the example of cattle ranchers–cum–cotton growers, marijuana intermediaries and exporters—popularly known as *marimberos*—also used vallenato music and its particular form of festivity, the *parranda,* as vehicles to project onto the regional public sphere an idealized image of themselves as men of stature and successful entrepreneurs. The vallenato *parranda* became an essential component of the marijuana cycle as it marked the end of an export operation and the beginning of another. It offered a space for the recognition of hierarchies, the discouragement of conflict, and the transmutation of newly acquired economic capital into social and cultural gains. The emotional, financial, and social investments that *marimberos* lavished on vallenato artists helped create a more danceable and commercial sound and expand the existing national market for this musical genre. Together, cotton growers, *marimberos,* and vallenato artists made this music the most autochthonous contribution of the region to the nation and a sonorous emblem of modern Colombia.

Similar to the banana industry in the western watershed of the Sierra Nevada and the Santa Marta bay area, the marijuana business relied on technological transfers and external financial sources, mostly from the United States, and it employed large contingents of agricultural workers who were foreign to the region and had experience in producing export commodities. Local pioneers, in association with US buyers, encouraged Colombia's destitute masses who originally tried to colonize these agricultural frontiers to grow marijuana crops exclusively for the United States. By providing financing and transferring technological knowledge, they made the Sierra Nevada the number-one supplier for the US counterculture, then the largest marijuana market in the world. The rapid spread of the new cash crop forced entrepreneurs to introduce another technological transfer, the use of air transportation. Veterans of US counterinsurgent wars in Southeast Asia who had the necessary training and skills found adventure and fortune smuggling marijuana from the Sierra Nevada to Florida and the Gulf Coast. The Colombian marijuana belt was therefore a horizon of possibilities for not only Colombian peasants, rural and urban proletarians, and middle and upper classes, but also for intrepid US war veterans, smugglers, and adventurers looking for ways to be a part of the US capitalist society on their own terms.

Although the cocaine export business prompted similar changes in the following two decades, marijuana was the commodity that originally updated Colombia's agrarian traditions to satisfy burgeoning demand from US drug markets. In other words, it was the cultivation, commercialization, and exportation of marijuana—not coca or cocaine—that initially articulated capitalist and noncapitalist modes of production and exchange, and temporarily provided the agricultural innovation, upward mobility, urbanization, and social recognition that modernizing state reforms promised but failed to deliver.

As in the beginning, US interests played a fundamental role in the end. Discussions about the United States' involvement in Colombia have primarily focused on economic and military penetration. These elements were certainly present in the history of the rise and fall of the marijuana boom; however, they were only part of the picture. Other types of interventions were also crucial components of US-Colombian relations. If US smugglers, travelers, and consumers participated actively in the marijuana boom's ascendance and peak—bringing in capital, expertise, ideas, and values to a society undergoing critical changes—US legislators, diplomats, antinarcotics agents, and journalists did their part to urge its decline. With tensions rising between the United States and the Soviet Union, civil wars and revolutions happening in Central America, negotiations over the interoceanic canal taking place in Panama, and decolonization and migration reconfiguring the insular Caribbean, the US federal government deemed the Colombian Caribbean coast an area of utmost geostrategic importance. The marijuana boom offered a unique opportunity for US and Colombian states to reassert cooperation between governments, inaugurate a laboratory for constructing of a new type of "internal enemy," and enlarge military bureaucracies by ushering in a combination of counterinsurgency and antinarcotics efforts. The consensus making behind the Two Peninsulas campaign represented a turning point in interstate relations, as it offered drugs control a major role in diplomacy and foreign policy, opened new areas of interaction and investment, and allowed the transnationalization of technologies and ideologies of war. The narcotization of US-Colombian relations from which the fight against marijuana in Colombia stemmed laid the foundation for an era in which the fight against drug trafficking became a powerful ideological axis around which the US established its role in the hemisphere in the late Cold War and beyond.

One of the most important corollaries of this low-intensity warfare between marijuana producers and traffickers on one side and the Colombian and US governments on the other materialized as a discursive battle to define the divide between what was legal and what was legitimate. Politicians, intellectuals, and the mass media created images and narratives to explain to the public the chaos and bloodshed in the region, and in so doing, this diverse bunch of experts traced the violence to the supposedly primitive men involved in the trafficking. The racialized interpretations were part and parcel of a national crisis of meaning about the authority and legitimacy of the state, a turning point that embodied a precarious effort on the part of a society in transition to something new and unknown to assign responsibility for, and determine the causes of, its current upheaval. Soon these attempts were interrupted by a deeper crisis, when the undercurrent of cocaine trafficking gained momentum and came to the surface in the form of a protracted war between the state and the leaders of the organizations that monopolized the alkaloid's exportation to and wholesale distribution in the United States. After this war hijacked national life, cocaine dominated public and academic debates about the country's politics, economy, and society. Meanwhile the prior marijuana boom vanished from national memory.

Only recently has the marijuana boom gained some attention. The context is yet another opening in the public sphere occasioned by the peace talks between the Revolutionary Armed Forces of Colombia (FARC) and the government of President Juan Manuel Santos (2010–18), which culminated in the demobilization of the oldest guerrilla organization in the Americas, and impelled Colombians to explore the nation's past. Although academics continued to focus on the cocaine business, journalists and artists who seem enchanted by the ostensible "magical realism" of the *bonanza marimbera* have resuscitated the subject. This book is my analytical contribution to these renewed endeavors. My intention is not only to interpret an old story with a new perspective but also to remove the aura of exoticism that has covered it. As the climax of a long-term process of regional and national formation, a process that involved integration with US markets and politics, Colombia's first drug boom was never a paradise—neither found nor fallen—much less the result of a barbarian invasion from outside the national polity. If anything, it was the bastard creature of the discontents of a series of reforms in pursuit of agrarian development, a creative response to modernization on its very own terms.

Appendix

COMMENT ON ORAL SOURCES

Conducting research about illicit activities is a dangerous endeavor because protagonists are prepared to pay cash or resort to violence in order to keep their affairs secret. Assuming this as the one and only truth, I approached the subject indirectly when I visited my grandmother Nina in San Juan del Cesar in early 2004 to explore the possibility of writing an MA thesis in anthropology on the culture and memory of the *bonanza marimbera,* a story that has fascinated me since I was child. Long conversations with relatives, neighbors, and family friends revealed that my assumption about the dangerousness of this history was only part of the picture. During the initial years of the boom, silence and secrecy were mandatory. But then rumor and gossip soon prevailed, and decades later, when the business was long past, those who had nothing to lose—no savings, no property, no political capital—were actually willing to talk. And that was the case with the vast majority of participants, which meant that the ins and outs of the boom were public (albeit unpublished) knowledge. Aunts, uncles, and cousins brainstormed about the names of people who they knew could share with me their insights and firsthand information.

With that general sense concerning themes, locations, and timeframes, I came back months later with my *compañero* and established headquarters in Riohacha, from which I traveled the region conducting fieldwork. When working in localities near San Juan del Cesar, my uncle Arique, who is famous for his encyclopedic knowledge of the Guajira's past and present, opened doors for me by introducing me to people. Occasionally, my aunts Marujita, Estela, and Juana did the same with people in town. When I was away from Nina's home, I was assisted by family friends, and friends of friends. In many cases, the interviewee sent me to a family member, a neighbor, a *compadre*. This research felt like jumping into a river of kinship and friendship and letting its currents take me to different places on my way to the ocean. After four months of fieldwork in early 2005, I left the country again and returned at least once every year, each time with a different perspective and a new inquiry. Although I conducted many more interviews over the course of a decade, I split my time between talking to people and canvasing libraries, archives, and bookstores in Colombia and the United States to explore questions that oral sources inspired but could not illuminate.

In interviews with those who directly participated in the boom—farmers, intermediaries, exporters, vallenato musicians, drivers, guards, sailors—I followed this protocol: After my host or hostess vouched for me and explained the purpose of my research, I introduced myself and the book project. I framed it as a history of the region in the 1970s, with special interest in the *bonanza marimbera,* and I promised to protect their identities by not revealing their names. (I used only first names or nicknames throughout the text when citing interviews with participants.) Once the person gave me his or her consent—and invariably offered me coffee—we sat in a quiet place along with my host or hostess. Whether or not they own air conditioners or fans, people prefer the fresh air, and thus most of my interviews took place on patios or porches or in backyards, which attracted the attention of other members of the household (including children and pets) or neighbors. After opening my notebook and turning on the recorder, I nearly always found myself in an improvised, public class on history in which I was not the only audience. Sporadically, a listener would chime in or interject, but it was astounding to see the solemnity with which people approached these memory exercises, as if giving their personal testimonies was a ritual they honored with a generosity of their time and spirit. None of the people I interviewed asked for anything in return, and only in one instance did someone request a pack of cigarettes and a pound of coffee in exchange for his time.

My protocol was quite different when I interviewed experts (i.e., intellectuals, journalists, and scholars). Those conversations generally took place one-on-one and indoors, be it in a living room, office, library, archive, bookstore, or café. These expert interviews were concise and unfolded in a more expedient manner. I did not offer, and was not asked to protect, the interlocutor's identity. But again, without exception, I was unfailingly offered coffee.

I conducted two types of interviews: thematic and life-history. I based my decision about which type of interview to conduct on a combination of factors, from interviewee's time availability, my own curiosity on what they had to say, and our rapport. With experts, I did only thematic interviews, though I included general personal questions in order to understand how they had become interested in the subject, when, and why. I did not use questionnaires, but instead built my own list of keywords as guidelines for pacing the conversation. When doing life history, I let the interviewee determine how much he or she wanted to share. Of course, I questioned their silences and signaled their blind spots, but I did not push boundaries. When these interviews failed to satisfy my curiosity, I looked for other, different sources, and in some cases I resorted to alternative methodologies such as mapmaking and seeing through photographs.

The time-intensive task of transcribing interviews took place later on and in batches. This intermission from interviews helped me get some distance from the fieldwork and the sources themselves so that I could construct panoramic views of the evidence collected and thereby identify leitmotivs. I preserved the vocabulary, pronunciation, and sequence of exposition of ideas verbatim, and the only interventions I made to the text was to underline or highlight recurring topics, which later helped me to decide which testimonies to include. I did not include all the interviews I conducted, only those that helped me to advance the narrative. The greatest challenge was translating from Spanish to English, because that required standardizing their voices, idiomatic expressions, and idiosyncrasies. All that is lost in translation is my sole responsibility.

Besides the limits of the interviewees' testimonies and memories, there were those that I imposed on myself in order to protect my safety and integrity. As a journalist I wrote for a magazine in Spain and a newspaper in Bolivia about the heated strife of political and social life in the region stemming from the advance of paramilitary armies onto the peninsula, into the Sierra Nevada, and everywhere in between. After a month or so of reporting on the campaign of terror, the displacement of populations, and the humanitarian crisis, I received veiled threats from the civilian wing of the paramilitaries, whose members let me know what line of questioning they did not like. After taking a time out, I returned to fieldwork but quit journalism and focused exclusively on history. Colleagues from Riohacha whose works I cite in these pages were the ones who helped me figure out how to deal with the risks inherent in my endeavor. During informal conversations that I recorded in my notebooks, a few of them shared their own experiences with publishing essays on the subject, and helped me to realize how being both an insider and an outsider—that is, half *guajira* and half *paisa* living abroad—counted in my favor. After assessing potential future risks to interviewees and myself that might arise under different political scenarios, I decided not to pursue interviews with those who still have something at stake—either money, status, or political power—especially the few former marijuana intermediaries and exporters who transitioned to cocaine trafficking, in order to avoid asking questions that could attract unwanted attention from those who controlled the current cocaine business. That is how I ended up focusing instead on the anonymous masses, examined their various roles in depth, and developed one of the central arguments of the book.

All of these contingencies and considerations shaped my decision not to make the interviews available to the general public. In doing so, I would have made it harder to get people to talk to me or record their voices, in addition to violating my promise to protect their identities. In this sense, the oral history in this book is more in tune with social history traditions than with archival history trends; that is, my priority was to shed light on the lived experience of those who had been ignored rather than to fill a perceived vacuum in the record and produce a public archive.[1]

These layers of limits and opportunities shaped the qualitative, semistructured, and interdisciplinary methodology behind this book. In finding tools appropriate to the immediate challenges before me, I combined methods from journalism, anthropology, and history, complementing and compensating the restrictions of one with the possibilities of another, and leaving behind old controversies about the validity of oral sources and embracing them for what they do offer. I learned to value the flickering nature of individual memory and the subjectivity of eyewitness accounts as vantage points from which to examine how history and memory have contended for social meaning, like windows onto the trials and tribulations of people's interpretations of a turbulent past.[2] This does not mean that I did not use the content of the interviews as information; rather, it means that doing so required more exhaustive cross-referencing and corroboration, as well as an honest calibration of my ambitions. More importantly, however, it demanded a different set of values to appreciate "the truth of the telling versus telling the truth."[3] This book is thus a testament to what oral history can do in the study of clandestine and illicit activities in contexts of social and political violence.

NOTES

ABBREVIATIONS

AGN	Archivo General de la Nación (National General Archive)
ANIF	Asociación Nacional de Instituciones Financieras (National Association of Financial Institutions)
ANUC	Asociación Nacional de Usuarios Campesinos (National Peasant Association)
DAS	Departamento Administrativo de Seguridad (Administrative Department of Security)
DEA	US Drug Enforcement Administration
Inderena	Instituto Nacional de Recursos Naturales (National Institute of Natural Resources)
Incora	Instituto Nacional de Reforma Agraria (National Institute of Agrarian Reform)
JCPL	Jimmy Carter Presidential Library
NARA	National Archives and Records Administration
RG	Record Group
SCNAC	US House of Representatives, Select Committee on Narcotics Abuse and Control
Unesco	United Nations Educational, Scientific and Cultural Organization

1. For a summary of these academic and political debates, see Asociación Nacional de Instituciones Financieras (ANIF), *Marihuana: Legalización o represión* (Bogotá: Biblioteca ANIF de Economía, 1979); and Asociación Nacional de Instituciones Financieras ANIF, *La legalización de la marihuana* (Bogotá: Serie Estudios ANIF, 1980). For a summary of mass-media discourses, see José Cervantes Angulo, *La noche de las luciérnagas* (Bogotá: Plaza y Janés, 1980).

2. Margarita Serje, "El mito de la ausencia del Estado: La incorporación económica de las 'zonas de frontera' en Colombia," *Cahiers des Ameriques Latines* 71 (2012): 95–117.

3. Paul Gootenberg and Isaac Campos, "Toward a New Drug History of Latin America: A Research Frontier at the Center of Debates," *Hispanic American Historical Review* 91, no. 1 (February 2015): 16.

4. Alfredo Iriarte, "Prefacio," in Eduardo Zalamea Borda, *Cuatro años a bordo de mi mismo: Diario de los cinco sentidos* (1934; reprint, Medellín: Editorial Bedout, 1982), 5.

5. Zalamea Borda, *Cuatro años a bordo de mi mismo,* 18, 22 (translation by the author).

6. Jaime Alejandro Rodríguez Ruíz, "Deconstrucción de códigos modernos: *Cuatro años a bordo de mí mismo,*" *Universitas Humanistica* 53, no. 53 (2002): 49–61. See also J. Eduardo Jaramillo Zuluaga, "4 años a bordo de mí mismo: Una poética de los sentidos," in *El mausoleo iluminado: Antología del ensayo en Colombia,* ed. Óscar Torres Duque (Bogotá: Presidencia de la República, 1997).

7. For some pioneering works, see Roberto Pineda Giraldo, "Indigenismo: Informe preliminar sobre aspectos sociales y económicos de la Guajira: Expedición 1947," *Boletín de Arqueología* 2, nos. 5–6 (1947): 529–72; Virginia Gutiérrez de Pineda, "Organización social en la Guajira," *Revista del Instituto Etnológico Nacional* 3, no. 2 (1948): 1–255; Milciades Chaves, "La Guajira: Una región y una cultura de Colombia," *Revista Colombiana de Antropología* 1 (1953): 123–95. See also Henry Candelier, *Riohacha y los indios guajiros* (1892; reprint, Riohacha, Colombia: Gobernación de la Guajira, 1994); Gustaf Bolinder, *Indians on Horseback* (London: Dennis Dobson, 1957); and Ernesto Guhl et al., *Indios y blancos en la Guajira: Estudio socioeconómico* (Bogotá: Tercer Mundo Editores, 1963).

8. "Memorandum from Minister of Education," Bogotá, June 16, 1960; "Official Communication from the Government of Colombia to the Unesco's Conference on Arid Zones," Paris, May 11–18, 1960, both in Archivo General de la Nación (AGN), Ministerio del Interior (Min. Int.), Secretaría General, box 11, folder 4, folios 25–26, 71–72. For reports on the Unesco representatives' visit to the Guajira in September 1960, see "Telegrams" and "Report from Eduardo Zalamea Borda," Paris, May 23, 1960, both in AGN, Min. Int., Sec. General, box 11, folder 4, folios 78–80, 28–30. See also "Decree of 1960 for the creation of the Corporación de Desarrollo Integral de la Guajira," AGN, Min. Int., Sec. General, box 11, folder 4, folios 73–77.

9. Germán Russi Laverde, "Notas para una investigación etnológica sobre una situación de cambio económico y social en la comunidad indígena de la Guajira" (honors thesis, anthropology, Universidad Nacional de Colombia-Medellín, 1972).

10. Elisée Reclus, *Viaje a la Sierra Nevada de Santa Marta* (Bogotá: Biblioteca Popular de Cultura Colombiana, 1947), 51, 67. See also Nicolás Ortega Cantero, "El viaje iberoamericano de Elisée Reclus," *Ería: Revista de Geografía* 28 (1992): 125–34; and Álvaro Rodríguez Torres, "Eliseo Reclus: Geógrafo y anarquista," *Revista Credencial Historia* 35 (November 1992): 8–10.

11. For an example, see Luis Striffler, *El río Cesar: Relación de un viaje a la Sierra Nevada* (1876; reprint, London: British Library, 2001). On Jorge Isaacs, one of Colombia's most respected poets and intellectuals, and his 1884 report on the Sierra Nevada, see José Antonio Figueroa, "Excluidos y exiliados: Indígenas e intelectuales modernistas en la Sierra Nevada de Santa Marta," in *Modernidad, identidad y desarrollo: Construcción de sociedad y recreación cultural en contextos de modernización,* ed. María Luisa Sotomayor (Bogotá: Instituto Colombiano de Antropología e Historia, 1998). On Bishop Rafael Celedón, director of the Catholic mission charged with the Christianization of the peoples of the Guajira and the Sierra Nevada, and his 1886 books on the grammar of indigenous languages, see Carlos Alberto Uribe Tobón, "Pioneros de la antropología en Colombia: El padre Rafael Celedón," *Boletín Museo del Oro* 17 (1986): 3–31. See also A. F. R. Wollaston, "The Sierra Nevada of Santa Marta, Colombia," *Geographical Journal* 66, no. 2 (1925): 97–106.

12. On "savage frontiers," see Margarita Serje, *El revés de la nación: Territorios salvajes, fronteras y tierras de nadie* (2005; reprint, Bogotá: Ediciones Uniandes, 2011). See also José Antonio Figueroa, *Del nacionalismo al exilio interior: El contraste de la experiencia modernista en Cataluña y los Andes americanos* (Bogotá: Convenio Andrés Bello, 2000). On chorographic commissions in Colombia, see Nancy Appelbaum, *Mapping the Country of Regions: The Chorographic Commission of Nineteenth-Century Colombia* (Chapel Hill: University of North Carolina Press, 2016).

13. Christine Lauriére, "Padre fundador de la etnología francesa, americanista apasionado, verdadero colombianista: Paul Rivet, un antropólogo polifacético," in *Arqueología y etnología en Colombia: La creación de una tradición científica,* ed. Carl Henrik Langebaek and Clara Isabel Botero (Bogotá: Ediciones Uniandes–CESO, Museo del Oro, Banco de la República, 2009).

14. For their most influential and ambitious work, see Gerardo Reichel-Dolmatoff and Alicia Reichel-Dolmatoff, *The People of Aritama: The Cultural Personality of a Colombian Mestizo Village* (Oxford: Routledge, 1961).

15. On Gerardo Reichel-Dolmatoff, see Carlos Alberto Uribe Tobón, "De Gran Jaguar a padre simbólico: La biografía 'oficial' de Gerardo Reichel-Dolmatoff," *Antípoda* 27 (January–April 2017): 35–60. On Alicia Dussán, see Marcela Echeverri, "Antropólogas pioneras y nacionalismo liberal en Colombia, 1941–1949," *Revista Colombiana de Antropología* 43 (2007): 61–90.

16. Figueroa, "Excluidos y exiliados."

17. Here I take inspiration from Thomas Miller Klubock, *La Frontera: Forests and Ecological Conflict in Chile's Frontier Territory* (Durham, NC: Duke University

Press, 2014), 14. See also Darío Fajardo, "Fronteras, colonizaciones y construcción social del espacio," in *Fronteras y poblamiento. Estudios de historia y antropología de Colombia y Ecuador,* ed. Chantal Caillavet and Ximena Pachón (Bogotá: Instituto Francés de Estudios Andinos [IFEA], Instituto de Investigaciones Amazónicas, Sinchi, Ediciones Uniandes, 1996); and Clara Inés García ed., *Fronteras: Territorios y metáforas* (Medellín: Instituto de Estudios Regionales, 2003).

18. Fernando Coronil, *The Magical State: Nature, Money, and Modernity in Venezuela* (Chicago: University of Chicago Press, 1997), 14–15.

19. Fabio Zambrano Pantoja, "Historia del poblamiento del territorio de la región Caribe de Colombia," in *Poblamiento y ciudades del Caribe colombiano,* ed. Alberto Abello Vives and Silvana Giaimo Chávez (Bogotá: Observatorio del Caribe Colombiano, Editorial Gente Nueva, 2000), 21.

20. On the term "Caribbean without plantation," see Alberto Abello Vives, ed., *Un Caribe sin plantación* (San Andrés: Universidad de Colombia y Observatorio del Caribe, 2006). On contraband, see Lance Grahn, *The Political Economy of Smuggling: Regional Informal Economies in Early Bourbon New Granada* (Boulder, CO: Westview Press, 1997); and Rodolfo Segovia, "El contrabando en el Nuevo Reino de Granada, 1700–1739," *Boletín Cultural y Bibliográfico* 39, no. 61 (2002): 34–55. On cattle ranching and haciendas, see Hermes Tovar Pinzón, *Grandes empresas agrícolas y ganaderas: Su desarrollo en el siglo XVII* (Bogota: Ediciones Ciec, 1980); and Eduardo Posada Carbó, *The Colombian Caribbean: A Regional History, 1870–1950* (New York: Oxford University Press, 1996), 105–10. For discussions of the Gobernación de Santa Marta more generally, see Marta Herrera Ángel, *Ordenar para controlar: Ordenamiento especial y control político en las llanuras del Caribe y en los Andes centrales neogranadinos, siglo XVIII* (Bogotá: Instituto Colombiano de Antropología e Historia, 2000); Aline Helg, *Liberty and Equality in Caribbean Colombia, 1770–1835* (Chapel Hill: University of North Carolina Press, 2004); Steinar A. Saether, "Independence and the Redefinition of Indianness around Santa Marta, Colombia, 1750–1850," *Journal of Latin American Studies* 37, no. 1 (February 2005): 55–80; and Juan Manuel Martínez Fonseca, "Santa Marta en la Independencia: Entre el pragmatismo y la insurrección," *Folios* 32 (2010): 61–72. For the Guajira in particular, see Eduardo Barrera Monroy, *Mestizaje, comercio y resistencia: La Guajira durante la segunda mitad del siglo XVIII* (Bogotá: Instituto Colombiano de Antropología e Historia, 2000); José Polo Acuña, *Indígenas, poderes y mediaciones en la Guajira en la transición de la colonia a la república* (Bogotá: Universidad de los Andes, 2012); and Forrest Hylton, "'The Sole Owners of the Land': Empire, War, and Authority in the Guajira Peninsula, 1761–1779," *Atlantic Studies* 13, no. 3 (2016): 315–44.

21. *Mestizaje* is perhaps one of the most controversial and debatable concepts in Latin American history. For a classic work, see Magnus Mörner, *Race Mixture in the History of Latin America* (Boston: Little Brown, 1967). For a more recent work, see Serge Gruzinski, *The Mestizo Mind: The Intellectual Dynamics of Colonization and Globalization* (New York: Routledge, 2002).

22. Nancy Appelbaum, *Muddy Waters: Race, Region, and Local History in Colombia, 1846–1948* (Durham, NC: Duke University Press, 2003), 11. See also Jaime

Jaramillo Uribe, "Nación y región en los orígenes del Estado nacional en Colombia," in *Ensayos de historia social, temas americanos y otros ensayos,* vol. 2 (Bogotá: Tercer Mundo Editores, Ediciones Uniandes, 1989); David Bushnell, *The Making of Modern Colombia: A Nation in Spite of Itself* (Berkeley: University of California Press, 1993); and Joanne Rappaport, *The Disappearing Mestizo: Configuring Difference in the Colonial New Kingdom of Granada* (Durham, NC: Duke University Press, 2014). On the coffee republic, see Charles Bergquist, *Coffee and Conflict in Colombia, 1886–1910* (Durham, NC: Duke University Press, 1986); Frank Safford and Marco Palacios, *Colombia: Fragmented Land, Divided Society* (Oxford: Oxford University Press, 2002); and Marco Palacios, *Between Legitimacy and Violence: A History of Colombia, 1875–2002* (Durham, NC: Duke University Press, 2006). On processes of regionalization in the nineteenth-century Caribbean coast, see Jorge Conde Calderón, "Identidades políticas y grupos de poder en el Caribe colombiano, 1828–1848," in *Historia, identidades, cultura popular y musica tradicional en el Caribe colombiano,* ed. Hugues R. Sánchez and Leovedis Martínez (Valledupar, Colombia: Ediciones Unicesar, 2004); and Eduardo Posada Carbó, "Progreso y estancamiento, 1850–1950," in *Historia económica y social del Caribe colombiano,* ed. Nicolás del Castillo Mathieu et al. (Barranquilla, Colombia: Ediciones Uninorte and ECOE Ediciones, 1994).

23. Serje, *El revés de la nación.*

24. Peter Wade, *Blackness and Race Mixture: The Dynamics of Racial Identity in Colombia* (Baltimore: Johns Hopkins University Press, 1993); and Palacios, *Between Legitimacy and Violence,* 174.

25. Safford and Palacios, *Colombia,* 17.

26. On US interests in Colombia, see Stephen Randall, *Colombia and the United States: Hegemony and Interdependence* (Athens: University of Georgia Press, 1992).

27. Gilbert Joseph, "Close Encounters: Toward a New Cultural History of US–Latin American Relations," in *Close Encounters of Empire: Writing the Cultural History of US–Latin American Relations,* ed. Gilbert Joseph, Catherine C. LeGrand, and Ricardo D. Salvatore (Durham, NC: Duke University Press, 1998), 15–16.

28. For a synthesis of the literature, see Álvaro Camacho Guizado and Andrés López Restrepo, "Perspectives on Narcotics Traffic in Colombia," *International Journal of Politics, Culture, and Society* 14, no. 4 (2000): 151–82. For some examples of this research, see Álvaro Camacho Guizado, *Drogas, corrupción y poder: Marihuana y cocaína en la sociedad colombiana* (Cali, Colombia: Universidad del Valle, CIDE, 1981); Mario Arango and Jorge Child, *Narcotráfico: Imperio de la cocaína* (Medellín: Editorial Diana, 1987); Álvaro Camacho Guizado, *Droga y sociedad en Colombia: El poder y el estigma* (Bogotá: CEREC, CIDSE, Universidad del Valle–Fondo Editorial, 1988); Hernando José Gómez, "La economía ilegal en Colombia: Tamaño, evolución, características e impacto económico," *Coyuntura Política* 18, no. 3 (1988): 93–113; Libardo Sarmiento and Carlos Moreno, "Narcotráfico y sector agropecuario en Colombia," *Economía Colombiana* 226–27 (1990): 29–37; Salomón Kalmanovitz, "La economía del narcotráfico en Colombia," *Economía Colombiana* 226–27 (1990): 18–28; Carlos G. Arrieta et al., eds., *Narcotráfico en Colombia: Dimensiones políticas, económicas, jurídicas e internacionales* (Bogotá: Tercer Mundo Editores, Ediciones

Uniandes, 1990); and Juan G. Tokatlian and Bruce Bagley, eds., *Economía y política del narcotráfico* (Bogotá: Ediciones Uniandes, 1990). For perspectives from below, see Jaime Jaramillo Uribe, Leonidas Mora, and Fernando Cubides, *Colonización, coca y guerrilla* (Bogotá: Universidad Nacional de Colombia, 1986); Alfredo Molano Bravo, *Selva adentro: Una historia oral de la colonización del Guaviare* (Bogotá: El Áncora Editores, 1987); Molano Bravo, *Aguas arriba: Entre la coca y el oro* (Bogotá: El Áncora Editores, 1990); Alonso Salazar, *No nacimos pa semilla* (Bogota: CINEP, 1990); Mario Arango, *El impacto del narcotráfico en Antioquia* (Medellín: J.M. Arango, 1988); and Víctor Gaviria, *El pelaíto que no duró nada* (Bogotá: Editorial Planeta, 1991).

29. For a pioneering work along this line of interpretation, see Francisco Thoumi, *Illegal Drugs, Economy, and Society in the Andes* (Washington, DC: Woodrow Wilson Center Press; Baltimore: Johns Hopkins University Press, 2003), 265–97. See also Eduardo Sáenz Rovner, "La prehistoria del narcotráfico en Colombia," *Innovar* 8 (1996): 65–92; and Mary Roldán, "Cocaine and the 'Miracle' of Modernity in Medellín," in *Cocaine: Global Histories,* ed. Paul Gootenberg (London: Routledge, 1999).

30. This is the main argument in Darío Betancourt and Martha Luz García, *Contrabandistas, marimberos y mafioso: Historia social de la mafia colombiana, 1965–1992* (Bogotá: Tercer Mundo Editores, 1994).

31. For some examples of this literature, see Alonso Salazar, *La cola del lagarto: Drogas y narcotráfico en la sociedad colombiana* (Medellín: Corporación Región, 1998); Francisco Thoumi, *Economía política y narcotráfico* (Bogotá: Tercer Mundo Editores, 1994); Salomón Kalmanovitz, Ricardo Vargas, and Camilo Borrero, eds., *Drogas, poder y región en Colombia* (Bogotá: CINEP, 1994); Francisco Thoumi et al., eds., *Drogas ilícitas en Colombia. Su impacto económico, político y social* (Bogotá: Editorial Ariel, 1997).

32. For an important exception, see Eduardo Sáenz Rovner, "La prehistoria de la marihuana en Colombia: Consumo y cultivos entre los años 30 y 60," *Cuadernos de Economía* 26, no. 47 (2007): 207–22.

33. Vladimir Daza Villar, *La Guajira: El tortuoso camino a la legalidad* (Bogotá: Naciones Unidas, 2003); Santiago González Plazas, *Pasado y presente del contrabando en la Guajira: Aproximaciones al fenómeno de ilegalidad en la región* (Bogotá: Centro de Estudios y Observatorio de Drogas y Delitos, Facultad de Economía, Universidad del Rosario, 2008).

34. Giangina Orsini Aarón, *Poligamia y contrabando: Nociones de legalidad y legitimidad en la frontera guajira, siglo XX* (Bogotá: Ediciones Uniandes, 2007); Anne Marie Losonczy, "De cimarrones a colonos y contrabandistas," in *Afrodescendientes en las Américas. Trayectorias sociales e identitarias,* ed. Claudia Mosquera, Mauricio Pardo, and Odile Hoffmann (Bogotá: Universidad Nacional de Colombia e Instituto Colombiano de Antropología e Historia, 2002), 235–36.

35. Karen Beatriz López Hernández, "Sociopatología de la vida cotidiana en tres tiempos," in *La Guajira, pluriétnica y multicultural* (Riohacha, Colombia: Fondo Mixto para la Promoción de la Cultura y las Artes de La Guajira, 2000); Yoleida Mercado, Seili Quintero, and Yenis Sierra, *Riohacha en tiempos de marimba* (honors thesis, ethno-education, Universidad de la Guajira, 2000); Martín López González,

"Cambios en los procesos académicos, políticos y culturales de la sociedad riohachera producto de la bonanza marimbera, 1975–1985" (master's thesis, social psychology, Universidad Naciona Abierta y a Distancia, 2008).

36. Ángel Acosta Medina, "El hombre guajiro: Descubrimiento y nacionalización," in *La Guajira, pluriétnica y multicultural* (Riohacha, Colombia: Fondo Mixto para la Promoción de la Cultura y las Artes de La Guajira, 2000); Fredy González Zubiría, *Cultura y sociedad criolla de La Guajira* (Riohacha, Colombia: Gobernación de La Guajira, Fondo Mixto para la Promoción de la Cultura y las Artes de La Guajira, 2005); and Guillermo José Daza Sierra, "Marihuana, sociedad y Estado en la Guajira" (honors thesis, sociology, Universidad Nacional de Colombia, 1988).

37. Peter Evans, Dietrich Rueschemeyer, and Theda Skocpol, eds., *Bringing the State Back In* (New York: Cambridge University Press, 1985).

38. Alan Knight, "The Weight of the State in Modern Mexico," in *Studies in the Formation of the Nation-State in Latin America,* ed. James Dunkerley (London: University of London Press, 2002), 213.

39. Forrest Hylton, *Evil Hour in Colombia* (London: Verso, 2006), 9. For discussion of Colombia in the Andean context, see Brooke Larson, *Trials of Nation Making: Liberalism, Race, and Ethnicity in the Andes, 1810–1910* (Cambridge: Cambridge University Press, 2004). For a synthesis, see John Coatsworth, "The Roots of Violence in Colombia," *ReVista: Harvard Report on the Americas* 2, no. 3 (spring 2003): 8–12.

40. On the notion of a "nation in spite of itself," see Bushnell, *The Making of Modern Colombia.* On the region as the "patria chica," see Fabio Zambrano Pantoja, *Colombia, país de regiones* (Bogotá: CINEP, 1998); Juan Guillermo Restrepo Arteaga, *El Caribe colombiano: Aproximación a la región y el regionalismo* (Barranquilla, Colombia: Universidad del Norte, 2000); Jaime Vidal Perdomo, *La región en la organización territorial del Estado* (Bogotá: Universidad del Rosario, 2001); Carmén Adriana Ferreira, *Región, historia y cultura* (Bucaramanga, Colombia: Universidad Industrial de Santander, 2003); and Gustavo Bell Lemus, ed., *La región y sus orígenes: Momentos de la historia económica y política del Caribe colombiano* (Bogotá: Maremagnum, 2007).

41. On "decentralized sites of struggles," see Florencia Mallon, *Peasant and Nation: The Making of Postcolonial Mexico and Peru* (Berkeley: University of California Press, 1995), 9. For discussion of hegemony in Latin America, see William Roseberry, *Anthropologies and Histories: Essays in Culture, History, and Political Economy* (New Brunswick, NJ: Rutgers University Press, 1994), 80–121. On "centralized institutions of sovereign authority," see William Taylor, "Between Global Process and Local Knowledge: An Inquiry into Early Latin America Social History, 1500–1900," in *Reliving the Past: The World of Social History,* ed. Olivier Zunz (Chapel Hill: University of North Carolina Press, 1985), 147. See also James Scott, "Foreword," in *Everyday Forms of State Formation: Revolution and the Negotiation of Rule in Modern Mexico,* ed. Gilbert Joseph and Daniel Nugent (Durham, NC: Duke University Press, 1994); and James Dunkerley, "Preface," in Dunkerley, *Studies in the Formation of the Nation-State in Latin America,* 2.

42. Itty Abraham and Willem van Schendel call for spatially and temporally rescaling the analysis of "international crime" in "Introduction: The Making of

Illicitness," in *Illicit Flows and Criminal Things: States, Borders, and the Other Side of Globalization,* ed. Willem van Schendel and Itty Abraham (Bloomington: Indiana University Press, 2005), 6.

43. Steve Stern, "The Decentered Center and the Expansionist Periphery: The Paradoxes of Foreign-Local Encounter," in Joseph, LeGrand, and Salvatore, *Close Encounters of Empire.*

44. For academic works on women's role in the drug trade, see Paul Gootenberg, *Andean Cocaine: The Making of a Global Drug* (Chapel Hill: University of North Carolina Press, 2008), 245–90; Elaine Carey, *Women Drug Traffickers: Mules, Bosses, and Organized Crime* (Albuquerque: University of New Mexico Press, 2014); and Jennifer Fleetwood, *Drug Mules: Women in the International Cocaine Trade* (London: Palgrave Macmillan, 2015). For nonfiction and fiction literature, see, for example, Arturo Pérez Reverte, *La Reina del Sur* (Madrid: Alfaguara, 2002); and Jorge Franco, *Rosario Tijeras* (Bogotá: Editorial Norma, 1999). For documentary and feature films, see, for example, *Maria Full of Grace* (Joshua Marston, dir.; 2004) and *Cocaine Cowboys* (Billy Corben, dir.; 2006).

45. On the war between paramilitary commanders, search on "Hernán Giraldo" and "Rodrigo Tovar Pupo, alias Jorge 40," in www.verdadabierta.com.

46. Fictive kinship, such as *compadrazgo,* binds people together through mutual rights and obligations in many parts of Latin America and the Caribbean. Anthropologists have traced this custom to colonial times, and have even found pre-Conquest analogues; see Daniel Balderstone, Mike Gonzalez, and Ana M. López, eds., *Encyclopedia of Contemporary Latin American and Caribbean Cultures* (New York: Routledge, 2000); and Harry Sanabria, *The Anthropology of Latin America and the Caribbean* (New York: Pearson Education, 2007). On Uncle Arique as a renowned storyteller and civic leader, see "Rafael Enrique Brito Molina, 'Arique,' un símbolo del civismo sanjuanero," *Diario del Norte* (March 14, 2017), 10–11.

47. The massacre of Bahía Portete took place on April 18, 2004. See Informe del Grupo de Memoria Histórica, *La masacre de Bahía Portete: Mujeres Wayuu en la mira* (Bogotá: Comisión Nacional de Reparación y Reconciliación, Taurus Editores, 2010).

48. Luis Alejandro Astorga, *Mitología del narcotraficante en México* (México, DF: Plaza y Valdés, 1995), 12–13.

49. Roseberry, *Anthropologies and Histories,* 147.

50. On the impact of hurricanes in colonial Guajira, see Weildler Guerra Curvelo, "Riohacha: Ciudad inconclusa," in Abello Vives and Giaimo Chávez, *Poblamiento y ciudades del Caribe colombiano.* On hurricanes in the Greater Caribbean, see Stuart B. Schwartz, *Sea of Storms: A History of Hurricanes in the Greater Caribbean, from Columbus to Katrina* (Princeton, NJ: Princeton University Press, 2015).

51. Here I take inspiration from Mike Davis, *Ecology of Fear: Los Angeles and the Imagination of Disaster* (New York: Vintage Books, 1999).

52. From 1953 to 1979 hurricanes had only female names; see "Tropical Cyclone Naming," World Meteorological Organization, available at, https://public.wmo.int/en/About-us/FAQs/faqs-tropical-cyclones/tropical-cyclone-naming.

53. Alex Halperin, "Marijuana: Is It Time to Stop Using a Word with Racist Roots?" *The Guardian,* January 29, 2018.

54. Nicolás del Castillo Mathieu, "El léxico negro-africano de San Basilio de Palenque," *Thesaurus* 39, nos. 1–3 (1984): 143. See also Andrés López Restrepo, "El control del cannabis: De las políticas nacionales al régimen global" (forthcoming).

55. Carolyn Merchant, *Reinventing Eden: The Fate of Nature in Western Culture* (London: Routledge, 2003).

56. For "tropical gaze," see Jefferson Dillman, *Colonizing Paradise: Landscape and Empire in the British West Indies* (Tuscaloosa: University of Alabama Press, 2015), 3.

57. For marijuana as the "forbidden plant," see Michael Pollan, *The Botany of Desire: A Plant's-Eye View of the World* (New York: Random House, 2001), 178.

58. For Liberalism and Conservatism in Colombia as doctrines of the Liberal and Conservative Parties, see Gerardo Molina, *Las ideas liberales en Colombia,* Vol. 2, *1915–1934* (Bogotá: Tercer Mundo Editores, 1974); and Javier Ocampo López, *Qué es el conservatismo colombiano* (Bogotá: Plaza y Janés, 1990).

CHAPTER I. WHEELS OF PROGRESS

1. Joaquín Viloria de la Hoz, *Café Caribe: La economía cafetera en la Sierra Nevada de Santa Marta,* Documentos de trabajo sobre economía regional (Cartagena de Indias: Centro de investigaciones económicas del Caribe colombiano, Banco de la República, 1997), 3, 6–7.

2. Judith White, *Historia de una ignominia: La United Fruit Co. en Colombia* (Bogotá: Editorial Presencia, 1978), 15.

3. Joaquín Viloria de la Hoz, "Historia empresarial del guineo: Empresas y empresarios bananeros en el departamento del Magdalena, 1870–1930," *Cuadernos de historia económica y empresarial* 23, 45.

4. Joaquín Viloria de la Hoz, *Sierra Nevada de Santa Marta: Economía de sus recursos naturales,* Documentos de trabajo sobre economía regional (Cartagena de Indias: Centro de Estudios Económicos Regionales, Banco de la República, 2005), 39–40.

5. José Benito Vives, *Pepe Vives cuenta su vida* (Santa Marta, Colombia: Editorial Mejoras, 1981), 57–67.

6. William Roseberry, "Introduction," in *Coffee, Society, and Power in Latin America,* ed. William Roseberry, Lowell Gudmundson, and Mario Samper Kutschbach (Baltimore: The Johns Hopkins University Press, 1995), 4–8.

7. Viloria de la Hoz, "Historia empresarial del guineo," 8–15; Marcelo Bucheli, *Bananas and Business: The United Fruit Company in Colombia, 1899–2000* (New York: New York University Press, 2005), 151.

8. Salomón Kalmanovitz and Enrique López Enciso, *La agricultura colombiana en el siglo XX* (Bogotá: Fondo de Cultura Económica y Banco de la República, 2006), 79; Michael F. Jiménez, "At the Banquet of Civilization: The Limits of Planter Hegemony in Early-Twentieth-Century Colombia," in Roseberry, Gudmundson and Kutschbach, eds., *Coffee, Society, and Power in Latin America.*

9. Viloria de la Hoz, "Historia empresarial del guineo," 20–22.

10. Viloria de la Hoz, *Café Caribe,* 21–26; White, *Historia de una ignominia,* 15; Viloria de la Hoz, "Historia empresarial del guineo," 45; Bucheli, *Bananas and Business,* 151.

11. Joaquín Viloria de la Hoz, *Empresarios del Caribe colombiano: Historia económica y empresarial del Magdalena Grande y del Bajo Magdalena, 1870–1930* (Bogotá: Colección de Economía Regional, Banco de la República, 2014), 102; Peter Chapman, *Bananas: How the United Fruit Company Shaped the World* (New York: Canongate, 2007), 43–58.

12. Bucheli, *Bananas and Business,* 89; Viloria de la Hoz, "Historia empresarial del guineo," 33.

13. White, *Historia de una ignominia,* 24; Bucheli, *Bananas and Business,* 47; Viloria de la Hoz, *Empresarios del Caribe colombiano,* 103.

14. Bergquist, *Coffee and Conflict in Colombia,* 223–24.

15. Acosta Medina, "El hombre guajiro," 72.

16. Bushnell, *The Making of Modern Colombia,* 156.

17. Salomón Kalmanovitz, *Economía y nación: Una breve historia de Colombia* (Bogotá: CINEP, Siglo Veintiuno Editores, 1988), 247–48; Bushnell, *The Making of Modern Colombia,* 156; Luis Javier Orjuela, "Tensión entre tradición y modernidad (1904–1945)," in *Historia de las ideas políticas en Colombia: De la independencia hasta nuestros días,* ed. José Fernando Ocampo (Bogotá: Instituto de Estudios Sociales PENSAR y Taurus, 2008), 188–89.

18. Bergquist, *Coffee and Conflict in Colombia,* 248.

19. Steven C. Topik and Allen Wells, "Introduction: Latin America's Response to International Markets during the Export Boom," *The Second Conquest of Latin America: Coffee, Henequen, and Oil during the Export Boom, 1850–1930,* ed. Steven C. Topik and Allen Wells (Austin: University of Texas Press, 1998), 15.

20. César Augusto Bermúdez Torres, "La doctrina *respice polum* ('Mirar hacia el norte') en la práctica de las relaciones internacionales de Colombia durante el siglo XX," *Memorias: Revista digital de historia y arqueología desde el Caribe colombiano* 12 (July 2010): 195.

21. Palacios, *Between Legitimacy and Violence,* 53.

22. Kalmanovitz and López Enciso, *La agricultura colombiana en el siglo XX,* 80–81.

23. Mariano Arango, *Café e industria, 1850–1930* (Bogotá: Carlos Valencia Editores, 1981), 197.

24. Bergquist, *Coffee and Conflict,* 247–62; Arango, *Café e industria,* 132–34; Palacios, *Between Legitimacy and Violence,* 51–52.

25. On *Yunai,* see Adriana Corso, "Santa Marta, la habilidad para sobrevivir," in *Poblamiento y ciudades del Caribe colombiano,* ed. Alberto Abello Vives and Silvana Giaimo Chávez (Bogotá: Observatorio del Caribe Colombiano, FONADE, Universidad del Altántico, 2000), 397.

26. Catherine LeGrand, "Living in Macondo: Economy and Culture in a United Fruit Company Enclave," in Joseph, LeGrand, and Salvatore, eds., *Close Encounters of Empire,* 339.

27. Viloria de la Hoz, "Historia empresarial del guineo," 23–26; Bucheli, *Bananas and Business,* 20–22; Viloria de la Hoz, *Empresarios del Caribe colombiano;* Chapman, *Bananas,* 43–58.

28. Vives, *Pepe Vives cuenta su vida,* 161–73.

29. Adolfo Meisel Roca, "Ciénaga: La economía después del banano," in *Economías locales en el Caribe colombiano: Siete estudios de caso,* ed. María M. Aguilera Díaz (Bogotá: Banco de la República, 2005), 189.

30. Vives, *Pepe Vives cuenta su vida,* 239.

31. LeGrand, "Living in Macondo," 342–47.

32. Palacios, *Between Legitimacy and Violence,* 87. See also Catherine LeGrand, *Frontier Expansion and Peasant Protest in Colombia, 1850–1936* (Albuquerque: University of New Mexico Press, 1986), 92.

33. Vernon Lee Fluharty, *Dance of the Millions: Military Rule and the Social Revolution in Colombia, 1930–1956* (Pittsburgh: University of Pittsburgh Press, 1957), 33; Harvey Kline, *Colombia: Portrait of Unity and Diversity* (Boulder: Westview Press, 1983), 41–43.

34. Palacios, *Between Legitimacy and Violence,* 84; W. John Green, "Vibrations of the Collective: The Popular Ideology of Gaitanismo on Colombia's Atlantic Coast, 1944–1948," *Hispanic American Historical Review* 76, no. 2 (1996): 283–311; Green, *Gaitanismo, Left Liberalism, and Popular Mobilization in Colombia* (Gainesville: University Press of Florida, 2003), 25–26.

35. Viloria de la Hoz, "Historia empresarial del guineo," 49; Palacios, *Between Legitimacy and Violence,* 81–85; LeGrand, *Frontier Expansion and Peasant Protest in Colombia,* 105.

36. Viloria de la Hoz, "Historia empresarial del guineo," 52–53.

37. Palacios, *Between Legitimacy and Violence,* 84; Bushnell, *The Making of Modern Colombia,* 180. For the debate about the numbers killed, see "La masacre de las bananeras: ¿Cuántos muertos hubo?" *Semana,* November 25, 2018.

38. Gabriel García Márquez, *Cien años de soledad* (Buenos Aires: Editorial Sudamericana, 1967), chapter 15.

39. Eduardo Posada Carbó, "Fiction as History: The *Bananeras* and Gabriel García Márquez's *One Hundred Years of Solitude," Journal of Latin America Studies* 30, no. 2 (May 1998): 400; Marco Palacios, *¿De quién es la tierra? Propiedad, politización y protesta campesina en la década de 1930* (Bogotá: Universidad de los Andes y Fondo de Cultura Económica, 2011), 160–63; Molina, *Las ideas liberales en Colombia,* 2: 234–35; Bushnell, *The Making of Modern Colombia,* 180; Green, *Gaitanismo, Left Liberalism, and Popular Mobilization,* 60–62.

40. Adriana Mercedes Corso, "El gravamen bananero: Un caso de historia política en el departamento del Magdalena" *Investigación y Desarrollo* 7(1998): 89–103.

41. Marcelo Bucheli, "La crisis del enclave bananero del Magdalena en los 60s," *Historia Crítica* 5 (January–July 1991): 113; Bucheli, *Bananas and Business,* 100; Mark Moberg and Steve Striffler, "Introduction," in *Banana Wars: Power, Production, and History in the Americas,* ed. Steve Striffler and Mark Moberg (Durham,

NC: Duke University Press, 2003), 7; Viloria de la Hoz, *Empresarios del Caribe colombiano*, 123.

42. LeGrand, "Living in Macondo," 345; Vives, *Pepe Vives cuenta su vida*, 197; White, *Historia de una ignominia*, 117; LeGrand, *Frontier Expansion and Peasant Protest in Colombia*, 115.

43. William L. Partridge, "Banana County in the Wake of United Fruit: Social and Economic Linkages," *American Ethnologist* 6, no. 3 (August 1979): 491–509.

44. For a similar case in Puerto Limón, United Fruit Company's first banana enclave in Latin America, see Lara Putnam, *The Company They Kept: Migrants and the Politics of Gender in Caribbean Costa Rica, 1870–1960* (Chapel Hill: University of North Carolina Press, 2002).

45. Moberg and Striffler, "Introduction," 5–9.

46. Posada Carbó, *The Colombian Caribbean*, 54; Kalmanovitz, *Economía y nación*, 245.

47. Posada Carbó, *The Colombian Caribbean*, 209–12.

48. For a revisionist interpretation of banana districts as "enclaves," see Dario Euraque, *Reinterpreting the Banana Republic: Region and State in Honduras, 1870–1972* (Chapel Hill: University of North Carolina Press, 1997).

49. LeGrand, "Living in Macondo," 336–37.

50. On the term "contact zone" see LeGrand, "Living in Macondo," 336.

51. For Olaya Herrera's interventions in the Greater Magdalena's banana district, see Molina, *Las ideas liberales en Colombia*, 240; Bushnell, *The Making of Modern Colombia*, 182–84; Thomas Charles Tirado, *Alfonso López Pumarejo, el conciliador: Su contribucion a la paz política en Colombia* (1977; reprint, Bogotá: Editorial Planeta, 1986), 86; Green, *Gaitanismo, Left Liberalism, and Popular Mobilization*, 70; and Marcelo Bucheli and Luis Felipe Sáenz, "Export Protectionism and the Great Depression: Multinational Corporations, Domestic Elite, and Export Policies in Colombia," in *The Great Depression in Latin America*, ed. Paulo Drinot and Alan Knight (Durham, NC: Duke University Press, 2014).

52. For López Pumarejo's words, see Bushnell, *The Making of Modern Colombia*, 185.

53. Carlos Lleras Restrepo, *Borradores para una historia de la República Liberal* (Bogotá: Editorial Nueva Frontera, 1975), 1:228–31. See also Green, *Gaitanismo, Left Liberalism, and Popular Mobilization*, 85–110.

54. On the Revolution on the March as the end of oligarchical democracy, see Molina, *Las ideas liberales en Colombia*; Alvaro Tirado Mejía, *Aspectos políticos del primer gobierno de Alfonso López Pumarejo, 1934–1938* (Bogotá: Instituto Colombiano de Cultura, 1981); Bushnell, *The Making of Modern Colombia*, 190–91; and Tirado, *Alfonso López Pumarejo*, 111. For the Revolution on the March as a handbrake on popular mobilization, see Richard Stoller, "Alfonso López Pumarejo and Liberal Radicalism in 1930s Colombia," *Journal of Latin American Studies* 27 (1995), 367–97; and Eduardo Sáenz Rovner, "Industriales, proteccionismo y política en Colombia: Intereses, conflictos y violencia," *Historia Crítica* 3 (January–June 1990), 85–105.

55. Marco Palacios, *Parábola del liberalism* (Bogotá: Grupo Editorial Norma, 1999), 96. On Law 200 of 1936, see Centro de Investigación y Educación Popular, ed., *Campesinado y capitalismo en Colombia* (Bogotá: Centro de Investigación y Educación Popular, 1981); LeGrand, *Frontier Expansion*, 149–53, 156–61; Absalón Machado, *Problemas agrarios colombianos* (Bogotá: Corporación de Estudios Ganaderos y Agrícolas, 1986); Leon Zamosc, *The Agrarian Question and the Peasant Movement in Colombia* (Cambridge: Cambridge University Press; Geneva: United Nations Institute for Social Development, 1986); Darío Fajardo Montaña, *Para sembrar la paz hay que aflojar la tierra* (Bogotá: Universidad Nacional de Colombia, 2002), 50–51.

56. Consuelo Araújo Noguera, "Rafael Escalona, el hombre y el mito," in *Trilogía vallenata* (1988; reprint, Bogotá: Ministerio de Cultura, 2002), 156.

57. Pepe Castro Castro, *Crónicas del Valle de Upar* (Bogotá: Zona Ltda., 2000), 145.

58. Araújo Noguera, "Rafael Escalona, el hombre y el mito," 157.

59. Alfonso López Michelsen, "Buscando el rostro de mi abuela," *Revista del Festival de la Leyenda Vallenata* 29 (1996), 68; Alfonso López Michelsen, "Prólogo," in Pepe Castro Castro, *Crónicas de la Plaza Mayor* (Bogotá: Cargraphics, 1998), 18.

60. Topik and Wells, "Introduction," 11.

61. For discussion of patronage and nepotism, see Safford and Palacios, *Colombia*, 156; and Posada Carbó, *The Colombian Caribbean*, 245.

62. Palacios, *Between Legitimacy and Violence*, 103.

63. Viloria de la Hoz, "Historia empresarial del guineo," 24–25.

64. Vives, *Pepe Vives cuenta su vida*, 198–202.

65. "El nuevo gobernador del Magdalena," *El Tiempo*, April 21, 1935.

66. Palacios, *Between Legitimacy and Violence*, 104; Álvaro Tirado Mejía, "López Pumarejo: La Revolución en Marcha," in *Nueva Historia de Colombia*, Vol. 1: *Historia Política, 1886–1946*, ed. Álvaro Tirado Mejía, Jorge Orlando Melo, and Jesús Antonio Bejarano (Bogotá: Editorial Planeta, 1989), 334. See also Special Decree 2298 of December 24, 1935, in Orsini Aarón, *Poligamia y contrabando*, 81.

67. Eduardo Sáenz Rovner, *La ofensiva empresarial: Industriales, políticos y violencia en los años 40 en Colombia* (Bogotá: Universidad Nacional de Colombia, CES, 2007), 18; Orsini Aarón, *Poligamia y contrabando*, 81. See also Lars Schoulz, *Beneath the United States: A History of US Policy toward Latin America* (Cambridge, MA: Harvard University Press, 1998), 305.

68. Juan Lázaro Robles to Minister of Public Works, Riohacha, April 30, 1924, in AGN, Ministerio de Obras Públicas, box 1447, fol. 6R–9R.

69. Benjamín Ezpeleta Ariza, *La verdadera historia de Riohacha* (Riohacha, Colombia: Aarón Impresores, 2000), 240.

70. On the term *criollos* in the Guajira, see González Zubiría, *Cultura y sociedad criolla de La Guajira*.

71. Lázaro Diago Julio, *Riohacha, fénix del Caribe* (Riohacha, Colombia: Fondo Mixto para la Promoción de la Cultura y de las Artes de la Guajira, 2005), 265–82.

72. Palacios, *Between Legitimacy and Violence,* 114.

73. For an account of Pepe Vives as governor, see Vives, *Pepe Vives cuenta su vida,* 198, 205, 246, 299–306, 340. For the Sigatoka disease, see Marcelo Bucheli, *Empresas multinationals y enclaves agrícolas: El caso de United Fruit en Magdalena y Urabá, Colombia (1948–1968),* Monografías 40 (Bogotá: Universidad de los Andes, Tercer Mundo Editores, 1994), 29–30.

74. Bucheli, "La crisis del enclave bananero del Magdalena en los 60s," 113; Bucheli, *Bananas and Business,* 100.

75. "Memorandum," July 16, 1940, National Archives and Records Administration (hereafter NARA), Record Group (RG) 84, box 1. See also Joseph Smith, *The United States and Latin America: A History of American Diplomacy, 1776–2000* (New York: Routledge, 2005), 102.

76. "Enclosure No. 2," October 10, 1941; "Letter No. 5," Riohacha, October 17, 1941; "Memorandum on Generoso and Vicente Ricciulli," Riohacha, September 29, 1942; and "Letter by Donato Pugliese," Riohacha, August 20, 1942, all in NARA, RG 84, box 1; "Lista de italianos sospechosos," Bogotá, November 13, 1940, AGN, Ministerio de Relaciones Exteriores, Fondo 33, No. Trans. 8 (Diplo. Cons.), Actividades Nazis, box 22, fol. 172, folios 87–93.

77. "Letter from R Kenneth Oakley, American Vice-Consul, to George C. Howard, American Commercial Attaché," Santa Marta, May 31, 1942, NARA, RG 84, box 1.

78. Nancy Mitchell, *The Danger of Dreams: German and American Imperialism in Latin America* (Chapel Hill: University of North Carolina Press, 1999), 9–63.

79. Max Paul Friedman, *Nazis and Good Neighbors: The United States Campaign against the Germans in Latin America in WWII* (Cambridge: Cambridge University Press, 2003), 84.

80. Luis Eduardo Bosemberg, "The US, Nazi Germany, and the CIAA [Coordinator of Inter-American Affairs] in Latin America during WWII," in Rockefeller Archive Center, *Publications Research Reports: Research Reports Online* (New York: Rockefeller Archive Center, 2009), 4.

81. Friedman, *Nazis and Good Neighbors,* 4.

82. Mitchell, *The Danger of Dreams,* 42.

83. "Memorandum-Copy," July 16, 1940; "Air Mail, Investigation of Activities in Colombia by a German by the Name of Moeller [*sic*]," Barranquilla, August 15, 1940, both in NARA, RG 84, box 1.

84. "Cover Memorandum with Letter No. 152," Barranquilla, June 17, 1941; "Letter signed by Gratiniano Gómez (in Spanish) attached to Memorandum with Letter No. 152," Barranquilla, June 17, 1941, both in NARA, RG 84, box 1. See also Orlando Essau Vidal Joiro, *Cuentos, relatos y personajes de mi tierra* (Riohacha, Colombia: Editorial Antorcha Guajira, 2000), 122.

85. "Letter signed by Gratiniano Gómez (in Spanish)," "Memorandum with Letter No. 152," and "Letter No. 3," Riohacha, October 10, 1941, all in NARA, RG 84, box 1.

86. "Air Mail to Sec. of State," Riohacha, January 29, 1942, NARA, RG 84, box 1. For more on Luis Cotes Gómez, see Julian A. Weston, *The Cactus Eaters* (London: H. F. & G. Witherby, Ltd., 1937), 61.

87. "Datos significativos del comercio Colombo-Alemán, Contraloría de la República," *Anuario General de Estadística y Anuario del Comercio Exterior,* in AGN, Ministerio de Relaciones Exteriores, Fondo 33, No. Trans. 8 (Diplo. Cons.), Actividades Nazis, box 23, folder 184, folio 9. See also "Memorandum-Copy," July 16, 1940, NARA, RG 84, box 1; and "Confidencial. Actividades Nazi in Colombia," Havana, March 21, 1941, AGN, Ministerio de Relaciones Exteriores, Fondo 33, No. Trans. 8 (Diplo. Cons.), Actividades Nazis, box 22, folder 175, folio 30.

88. For industrial and medicinal uses of divi-divi in the Guajira, see Jairo Rosado, "El proceso industrial, terapéutico y biológico del dividivi," in *Memorias del foro el dividivi como árbol y el dividivi como festival* (Riohacha, Colombia: Fondo Mixto para la Promoción la Cultura y las Artes de la Guajira, 1994), 17–19.

89. "Resolución No. 5," 1935; "Relaciones de Compras Locales," both in AGN, Ministerio de Obras Públicas, box 3561.

90. George M. Lauderbaugh, "Bolivarian Nations: Securing the Northern Frontier," in *Latin America during World War II,* ed. Thomas M. Leonard and John F. Bratzel (New York: Rowman & Littlefield, 2007), 115; Andrés Felipe Mesa Valencia, "El papel de Colombia en la Segunda Guerra Mundial: Desde el inicio de la conflagración haste el ataque japonés a Pearl Harbor," *Historia Caribe* 10, no. 26 (January–June 2015): 291–319.

91. Nicola Foote and Michael Goebel, *Immigration and National Identities in Latin America* (Gainesville: University Press of Florida, 2014); Walter Nugent, *Crossings: The Great Transatlantic Migrations, 1870–1914* (Bloomington: Indiana University Press, 1992).

92. Federal Bureau of Investigation, "Totalitarian Activities: Colombia. Today" (March 1942), 22, National Security Archives (hereafter NSA), Bradley Lynn Coleman Collection, box 3. Coleman reproduced this document, originally from FBI Reports, Papers of Harry L. Hopkins Special Assistant to the President, box 141, Franklin D. Roosevelt Presidential Library, Hyde Park, NY. See also Max Paul Friedman, "Specter of a Nazi Threat: United States–Colombian Relations, 1939–1945," *The Americas* 56, no. 4 (2000): 564.

93. Bradley Lynn Coleman, *Colombia and the United States: The Making of an Inter-American Alliance, 1939–1960* (Kent, OH: Kent State University Press, 2008), 21.

94. Bosemberg, "The US, Nazi Germany, and the CIA," 12. See also David Bushnell, *Eduardo Santos and the Good Neighbor, 1938–1942* (Gainesville: University of Florida Press, 1967), 50–66; Silvia Galvis and Alberto Donadío, *Colombia Nazi, 1939–1945* (Bogotá: Editorial Planeta, 1986), 60–99; Germán Arciniegas, "Eduardo Santos," in Tirado Mejía, Melo, and Bejarano, eds., *Nueva Historia de Colombia,* vol. 1.

95. Coleman, *Colombia and the United States,* 7–12, 21. See also Spruille Braden, *Diplomats and Demagogues: The Memoirs of Spruille Braden* (New Rochelle, NY: Arlington House, 1971), 207–9.

96. Coleman, *Colombia and the United States,* 32.

97. Braden, *Diplomats and Demagogues,* 193. See also Friedman, *Nazis and Good Neighbors,* 80; Galvis and Donadío, *Colombia Nazi,* 61–62.

98. On the nationalization of SCADTA, see Braden, *Diplomats and Demagogues,* 231–41; as well as "David L. Stone," November 14, 1939; "Airmail to Laurence Duggan," Bogotá, November 13, 1940; and "Letter no. 3288," Bogotá, November 19, 1941, all in Columbia University, Rare Book and Manuscript Library, Spruille Braden Papers, box 7 (Correspondence, Diplomatic, 1939–1941), folders 1939 and 1940. See also Stephen Randall, *The Diplomacy of Modernization: Colombian-American Relations, 1920–1940* (Toronto: University of Toronto Press, 1977), 146–61.

99. "Air Mail; Explanation of the Delay in Opening the Vice-Consulate at Riohacha," August 30, 1941, NARA, RG 84, vol. 2. See also "Memorandum," December 1, 1941, NARA, RG 84, box 1; and "Enclosure No. 2," October 10, 1941, NARA, RG 84, box 1, fol. 8.

100. Enclosure No. 1, March 1, 1941, NARA, RG 84, box 1.

101. "Memorandum, Subject: The General Situation in Rio Hacha [*sic*]," December 5, 1941, in NARA, RG 84, box 1.

102. Leonard to Spruille Braden, Riohacha, November 26, 1941, NARA, RG 84, box 1.

103. "Letter No. 45 by Consul Thomas Robinson to Vice-Consul Braggiotti," Barranquilla, July 1, 1942, NARA, RG 84, box 1. Miguelito Cotes, one of Luis Cotes Gómez's sons, sent a "flood of unsolicited telegrams" to British and American consular services, including letters signed "V," targeting merchants who did not belong to the pool of smugglers who worked with his father. See folder "Cotes B, Miguel," NARA, RG 84, box 1. See also "Letter by Miguel Cotes Barros to Eleazar Matiz Díaz, Inv. Nacional [National Police detective]," Riohacha, June 24, 1942; "Letter by Miguel Cotes Barros to Consul Nelson Park," Riohacha, April 21, 1942, both in NARA, RG 84, box 1.

104. "Subject: Reported Sighting of Two Submarines Off Cabo de la Vela, by Vice-Consul at Riohacha, Guajira Peninsula," July 24, 1942; "Letter to American Consul Thomas Robinson, Riohacha," June 25, 1942, both in NARA, RG 84, box 1. See also Letter No. 55, Barranquilla, July 11, 1942, NARA, RG 84, box 1; and "Report on Trip Made From Riohacha to Dibulla on September 4, 1942, and From Riohacha Into the Guajira, September 26 to October 3rd 1942," and Letter No. 13, Riohacha, December 11, 1942, both in NARA, RG 84, box 1.

105. For a detailed account of the battle for the Guajira and German U-boats, see Lina Britto, "El eje guajiro: Nazis, contrabandistas y diplomáticos durante la Segunda Guerra Mundial, Riohacha, 1940–1943," in *Pensamiento Poscolonial: Cambio social y relaciones subalternas en América Latina,* ed. Ricardo Oviedo (Pasto, Colombia: Universidad de Nariño, 2014).

106. Ezpeleta Ariza, *La verdadera historia de Riohacha,* 242–43.

107. Catalina Muñoz, "'A Mission of Enormous Transcendence': The Cultural Politics of Music during Colombia's Liberal Republic, 1930–1946," *Hispanic American Historical Review* 94, no. 1 (2014): 79.

108. Pepe Castro Castro, "Cuando las cosas no eran tan fáciles para ir a estudiar," in Pepe Castro Castro, *Crónicas de Pepe* (Bogotá: El Malpensante, 2002), 31–42; Pepe Castro Castro Castro, "Educación durante la República Liberal," in Castro Castro, *Crónicas de la Plaza Mayor,* 74–79; Ciro Quiroz Otero, "Prólogo," in Castro Castro, *Crónicas del Valle de Upar,* 14; Pepe Castro Castro, *Crónicas y cuentos* (Bogotá: La Silueta Ediciones, 2005), 97; Pepe Castro Castro, *Iglesia Nuestra Señora de la Concepción y la familia vallenata* (Bogotá: Tradelink Ltda., 2007), 82; Jorge Dangond Daza, *De París a Villanueva: Memorias de un vallenato* (Bogotá: Plaza & Janés, 1990), 78.

109. Pepe Castro Castro, interview by the author, Valledupar, Cesar, Colombia, February 1, 2011.

110. Castro Castro, *Crónicas de la Plaza Mayor,* 76.

111. Castro Castro, *Crónicas de la Plaza Mayor,* 77.

112. Castro Castro, *Crónicas del Valle de Upar,* 233.

113. Castro Castro, *Crónicas del Valle de Upar,* 219–26.

114. Pepe Castro Castro, *El cuento de Pepe* (Bogotá: Tradelink Ltda., 2003), 1:47–53.

115. Castro Castro, *Crónicas del Valle de Upar,* 215–64. On *tertulias,* see Aníbal Martínez Zuleta, *Escolios y croniquillas del país vallenato* (n.p.: Tefa Comercializadora, 1999), 169.

116. Alfonso Sánchez Baute, *Líbranos del bien* (Bogotá: Alfaguara, 2008), 64.

117. Britto, "El eje guajiro." See also Alfredo Molano, Fernando Rozo, Juana Escobar, and Omayra Mendiola, "Diagnóstico de la Sierra Nevada de Santa Marta, Área Social: Aproximación a una historia oral de la colonización de la SNSM, Descripción testimonial (Agosto 1988)," Documento de Trabajo (unpublished manuscript), Fundación ProSierra Nevada de Santa Marta, 91–92; "Destacados personajes extranjeros que llegaron a Valledupar," in Castro Castro, *Crónicas del Valle de Upar,* 425; and "Enclosure No. 5," October 10, 1941, NARA, RG 84, box 1.

118. Palacios, *Between Legitimacy and Violence,* 120–21.

119. Darío Betancourt and Martha Luz García, *Matones y cuadrilleros: Origen y evolución de la violencia en el occidente colombiano, 1946–1965* (Bogotá: Tercer Mundo Editores, 1990), 57–61.

120. Jon V. Kofas, *Dependence and Underdevelopment in Colombia* (Tempe: Arizona State University, 1986), 20–41; Jesús Antonio Bejarano, "Industrialización y Política Económica, 1950–1976," in *Colombia Hoy,* ed. Jorge Orlando Melo (1978, reprint; Bogotá: Imprenta Nacional, 1996), 211–54; Antonio Abello Roca, "El algodón en Colombia," in *El sector agropecuario en el desarrollo de la Costa Caribe: Memorias del foro,* ed. Uriel Ramírez Bolívar (Bogotá: Fondo de Publicaciones Universidad del Atlántico, 1999), 212.

121. Posada Carbó, *The Colombian Caribbean,* 62–65; Will Calderón Guerra, *Bonanza y crisis del algodón en el Cesar, 1950–2010* (Valledupar, Colombia: Imagen Visual Ltda., 2010), 21. See also José Antonio Ocampo and Santiago Montenegro, *Crisis mundial, protección e industrialización* (Bogotá: CEREC, 1984).

122. Fernando Bernal Castillo, *Crisis algodonera y violencia en el departamento del Cesar* (Bogotá: PNUD, 2004), 25; Marcela Wagner Medina, "Las huellas

ambientales del oro blanco: La expansión algodonera en el valle del río Cesar, 1950–1980" (master's thesis, geography, Universidad de los Andes, 2011), 22.

123. Arturo Guerrero, "Algodón, la historia de un largo esfuerzo frustrado," *Nueva Frontera* 380 (1982): 8.

124. "Letter from Mariano Ospina Pérez to Alfonso López Pumarejo," quoted in Sáenz Rovner, "Industriales, proteccionismo y política en Colombia," 93.

125. Sáenz Rovner, "Industriales, proteccionismo y política en Colombia," 96. See also Sáenz Rovner, *La ofensiva empresarial*. For a similar case in nineteenth-century Mexico, see Sven Beckert, *Empire of Cotton: A Global History* (New York: Alfred A. Knopf, 2014), 160.

126. Public works constructed while Castro Monsalvo was governor include the Vocational Technical School, the Experimental Cattle Farm, the irrigation ditch, the Salguero Bridge, a web of paved roads that connected Valledupar with the towns of the *provincia* and the banana district, the expansion of the airport, and the beginning of the public hospital's construction. See "Letter," Valledupar, May 19, 1942, in AGN, Ministerio de Obras Públicas, Edificios Nacionales-Hospitales, 1941–1942, box 877; and Tomas Darío Gutiérrez, *Valledupar: Música de una historia* (Bogotá: Editorial Grijalbo, 2000), 344.

127. Yin Daza Noguera, *Itinerario de un periodista* (Bogotá: Colección de Autores Guajiros, Secretaría de Educación-Divulgación Cultural, Departamento de la Guajira, 1983), 227.

128. Álvaro Castro Socarrás, *Episodios históricos del Cesar* (Bogotá: Plaza & Janés, 1997), 306. On Castro Monsalvo's election to the Magdalena departmental assembly, see Castro Castro, *Iglesia Nuestra Señora de la Concepción y familia vallenata,* 99. On Castro Monsalvo and the Agrarian Bank, see José Vicente Lafaurie Acosta, "El desarrollo del Cesar," in *Cesar, 20 años, 1967–1987* (Valledupar: Impresos de la Costa Ltda, Gobernación del Cesar, 1988), 41; Antonio Araújo Calderón, *Cuaderno de la historia provincial* (Bogotá: Contraloría General de la República, 1978), 71.

129. On the resignation of Minister Castro Monsalvo and others, see Kofas, *Dependence and Underdevelopment in Colombia,* 41.

130. Jorge García García, *El cultivo de algodón en Colombia entre 1953 y 1978: Una evaluación de las políticas gubernamentales,* Documentos de trabajo sobre economía regional 44 (Cartagena de Indias: Centro de investigaciones económicas del Caribe colombiano, Banco de la República, 2004), 4. See also Wagner Medina, *Las huellas ambientales del oro blanco,* 22.

131. Calderón Guerra, *Bonanza y crisis del algodón en el Cesar,* 24.

132. Luis Bértola and José Antonio Ocampo, *The Economic Development of Latin America since Independence* (Oxford: Oxford University Press, 2012), 138–97.

133. Lafaurie Acosta, "El desarrollo del Cesar," 39; Calderón Guerra, *Bonanza y crisis del algodón en el Cesar,* 28–30.

134. Lafaurie Acosta, "El desarrollo del Cesar," 42.

135. Dangond Daza, *De París a Villanueva,* 84–89.

136. Jorge Dangond Daza, *Renacimiento de Valledupar: Así nació el Cesar* (Barranquilla, Colombia: Editorial Antillas, 2002), 56–57. On poor peasants dying of sadness, see Tomás Darío Gutiérrez, "Los conflictos sociales en la historia de la cultura vallenata," in *Historia, identidades, cultura popular y música tradicional en el Caribe colombiano,* ed. Leovedis Martínez Durán and Hugues Sánchez Mejía (Valledupar, Colombia: Ediciones Unicesar, 2004), 43.

137. Dangond Daza, *Renacimiento de Valledupar,* 15.

138. Dangond Daza, *De París a Villanueva,* 80.

139. Fabio López de la Roche, "Cultura política de las clases dirigentes en Colombia: Permanencias y rupturas," *Controversia: Ensayos sobre cultura política colombiana,* nos. 162–63 (1990): 112. See also Fabio López de la Roche, "Tradiciones de cultura política en el siglo XX," in *Modernidad y sociedad política en Colombia,* ed. Miguel Eduardo Cárdenas Rivera (Bogotá: FESCOL, IEPRI, Ediciones Foro Nacional por Colombia, 1993), 108–19.

140. David Harrison, *The Sociology of Modernization and Development* (New York: Routledge, 1988), 8.

141. Mark T. Berger, *Under Northern Eyes: Latin American Studies and US Hegemony in the Americas, 1898–1990* (Bloomington: Indiana University Press, 1995), 75–86; and Kofas, *Dependence and Underdevelopment in Colombia,* 43–66.

142. On Rojas Pinilla's hacienda near Riohacha, see Molano et al., "Diagnóstico de la Sierra Nevada de Santa Marta, Descripción testimonial," 5. See also Santiago Araoz, *Historia del Frente Nacional y otros ensayos* (Bogotá: Editorial Presencia, 1977), 19.

143. José Ignacio Vives, *La Guajira ante el Congreso de Colombia: Historia de un proceso* (Bogotá: Senado de la República, Imprenta Nacional, 1965), 31.

144. Jaime Dangond Ovalle, *El Cesar, hijo del amor: En el veinte aniversario del Departamento del Cesar* (Barranquilla, Colombia: Gráficas del Litoral, 1987), 28.

145. Consuelo Araújo Noguera, "Vallenatología: Orígenes y fundamentos de la música vallenata," in *Trilogía vallenata* (1973; reprint, Bogotá: Ministerio de Cultura, 2002), 30.

146. Yim Daza Noguera, interview by the author, San Juan del Cesar, Guajira, Colombia, March 24, 2005.

147. Calderón Guerra, *Bonanza y crisis del algodón en el Cesar,* 31; Bernal Castillo, *Crisis algodonera y violencia en el departamento del Cesar,* 27.

148. Enrique Orozco Daza, Oswaldo Villalobos Hincapié, and Alberto Yurcowiez Melendez, "Implicaciones socio-económicas del cultivo del algodón en la zona de San Juan del Cesar, Guajira" (honors thesis, agricultural economy, Universidad Tecnológica del Madgalena, Santa Marta, 1983), 24–28. On cotton cultivation's stages, see Wagner Medina, *Las huellas ambientales del oro blanco,* 33–38.

149. Fernando Herrera Araújo, "Prólogo," in Bernal Castillo, *Crisis algodonera y violencia en el departamento del Cesar,* 14.

150. Herbert Stewart et al., "El desarrollo agrícola de Colombia: Informe de la Misión organizada por el Banco de Reconstrucción y Fomento a solicitud del Gobierno de Colombia," *Revista Cafetera de Colombia* 13, no. 30 (January 1957). See also

Lauchlin Currie and Julio Bejarano, *El algodón en Colombia: Problemas y oportunidades* (Bogotá: Federación Nacional de Algodoneros y Fundación Para el Progreso de Colombia, 1963).

151. Calderón Guerra, *Bonanza y crisis del algodón en el Cesar,* 41; García García, "El cultivo de algodón en Colombia entre 1953 y 1978," 3.

152. John H. Perkins, *Geopolitics and the Green Revolution: Wheat, Genes, and the Cold War* (Oxford: Oxford University Press, 1997), 108–9.

153. LeGrand, *Frontier Expansion,* 33–62.

154. Blanca Nubia Zapata, "Empresas comerciales del municipio de Valledupar, 1950–1980," in Observatorio del Caribe Colombiano, *Becas culturales en investigación sociocultural en historia regional y/o local del Departamento del Cesar* (Bogotá, 2006), 151.

155. Dangond Daza, interview by Zapata, quoted in "Empresas comerciales del municipio de Valledupar," 123.

156. Zapata, "Empresas comerciales del municipio de Valledupar," 151–56. On his many business ventures, see Dangond Daza, *Renacimiento de Valledupar,* 2002.

157. Jacobo "El Pano" Mejía, interview by the author, San Juan del Cesar, Guajira, Colombia, August 8, 2008.

158. Alfredo Chinchilla, interview by Wagner Medina, quoted in *Las huellas ambientales del oro blanco,* 24.

159. Castro Castro, *El cuento de Pepe,* 2:193. See also Orozco, Villalobos Hincapié, and Yurcowiez Melendez, *Implicaciones socio-económicas del cultivo del algodón en la zona de San Juan del Cesar, Guajira,* 64.

160. Bernal Castillo, *Crisis algodonera y violencia en el departamento del Cesar,* 32.

161. Manuel Germán Cuello, interview by Zapata, quoted in "Empresas comerciales del municipio de Valledupar," 123.

162. On *socas* (cotton residue), see Wagner Medina, *Las huellas ambientales del oro blanco,* 38.

163. Dangond Ovalle, *El Cesar, hijo del amor,* 9, and 28.

164. Dangond Ovalle, *El Cesar, hijo del amor,* 27.

165. Dangond Ovalle, *El Cesar, hijo del amor,* 10.

166. Diana Rojas, "Colombia como 'vitrina' de la Alianza para el Progreso," in *50 años de la Alianza para el Progreso: Lecciones para el presente, relatoría del evento,* Documentos del Departamento de Ciencia Política 11 (Bogotá: Universidad de los Andes, 2011), 6–8; Coleman, *Colombia and the United States;* "Memorandum August 3, 1960," NARA, RG 59 (Records Relating to Colombia; Comp 1955–1964), box 2.

167. Amy C. Offner, *Sorting Out the Mixed Economy: The Rise and Fall of Welfare and Developmental States in the Americas* (Princeton, NJ: Princeton University Press, 2019). See also Timothy W. Lorek, "Imagining the Midwest in Latin America: US Advisors and the Envisioning of an Agricultural Middle Class in Colombia's Cauca Valley, 1943–1946," *The Historian* 75, no. 2 (summer 2013): 283–305.

168. Tatiana Acevedo, "No te metas con la tierra," *El Espectador,* April 20, 2011.

169. For the argument that the fiercest resistance against the agrarian reform came from within the Liberal Party, see César Augusto Ayala, *Resistencia y oposición al establecimiento del Frente Nacional: Los orígenes de la Alianza Nacional Popular, ANAPO, Colombia, 1953–1964* (Bogotá: Universidad Nacional de Colombia, 1996).

170. Pedro Castro Monsalvo, speech of May 25, 1961, in Pedro Castro Monsalvo, *Un campesino previno al país* (Bogotá: Ediciones Tercer Mundo, 1972), 108–16. See also Pedro Castro Monsalvo, Raimundo Emiliani Román, and Benjamín Burgos Puche, *El INCORA y la ejecución de la Reforma Agraria: Informe de la Comisión del Senado* (Bogotá: Senado de la República, 1967).

171. Castro Monsalvo, *Un campesino previno al país,* 84.

172. Pedro Castro Monsalvo, speech of September 27, 1960, in Castro Monsalvo, *Un campesino previno al país,* 53–54.

173. Berger, *Under Northern Eyes,* 76.

174. Joseph Cotter, *Troubled Harvest: Agronomy and Revolution in Mexico, 1880–2002* (Westport, CT: Praeger, 2003), 35–36. For the paradigmatic case of Sonora, Mexico, see Jayson Maurice Porter, "Plagas, pesticidas y ciencias agrícolas entre revoluciones," *Boletín* 89 (September–December 2018): 1–44.

175. "Miscellaneous Notes," March 26–31, 1961, NARA, RG 59 (Records Relating to Colombia; Comp. 1955–1964), box 2.

176. Pedro de Andreis, interview by the author, Santa Marta, Magdalena, Colombia, January 20, 2011.

177. César Ayala, "Fiesta y golpe de Estado en Colombia," *Anuario Colombiano de Historia Social y de la Cultura,* vol. 25 (Bogotá: Universidad Nacional de Colombia, 1998); and Medófilo Medina, *Juegos de rebeldía:. La trayectoria política de Saúl Charris de la Hoz (*Bogotá: Universidad Nacional de Colombia, CINDEC, 1997).

178. "Palabras de Juan Carlos Vives Menotti en la traída de las cenizas de su padre Nacho Vives a Santa Marta," n.d., in Luz Marina Vives personal archive, Santa Marta; Luz Marina Vives (Nachos Vives's daughter), interview by the author, Santa Marta, Magdalena, Colombia, January 24, 2011. See also Vives, *Pepe Vives cuenta su vida,* 178.

179. On "language of contention," in the sense of a shared set of ideas and ideals used by most interest groups in a given society to communicate with one another and among themselves and advance their claims and agendas in specific political battles, see William Roseberry, "Hegemony and the Language of Contention," in Joseph and Nugent, *Everyday Forms of State Formation.*

180. Partridge, "Banana County in the Wake of United Fruit," 500.

181. "Telegram," December 26, 1959, AGN, Ministerio del Interior, Secretaría General, box 227, fol. 2129, roll 212, folio 1R; "Prosperous capitalist Daza and company invaded with a gang of workers plots in Calle Ancha (Main Street)," April 2, 1959, AGN, Min. Interior, Sec. Gen., box 227, folder 2129, roll 212, folio 11R.

182. "Marconigram," April 6, 1960, AGN, Min. Interior, Sec. Gen., box 227, folder 2129, roll 212, folio 114R.

183. "Telegram," January 1962, AGN, Ministerio del Interior, Varios, box 262, folder 2485, folio 26.

184. Partridge, "Banana County in the Wake of United Fruit," 503–4.

185. "Letter," February 2, 1960, in AGN, Min. Interior, Sec. Gen., box 227, folder 2129, roll 212, folio 139R.

186. "Letter," February 26, 1960, in AGN, Min. Interior, Sec. Gen., box 227, folder 2129, roll 212, folios 29R–31R.

187. On *combos,* see Molano et al., "Diagnóstico de la Sierra Nevada de Santa Marta, Descripción testimonial," 42.

188. "Letter," October 21, 1960, AGN, Min. Interior, Sec. Gen., box 227, folder 2129, roll 212, folios 68R, 68V.

189. "Letter," February 25, 1960, AGN, Min. Interior, Sec. Gen., box 227, folder 2129, roll 212, folios 35R–36R.

190. "Telegram," January 21, 1960, AGN, Min. Interior, Sec. Gen., box 227, folder 2130, roll 218, folio 168R.

191. "Telegram," May 18, 1960, AGN, Min. Interior, Sec. Gen., box 227, folder 2129, roll 212, folio 189R.

192. "Letter," January 14, 1960, AGN, Min. Interior, Sec. Gen., box 227, folder 2129, roll 212, folio 145R.

193. "Memorandum," n.d., AGN, Min. Interior, Sec. Gen., box 227, folder 2129, roll 212, folios 31R and 32R.

194. "Letter," July 14, 1960, in AGN, Min. Interior, Sec. Gen., box 227, folder 2129, roll 212, folios 100R, 100V.

195. "Letter,"n.d., in AGN, Min. Interior, Varios, box 262, folder 2485, folio 27.

196. The shantytowns where Vives began his career were Pescaíto, Manzanares, Cundí, Olivos, Casco Viejo, Mamatoco, Taganga, and Gaira. Pedro de Andreis, interview by the author; Luz Marina Vives, interview by the author.

197. Alfonso López Michelsen, "Los intelectuales y la revolución" (speech given to a group of artists and intellectuals, March 1962), in Alfonso López Michelsen, *Colombia en la hora cero* (Bogotá: Ediciones Tercer Mundo, 1963), 107; Alfonso López Michelsen, "El oficialismo liberal como partido al servicio de los factores del poder y como promotor de la Mano Negra" (speech given during the Liberal National Convention, Febraury 24, 1961), in López Michelsen, *Colombia en la hora cero,* 11–37.

198. "Memorandum," August 3, 1960, in NARA, RG 59 (Records Relating to Colombia; Comp. 1955–1964), box 2; Alfonso López Michelsen, "La Reforma Agraria del Frente Nacional no es revolucionaria y va contra la historia" (speech given in Pereira, 1961), in López Michelsen, *Colombia en la hora cero,* 41; and Alfonso López Michelsen, "El problema del Comunismo," in López Michelsen, *Colombia en la hora cero,* 217.

199. Throughtout the 1960s, Vives won seats in the municipal councils of Santa Marta, Ciénaga, and Aracataca—in Santa Marta province—and in San Sebastián, Chimichagua, La Gloria, Tamalameque, and Río de Oro—in Valledupar province; see "Nacho Vives C.V.," in Luz Marina Vives personal archive.

200. For an intelligence report on Vives's congressional campaign in the Guajira with Eduardo Abuchaibe Ochoa as his running mate, see "Boletín Informativo #65," October 13, 1961, Informes sobre orden público, Departamento Administrativo de Seguridad (hereafter DAS), 1960–1961, AGN, Ministerio del Interior, Secretaría General, box 229, folder 2154.

201. Castro Socarrás, *Episodios históricos del Cesar*, 222.

202. Vives, *La Guajira ante el Congreso de Colombia*, 44.

203. Vives, *La Guajira ante el Congreso de Colombia*, 15. "Nowadays [1962] an incomplete census of Guajiro professionals shows: 50 doctors, 65 lawyers, 20 engineers, 17 dentists, 9 agronomists, 5 veterinarians, 6 professors, 5 bacteriologists, 2 economists, and a considerable number of high school and college students." Vives, *La Guajira ante el Congreso de Colombia*, 27.

204. Vives, *La Guajira ante el Congreso de Colombia*, 16.

205. Meña Melo, interview by the author, Riohacha, Guajira, Colombia, August 2, 2008.

206. "Palabras en homenaje al doctor José Ignacio Vives Echeverría, al mes de su fallecimiento," Riohacha, August 6, 2007, in Luz Marina Vives personal archive.

207. Interview with José Antonio Murgas, who presented the second bill in Congress, February 1997, quoted in Castro Socarrás, *Episodios históricos del Cesar*, 221. With Decree 029 of March 5, 1963, Valledupar's mayor, Jaime Dangond Ovalle, appointed López Michelsen representative of the initiative in Bogotá. See Dangond Ovalle, *El Cesar, hijo del amor*, 15.

208. Castro Socarrás, *Episodios históricos del Cesar*, 224.

209. On López Michelsen and Lleras Restrepo's many battles, see Alfonso López Michelsen, "La revolución colombiana," in López Michelsen, *Colombia, la hora cero*, 241; and López Michelsen, "Los responsables de la violencia," ibid., 98.

210. For the roster, and transcriptions of speeches, see Dangond Ovalle, *Cesar, hijo del amor.*

211. César Augusto Ayala, *El populismo atrapado, la memoria y el miedo: El caso de las elecciones de 1970* (Medellín: Universidad Nacional de Colombia y La Carreta Ediciones, 2006), 87. On Vives's power in Tamalameque, in particular, see "Telegram," December 5, 1960, AGN, Min. Interior, Sec. Gen., box 227, folder 2129, roll 212, folios 133R–134R. On other towns where Vives was the *cacique*, see "Letter," January 19, 1960, AGN, Min. Interior, Sec. Gen., box 227, folder 2129, roll 212, folios. 131R, 131V; and "Telegram," August 5, 1960 in AGN, Min. Interior, Sec. Gen., box 227, folder 2130, roll 218, folio 62R.

212. "Levantada inmunidad a Vives," *El Tiempo* (September 12, 1969), 6.

213. José Ignacio Vives, "Las banderas no se encarcelan," *Seneca* 9 (October 1969); Congressional Debate, July 23, 1969, track 2, both reprinted in Hugo Vélez, *El debate en gráficas de Nacho Vives ante el Senado* (Bogotá: Hugo Vélez O, 1969), no page numbers in the copy in Luz Marina Vives's personal archive. See also Ayala, *El populismo atrapado, la memoria y el miedo*, 89.

214. On the Pact of Chicoral, reversing the agrarian reform law, see Cristina Escobar and Francisco de Roux, "Movimientos populares en Colombia, 1970–1983,"

in *Los movimientos populares en América Latina,* eds. Daniel Camacho and Rafael Menjívar (Mexico: Siglo XXI Editores 1989), 160.

215. Moberg and Striffler, "Introduction," 3–4; Topik and Wells, "Introduction," 16.

CHAPTER 2. COMING FROM THE MOUNTAIN

1. This paragraph is based on Justiniano Mendoza, interview by the author, February 23, 2005, San Juan del Cesar, Guajira, Colombia; Rafael Enrique "Arique" Britto, interview by the author, no. 2, February 23, 2005, San Juan del Cesar, Guajira, Colombia; Rafael Enrique "Arique" Britto, interview by the author, no. 3, February 24, 2005, on road Villanueva–San Juan del Cesar, Guajira, Colombia; Daza Noguera, interview by the author; and Rafael Enrique "Arique" Britto, interview by the author, no. 4, December 5, 2014, on road La Junta–San Juan del Cesar, Guajira, Colombia. On the use of trucks in the smuggling business, see González Plazas, *Pasado y presente del contrabando en la Guajira,* 53.

2. On the "long sixties," see Tamara Chaplin and Jadwiga E. Pieper Mooney, "Introduction," in *The Global 60s: Convention, Contest, and Counterculture,* ed. Tamara Chaplin and Jadwiga E. Pieper Mooney (New York: Routledge, 2018), 2–4; and Martin Klimke and Mary Nolan, "Introduction: The Globalization of the Sixties," in *The Routledge Handbook of the Global Sixties: Between Protest and Nation-Building,* ed. Chen Jian, Martin Klimke, Masha Kirasirova, Mary Nolan, Marilyn Young, and Joanna Waley-Cohen (New York: Routledge, 2018), 4–5.

3. For the case for expanding the narrow notion of the "political" in the study of the "global sixties," see Vania Markarian, "To the Beat of 'The Walrus': Uruguayan Communists and Youth Culture in the Global Sixties," *The Americas* 70, no. 3 (January 2014): 363–92.

4. On youth and generation as main markers of identity, see Patrick Barr-Melej, *Psychedelic Chile: Youth, Counterculture, and Politics on the Road to Socialism and Dictatorship* (Chapel Hill: University of North Carolina Press, 2017), 5–6.

5. On the "global sixties" as a heuristic tool for understanding local change within a transnational framework, see Eric Zolov, "Introduction: Latin America in the Global Sixties," *The Americas* 70, no. 3 (January 2014): 349–62.

6. On 1946 to 1953 as the bloodiest phase of La Violencia, see Germán Gustavo Guzmán, Orlando Fals Borda, and Eduardo Umaña, *La Violencia en Colombia: Estudio de un proceso social* (Bogotá: Ediciones Tercer Mundo, 1963).

7. On labor in the cotton belt, see Partridge, "Banana County in the Wake of United Fruit," 494; Bernal Castillo, *Crisis algodonera y violencia en el departamento del Cesar,* 33–34; Wagner Medina, "Las huellas ambientales del oro blanco," 37–38. By 1953 the United Fruit Company had sold out to private owners and turned over to the government seven thousand hectares of irrigated lands; by 1965 it concluded its withdrawal. See Bucheli, *Empresas multinacionales y enclaves agrícolas,* 29–30; and Partridge, "Banana Country in the Wake of United Fruit," 497.

8. Molano et al., "Diagnóstico de la Sierra Nevada de Santa Marta, Descripción testimonial," 42.

9. Alfredo Molano, Fernando Rozo, Juana Escobar, and Omayra Mendiola, "Diagnóstico de la Sierra Nevada de Santa Marta, Área Social: Aproximación a una historia oral de la colonización de la SNSM, Recuento analítico (Agosto 1988)," Documento de Trabajo (unpublished manuscript), Fundación ProSierra Nevada de Santa Marta, 93.

10. Viloria de la Hoz, *Café Caribe,* 29.

11. Molano et al., "Diagnóstico de la Sierra Nevada de Santa Marta, Descripción testimonial," 131.

12. Luisa Fernanda Herrera de Turbay, "La actividad agrícola en la SNSM (Colombia): Perspectiva histórica," in *Studies on Tropical Andean Ecosystems/Estudios de ecosistemas Tropoandinos,* vol. 2: *La Sierra Nevada de Santa Marta,* ed. Thomas Van Der Hammen and Pedro M. Ruiz (Berlin: J. Cramer, 1986), 501–2. See also Gene Logsdon, "The Importance of Traditional Farming Practices for a Sustainable Modern Agriculture," in *Meeting the Expectations of the Land: Essays in Sustainable Agriculture and Stewardship,* ed. Wes Jackson, Wendell Berry, and Bruce Colman (San Francisco: North Point Press, 1984), 7.

13. Molano et al., "Diagnóstico de la Sierra Nevada de Santa Marta, Descripción testimonial," 4.

14. In the original Spanish: "Vengo de la montaña / de allá de la cordillera, / allá dejé mi compañera / junto con mis dos hijitos. / Yo me traje bien cargado mi burrito, / vendo mi carga y me alisto / porque mi mujer me espera. / Tengo pensado regresarme muy temprano / porque ella me está esperando con algunos alimentos, / mi pobre compañera que con tanto sufrimiento, / amarguras y tormentos me acompaña en esas tierras." Máximo Movil, "Mujer conforme," in Jorge Oñate, *La parranda y la mujer,* 1975.

15. Kalmanovitz and López Enciso, *La agricultura colombiana en el siglo XX,* 83. See also Margarita Jiménez and Sandro Sideri, *Historia del desarrollo regional en Colombia* (Bogotá: Fondo Editorial CEREC, 1985), 112.

16. Sáenz Rovner, *La ofensiva empresarial,* 189–202. See also Francisco Rodríguez Vargas, "Las organizaciones del sector cafetero colombiano," *Innovar* 7 (1996): 7–26.

17. Sáenz Rovner, *La ofensiva empresarial,* 212.

18. On the plunder of coffee farms, see Carlos Miguel Ortiz Sarmiento, *Estado y subversion en Colombia: La Violencia en el Quindío, años 50* (Bogotá: CIDER-Uniandes; Fondo Editorial CEREC, 1985), 294–99. See also Robert A. Karl, *Forgotten Peace: Reform, Violence, and the Making of Contemporary Colombia* (Oakland: University of California Press, 2017), 98; and Mariano Arango, *El café en Colombia, 1930–1958: Producción, circulación y política* (Bogotá: Carlos Valencia Editores, 1982), 252–56.

19. Charles Bergquist, *Labor in Latin America: Comparative Essays on Chile, Argentina, Venezuela, and Colombia* (Palo Alto, CA: Stanford University Press, 1986), 328.

20. The other area involved was the Andean department of Norte de Santander, bordering Venezuela; see Comité Nacional de Cafeteros, "El contrabando de café: Comunicado de la Secretaría del Comité Nacional de Cafeteros, Diciembre 14 de 1956," *Revista Cafetera de Colombia* 13, no. 130 (January 1957): 62. See also Iván Cadavid Orozco and Hugo Molina Muñoz, *El delito de contrabando* (Bogotá: Editorial Súper, 1979), 73–74.

21. Viloria de la Hoz, *Café Caribe,* 18.

22. On contraband as a creation of the state, see Peter Andreas, *Smuggler Nation: How Illicit Trade Made America* (Oxford: Oxford University Press, 2013), 2.

23. James D. Henderson, *Las ideas de Laureano Gómez* (Bogotá: Ediciones Tercer Mundo, 1985), 54, 255; Bushnell, *The Making of Modern Colombia,* 212–13.

24. Jorge Dangond Castro, *Tierra nuestra: Crónicas de frontera* (Barranquilla, Colombia: Editorial Antillas, 2001), 38. See also Margarita Serje, "El 'Almirante Padilla' en Corea: Una crónica del legendario buque de la Armada Nacional de Colombia," *Expedición Padilla,* May 2012, available at https://www.academia.edu/3792656/El_Almirante_Padilla_en_Corea_Una_crónica_del_legendario_buque_de_la_Armada_Nacional_de_Colombia.

25. Fredy González Zubiría, *Crónicas del cancionero vallenato* (Riohacha, Colombia: Dirección Departamental de Cultura de la Guajira, 2011), 14; Abel Medina Sierra, "Escalona y su aventura en La Guajira," *Aguaita* 21 (December 2009): 112; Héctor Castillo Castro, "Música de acordeón, frontera y contrabando en La Guajira, 1960–1980," *Educación y Ciencia* 10 (2007): 73–88.

26. In the original Spanish: "Allá en La Guajira arriba, / donde nace el contrabando, / el Almirante Padilla llegó a Puerto López / y lo dejó arruinado . . . / barco pirate bandido, / que Santo Tomás lo vea, / prometí hacerle una fiesta / cuando un submarino lo voltee en Corea." Rafael Escalona, "El almirante Padilla," in Bovea y sus Vallenatos, *Los cantos vallenatos de Escalona,* 1962.

27. "Pobre Tite, pobre Tite / pobre Tite Socarrás / ahora se encuentra muy triste / lo ha perdido todo por contrabandear." Escalona, "El almirante Padilla."

28. Orsini Aarón, *Poligamia y contrabando,* 99.

29. Eduardo Sáenz Rovner, *Colombia años 50: Industriales, política y diplomacia* (Bogotá: Universidad Nacional de Colombia, 2002), 137–48; and Robert Karl, "From 'Showcase' to 'Failure': Democracy and the Colombian Developmental State in the 1960s," in *State and Nation Making in Latin America and Spain: The Rise and Fall of the Developmental State,* ed. Miguel A. Centeno and Agustin E. Ferraro (Cambridge: Cambridge University Press, 2018), 73–104.

30. Comité Nacional de Cafeteros, "El contrabando de café," 59–60; Arango, *El café en Colombia,* 260.

31. Roberto Junguito and Carlos Caballero, "La otra economía," *Coyuntura Económica* 8, no. 4 (1978): 124.

32. Orsini Aarón, *Poligamia y contrabando,* 98.

33. Callo, interview by the author, March 18, 2005, Riohacha, Guajira, Colombia. I have also drawn on the following sources: Enrique Herrera Barros (journalist),

interview by the author, February 8, 2005, Riohacha, Guajira, Colombia; Yim Daza Noguera, interview by the author; Edgar Ferrucho Padilla (journalist and former mayor of Maicao), interview by the author, no. 1, February 16, 2005, Riohacha, Guajira, Colombia.

34. Yim Daza Noguera, interview by the author.

35. Chijo, "recordings," family archive, n.d. (hereafter "Chijo's recordings"), tape 4, side B; and Arique Britto, interview by the author, no. 3.

36. Raúl, interview by the author, March 16, 2005, Riohacha, Guajira.

37. Silvio, interview by the author, March 15, 2005, Riohacha, Guajira.

38. Araújo Noguera, "Rafael Escalona, el hombre y el mito," 279.

39. Justiniano Mendoza, interview by the author.

40. Raúl, interview by the author.

41. On coffee consumption, see Michael Jiménez, "From Plantation to Cup: Coffee and Capitalism in the United States, 1830–1930," in *Coffee, Society, and Power in Latin America,* ed. William Roseberry, Lowell Gudmundson, and Mario Samper Kutschbach (Baltimore: Johns Hopkins University Press, 1995), 38–63.

42. Eric Hobsbawm, *Primitive Rebels: Studies in Archaic Forms of Social Movement in the 19th and 20th Centuries* (Manchester: Manchester University Press, 1959), 24.

43. Orsini Aarón, *Poligamia y contrabando,* 97; Losonczy, "De cimarrones a colonos y contrabandistas," 235–36.

44. Justiniano Mendoza, interview by the author.

45. Justiniano Mendoza, interview by the author.

46. González Plazas, *Pasado y presente del contrabando en La Guajira,* 53.

47. Rafael Enrique "Arique" Britto, interview by the author, no. 1, January 16, 2005, San Juan del Cesar, Guajira, Colombia.

48. Arique Britto, interview by the author, no. 2. Here are the song's lyrics: "Ahí viene la perra / que me iba mordiendo,/ perra valiente / que mordió a su dueño." Alejo Durán, "La perra," in Alejo Durán, *Lo Mejor de Alejo Durán,* n.d. For more on this song, see Bernardo A. Ciro Gómez, "'Murió don Heriberto y los tambores y los cantos cesaron': Una aproximación a la tambora en el contexto de las políticas culturales de la Revolución en Marcha en Colombia, 1930–1946," *Trashumante. Revista Americana de Historia Social* 14 (2019): 156.

49. On smugglers as aspirational figures, see Orsini Aarón, *Poligamia y contrabando,* 101.

50. On Juya and Pulowi, see Michel Perrin, *The Way of the Dead Indians: Guajiro Myths and Symbols* (1976; reprint, Austin: University of Texas, 1987), 83–84. On "counter-acculturation" in the Guajira, see Acosta Medina, "El hombre guajiro," 73.

51. On "*la mosca,*" see "Intelligence Report No. 4 on Coffee Contraband in Colombia by National Customs, Special Investigations Division," October 28, 1975, in AGN, Min. Interior, Sec. Gen., box 85, folder 3, folio 139.

52. Justiniano Mendoza, interview by the author.

53. Orsini Aarón, *Poligamia y contrabando,* 102–3.

54. Diana Bocarejo, "Thinking with (Il)legality: The Ethics of Living with Bonanzas," *Current Anthropology* 59, no. 18 (April 2018): 49.

55. Here I take inspiration from a similar argument that Charles Bergquist makes about coffee growers in the *eje cafetero,* in *Labor in Latin America,* 324–25.

56. For the Wayuu code of honor see Wilder Guerra Curvelo, *La disputa y la palabra: La ley en la Sociedad Wayuu* (Bogotá: Ministerio de Cultura, 2001).

57. Losonczy, "De cimarrones a colonos y contrabandistas," 238.

58. Molano et al., "Diagnóstico de la Sierra Nevada de Santa Marta, Descripción testimonial," 140.

59. Arique Britto, interview by the author, no. 2.

60. Justiniano Mendoza, interview by the author; Arique Britto, interview by the author, no. 2.

61. Arique Britto, interview by the author, no. 3.

62. Justiniano Mendoza, interview by the author; Arique Britto, interview by the author, no. 3; Daza Noguera, interview by the author.

63. Edward Muir, *Mad Blood Stirring: Vendetta in Renaissance Italy* (Baltimore: Johns Hopkins University Press, 1993), 31–32.

64. Acosta Medina, "El hombre guajiro," 74.

65. Molano et al., "Diagnóstico de la Sierra Nevada de Santa Marta, Descripción testimonial," 9.

66. Molano et al., "Diagnóstico de la Sierra Nevada de Santa Marta, Descripción testimonial," 9; Losonczy, "De cimarrones a colonos y contrabandistas," 237.

67. Losonczy, "De cimarrones a colonos y contrabandistas," 232.

68. Michael Taussig, *The Devil and Commodity Fetishism in South America* (1980; reprint, Chapel Hill: University of North Carolina Press, 2010), 18.

69. Jorge Alejandro González Cuello, *Aquel Corral de Piedras: Un legado de la humanidad* (Bogotá: Editorial Carrera 7a, Ltda., 2003).

70. Sáenz Rovner, "La prehistoria del narcotráfico en Colombia."

71. John Charles Chasteen, *Getting High: Marijuana through the Ages* (New York: Rowman & Littlefield, 2016), 59.

72. Vera Rubin and Lambros Comitas, *Ganja in Jamaica: A Medical Anthropological Study of Chronic Marijuana Use* (The Hague: Mouton, 1975).

73. All quotations from Pebo, interview by the author, June 25, 2006, Taganga, Magdalena, Colombia.

74. William Partridge, "Exchange Relations in a Community on the North Coast of Colombia, with Special Reference to Cannabis" (PhD dissertation, University of Florida, 1974), 42–43; Molano et al., "Diagnóstico de la Sierra Nevada de Santa Marta, Descripción testimonial," 5; Augusto Pérez Gómez, ed., *Sustancias psicoativas: Historia del consumo en Colombia,* 2nd ed. (1988; reprint, Bogotá: Tercer Mundo Editores, 1994), 47.

75. Sáenz Rovner, "La prehistoria de la marihuana en Colombia," 212–15.

76. Arango and Child, *Narcotráfico,* 75; Saénz Rovner, "La prehistoria de la marihuana en Colombia."

77. Fernando Vallejo, *Barba Jacob el mensajero* (México, DF: Editorial Séptimo Círculo, 1984), 68.

78. Manuel Mejía Vallejo, *El hombre que parecía un fantasma* (Medellín: Biblioteca Pública Piloto, 1984).

79. María Mercedes Carranza, "Porfirio Barba Jacob: El hombre que parecía un caballo," *El País,* March 9, 2002.

80. On "La dama de los cabellos ardientes," see Porfirio Barba Jacob, *Poesía completa* (Bogotá: Arango Editores, El Áncora Editores, 1988).

81. Vallejo, *Barba Jacob el mensajero,* 125.

82. Arango and Child, *Narcotráfico,* 81.

83. On the Geneva Convention of 1925, see William C. Plouffe Jr., "1925 Geneva Convention on Opium and Other Drugs," in *Encyclopedia of Drug Policy,* ed. Mark A. Kleiman and James E. Hawdon (Washington DC: Sage, 2011); and on the Geneva Convention of 1931, see Quincy Wright, "The Narcotics Convention of 1931," *American Journal of International Law* 28, no. 3 (July 1934): 475–86. For Colombia's ratification of Geneva Conventions, see "Decreto 896 de 1947," *Diario oficial* año LXXXII, no. 26387 (March 25, 1947), 6.

84. "Decreto 896 de 1947"; "Decreto 1858, 1951," *Diario oficial* año LXXXVIII, no. 27817 (January 31, 1952), 1.

85. "Decreto 14 de 1955," *Diario oficial* año XCI, no. 28661 (January 19, 1955), 1.

86. Alonso Salazar, *La cola del lagarto: Drogas y narcotráfico en la sociedad colombiana* (Medellín: Corporación Región, 1998), 19.

87. AGN, Colonial Penal Araracuara, no. 95, box 1; no. 196, box 6; no. 244, box 8; no. 245, box 8; no. 329, box 10; no. 385, box 12; no. 417, box 13; no. 428, box 13; no. 451, box 14; no. 453, box 14; no. 496, box 15; no. 533, box 16; no. 615, box 18; no. 617, box 18; no. 629, box 19; no. 706, box 21; no. 747, box 22; no. 770, box 23; no. 775, box 23; no. 808, box 24; no. 841, box 25; no. 1005, box 29; no. 1092, box 32; no. 1108, box 32, no. 1214, box 35.

88. Case 706, 1954–1958, in AGN, Colonia Penal Araracuara, no. 45, box 21.

89. Sáenz Rovner, "La prehistoria de la marihuana en Colombia," 215–17.

90. For a similar case of peasant soldiers smoking marijuana in Mexico during the Revolution, see Curtis Marez, *Drug Wars: The Political Economy of Narcotics* (Minneapolis: University of Minnesota Press, 2004), 105–45.

91. Hobsbawm, *Primitive Rebels,* 13–29.

92. Carlos Aguirre and Ricardo D. Salvatore, "Writing the History of Law, Crime, and Punishment in Latin America," in *Crime and Punishment in Latin America: Law and Society since Late Colonial Times,* ed. Gilbert Joseph, Carlos Aguirre, and Ricardo D. Salvatore (Durham, NC: Duke University Press, 2001), 13.

93. Gonzalo Sánchez and Donny Meertens, *Bandoleros, gamonales y campesinos: El caso de La Violencia en Colombia* (Bogotá: El Áncora Editores, 1983), 54.

94. Sánchez and Meertens, *Bandoleros, gamonales y campesinos,* 47–48.

95. On "moral panic" and the media, see Erich Goode and Nachman Ben-Yehuda, *Moral Panics: The Social Construction of Deviance* (1994; reprint, Malden, MA: Wiley-Blackwell, 2009), 88–108.

96. Álvaro Tirado Mejía, "Cambios económicos, sociales y culturales en los años sesenta del siglo XX," *Historia y Memoria* 12 (January–June 2016): 302.

97. Daniel Llano Parra, *Enemigos públicos: Contexto intelectual y sociabilidad literaria del movimiento nadaísta, 1958–1971* (Medellín: Universidad de Antioquia, 2015), 25.

98. Juan Carlos Galeano, "El Nadaísmo y 'La Violencia' en Colombia," *Revista Iberoamericana* 59, no. 164 (July 1993): 647.

99. "Yo, un poeta, en las mismas circunstancias de opresión, miseria, miedo y persecución, también habría sido bandolero. Creo que hoy me llamaría 'General Exterminio.' Por eso le hago esta elegía a 'Desquite,' porque con las mismas posibilidades que yo tuve, él se habría podido llamar Gonzalo Arango." See Gonzalo Arango, *Obra Negra* (Bogotá: Plaza & Janés, 1993), 42–44.

100. Galeano, "El Nadaísmo y 'La Violencia' en Colombia," 647.

101. Brahiman Saganogo, "Nadaísmo colombiano: Ruptura socio-cultural o extravagancia expresiva," *Espéculo: Revista de Estudios Literarios* 38 (March–June 2008), available at Universidad Complutense de Madrid, available at http://webs .ucm.es/info/especulo/numero38/nadaism.html.

102. Here I am paraphrasing Barba Jacob's aforementioned poem, "La dama de cabellos ardientes."

103. Colombia's demographic transition finally took off in 1951; by 1964, people between the ages of fifteen and twenty-four constituted 18.2 percent of the population, a proportion that kept growing. See Rodrigo Parra Sandoval, *Ausencia de Futuro. La juventud colombiana* (Bogotá: Plaza & Janés, 1978), 26.

104. Cited in James D. Henderson, *Colombia's Narcotics Nightmare: How the Drug Trade Destroyed Peace* (2012; reprint, Jefferson, NC: McFarland, 2015), 27.

105. On 1967 as the year when marijuana consumption first boomed in the United States, see Institute of Medicine, Division of Health Sciences Policy, *Marijuana and Health* (Washington DC: National Academy Press, 1982), 38.

106. Paul Stares, *Global Habit: The Drug Problem in a Borderless World* (Washington, DC: Brookings Institution Press, 1996), 29; Richard Craig, "Operation Intercept: The International Politics of Pressure," *Review of Politics* 42, no. 4 (October 1980): 573; Richard Craig, "Colombian Narcotics and United States–Colombian Relations," *Journal of Interamerican Studies and World Affairs* 23, no. 3 (August 1981): 243–70; Barry Farrell, "The Marijuana Famine," *Life* Magazine 67, no. 8 (August 22, 1969): 20B; Peggy J. Murrell for *Wall Street Journal,* September 11, 1969, quoted in Edward M. Brecher, "The Consumers Union Report on Licit and Illicit Drugs," *Consumer Reports Magazine* (1972).

107. On the five regions involved in the smuggling of marijuana and cocaine, including Bogotá's international airport, see "Apreciación de criminalidad presentada al Consejo Nacional de Seguridad por Policia Nacional: Panorama general, 1967–1972," AGN, Min. Interior, Sec. Gen., box 67, folder 1.

108. Secretary of Health, Education, and Welfare and Subcommittee on Alcoholism and Narcotics, *Marijuana and Health: Second Annual Report to Congress* (Washington DC: US Government Printing Office, 1972), 9.

109. "CND, Agenda Item 6," and "Telegram, 12 OCT 71," in NARA, RG 59 (Bureau of International Narcotics Matters), box 1.

110. Betancourt and García, *Contrabandistas, marimberos y mafiosos,* 48.

111. Rodrigo Echeverri, untitled, unpublished manuscript on the marijuana export sector for Inderena, n.d. (circa 1979), Santa Marta, Colombia, Rodrigo Echeverri's personal archive, Carmen de Viboral, Antioquia. See also Ariel Martínez (agronomist for Inderena), interview by the author, January 21, 2011, Santa Marta, Magdalena, Colombia.

112. Carlos, interview by the author, no. 1, March 9, 2005, Riohacha, Guajira, Colombia; Raúl, interview by the author; Callo, interview by the author; Rodrigo Echeverri, interview by the author, March 15, 2010, Carmen de Viboral, Antioquia, Colombia; Ariel Martínez, interview by the author.

113. Miguel Ángel López Hernández (Chijo's relative), interview by the author, March 10, 2005, Riohacha, Guajira, Colombia.

114. "Chijo's recordings," tape 4, side B.

115. Mantequilla, interview by the author, March 11, 2005, Riohacha, Guajira, Colombia.

116. "Letter from Luis Emilio Plata, officialist Liberal from Riohacha," September 17, 1962, AGN, Min. Interior, Despacho del Ministro, box 34, folder 290, roll 34, folios 23R, 24R; "Letter," October 2, 1962, ibid., folios 1R, 2R; "Telegram," September 25, 1962, ibid., folio 4R; "Letter," August 28, 1962, ibid., folio 41R; "Letter," September 26, 1962, ibid., folio 5R. See also Meña Melo (personal assistant of Guajira's *intendentes* and governors from 1962 to 1978), interview by the author.

117. Callo, interview by the author.

118. For police reports on Santa Marta and Valledupar as stopovers in the circuit of petty commerce in marijuana in the 1960s, see Sáenz Rovner, "La prehistoria de la marihuana en Colombia," 219.

119. Meco, interview by the author, January 17, 2005, San Juan del Cesar, Guajira, Colombia.

120. Enrique Herrera Barros, interview by the author, February 8, 2005, Riohacha, Guajira, Colombia.

121. Callo, interview by the author.

122. Ariel Martínez, interview by the author.

123. Catherine Cocks, *Tropical Whites: The Rise of the Tourist South in the Americas* (Philadelphia: University of Pennsylvania Press, 2013), 13, 51.

124. Jerry Kamstra, *Hierba: Aventuras de un contrabandista de marihuana* (1974; reprint, Mexico, DF: Editorial Grijalbo, SA, 1976), 37.

125. Secretary of Health, Education, and Welfare and Subcommittee on Alcoholism and Narcotics, *Marijuana and Health,* 30.

126. Juan "Ios" Vieira, interview by the author, March 30, 2005, Santa Marta, Magdalena, Colombia.

127. Howard S. Becker, "Marijuana Use and the Social Context," in *Marijuana,* ed. Erich Goode (New York: Atherton Press, 1970), 29.

128. Pablo Astorga, Ame R. Berges, and Valpy Fitzgerald, "The Standard of Living in Latin America during the Twentieth Century," *Economic History Review* 58, no. 4 (November 2005): 784. See also Ewout Frankema, "The Expansion of Mass Education in Twentieth-Century Latin America: A Global Comparative Perspective," *Revista de historia económica/Journal of Iberian and Latin American Economic History* 3 (winter 2009): 369; and Miguel Somoza Rodríguez, "Educación y movimientos populistas en América Latina: Una emancipación frustrada," *Historia de la Educación* 29 (2010): 175.

129. Martha Cecilia Herrera, "Historia de la educación en Colombia: la República Liberal y la modernización de la educación: 1930–1946," *Revista Colombiana de Educación* 26 (1993), available at https://doi.org/10.17227/01203916.5297. See also Laurence Gale, *Education and Development in Latin America, with Special Reference to Colombia and Some Comparison with Guyana, South America* (London: Routledge & Kegan Paul, 1969), 29.

130. Vives, *La Guajira ante el Congreso de Colombia*, 56–60.

131. In the original Spanish: "Con esta noticia le fueron a mi mamá / que yo de lo flaco ya me parecía un fideo. / Y es el hambre del liceo / que no me deja engordá." Rafael Escalona, "El hambre del liceo," 1948.

132. Martín López González, interview by the author, February 14, 2005, Riohacha, Guajira, Colombia.

133. López González, "Cambios en los procesos académicos, políticos y culturales de la sociedad riohachera producto de la bonanza marimbera"

134. "Chijo's recordings," tape 1, side A.

135. On "educational breach," see Parra Sandoval, *Ausencia de Futuro,* 59–60.

136. On rapid urbanization in the 1950s and 1960s, see Fabio Botero Gómez, *La ciudad colombiana* (Medellín: Ediciones Autores Antioqueños, 1991), 83–86.

137. Cervantes Angulo, *La noche de las luciérnagas,* 53.

138. Silvio, interview by the author. See also the documentary *Gamín,* directed by Ciro Durán (1977).

139. Silvio, interview by the author.

140. All quotations from Cervantes Angulo, *La noche de las luciérnagas,* 54–55.

141. Eduardo Galeano, *Memory of Fire,* Vol. 3: *Century of the Wind* (New York: W. W. Norton, 1988), 254.

142. On the value of oral history as providing meaning rather than factual information, see Alessandro Portelli, *The Death of Luigi Trastulli and Other Stories: Form and Meaning in Oral History* (Albany: State University of New York, 1991), 1–26; Daniel James, *Doña María's Story: Life, History, Memory, and Political Identity* (Durham, NC: Duke University Press, 2000), 119–56; and Ronald J. Grele, "Oral History as Evidence," in *History of Oral History: Foundations and Methodology,* ed. Thomas L. Charlton, Lois E. Myers, and Rebecca Sharpless (New York: Altamira Press, 2007).

143. Miguel Ángel López Hernández, interview by the author.

144. All quotations from "Chijo's recordings," tape 1, side A.

145. "Chijo's recordings," tape 4, side A.

146. Germán Rojas, interview by the author, March 28, 2005, Riohacha, Guajira, Colombia. On secrecy as rule of the business in its beginnings, see Esperanza Ardila Beltrán, Álvaro Acevedo Merlano, and Luis Martínez González, "Memoria de la bonanza marimbera en Santa Marta," *Oraloteca* 5 (2013): 55–79.

147. On Guajira's "juridical pluralism," see Orsini Aarón, *Poligamia y contrabando*, 103.

148. Valeria Manzano, *The Age of Youth in Argentina: Culture, Politics, and Sexuality from Perón to Videla* (Chapel Hill: University of North Carolina Press, 2014), 3.

CHAPTER 3. SANTA MARTA GOLD

1. Partridge, "Exchange Relations in a Community on the North Coast of Colombia," vi–vii.

2. On 1976 as the peak, see Ariel Martínez (agronomist for Inderena), interview by the author; ANIF, *Marihuana*, 74.

3. The US Drug Enforcement Administration estimated that in 1978 Colombia supplied 70 percent of the marijuana moved into the United States, a market comprising 26.6 million marijuana consumers. This represented 7,000 to 10,500 tons. See "The US Marihuana Market: Excerpt from the Narcotics Intelligence Estimate, December 1979," *Drug Enforcement* (March 1980), 16.

4. On agricultural frontiers as a "safety valve" for accumulated social tensions in Colombia's countryside, see LeGrand, *Frontier Expansion and Peasant Protest in Colombia*, xv.

5. Germán Arciniegas, *The Knight of El Dorado: The Tale of Don Gonzalo Jiménez de Quesada and His Conquest of New Granada, Now Called Colombia* (1939; reprint, New York: Viking Press, 1942), 38.

6. Arciniegas, *The Knight of El Dorado*, 37.

7. Partridge, "Exchange Relations in a Community on the North Coast of Colombia," 163–74.

8. Partridge, "Exchange Relations in a Community on the North Coast of Colombia," 37.

9. Partridge, Exchange Relations in a Community on the North Coast of Colombia," 133–34, 148–51.

10. Partridge, "Exchange Relations in a Community on the North Coast of Colombia," 151.

11. On the advantages of oral history as a method for recovering memories, meanings, and voices of underrepresented social groups, see Paul Thompson, "The Voice of the Past: Oral History," in *The Oral History Reader*, ed. Robert Perks and Alistair Thomson (New York: Routledge, 1988). For a discussion of conflictive narratives and orality, see Jeffrey Gould and Aldo Lauria-Santiago, *To Rise in Darkness: Revolution, Repression, and Memory in El Salvador, 1920–1932* (Durham, NC: Duke University Press, 2008).

12. Hernando Ruiz, interview by the author, February 16, 2010, Bogotá; Rodrigo Echeverri, interview by the author.

13. Martínez, interview by the author.

14. On contemporary scientific experiments with "native" marijuana varieties in the different microclimates of the Sierra Nevada de Santa Marta, see Alejandro Mazuera Navarro, "Una charla con el gurú de la Santa Marta Golden, la marihuana colombiana por excelencia," *Cartel Urbano,* September 28, 2017, available at https://cartelurbano.com/420/una-charla-con-el-guru-de-la-santa-marta-golden-la-marihuana-colombiana-por-excelencia.

15. Echeverri, interview by the author.

16. Pebo, interview by the author.

17. Molano et al., "Diagnóstico de la Sierra Nevada de Santa Marta, Descripción testimonial," 17.

18. Molano et al., "Diagnóstico de la Sierra Nevada de Santa Marta, Recuento analítico," 23.

19. Raúl, interview by the author.

20. Carlos, interview by the author, no. 1.

21. Josefina, interview by the author, July 4, 2006, Riohacha, Guajira, Colombia.

22. On workers' gaining control over the means of production and seizing the value of their own labor, see Bergquist, *Labor in Latin America,* 324–25; and Angus Wright, *The Death of Ramón González: The Modern Agricultural Dilemma* (Austin: University of Texas Press, 1990), 9.

23. Roseberry, *Anthropologies and Histories,* 163.

24. On new plant varieties as a knowledge set often accompanied by a panoply of other changes, see Perkins, *Geopolitics and the Green Revolution,* 15. For scientific and humanistic definitions of technology, see Mónica Cordovez, "Transfer of Technology to Latin America" (MA thesis, McGill University, 1991), 3.

25. Hernando Ruiz, "Implicaciones sociales y económicas de la producción de la marihuana," in ANIF, *Marihuana,* 116.

26. Echeverri, interview by the author; Ruiz, interview by the author.

27. Cervantes Angulo, *La noche de las luciérnagas,* 21. Indigenous peoples in the Sierra Nevada have not cultivated or consumed marijuana, but grow coca for a traditional ritual called *mambeo* (chewing coca leaves with lime made from seashells). For a foundational work on *mambeo,* see Gerardo Reichel Dolmatoff, "Los Kogis: Una tribu indígena de la Sierra Nevada de Santa Marta," *Revista del Instituto Etnológico Nacional* 1–2 (1950–51).

28. Víctor Mosquera Chaux, letter to the editor, *El Espectador,* July 23, 1984.

29. For the most influential works portraying Peace Corps volunteers as pioneers of the marijuana and cocaine businesses, see Arango and Child, *Narcotráfico,* 123–31; Camacho Guizado, *Droga y sociedad en Colombia*; Betancourt and Luz García, *Contrabandistas, marimberos y mafiosos,* 47–50; and Losonczy, "De cimarrones a colonos y contrabandistas," 227.

30. *Pájaros de verano* (Birds of Passage), directed by Ciro guerra and Cristina Gallego (2018). For critical reviews of the film, see Lina Britto, "La venganza guajira," *Universo Centro* 101 (October 2018): 12–13, https://www.universocentro.com /NUMERO101/La-venganza-guajira.aspx; and Aimar Arizmendi and Jacquelyn Kovarik, "'Birds of Passage:' Indigenous Communities Rewrite the Drug War," *NACLA,* March 11, 2019, https://nacla.org/news/2019/03/11/%E2%80%9Cbirds-passage%E2%80%9D-indigenous-communities-rewrite-drug-war.

31. Martínez, interview by the author.

32. Abby Wasserman, interview by the author via email, January 9, 2019.

33. Abby Wasserman, phone interview by the author, December 23, 2018. See also Abby Wasserman, "PCVs and Wayuu Blamed for Drug Trade," *Worldview Magazine* (spring 2019): 20–23.

34. Wasserman, interview by the author via email.

35. For the op-ed, see Maureen Orth, Abby Wasserman, and Arleen Cheston, "How Narco Movie 'Birds of Passage' 'Tramples the Truth,'" *Hollywood Reporter,* February 14, 2019, https://www.hollywoodreporter.com/news/how-narco-movie-birds-passage-tramples-truth-guest-column-1186566.

36. Maureen Orth, communication with the author via email, January 10, 2019.

37. Patrick Beach, "Drug Kingpin Jimmy Chagra's Daughter Recalls His Rise," *Austin Statesman,* December 26, 2013, https://www.statesman.com/article /20131227/NEWS/312279679; James C. McKinley Jr., "Jamiel A. Chagra, 63, Drug Kingpin, Dies," *New York Times,* July 29, 2008. See also Gary Cartwright, *Dirty Dealings: A True Story of Smuggling, Murder, and the FBI's Biggest Investigation* (Cambridge, MA: Atheneum Press, 1984).

38. Callo, interview by the author.

39. Molano et al., "Diagnóstico de la Sierra Nevada de Santa Marta, Recuento analítico," 23. See also Fundación ProSierra Nevada de Santa Marta (ProSierra), *Historia y geografía de la Sierra Nevada de Santa Marta* (Santa Marta, Colombia: Fundación ProSierra, 1991).

40. Margarita Serje, "La invención de la Sierra Nevada," *Antípoda: Revista de Antropología y Arquelogía* 7 (July–December 2008): 200.

41. Ismael, interview by the author, January 30, 2005, Santa Marta, Magdalena, Colombia.

42. Josefina, interview by the author.

43. Irma, interview by the author, March 30, 2005, Buritaca, Magdalena, Colombia.

44. "Telegram," Valledupar, January 12, 1973, AGN, Min. Interior, Sec. Gen., box 63, folder 1, folio 32.

45. Bienvenido Arroyo, interview by the author, February 4, 2011, Pueblo Bello, Cesar, Colombia.

46. Molano et al., "Diagnóstico de la Sierra Nevada de Santa Marta, Recuento analítico," 32.

47. "Yo tenía mi cafetal, / era una tierra muy generosa. . . . / Hasta que llegó un tipo gordo y muy bien trajeado / que no se quiso identificar. . . . / El tipo gordo me convenció / de que sembrara en mi cafetal / una semilla que me haría rico sin siquiera regarla." Álvaro Serrano, "Yo tenía mi cafetal," in Los Melódicos, *Los Melódicos en vallenato,* 1980.

48. Michael Latham, *Modernization as Ideology: American Social Science and Nation Building in the Kennedy Era* (Chapel Hill: University of North Carolina Press, 2000), 78, 84.

49. Latham, *Modernization as Ideology,* 92, 112; Elizabeth Cobbs-Hoffman, *All You Need Is Love: The Peace Corps and the Spirit of the 1960s* (Cambridge, MA: Harvard University Press, 1998), 71–72.

50. John F. Kennedy, Democratic National Convention Nomination Acceptance Address (July 15, 1960), *American Rhetoric,* http://www.americanrhetoric .com/speeches/jfk1960dnc.htm; Smith, *The United States and Latin America,* 124.

51. "Peace Corps Pilot Program," in NARA, RG 59 (Records Relating to Colombia, Comp. 1955–1964), box 3. See also Diana Rojas, "La Alianza para el Progreso en Colombia," *Revista Análisis Político* 23, no. 70 (September–December 2010): 91–124.

52. "Puntos básicos de coordinación aprobados por el comité coordinador de Cuerpos de Paz para Acción Comunal," July 21, 1967, AGN, Min. Interior, Asuntos Indígenas, box 43, folder 2.

53. Daniel Immerwahr, *Thinking Small: The United States and the Lure of Community Development* (Cambridge, MA: Harvard University Press, 2015), 40–65.

54. Wasserman, interview by the author via email.

55. Jasamin Rostam-Kolay, "'Beautiful Americans': Peace Corps Iran in the Global Sixties," in Jian et al., *The Routledge Handbook of the Global Sixties,* 304–5. See also Stephen G. Rabe, *The Most Dangerous Area in the World: John F. Kennedy Confronts Communist Revolution in Latin America* (Chapel Hill: University of North Carolina, 1999).

56. Molly Geidel, *Peace Corps Fantasies: How Development Shaped the Global Sixties* (Minneapolis: University of Minnesota Press, 2015), ix–xvi.

57. ProSierra, *Historia y geografía.*

58. Molano et al., "Diagnóstico de la Sierra Nevada de Santa Marta, Descripción testimonial," 8.

59. Fundación ProSierra Nevada de Santa Marta (ProSierra), *Los cultivos de marihuana en la Sierra Nevada de Santa Marta. Una reflexión sobre los métodos de erradicación* (Santa Marta: Fundación Pro Sierra Nevada Library, November 1993), 4.

60. Horace Campbell, *Rasta and Resistance: From Marcus Garvey to Walter Rodney* (Trenton, NJ: Africa World Press, 1987), 112; Stephen A. King, *Reggae, Rastafari, and the Rhetoric of Social Control* (Jackson: University Press of Mississippi, 2002), 116.

61. Betancourt and García, *Contrabandistas, marimberos y mafiosos,* 50.

62. "Report No. 2338 by National Police, Department of Guajira," Riohacha, August 26, 1975, AGN, Min. Interior, Sec. Gen., box 85, folder 3, folio 18. See also

"Indocumentados en Venezuela: Éxodo, miseria y muerte," *Alternativa* 204 (March 19–26, 1979), 4.

63. Ruiz, "Implicaciones sociales y económicas de la producción de la marihuana," 117.

64. Meco, interview by the author, January 17, 2005, San Juan del Cesar, Guajira, Colombia.

65. Callo, interview by the author.

66. Cervantes Angulo, *La noche de las luciérnagas,* 237.

67. "Report No. 1442 on Perception of Public Order, DAS," Riohacha, August 26, 1975, AGN, Min. Interior, Sec. Gen., box 85, folder 3, folio 24. See also Manuel Lineros (former head of Incora, Department of Magdalena), interview by the author, January 21, 2011, Santa Marta, Magdalena, Colombia.

68. José Agustín Llaguna, interview by the author, February 28, 2005, Conejo-Fonseca, Guajira, Colombia.

69. Betty Solórzano and Frida de Dangond, "Implicaciones socioeconómicas de la cannabiscultura en los departamentos del Magdalena y de la Guajira" (Honors thesis, agricultural economy, Universidad Tecnológica del Magdalena, 1978), 19.

70. On production patterns in the coffee region, see Bergquist, *Labor in Latin America,* 312–17.

71. ANIF, *La legalización de la marihuana,* 71.

72. Ruiz, "Implicaciones sociales y económicas de la producción de la marihuana," 142–43.

73. They cleared land between January and February; slashed and burned to prepare the soil; built nurseries for seedlings, replicating coffee techniques; transplanted the sprouts when they reached between one and two feet high, and planted them in rows from April to June, according to the rainy season's timing; controlled plagues by hand twice or three times during the growing phase; fertilized with urea and fumigated with DDT; separated out males to avoid pollination of females; harvested after approximately eight to nine months, sometimes five or six; and finally, cleaned the plot and let it lie fallow, as they rarely planted twice in a row in the same area. See Solórzano and Dangond, "Implicaciones socioeconómicas de la cannabiscultura," 22–23.

74. Solórzano and Dangond, "Implicaciones socioeconómicas de la cannabiscultura," 21.

75. ANIF, *Marihuana,* 74; Partridge, "Exchange Relations in a Community on the North Coast of Colombia," 133.

76. Solórzano and Dangond, "Implicaciones socioeconómicas de la cannabiscultura," 30–31. See also "Marihuana: La verdad económica," *Alternativa* 204 (March 19–26, 1979), 12–13.

77. Solórzano and Dangond, "Implicaciones socioeconómicas de la cannabiscultura," 31.

78. Ruiz, "Implicaciones sociales y económicas de la producción de la marihuana," 145.

79. Echeverri and his team at Inderena, after planting the same seed in different ecological niches under control conditions and obtaining different varieties,

concluded that cultivation methods generated the differences. Echeverri, interview by the author. Regardless of the variety, harvesting invariably comprised the same four steps: *raspado* (shaving), tying the plant a couple of inches up from its roots to accelerate maturation; cutting the plants and drying them in the sun to get the seeds; *ordeño* (milking), cutting the flowers by hand or with scissors; and packing in sacks of around thirty pounds each. See Echeverri, untitled, unpublished manuscript, 6–7, 12.

80. For a similar case in the coffee region, see Palacios, *Coffee in Colombia,* 197; and Bergquist, *Labor in Latin America,* 308.

81. Carlos, interview by the author, no. 1.

82. Carlos, interview by the author, no. 1.

83. Carlos, interview by the author, no. 1.

84. Echeverri, untitled, unpublished manuscript for Inderena chapter on commercialization, 9.

85. ANIF, *La legalización de la marihuana,* 76.

86. Partridge, "Exchange Relations in a Community on the North Coast of Colombia," 141.

87. Carlos, interview by the author; ANIF, *La legalización de la marihuana,* 76.

88. ANIF, *La legalización de la marihuana,* 22.

89. Ernesto Samper, "Marihuana: Entre la represión y la legalización," in ANIF, *Marihuana,* 3.

90. Solórzano and Dangond, "Implicaciones socioeconómicas de la cannabiscultura," 73.

91. Mantequilla, interview by the author.

92. "Report No. 2338 by National Police, Department of Guajira," AGN, folio 19.

93. Ruiz, "Implicaciones sociales y económicas de la producción de la marihuana," 166. See also "El tráfico de marihuana: Radiografía de un negocio no tan misterioso," *Alternativa* 168 (June 26–July 3, 1978): 2–4.

94. Carlos, interview by the author, no. 1.

95. Lineros, interview by the author.

96. "List of narcotraffickers" prepared by the Group for Anti-Narcotics Intelligence, Santa Marta (n.d.), in Fabio Castillo, *Los jinetes de la cocaína* (Bogotá: Editorial Documentos Periodísticos, 1987), 131–38.

97. Edgar Ferrucho Padilla, interview by the author, no. 2, February 18, 2005, Riohacha, Guajira, Colombia.

98. Germán Aguilar Epieyú, interview by the author, January 28, 2011, Maicao, Guajira, Colombia.

99. Herrera Barros, interview by the author.

100. Carlos, interview by the author; Raúl, interview by the author; Callo, interview by the author; Echeverri, interview by the author; Martínez, interview by the author.

101. "Report No. 2338 by National Police, Department of Guajira," AGN, folios 17–18.

102. Ferrucho Padilla, interview by the author, no. 2.

103. Alberto Abello Vives and Silvana Giaimo Chávez, eds., *Poblamiento y ciudades del Caribe colombiano* (Bogotá: Observatorio del Caribe Colombiano y Editorial Gente Nueva, 2000).

104. "Report on Criminality in Magdalena from National Police, Department of Magdalena," n.d., AGN, Min. Interior, Sec. Gen., box 85, folder 3, folio 62.

105. Chucho, interview by the author, July 4, 2005, La Paz, Bolivia.

106. Chucho, interview by the author.

107. Arturo Escobar, *Encountering Development: The Making and Unmaking of the Third World* (Princeton, NJ: Princeton University Press, 1995), 9.

108. Elber, interview by the author.

109. José Luis, interview by the author, January 17, 2005, San Juan del Cesar, Guajira, Colombia.

110. Silvio, interview by the author.

111. Martínez, interview by the author.

112. Chucho, interview by the author; José Luis, interview by the author; Herrera Barros, interview by the author; Meco, interview by the author; Rojas, interview by the author.

113. Chucho, interview by the author.

114. Silvio, interview by the author. For more on maritime routes, see *United States v. Cadena,* 585 F.2d 1252, *American Journal of International Law* 73, no. 2 (1979): 302–4; *United States v. Warren,* 578 F.2d. 1058, *American Journal of International Law* 73, no. 1 (January 1979): 143–44; *United States v. Cortes,* 588 F.2d 106, *American Journal of International Law* 73, no. 3 (July 1979): 514–15; *United States v. Williams,* 589 F.2d 210, *American Journal of International Law* 73, no. 4 (October 1979): 701–2.

115. Jeremy Kuzmarov, *The Myth of the Addicted Army: Vietnam and the Modern War on Drugs* (Amherst: University of Massachusetts Press, 2009). See also Lucasz Kamiénski, *Shooting Up. A Short History of Drugs and War* (Oxford: Oxford University Press, 2016), 187–217.

116. On "sky as frontier," see David T. Courtright, *Sky as Frontier: Adventure, Aviation, and Empire* (College Station: Texas A&M University Press, 2005). On the airplane as a tool of US hegemony in the Caribbean, see Eric Paul Roorda, "The Cult of the Airplane among U.S. Military Men and Dominicans during the U.S. Occupation and the Trujillo Regime," in Joseph, LeGrand, and Salvatore, *Close Encounters of Empire,* 271. See also Jenifer Van Vleck, *Empire of the Air: Aviation and the American Ascendancy* (Cambridge, MA: Harvard University Press, 2013), 5.

117. All quotations from K. "Hawkeye" Gross, *Reefer Warrior: How My Friends and I Found Adventure, Wealth, and Romance Smuggling Marijuana—Until We All Went to Jail* (Boulder, CO: Paladin Press, 1998), 49.

118. Yo soy entre las aves el más volador, / porque en las alas tengo más poder, / porque cargo mi pico con disposición / pa' el que me quiera jugar una traición / y con mis garras me sé defender. / Yo soy El Gavilán Mayor / que en el espacio soy el rey." See Hernando Marín, "El gavilán mayor," in Diomedes Díaz and Colacho Mendoza, *Dos Grandes,* 1978.

119. Here I take inspiration from Lowell Gudmundson, "Peasant, Farmer, Proletarian: Class Formation in a Smallholder Coffee Economy, 1850–1950," in *Coffee, Society, and Power in Latin America,* ed. William Roseberry, Lowell Gudmundson, and Mario Samper Kutschbach (Baltimore: Johns Hopkins University Press, 1995), 128. For a contrasting case, see Putnam, *The Company They Kept,* 200–203.

CHAPTER 4. PARTY ANIMALS

1. "Chijo's recordings," tape 2, side A.

2. For the telenovela, see *Diomedes, el cacique de la Junta* (prod. RCN televisión, Colombia, 2015).

3. On smugglers who imported accordions through the Guajira in the late nineteenth century, see Joaquín Viloria de la Hoz, *Acordeones, cumbiamba y vallenato en el Magdalena Grande: Una historia cultural, económica y política, 1870–1960* (Santa Marta: Editorial Unimagdalena, 2018), 25–32.

4. Quotations in Tomás Darío Gutiérrez, *Cultura vallenata: Origen, teoría y pruebas* (Bogotá: Plaza & Janés, 1992), 217–18. See also Peter Wade, "Man the Hunter: Gender and Violence in Music and Drinking Contexts in Colombia," in *Sex and Violence: Issues in Representation and Experience,* ed. Penelope Harvey and Peter Gow (London: Routledge, 1994).

5. Here I take inspiration from Roseberry, *Anthropologies and Histories,* 37–49.

6. Rafael José de Menezes Bastos, "Situación del músico en la Sociedad," in *América Latina en su música,* ed. Isabel Aretz (México City: Siglo XXI, 1980); Thomas Turino, "Nationalism and Latin American Music: Selected Case Studies and Theoretical Considerations," *Latin American Music Review* 24, no. 2 (2003): 169–209; Bryan McCann, *Hello, Hello Brazil: Popular Music in the Making of Modern Brazil* (Durham, NC: Duke University Press, 2004).

7. Peter Wade, "Racial Identity and Nationalism: A Theoretical View from Latin America," *Ethnic and Racial Studies* 24, no. 5 (2001): 845–65.

8. On popular Liberalism on the Caribbean coast, see Green, "'Vibrations of the Collective.'" See also Green, *Gaitanismo, Left Liberalism, and Popular Mobilization in Colombia.*

9. Peter Wade, *Music, Race, and Nation, Música Tropical in Colombia* (Chicago: University of Chicago Press, 2000), 5.

10. Araújo Noguera, "Vallenatología". See also Viloria de la Hoz, *Acordeones, cumbiamba y vallenato en el Magdalena Grande.*

11. For the lyrics of some of these songs, see Julio Oñate Martínez, *El ABC del vallenato* (Bogotá: Tauros Editores, 2003), 207–38.

12. "Me llaman Compae Chipuco / y vivo a orillas del río Cesar / soy vallenato de verdá, / tengo las patas bien pintá, / un sombrero bien alón / y pa' remate me gusta el ron . . . / Soy vallenato de verdá, / no creo en cuentos, no creo en ná, / solamente en Pedro Castro, Alfonso López y nadie más;" José María "Chema" Gómez, *Compae Chipuco,* 1938. On the composition of *Compae Chipuco* in 1938, see

Héctor González, *Vallenato: tradición y comercio* (Cali, Colombia: Universidad del Valle, 2007), 35; on *Compae Chipuco*'s first recording, in 1949, an instrumental version, see Egberto Bermúdez, "¿Qué es y qué no es vallenato?" in *Historia, identidades, cultura popular y música tradicional en el Caribe colombiano,* ed. Leovedis Martínez Durán and Hugues Sánchez Mejía (Valledupar, Colombia: Ediciones Unicesar, 2004), 69.

13. Wade, *Music, Race, and Nation,* 39.

14. Bermúdez, "¿Qué es y qué no es vallenato?" 19–39; Abel Medina Sierra, *El vallenato: Constante espiritual de un pueblo* (Riohacha, Colombia: Fondo Mixto para la Promoción de la Cultura y las Artes en La Guajira, 2002); Guillermo Henríquez Torres, "La música del Magdalena Grande en el siglo XIX: Eulalio Meléndez," in *Historia, identidades, cultura popular y música tradicional en el Caribe colombiano*; Hugues R. Sánchez Mejía, "De bundes, cumbiambas y merengues vallenatos: Fusiones, cambios y permanencias en la música y danzas en el Magdalena Grande, 1750–1970," in *Música y sociedad en Colombia: Traslaciones, legitimaciones e identificaciones,* ed. Mauricio Pardo Rojas (Bogotá: Editorial Universidad del Rosario, 2009); Egberto Bermúdez, "¿Qué es y qué no es vallenato? Una aproximación musicológica," in *Ensayos: Historia y Teoría del Arte* 9 (2004): 11–62; Egberto Bermúdez, "Beyond Vallenato: The Accordion Traditions in Colombia," in *The Accordion in the Americas: Klezmer, Polka, Tango, Zydeco, and More!,* ed. Helena Simonett (Urbana: University of Illinois Press, 2012); Castillo Castro, "Música de acordeón, frontera y contrabando en La Guajira."

15. Gustavo Gutiérrez Cabello, interview by the author, February 4, 2005, Riohacha, Guajira, Colombia. On Gutiérrez Cabello's work, see Hernán Urbina Joiro, *Lírica vallenata: De Gustavo Gutiérrez a las fusiones modernas* (Bogotá: Convenio Andrés Bello, 2003).

16. Abel Medina Sierra, *Seis cantores vallenatos y una identidad* (Riohacha, Colombia: Fondo Mixto para la Promoción de la Cultura y las Artes de la Guajira, 2004), 23.

17. Víctor Hugo Guzmán Lengua, Rosa Esther Pacheco Núñez, and Hermana Josefina Zúñiga Deluque, *Historia de la música en la ciudad de Riohacha, siglos XIX y XX* (Riohacha, Colombia: Fondo Mixto de Promoción de la Cultura y las Artes de la Guajira, 1998).

18. Herrera Barros, interview by the author.

19. Fredy González Zubiría, *Manuel Boy Magdaniel: Alegría, canto y parranda* (Riohacha, Colombia: Fondo Mixto para la Promoción de la Cultura y las Artes de la Guajira; Dirección de Cultura y Juventud Departamental, 2010), 17–22.

20. Alejandra Bronfman, *Isles of Noise: Sonic Media in the Caribbean* (Chapel Hill: University of North Carolina Press, 2016), 4–6.

21. Gutiérrez Cabello, interview by the author.

22. On Ondas de Riohacha, see Ismael Darío Fernández Gámez and Dilia Rosa Gnecco de Daza, *Historia de la radiodifusión en La Guajira* (Barranquilla, Colombia: Editorial Antillas, 2002).

23. Édison Hernández, interview by the author, February 10, 2005, Riohacha, Guajira, Colombia. On Lucho Bermúdez and Bovea y sus Vallenatos, see Wade, *Music, Race, and Nation,* 96–105, 123–24.

24. Darío Blanco Arboleda, "De melancólicos a rumberos . . . de los Andes a la costa: La identidad colombiana y la música caribeña," *Boletín de Antropología Universidad de Antioquia* 23, no. 40 (2009): 102–28.

25. Wade, *Music, Race, and Nation,* 229.

26. For a discussion of hegemonic and subordinate masculinities in Colombia, see Mara Viveros Vigoya, "Masculinidades: Diversidades regionales y cambios generacionales en Colombia," in *Hombres e identidades de género: Investigaciones desde América Latina,* ed. Mara Viveros, José Olavarría, and Norma Fuller (Bogotá: CES, Universidad Nacional de Colombia, 2001), 53–54.

27. González Zubiría, *Cultura y sociedad criolla de la Guajira,* 129. On *bacanería* in Barranquilla, see the documentary film *La bacanería, un estilo de vida,* directed by Hugo González Montalvo (1999).

28. Callo, interview by author.

29. Guillermo Henríquez Torres, *Cienagua: La música del otro valle; Zona bananera del Magdalena, siglos XVIII, XIX, XX* (Barranquilla, Colombia: Editorial La Iguana Ciega, 2013).

30. *Vallenato* scholar Tomás Darío Gutiérrez disagrees with Araújo Noguera about the common origins of *colitas* and *vallenato* music. According to Gutiérrez *colitas* were animated with accordion, bass guitar, and snare drums, three instruments used not to play *vallenato* music but only Europeans genres such as waltzes and fox trots. In addition, *colitas* were a tradition only in the heart of the great valley, between Valledupar and Fonseca, and never spread to the rest of the Greater Magdalena region, as Araújo Noguera suggested. See Gutiérrez, *Valledupar.*

31. Araújo Noguera, "Vallenatología," 30.

32. José Antonio Figueroa, *Realismo mágico, vallenato y violencia política en el Caribe colombiano* (Bogotá: Instituto Colombiano de Antropología e Historia, 2009), 132–34.

33. Oñate Martínez, *El ABC del vallenato,* 139–44.

34. Araújo Noguera, "Vallenatología," 32–38.

35. Gutiérrez Cabello, interview by the author.

36. Araújo Noguera, "Vallenatología," 38.

37. Araújo Noguera, "Vallenatología," 38. See also Deibys Carrasquilla Baza, "Entre las tradiciones de la tierra y los sonidos industrializados: Música tradicional e industrias culturales en el Caribe colombiano," in *Pensando la región: Etnografías propias para la construcción de un discurso regional,* ed. Fabio Silva Vallejo (Santa Marta, Colombia: Universidad del Magdalena, 2007).

38. Figueroa, *Realismo mágico, vallenato y violencia política en el Caribe colombiano,* 130–40.

39. Figueroa, *Realismo mágico, vallenato y violencia política en el Caribe colombiano,* 139.

40. Araújo Noguera, "Vallenatología," 74.

41. Gutiérrez Cabello, interview by the author.

42. One school maintains that the word *vallenato* has colonial origins and was used to distinguish the Indians of the hinterlands from those of other areas along the coast, and literally meant "native from the valley" (*nato del valle*, or *valle-nato*). The other school argues that the term emerged in republican times as a pejorative given to cowboys because popular belief had it that mosquito bites infected them with vitiligo, making their skins look like those of baby whales (*ballenatos* in Spanish). See Viloria de la Hoz, *Acordeones, cumbiamba y vallenato en el Magdalena Grande*, 71-86. See also Gutiérrez, *Cultura vallenata: Origen, teoría y pruebas*; Ciro Quiroz Otero, *Vallenato, hombre y canto* (Bogotá: Ícaro Editores, 1983); and Álvaro Castro Socarrás, "Mitos, leyendas y tradiciones vallenatas," *Desarrollo Indoamericano* 34 (2000): 67–73.

43. Gutiérrez Cabello, interview by the author.

44. On *Vallenatología* as the foundational scholarly work on vallenato, see Marina Quintero, "La palabra de 'La Cacica': Exégesis de una tradición," in *Identidad vallenata* (Medellín: Facultad de Educación, Universidad de Antioquia, 2006).

45. Oñate Martínez, *El ABC del vallenato*, 226.

46. Alfonso López Michelsen, "Elogio del vallenato," in *Los últimos días de López y otros escritos* (Bogotá: Banco Popular, 1974), 311–21.

47. Araújo Noguera, "Vallenatología," 30–33.

48. Jacques Gilard, "Vallenato, ¿cuál tradición narrativa?" in *Huellas: Revista de la Universidad del Norte* 19 (1987): 59–68; Ana María Ochoa Gautier, "García Márquez, Macondismo, and the Soundscapes of Vallenato," *Popular Music* 24, no. 2 (2005): 207–22.

49. Jacques Gilard, "¿Crescencio o don Toba? Falsos interrogantes y verdaderas respuestas sobre el vallenato," *Huellas: Revista de la Universidad del Norte* 37 (1993): 28–34.

50. Wade, *Music, Race, and Nation*, 105. On popular music and literary production, see Ana María Ochoa Gautier, "Sonic Transculturation, Epistemologies of Purification, and the Aural Public Sphere in Latin America," *Social Identities* 12, no. 6 (November 2006): 803–25.

51. "Alerta, alerta, Vallenato, / mira que ahí viene la Guajira / lo comentaba Pedro Castro / lo comentaba Pedro Castro / que el gran desierto se avecina ... Y entonces, / el pasto verde que hay en tu región / será cambiado por tuna y cardón / y el verde intenso de tu algodonal / no será visto allá en Valledupar (bis) ... / Destruyeron de manera irresponsable / los bosques de dividivi, tu barrera natural / y tumbaron esos grandes cafetales." Julio Oñate, "La profecía," in Hermanos Zuleta, *Tierra de cantores*, 1978.

52. Here I take inspiration from Roseberry, *Anthropologies and Histories*, 37.

53. For drug trafficking and the failed promises of modernization, see Roldán, "Cocaine and the 'Miracle' of Modernity in Medellín."

54. Carlos, interview by the author, no. 2, March 11, 2005, Riohacha, Guajira, Colombia.

55. "Suggestions on national security, DAS, Department of Cesar," Valledupar, August 26, 1975, AGN, Min. Interior, Sec. Gen., box 85, folder 3, folio 32.

56. López González, interview by the author. See also López González, "Cambios en los procesos académicos, políticos y culturales de la sociedad riohachera producto de la bonanza marimbera, 1975–1985."

57. López Hernández, "Sociopatología de la vida cotidiana en tres tiempos"; and González Zubiría, *Cultura y sociedad criolla de la Guajira.*

58. Callo, interview by the author.

59. Daza Sierra, "Marihuana, sociedad y Estado en la Guajira," 53.

60. Carlos, interview by the author, no. 1.

61. "Chijo's Recordings," tape 2, side A.

62. Germán Barros (cockfight pit owner), interview by the author, July 2, 2006, Riohacha, Guajira, Colombia; Abel Medina Sierra (cultural critic and vallenato scholar), interview by the author, June 28, 2006, Riohacha, Guajira, Colombia. On the term *culo-pullú,* see Abel Medina Sierra, "El cachafuera: Radiografía de un estilo de vida," *Jepiriana* 2, no. 2 (1999): 8–12.

63. Pierre Bourdieu, *Distinction: A Social Critique of the Judgement of Taste* (Cambridge, MA: Harvard University Press, 1984), 5–6.

64. Wilfredo Deluque, interview by the author, March 18, 2005, Riohacha, Guajira, Colombia.

65. Oscar Escamilla, *Narcoextravagancia: Historias insólitas del narcotráfico* (Bogotá: Aguilar, 2002), 89.

66. Juan Gossaín, *La mala hierba* (Bogotá: Plaza y Janés, 1981), 169.

67. Escamilla, *Narcoextravagancia,* 127–28.

68. On renown as a *parrandero* as a great source of prestige for men on the Colombian Pacific and Caribbean coasts, see Wade, "Man the Hunter," 124.

69. Rojas, interview by the author.

70. On *piqueria,* see Oñate Martínez, *El ABC del vallenato,* 155–206. On the legendary *piqueria* between Emiliano 'El Viejo Mile' Zuleta and Lorenzo Morales, which occurred in episodes over a decade and produced the internationally famous song "La gota fría," see Alberto Salcedo Ramos, *La eterna parranda: Crónicas 1997–2011* (Bogotá: Aguilar, 2011), 39–81.

71. Sergio Moya Molina, interview by the author, February 3, 2011, Valledupar, Cesar, Colombia.

72. Moya Molina, interview by the author.

73. For examples, listen to Hernando Marín, "Lluvia de verano," in Diomedes Díaz and Juancho Rois, *La locura,* 1978; Euclides Enrique Coronado, "Adiós a un amigo," and Isaac "Tijito" Carrillo, "Mi primo," both in Hermanos Zuleta, *Dinastía y folclor,* 1979; Armando Zabaleta, "Jaime Luis," in Hermanos Zuleta, *Volumen 12,* 1979; Juancho Rois, "Homenaje sincero," in Jorge Oñate and Juancho Rois, *Ruiseñor de mi valle,* 1981; Romualdo Brito, "Los ojos no mienten," in Binomio de Oro, *Superior,* 1985; and Diomedes Díaz, "Mi compadre," in Diomedes Díaz and Juancho Rois, *El cóndor herido,* 1989.

74. Lenín Bueno Suárez, interview by the author, February 10, 2005, Riohacha, Guajira.

75. Abel Medina Sierra, "El otro discurso de nuestra música emblemática," in *Primer Encuentro Nacional de Investigadores de Música Vallenata* (Valledupar, Colombia: Universidad Popular del Cesar; La Piedra en el Zapato, 2012).

76. "¡Ay, no joñe! No me importa qué diga la gente / que yo soy un borracho perdido, / sólo quiero que tengan pendiente / que trabajo y que a nadie le pido. / Soy parrandero y qué, / a nadie le importa, / yo soy Lucky . . . oiga, / a nadie le importa, / si hago mi parranda es porque / la vida es bien corta." Lenín Bueno Suárez, "Soy parrandero y qué," in Los Hermanos Zuleta, *Dos estrellas,* 1977.

77. Bueno Suárez, interview by the author.

78. Medina Sierra, interview by the author.

79. Mark Cameron Edberg, *El Narcotraficante: Narcocorridos and the Construction of a Cultural Persona on the US-Mexico Border* (Austin: University of Texas Press, 2004). See also Helena Simonett, "Narcocorridos: An Emerging Micromusic of Nuevo LA," *Ethnomusicology* 45, no. 2 (2001): 315–37.

80. Rito Llerena Villalobos, *Memoria cultural en el vallenato: Un modelo de textualidad en la canción folclórica* colombiana (Medellín: Centro de Investigaciones, Facultad de Ciencias Humanas, Universidad de Antioquia, 1985), 71–112; Consuelo Posada Giraldo, *Canción vallenata y tradición oral* (Medellín: Universidad de Antioquia, 1986).

81. Julio Escamilla Morales, Efraín Morales Escorcia, and Grandfield Henry Vega, *La canción vallenata como acto discursivo* (Barranquilla, Colombia: Universidad del Atlántico, 2005).

82. "Hoy me llaman *marimbero* / por cambiar de situación, / sin saber que yo primero / fui gamín y pordiosero / sin ninguna educación. / Hoy porque tengo dinero, / raudo me sigue el gobierno / queriendo saber quién soy . . . / De nada qué avergonzarme / pueden con gusto llamarme / *marimbero* y ricachón." Romualdo Brito, "El Marimbero," in Roberto Torres, featuring Daniel Santos, *La Charanga Vallenata,* 1981. See also Ismael Darío Fernández Gámez, *Romualdo Brito: Vivencias de un compositor vallenato* (Barranquilla, Colombia: Editorial Antillas, 1999).

83. Llerena Villalobos, *Memoria cultural en el vallenato,* 108.

84. On *vallenato*'s second golden age, in the 1970s, see Adlai Stevenson Samper, "El vallenato en tiempos de difusión," in *Huellas: Revista de la Universidad del Norte* 67–68 (2003): 55–64; Marcos Fidel Vega Seña, *Vallenato: Cultura y sentimiento* (Bogotá: Universidad Cooperativa de Colombia, 2005); González, *Vallenato, tradición y comercio;* and Jorge Nieves Oviedo, *De los sonidos del patio a la música mundo: Semiosis nómadas en el Caribe* (Bogotá: Convenio Andrés Bello, 2008).

85. Bueno Suárez, interview by the author.

86. Roger Bermúdez, interview by the author, March 11, 2005, Riohacha, Guajira.

87. Bueno Suárez, interview by the author.

88. Herrera Barros, interview by the author.

89. Mantequilla, interview by the author.

90. "El festival vallenato: 'Lo ancho pa ellos, lo angosto pa uno,'" *Alternativa* 161 (May 1978): 16–17.

91. Moya Molina, interview by the author.

92. Marina Quintero, interview by the author, October 19, 2010, Medellín, Antioquia, Colombia. On the role of students from the coast who migrated to the cities of the Andean interior as composers, musicians, and listeners of vallenato music during its second golden age, in the 1970s, see Marina Quintero, "Octavio Daza: El cantor del Río Badillo, entre el poder liberador de la imaginación y la fuerza evocadora de la nostalgia; Años 70, la invención de una retórica amorosa para la canción vallenata," in Quintero, *Identidad vallenata,* 191–206.

93. Quintero, interview by the author. The quoted lines of the song in the original Spanish: "Salí preocupado / pa' la gran ciudad, / yo venía del pueblo / trayendo en mi pecho / aquellos recuerdos que no volverán." Octavio Daza, "Dime pajarito," in Binomio de Oro, *Clase aparte,* 1980.

94. Quintero, interview by the author.

95. "Me siento orgulloso de este arte / hoy en día mi bella profesión, / desempeño el cargo como autor / algo muy bonito de mi parte / y ahora tengo base pa' cantante. . . . / Y como no tuve pa' estudiar / fueron imposibles mis estudios. / Pero hay cosas bellas en el mundo / que es la inteligencia natural / y cualquier hombre puede triunfar / después brindarlo con orgullo. / No fueron completos mis estudios, / pero soy un buen profesional." Diomedes Díaz, "El profesional," in Diomedes Díaz and Colacho Mendoza, *Los profesionales,* 1979.

96. A reproduction of the diamond-encrusted implant is displayed at Diomedes Díaz House Museum in Carrizal, San Juan del Cesar, Guajira, Colombia.

97. Notes on visit to Zuñiga family, Chijo's next-door neighbors, author's fieldwork notebook, San Juan del Cesar, Guajira, August 11, 2018.

98. Mantequilla, interview by the author.

99. Guillermo Velandia, interview by the author, February 12, 2005, Riohacha, Guajira, Colombia.

100. Moya Molina, interview by the author.

101. Wade, "Man the Hunter."

102. "La parranda es pa' amanecer, / el que se duerma lo motilamos." Lenín Bueno Suárez, "La parranda es pa' amanecer," in Binomio de Oro, *Enamorado como siempre,* 1978.

103. Mantequilla, interview by the author.

104. On *"sentimiento vallenato,"* see Gutiérrez, *Cultura vallenata,* 246.

105. Medina Sierra, "El otro discurso de nuestra música emblemática," 10.

106. "Chijo's recordings," tape 3, side A.

107. "Cuando salga de mi casa/ y me demore por la calle, / no te preocupes, Juanita, / que tú muy bien lo sabes /que me gusta la parranda / y tengo muchas amistades. / Y si acaso no regreso por la tarde, / volveré al siguiente día en la mañanita." Sergio Moya Molina, "La celosa," in Hermanos Zuleta, *Río crecido,* 1974; Moya Molina, interview by the author.

108. Ferrucho Padilla, interview by the author, no. 1.

109. Callo, interview by the author.

110. Moya Molina, interview by the author.

111. Ferrucho Padilla, interview by the author, no. 1.

112. Oscar Hernández Salgar, "Colonialidad y postcolonialidad musical en Colombia," *Latin American Music Review* 28, no. 2 (2007): 242–70; Daniel H. Levine, "Constructing Culture and Power," in *Constructing Culture and Power in Latin America,* ed. Daniel H. Levine (Ann Arbor: University of Michigan Press, 1993).

113. Bueno Suárez, interview by the author.

114. Araújo Noguera, "Vallenatología," 27.

115. Notes on Chijo's wake and *novena,* author's fieldwork notebook, Riohacha, March 14, 2005; Mantequilla, interview by author; and Doris Paulina Zuñiga (Chijo's next-door neighbor), interview by the author, August 11, 2018, San Juan del Cesar, Guajira, Colombia.

116. "Chijo's recordings," tape 4, side B.

117. Wade, *Music, Race, and Nation,* 61.

118. Here I take inspiration from Linden Lewis, "Caribbean Masculinity at the Fin de Siècle," in *Interrogating Caribbean Masculinities: Theoretical and Empirical Analyses,* ed. Rhoda E. Reddock (Kingston, Jamaica: University of the West Indies Press, 2004).

CHAPTER 5. TWO PENINSULAS

1. Donald Neff, "The Colombian Connection," *Time* (January 29, 1979), 22–27.

2. Greg Grandin, *Empire's Workshop: Latin America, the United States, and the Rise of New Imperialism* (New York: Henry Holt, 2007). See also Greg Grandin, "Off the Beach: The United States, Latin America, and the Cold War," in *A Companion to Post-1945 America,* ed. Jean-Christophe Agnew and Roy Rosenzweig (Malden, MA: Blackwell, 2002).

3. Daniel Sargent, *A Superpower Transformed: The Remaking of American Foreign Relations in the 1970s* (New York: Oxford University Press, 2015), 310.

4. William Appleman Williams, *The Tragedy of American Diplomacy* (Cleveland: World Publishing, 1959), 136.

5. On US public aversion to anything that resembled Vietnam, see Michelle Denise Reeves, "The Evolution of 'Narcoterrorism': From the Cold War to the War on Drugs," in *Beyond the Eagle Shadow: New Histories of Latin America's Cold War,* ed. Virginia Garrard-Burnett, Mark Atwood Lawrence, and Julio E. Moreno (Albuquerque: University of New Mexico Press, 2013), 283. On the "illegal drugs portfolio," see Kathleen J. Frydl, *The Drug Wars in America, 1940–1973* (Cambridge: Cambridge University Press, 2013), 10–12. On the early Cold War formulation of US drug control, see Matthew Pembleton, "The Voice of the Bureau: How Frederic Sondern and the Bureau of Narcotics Crafted a Drug War and Shaped Popular

Understanding of Drugs, Addiction, and Organized Crime in the 1950s," *Journal of American Culture* 38, no. 2 (June 2015): 114.

6. Daniel Weimer, *Seeing Drugs: Modernization, Counterinsurgency, and US Narcotics Control in the Third World, 1969–1976* (Kent, OH: Kent University Press, 2011), 215–28.

7. Aileen Teague, "Mexico's Dirty War on Drugs: Source Control and Dissidence in Drug Enforcement," *Social History of Alcohol and Drugs* 33, no. 1 (spring 2019): 63–87.

8. Sáenz Rovner, "La prehistoria de la marihuana en Colombia," 207.

9. Sáenz Rovner, "La prehistoria del narcotráfico en Colombia," 84.

10. Kate Doyle, "Operation Intercept: The Perils of Unilateralism," *The National Security Archive,* posted April 13, 2003, http://www.gwu.edu/~nsarchiv/NSAEBB /NSAEBB86/.

11. Robert D. Schulzinger, "Détente in the Nixon-Ford Years, 1969–1976," in *The Cambridge History of the Cold War,* ed. Melvyn P. Leffler and Odd Arne Westad (Cambridge: Cambridge University Press, 2010), 373.

12. Craig, "Operation Intercept." See also unclassified documents in the *National Security Archive*'s Mexico Project (Kate Doyle, dir.), at http://www.gwu .edu/~nsarchiv/mexico/; and Richard Nixon, "Special Message to the Congress on Control of Narcotics and Dangerous Drugs," July 14, 1969, *The American Presidency Project,* https://www.presidency.ucsb.edu/node/239611.

13. Robert S. Litwak, *Détente and the Nixon Doctrine: American Foreign Policy and the Pursuit of Stability, 1969–1976* (Cambridge: Cambridge University Press, 1984), 50.

14. For a fuller discussion of détente, see Schulzinger, "Détente in the Nixon-Ford Years," 374–75.

15. Michael Latham, "The Cold War in the Third World, 1963–1975" in *The Cambridge History of the Cold War,* 270–71.

16. Frydl, *The Drug Wars in America,* 344–65.

17. For "all-out offensive," see Richard Nixon's press conference on June 17, 1971: "Remarks about an Intensified Program for Drug Abuse Prevention and Control," *The American Presidency Project,* https://www.presidency.ucsb.edu/node/240238. See also Weimer, *Seeing Drugs,* 175.

18. US Senate, Committee on the Judiciary, *Controlled Dangerous Substances Act of 1969: Report of the Committee on the Judiciary, United States Senate, Together with Additional Views,* June 6, 1969 (Washington, DC: US Government Printing Office, 1969), 17–31.

19. G. Gordon Liddy, *Will: The Autobiography of G. Gordon Liddy* (New York: St. Martin's, 1991), 185–86.

20. Richard B. Craig, "Mexican Narcotics Traffic: Binational Security Implications," in *The Latin American Narcotics Trade and US National Security,* ed. Donald J. Mabry (New York: Greenwood, 1989), 28. See also Weimer, *Seeing Drugs*; and Ryan Gingeras, *Heroin, Organized Crime, and the Making of Modern Turkey* (Oxford: Oxford University Press, 2014).

21. For a discussion of definitions of "drug abuse" and the "drug problem," see Domestic Council Drug Abuse Task Force, *White Paper on Drug Abuse: A Report to the President* (Washington, DC: US Government Printing Office, 1975), 15.

22. "Review of the Twenty-Fourth Session of the Commission on Narcotic Drugs," United Nations Office on Drugs and Crime, January 1, 1972, https://www.unodc.org/unodc/en/data-and-analysis/bulletin/bulletin_1972-01-01_1_page004.html.

23. Craig, "Colombian Narcotics and United States–Colombian Relations," 250.

24. "Telegram, October 12, 1971," NARA, RG 59, Bureau of International Narcotics Matter, Colombia Country Files 1970–1978, box 1.

25. "CND, Agenda Item 6," NARA, RG 59, Bureau of International Narcotics Matter, Colombia Country Files 1970–1978, box 1.

26. Henderson, *Colombia's Narcotics Nightmare,* 27.

27. Smith, *The United States and Latin America,* 136.

28. Gootenberg, *Andean Cocaine,* 261–68.

29. On the narcotics coordinator in Bogotá, see "Memorandum on Colombia—Narcotics Program," January 14, 1974, NARA, RG 59, Bureau of International Narcotics Matters, Colombia Country Files 1970–1978, box 4. On the creation of the DEA, see Richard Nixon, "Executive Order 11727—Drug Law Enforcement," July 6, 1973, *The American Presidency Project,* https://www.presidency.ucsb.edu/node/255717.

30. Craig, "Colombian Narcotics and United States–Colombian Relations," 251.

31. "Airgram from American Embassy Bogota to Department of State," December 18, 1975, NARA, RG 59, Bureau of International Narcotics Matters, Colombia Country Files 1970–1978, box 4.

32. "Apreciación de criminalidad presentada al Consejo Nacional de Seguridad por Policía Nacional: Panorama General, 1967–1972," AGN, Min. Interior, Sec. Gen., box 67, folder 1.

33. "Telegram Bogotá 05340 Jun 73 from ambassador to sec of state," NARA, RG 59, Bureau of International Narcotics Matters, Colombia Country Files 1970–1978, box 5.

34. Decree 1188 of 1974, in *Diario Oficial,* No. 34.116, July 8, 1974, https://www.minjusticia.gov.co/portals/0/MJD/docs/decreto_1188_1974.htm; "Telegram from Embassy to Sec. of State," October 1974, NARA, RG 59, Bureau of International Narcotics Matter, Colombia Country Files 1970–1978, box 5.

35. For the extraordinary decree 659 of 1974, which reformed the National Security Council, see "Consejo de Seguridad, Acta No. 3 de 1974," AGN, Min. Interior, Sec. Gen., box 77, folder 1.

36. "Memorandum Colombia—Narcotics Program," January 14, 1974, NARA, RG 59, Bureau of International Narcotics Matters, Colombia Country Files 1970–1978, box 4.

37. "Telegram from NCAP," NARA, RG 59, Bureau of International Narcotics Matter, Colombia Country Files 1970–1978, box 5.

38. David Musto and Pamela Korsmeyer, *The Quest for Drug Control: Politics and Federal Policy in a Period of Increasing Substance Abuse, 1963–1981* (New Haven: Yale University Press, 2002), xx.

39. "Telegram from Sec. of State to Embassy," October 1974, NARA, RG 59, Bureau of International Narcotics Matters, Colombia Country Files 1970–1978, box 4.

40. "Telegram Bogota 08755" from Embassy to Secretary of State, October 1974, NARA, RG 59, Bureau of International Narcotics Matter, Colombia Country Files 1970–1978, box 5.

41. For his biography, see Fernando Mayorga García, *Alfonso López Michelsen, el retrato del intelectual* (Bogotá: Editorial Universidad del Rosario, 2008).

42. On *respice similia,* see Arlene Tickner and Sandra Borda, "Las relaciones internacionales en Colombia: Creación, consolidación y producción disciplinaria," in *Relaciones internacionales y política exterior de Colombia,* ed. Sandra Borda y Arlene Tickner (Bogotá: Universidad de los Andes, 2011), 28; and Luis Dallanegra Pedraza, "Claves de la política exterior de Colombia," *Latinoamérica: Revista de Estudios Latinoamericanos* 54 (August 2012): 37–73.

43. "Memorandum for the CCINC Coordinating Subcommittee," November 14, 1974, NARA, RG 59, Bureau of International Narcotics Matter, Colombia Country Files 1970–1978, box 5.

44. On Matallana's measures against corruption and complicity with the drug trade, see Eduardo Sáenz Rovner, "Estudio de caso de la diplomacia antinarcóticos entre Colombia y los Estados Unidos (gobierno de Alfonso López Michelsen, 1974–1978)," *Documento Escuela de Administración y Contaduría* 13 (July 2012): 7. On the US Embassy's satisfaction with López Michelsen's decision, see "Telegram Bogota OCT 74," NARA, RG 59, Bureau of International Narcotics Matter, Colombia Country Files 1970–1978, box 5. For more on counterinsurgency, see Francisco Leal Buitrago, *La inseguridad de la seguridad: Colombia, 1958–2005* (Bogotá: Planeta, 2006).

45. Agency for International Development (Office of Public Safety), "Termination Phase-Out Study: Public Safety Project, Colombia, April 1974," *National Security Archive,* box Colombia. For more on the NSA, https://nsarchive.gwu.edu/about.

46. For the full plan, see "Consejo de Seguridad, Acta No. 3 de 1974."

47. "Telegram de AMB a Sec. of State, NOV 75"; "Telegram," September 1975, both in NARA, RG 59, Bureau of International Narcotics Matter, Colombia Country Files 1970–1978, box 4.

48. Francisco Leal Buitrago, *El oficio de la guerra: La seguridad nacional en Colombia* (Bogotá: Tercer Mundo Editores and IEPRI, 1994), 12–22.

49. For a concise summary of the guerrillas' origins, see Hylton, *Evil Hour in Colombia,* 56–66. See also Eduardo Pizarro Leongómez, *Las FARC (1949–1966): De la autodefensa a la combinación de todas las formas de lucha* (Bogotá: Tercer Mundo Editores, 1991); Palacios, *Between Legitimacy and Violence,* 170–213; and Karl, *Forgotten Peace,* 207–13.

50. Harvey F. Kline, *The Coal of El Cerrejón: Dependent Bargaining and Colombian Policy-Making* (College Park: Pennsylvania State University Press, 1987).

51. For critical perspectives on El Cerrejón, see Amylkar Acosta, *Glosas al contrato del Cerrejón* (Medellín: Editorial Lealon, 1981); Luis Carlos Galán, *Los carbones de Colombia* (Bogotá: Editorial Oveja Negra, 1982); and Aviva Chomsky, Garry Leech, and Steve Striffler, *The People behind Colombian Coal* (Bogotá: Casa Editorial Pisando Callos, 2007).

52. See Letters from Congressman Miguel Pinedo to Minister of Government, in "Informe de visita del DAS a Mingueo," November 29, 1974, AGN, Min. Interior, Sec. Gen., box 75, folder 4.

53. For a journalistic account of the conflict, see "Campesinos en Mingueo: 'Nos quedaremos, pase lo que pase,'" *Alternativa* 41 (July 1975): 13.

54. Zamosc, *The Agrarian Question and the Peasant Movement in Colombia,* 76–77.

55. Zamosc, *The Agrarian Question and the Peasant Movement in Colombia,* 97–103. On ANUC's radicalization, see Silvia Rivera Cusicanqui, *Política e ideología en el movimiento campesino colombiano: El caso de la ANUC, Asociación Nacional de Usuarios Campesinos* (Bogotá: Instituto de Investigaciones de las Naciones Unidas para el Desarrollo Social, UNRISD; Centro de Investigación y Educación Popular CINEP, 1987), 81–212.

56. In 1971 there were 90 land invasions in Magdalena, 30 in Cesar, and 2 in Guajira. In 1974, there was 1 in Magdalena, 4 in Cesar, and 1 in Guajira (the one in Mingueo); see Zamosc, *The Agrarian Question and the Peasant Movement in Colombia,* 75, 111.

57. Zamosc, *The Agrarian Question and the Peasant Movement in Colombia,* 112.

58. Ferrucho Padilla, interview by the author, no. 1.

59. "Riohacha: Lo que tenía que suceder," *Alternativa* 20 (August 1974): 25; "Plomo a los 18," *Alternativa* 22 (September 1974): 10.

60. Ferrucho Padilla, interview by the author, no. 2.

61. "Informe de visita del DAS a Mingueo," November 29, 1974.

62. "Acta No. 10," November 28, 1974, AGN, Min. Interior, Sec. Gen., box 77, folder 1.

63. On the first guerrilla cells formed in various sectors of the Sierra Nevada in the early 1980s, see Adriana Montes Castilla, Luis Martínez González, Nestor Martínez González, William Renán Rodríguez, and Fabio Silva Vallejo, *Memorias y Narrativas: Tres décadas del conflicto armado en el Magdalena Grande* (Santa Marta, Colombia: Editorial Unimagdalena, 2014).

64. "Informe de visita del DAS a Mingueo," November 29, 1974. See also "Letter to Donald Ackerman from Jorge Restrepo Fontalvo, executive secretary of the National Narcotics Council," November 29, 1974, NARA, RG 59, Bureau of International Narcotics Matter, Colombia Country Files 1970–1978, box 5.

65. Alfonso López Michelsen, *El Gobierno del Mandato Claro,* vol. 3 (Bogotá: Imprenta Nacional, 1976), 96.

66. López Michelsen, *El Gobierno del Mandato Claro,* 3, 122.

67. Musto and Korsmeyer, *The Quest for Drug Control*, 165–70. On the visit to Bogotá of Lee Dogoloff, treatment leader of a study group for the Domestic Council Drug Abuse Task Force and one of the authors of the *White Paper*, see "Telegram, December 1975," NARA, RG 59, Bureau of International Narcotics Matter, Colombia Country Files 1970–1978, box 4.

68. "Telegram September 1975 (2)," NARA, RG 59, Bureau of International Narcotics Matter, Colombia Country Files 1970–1978, box 4.

69. "Gerald R. Ford's Special Message to the Congress on Drug Abuse" April 27, 1976, Gerald R. Ford Presidential Library and Museum, https://www.fordlibrary-museum.gov/library/speeches/760368.htm.

70. Douglas Clark Kinder, "Nativism, Cultural Conflict, Drug Control: United States and Latin American Antinarcotics Diplomacy through 1965," in *The Latin American Narcotics Trade and US National Security*, ed. Donald J. Mabry (New York: Greenwood Press, 1989), 12.

71. Kinder, "Nativism, Cultural Conflict, Drug Control," 21–23.

72. On Ford's "new realism" and military aid cuts, see Grandin, *Empire's Workshop*, 62–63.

73. "Operación UNITAS en Cartagena: Amores que matan," *Alternativa* 106 (November 1976): 19.

74. "Un funcionario como hay tantos," *Alternativa* 45 (August 1975): 11; "¿Quién es la mafia? Blanco es, gallina lo pone," *Alternativa* 106 (November 1976): 2–4; "Tormenta ética en la Policía: Rabos de paja a granel," *Alternativa* 80 (May 1976): 12–13; "Peculado en el DAS: ¿General a la cárcel?" *Alternativa* 92 (September 1976): 2–4; "FF.AA.: Negocios generales," *Alternativa* 118 (June 1977): 2–4. For internal correspondence regarding similar cases, see "Memorandums (various)," NARA, RG 5, Bureau of International Narcotics Matter, Colombia Country Files 1970–1978, boxes 4 and 5; and for the official position of the Colombian navy on corruption among its officers, see "Memorandum," June 30, 1975, NARA, RG 59, Bureau of International Narcotics Matter, Colombia Country Files 1970–1978, box 5.

75. "La corruptocracia, nuevo motor del sistema," *Alternativa* 118 (June 1977): 6–7. See also "Crimen y mafia en Colombia: Un sistema dentro del sistema," *Alternativa* 27 (February–March 1975): 2–3. And for articles in the *New York Times* and *Miami Herald*, see Sáenz Rovner, "Estudio de caso de la diplomacia antinarcóticos entre Colombia y los Estados Unidos."

76. Robert Pastor, *The Carter Administration and Latin America: A Test of Principle* (Atlanta: Carter Center of Emory University, 1992).

77. Peter Bourne, *Jimmy Carter: A Comprehensive Biography from Plains to Postpresidency* (New York: Scribner, 1997), 399; "Press clippings of *El Tiempo, El Siglo* and *La República*," June 9, 1977, Jimmy Carter Presidential Library (hereafter JCPL), First Lady's Office, Mary Hoyt's Foreign Trips Files (Press), box 25, folder Colombia, June 9, 1977.

78. Other diplomatic officials attending the meeting were Robert Drexler, chargé d'affaires; Joseph Lee, narcotics coordinator; Donald Johnston, political officer; David Burnett, special agent in charge, DEA; and James Megellas, director

of USAID. See "Memorandum of Conversation," June 9, 1977, JCPL, First Lady's Office, Mary Hoyt's Foreign Trips Files (Press), box 25, folder Colombia, June 9, 1977.

79. For more on the three helicopters, see Bruce Bagley, "Colombia and the War on Drugs," *Foreign Affairs* 67, no. 1 (fall 1988): 79.

80. Donald Johnston, US Embassy Political Officer, quoted in "Memorandum of Conversation," June 9, 1977.

81. Johnston, in "Memorandum of Conversation," June 9, 1977.

82. "Memorandum from Peter Bourne to President," June 20, 1977, JCPL, White House Central Files, Countries Files, box CO-20. See also "Memorandum from Peter Bourne to the Pres," May 1 1978, JCPL, Staff Offices—Office of Staff Secretary, Handwriting File, box 83, folder 5/1/78 [No. 1].

83. "Memorandum of Conversation," June 9, 1977.

84. "Memorandum from Warren Christopher to President," May 12, 1977, JCPL, Brzezinski Materials, Brzezinski Office File, box 122, folder 8.

85. "Memorandum from Secretary of State Vance Vaky to President," June 3, 1977, JCPL, Plains Files, box 12, folder 9.

86. "Memorandum from Peter Bourne to President," June 24, 1977, JCPL, President's Files—Staff Secretary, box 8, folder 10.

87. "Memorandum on Guatemala—State Department Latin American Narcotics Meeting," December 14, 1976, JCPL, Staff Offices—Special Assistance for Health Issues, box 8, folder 3; "Memorandum from Peter Bourne to President," June 2, 1977, JCPL, Staff Offices, Special Assistant to the President—Peter Bourne, box 32, folder Colombia Drug Traffic.

88. For Carter's message to Congress on August 2, 1977, see Jimmy Carter, "Drug Abuse Message to the Congress," *The American Presidency Project,* https://www.presidency.ucsb.edu/node/243653.

89. "Report on Cocaine Policy: Executive Summary from the Office of Drug Abuse Policy," JCPL, Staff Offices, Special Assistant to the President—Peter Bourne, box 32, folder Cocaine Policy.

90. "Cocaine Policy—draft," July 27, 1977, JCPL, Staff Offices, Special Assistant to the President—Peter Bourne, box 32, folder Cocaine Policy Paper, 7/28/77–8/9/77.

91. "Memorandum from Peter Bourne to President," June 2, 1977.

92. "Colombia: Discovery of Large Marijuana Field," June 1977, JCPL, Staff Offices, Special Assistant for Health Issues, box 2, folder 1.

93. "Memorandum," December 24, 1975; "Airgram," December 1975, both in NARA, RG 59, Bureau of International Narcotics Matters, Colombia Country Files 1970–1978, box 4. On Operations Kitchen and Funnel, see Sáenz Rovner, "Estudio de caso de la diplomacia antinarcóticos entre Colombia y los Estados Unidos," 12.

94. Palacios, *Between Legitimacy and Violence,* 239; Leal Buitrago, *El oficio de la guerra,* 67.

95. Alfonso López Michelsen, *El Gobierno del Mandato Claro,* vol. 4 (Bogotá: Imprenta Nacional, 1980), 292–93.

96. Echeverri, interview by the author.

97. On Wolff and Bensinger in the Vatican, see "Statement on Drug Abuse by His Holiness Pope VI," *Drug Enforcement* (December 1977): 45.

98. "Press Release," December 2, 1976, JCPL, Office of Congressional Liaison—Cable, box 259, folder Lester Wolff. See also "Message from Pope Paul VI to the Select Committee on Narcotics Abuse and Control"; "Profile of Lester Wolff (D-NY)," both in JCPL, Office of Congressional Liaison—Cable, box 259, folder Lester Wolff.

99. US House of Representatives, Select Committee on Narcotics Abuse and Control (hereafter SCNAC), *Problems of Law Enforcement and Its Efforts to Reduce the Level of Drug Trafficking in South Florida,* Report to the 95th Congress, 2nd sess., August 1978 (Washington, DC: US Government Printing Office, 1978), 1–4.

100. SCNAC, *Problems of Law Enforcement and Its Efforts to Reduce the Level of Drug Trafficking in South Florida,* 12.

101. Robin Kirk, *More Terrible than Death: Massacres, Drugs, and America's War in Colombia* (New York: PublicAffairs, 2003), 61.

102. Daniel Pécaut, *Crónicas de cuatro décadas de política colombiana* (Bogotá: Editorial Norma, 2006), 251–52.

103. "'Padrinos' militares: ¿Quién divide al Ejército?" *Alternativa* 37 (June 1975): 8–10; "Defensa nacional (1): Los militares y el derecho a opinar," *Alternativa* 48 (August 1975): 20–21. See also Leal Buitrago, *El oficio de la guerra,* 54.

104. "Cambios en las FF.MM. Ruleta de generals," *Alternativa* 109 (November–December 1976): 8–9.

105. "Matallana se enteró de su baja por la prensa," *El Tiempo* (December 4, 1977), 1, 12A.

106. "López habla sobre el retiro de Matallana," *El Tiempo* (December 7, 1977), 1, 8A.

107. For overviews of the controversy, see Pécaut, *Crónicas de cuatro décadas de política colombiana;* Leal Buitrago, *La inseguridad de la seguridad*; and "Retiro de otros dos generals," *El Tiempo* (December 5, 1977), 1, 6A.

108. "*Le Monde* denuncia a Varón Valencia," *Alternativa* 149 (January–February 1978): 10–11.

109. Tirado Mejía, "Cambios económicos, sociales y culturales," 308.

110. "El escándalo de la droga: La conexión colombiana," *Alternativa* 158 (April 1978): 2–4; "López y Turbay rechazan cargos de la TV americana sobre drogas," *El Tiempo* (April 4, 1978), 1B; "Enérgica replica de Turbay al programa," *El Tiempo* (April 4, 1978), 12A.

111. Henderson, *Colombia's Narcotics Nightmare,* 99. See also Sáenz Rovner, "Estudio de caso de la diplomacia antinarcóticos," 33.

112. Peter Bourne, interview by the author via email, May 26, 2014.

113. Bourne, interview by the author via email.

114. Bourne, interview by the author via email.

115. "North-South, LDC's, UN," n.d., JCPL, Plains Files, box 7, folder 2, page 2.

116. Jerry Carrier, *Hard Right Turn: The History and the Assassination of the American Left* (New York: Algora, 2015), 238; William C. Berman, *America's Right Turn: From Nixon to Clinton* (Baltimore: Johns Hopkins University Press, 1998), 42.

117. Patrick Anderson, *High in America: The True Story behind NORML and the Politics of Marijuana* (New York: Viking, 1981), 191–201.

118. On the Parent Movement, see Emily Dufton, *Grass Roots: The Rise and Fall and Rise of Marijuana in America* (New York: Basic Books, 2017), 107–42. On Bourne as a political amateur, see Anderson, *High in America*, 196.

119. Anderson, *High in America*, 7. For more on Bourne's trajectory in the White House and Carter's Office of Drug Abuse Policy, see Musto and Korsmeyer, *The Quest for Drug Control*, 185–233.

120. Jerry W. Sanders, *Peddlers of Crisis: The Committee on the Present Danger and the Politics of Containment* (Boston: Sound End Press, 1983), 241. See also Bruce M. Bagley, "Myths of Militarization: Enlisting Armed Forces in the War on Drugs," in *Drug Policy in the Americas,* ed. Peter H. Smith (Boulder, CO: Westview Press, 1992), 129.

121. "North-South, LDC's, UN."

122. "North-South, LDC's, UN," p. 5. See also "Economic and Political trends in the Caribbean, Key Judgments," April 1977, JCPL, Staff Material: North/South, Interagency Intelligence Memorandum, box 3, folder 8.

123. Pastor, *The Carter Administration and Latin America*; Joseph H. Stodder and Kevin F. McCarthy, *Profiles of the Caribbean Basin, 1960–1980: Changing Geopolitical and Geostrategic Dimensions* (Santa Monica, CA: RAND Corporation, 1983).

124. "Briefs: International Narcotics Bi-weekly Reviews from National-Foreign Assessment Center," June 7, 1978, JCPL, Staff Offices, Special Assistant for Health Issues, box 5, folder 3.

125. "Developing countries: Oil Potential, Policies, and Constraints; An intelligence assessment," November 1977, JCPL, Staff Material: Defense/Security.

126. "North-South, LDC's, UN," pp. 5–6.

127. Julio César Turbay Ayala, *Memorias de un cuatrenio, 1978–1982*, vol. 5 (Bogotá: Editorial Presencia, n.d.), 6–7.

128. Juan Gabriel Tokatlian, "Colombia: ¿La última oportunidad?" *El Tiempo* (June 6, 2007).

129. Decree 2144 of 1978, SUIN Juriscol, http://www.suin-juriscol.gov.co /viewDocument.asp?id=1871155.

130. E. Wilson Purdy, "Cooperation: The Decisive Factor in the War on Drug Abuse," *Drug Enforcement* (October 1979): 14–15.

131. Cervantes Angulo, *La noche de las luciérnagas,* 225–26, 246.

132. "Reply to Turbay," November 28 1978, sent on December 8, 1978, JCPL, White House Central File, Countries Files, box CO-20.

133. On aerial fumigations with paraquat in the Sierra Nevada in 1978 and 1981, see Liliana Dávalos and Adriana Bejarano, "Conservation in Conflict: Illegal Drugs and Habitat in the Americas," in *State of the Wild, 2008–2009: A Global Portrait of*

Wildlife, Wildlands, and Oceans, ed. Wild Life Conservation Society (Washington, DC: Island Press, 2008), 218–25. See also Fundación ProSierra Nevada de Santa Marta, *Los cultivos de marihuana en la Sierra Nevada de Santa Marta*; and Washington Office for Latin American Affairs (WOLA), *La aspersión de cultivos de usos ilícitos en Colombia: Una estrategia fallida* (Washington, DC: WOLA; Bogotá: Instituto de Estudios para el Desarollo y la Paz, 2008).

134. During the first few months, the Turbay administration announced that 27 airplanes and 59 ships were interdicted, 450 traffickers arrested, and tons of marijuana confiscated. Eight months later the numbers increased: detained Colombians, 1,127; detained foreigners, 188; confiscated long-range weapons, 152; short-range weapons, 477; rounds of ammunition, 19,226; vehicles, 268; airplanes, 75; ships, 74; seized marijuana, 2,610,338 kilos; and destroyed crops, 10,217 hectares. See Turbay Ayala, *Memorias de un cuatrenio,* 33. See also US Department of State, Bureau of Intelligence and Research, "President Turbay of Colombia: A six-month appraisal," *National Security Archive,* box Colombia.

135. Cervantes Angulo, *La noche de las luciérnagas,* 225.

136. "Colombia: An Overview of the Drug Problem," *National Security Archive,* box Colombia.

137. "Ejército, seguridad y política: Matallana a la palestra," *Alternativa* 199 (February 1979): 2–4.

138. For more on the ANIF conference, see Lina Britto, "'Legalización o represión': How a Debate in Colombia Steered the Fate of the 'War on Drugs,'" *Social History of Alcohol and Drugs* 33, no. 1 (spring 2019): 88–112. For memoirs of the event, see ANIF, *Marihuana;* and ANIF, *La legalización de la marihuana.*

139. ANIF, *Marihuana,* 9–12.

140. Echeverri, interview by the author; Hernando Ruiz, interview by the author. See also Juan G. Tokatlian, "La polémica sobre la legalización de drogas en Colombia, el Presidente Samper y los Estados Unidos," *Latin American Research Review* 35, no. 1 (2000): 37–83.

141. Ruiz, interview by the author. On these estimates, see Hernando Ruiz, "Implicaciones sociales y económicas de la producción de la marihuana," in ANIF, *Marihuana,* 38.

142. Ernesto Samper Pizano, "Marihuana U.S.A." in ANIF, *Marihuana,* 1–8.

143. Ruiz, interview by the author.

144. For a different interpretation as to why marijuana was the topic and not cocaine, see Tokatlian, "La polémica sobre la legalización de drogas en Colombia."

145. Ruiz, interview by the author.

146. For an alternative account of the controversy, see Tokatlian, "La polémica sobre la legalización de drogas en Colombia."

147. For the congressional debate, see *Anales del Congreso* 79 (September 26, 1979). See also "Héctor Echeverri Correa: Droga y la doble moral," *Alternativa* 236 (October 1979): 16–17.

148. "Hablan marimberos: No a la legalización," *Alternativa* 212 (May 1979): 3–5.

149. "Telegram from SecState to AmEmbassy Bogota, Subject: CODEL Wolff," March 1979, *National Security Archive*, box Colombia.

150. "Telegram from SecState to AmEmbassy Bogota, Subject: CODEL Wolff."

151. "Gringos y hierba: Al que no quiere caldo...," *Alternativa* 209 (April 1979): 14.

152. "Memorandum to several agencies, including DEA, from Narcotics Coordinator Shurtleff," NARA, RG 59, Bureau of International Narcotics Matter, Colombia Country Files 1970–1978, box 4. See also "Telegram Dec 75," NARA, RG 59, Bureau of International Narcotics Matter, Colombia Country Files 1970–1978, box 4; and "Unclassified memorandum from American Embassy in Bogota to Secretary of State in Washington," February 1979, NSA, box Colombia.

153. "Unclassified memorandum from American Embassy in Bogota to Secretary of State in Washington." See also "Unclassified memorandum from American Embassy in Bogota to the Secretary of State in Washington," December 1978, *National Security Archive*, box Colombia; and the case of William Higgins Jr. detailed in "Letter from Patricia Higgins," October 18, 1979, NSA, box Colombia.

154. Turbay Ayala, *Memorias de un cuatrenio*, 64.

155. On the wars over statistics in antinarcotics campaigns, see Paul Gootenberg, "Talking like a State: Drugs, Borders, and the Language of Control," in *Illicit Flows and Criminal Things: States, Borders, and the Other Side of Globalization*, ed. Willem van Schendel and Itty Abraham (Bloomington: Indiana University Press, 2005).

156. Diego Asencio, *Our Man Is Inside: Outmaneuvering the Terrorists* (Boston: Little, Brown, 1982), 6–16.

157. Bagley, "Colombia and the War on Drugs," 80.

158. Bagley, "Colombia and the War on Drugs," 80.

159. Winifred Tate, *Drugs, Thugs, and Diplomats: U.S. Policymaking in Colombia* (Stanford, CA: Stanford University Press, 2015), 12–13.

160. Arlene Tickner and Carolina Cepeda, "The Role of Illegal Drugs in Colombia-US Relations," in *Anti-drug Policies in Colombia: Successes, Failures, and Wrong Turns*, ed. Alejandro Gaviria and Daniel Mejía (2011; reprint, Nashville: Vanderbilt University Press, 2016), 145.

161. Tate, *Drugs, Thugs, and Diplomats*, 54.

CHAPTER 6. REIGN OF TERROR

1. This account of how Peralta met his end is based on Fredy González Zubiría, "Lisímaco Peralta y su 'Lluvia de verano,'" *Arte y Parte* 11–12 (January–February 2010): 12–15. For the song, listen to Marín, "Lluvia de verano."

2. For definitions of violence, see Alberto Concha-Eastman, "Urban Violence in Latin America and the Caribbean: Dimensions, Explanations, Actions," in *Citizens of Fear: Urban Violence in Latin America*, ed. Susana Rotker (New Brunswick, NJ: Rutgers University Press, 2002), 44.

3. Armando Montenegro and Carlos Esteban Posada, "Criminalidad en Colombia," *Borradores de Economía* 4 (October 1994): 1. See also Alvaro Tirado Mejía, "Violence and the State in Colombia," in *Colombia: The Politics of Reforming the State*, ed. Eduardo Posada Carbó (London: Institute of Latin American Studies, University of London; Macmillan Press, 1998), 117.

4. Henderson, *Colombia's Narcotics Nightmare*, 11–17.

5. Henderson, *Colombia's Narcotics Nightmare*, 187.

6. Peter Andreas and Joel Wallman, "Illicit Markets and Violence: What Is the Relationship?" *Crime, Law and Social Change* 52, no. 3 (September 2009): 225–29.

7. Peter Reuter, "Systemic Violence in Drug Markets," *Crime, Law and Social Change* 52, no. 3 (September 2009): 275–84.

8. On violence and competitive adaptation in the drug trade business, see Michael Kenney, *From Pablo to Osama: Trafficking and Terrorist Networks, Government Bureaucracies, and Competitive Adaptation* (University Park: Pennsylvania State University Press, 2007), 103.

9. Alan Knight, "War, Violence, and Homicide in Modern Mexico," in *Murder and Violence in Modern Latin America,* ed. Eric A. Johnson, Ricardo D. Salvatore, and Pieter Spierenburg (Chichester, UK: Wiley-Blackwell, 2013), 20–21.

10. José Luis, interview by the author.

11. Silvio, interview by the author.

12. Raúl, interview by the author.

13. "Report on Criminality in Magdalena, National Police, Department of Magdalena," AGN, Min. Interior, Sec. Gen., box 85, folder 3, folio 62. See also "Report No. 2202 of Assessment of Intelligence, DAS, Department of Magdalena to National Council of Security," Santa Marta, August 26, 1975, AGN, Min. Interior, Sec. Gen., box 85, folder 3, folio 35; and "Report on Appreciation of Intelligence, DAS Department of Cesar, Valledupar, August 27, 1975, AGN, Min. Interior, Sec. Gen., box 85, folder 3, folio 57.

14. On spontaneous urban growth in Latin America, see Jorge Balán, "Introduction," in Rotker, *Citizens of Fear*, 2.

15. Deluque, interview by the author.

16. Henri Lefebvre, *The Production of Space* (Malden, MA: Blackwell, 1991), 73–76.

17. Lefebvre, *The Production of Space,* 416.

18. Jorge Orlando Melo, "The Drug Trade, Politics, and the Economy: The Colombian Experience," in *Latin America and the Multinational Drug Trade,* ed. Elizabeth Joyce and Carlos Malamud (New York: Palgrave Macmillan, 1998), 87.

19. "Mafiosos encarecen vivienda," *El Tiempo* (March 12, 1979), 9B.

20. "Sector financiero: Válvula de escape del dinero sucio," *Alternativa* 254 (February 1980): 20–23.

21. On Barranquilla as a symbol of tropical modernity, see Carlos Bell Lemus, "Barranquilla y la modernización del delta del Río Magdalena, 1842–1935," *Revista M* 11, no. 1 (January–June 2014): 52–65. See also Posada Carbó, *The Colombian Caribbean*; and Wade, *Music, Race, and Nation*.

22. Christine Page, "A History of Conspicuous Consumption," in *Meaning, Measure, and Morality of Materialism,* ed. Floyd W. Rudmin and Marsha Richins (Provo, UT: Association of Consumer Research, 1992), 82–87. See also John Kenneth Galbraith, *The Affluent Society* (1958; reprint, Boston: Houghton Mifflin, 1998), 1–5. On conspicuous consumption as an obstacle to development, see Montenegro and Posada, "Criminalidad en Colombia," 20–22; and Camacho Guizado, *Drogas, corrupción y poder,* 11. For a discussion of conspicuous consumption in the context of underdevelopment, see Jorge Larraín, *Identity and Modernity in Latin America* (Malden, MA: Blackwell, 2000), 181.

23. Ken McCormick, "Duesenberry and Veblen: The Demonstration Effect Revisited," *Journal of Economic Issues* 17, no. 4 (1983): 1125–29.

24. Silvio, interview by the author.

25. Sonia Sánchez, "Causas y manifestaciones del delito en la costa norte del país: Departamentos del Atlántico, Magdalena y Guajira" (honors thesis, sociology, Universidad Nacional de Colombia, Bogotá, 1978), 175.

26. Carlos, interview by the author, no.1.

27. Helena Hansen, "The 'New Masculinity': Addiction Treatment as a Reconstruction of Gender in Puerto Rican Evangelist Street Ministries," *Social Science and Medicine* 74, no. 11 (June 2012): 1721–28.

28. Russell Belk, "Yuppies as Arbiters of the Emerging Consumption Style," *Consumer Research* 13 (1986): 514–19. See also Lee O'Bryan, "The Cost of Lacoste: Drugs, Style, and Money," in *Big Deal: The Politics of the Illicit Drug Business,* ed. Anthony Henman, Roger Lewis, and Tim Malyon (London: Pluto Press, 1985).

29. Page, "A History of Conspicuous Consumption," 86.

30. SL Farapi, *Drogas y género* (Vitoria-Gasteiez, Basque Country, Spain: Emakunde, Instituto Vasco de la Mujer, 2009), 68. See also Lotta Pettersson and Christoffer Carlsson, "Sex, Drugs, and Masculinities: A Life-Course Perspective," in *Masculinities in the Criminological Field: Control, Vulnerability, and Risk-Taking,* ed. Ingrid Lander, Signe Ravn, and Nina Jon (Burlington, VT: Ashgate, 2014), 243–44.

31. Jesús Martín Barbero, "The City: Between Fear and the Media," in Rotker, *Citizens of Fear,* 26.

32. Barbero, "The City," 32. See also Michel Maffesoli, *The Time of the Tribes: The Decline of Individualism in Mass Society* (London: SAGE, 1996), 72–102.

33. Callo, interview by the author.

34. Peter Wade, "Man the Hunter," 126–27. See also Henrietta Moore, "The Problem of Explaining Violence in the Social Sciences," in Harvey and Gow, *Sex and Violence,* 152–53.

35. Pablo Piccato, *City of Suspects: Crime in Mexico City, 1900–1931* (Durham, NC: Duke University Press, 2001), 99–101.

36. Laura Restrepo, *Leopardo al sol* (1989; reprint, Bogotá: Grupo Editorial Norma, 1997), 31–32. See also Françoise Bouvet, "*Leopardo al sol*: La monstruosidad desvelada de la Colombia del narcotráfico," *Amerika* 11 (2014), https://journals.openedition.org/amerika/5538.

37. Nicolás Cárdenas and Simón Uribe, *La guerra de los Cárdenas y los Valde-blánquez: Estudio de un conflicto mestizo en la Guajira* (Bogotá: Universidad Nacional de Colombia, IEPRI, 2007). This vendetta has been the subject of innumerable journalistic articles, in addition to two novels—Juan Gossaín's *La mala hierba* (1981) and Laura Restrepo's *Leopardo al sol* (1993)—and two telenovelas—*La Mala Hierba* (prod. Caracol Televisión, 1982) and *Guajira* (prod. RCN Televisión, 1996). See also "Historia de marimberos" *Semana,* May 7, 1982.

38. Anne Marie Losonczy, "De cimarrones a colonos y contrabandistas," 237–39.

39. "Oligarquía y mafia: Una llave indisoluble" and "Mafia en la Costa: Un fantasma con nombre y apellidos," *Alternativa* 49 (September 1975): 8–9, 12–13.

40. David Riches, "The Phenomenon of Violence," in *The Anthropology of Violence,* ed. David Riches (New York: Basil Blackwell, 1986), 10–11.

41. Cárdenas and Uribe, *La guerra de los Cárdenas y los Valdeblánquez,* 58–59.

42. "Se estrella avión en el Tayrona," *El Tiempo* (January 16, 1979), 7B; "Asesinados 4 arhuacos en la Sierra Nevada," *El Tiempo* (January 30, 1979), 14A; "20 muertos en 48 horas en Guajira," *El Tiempo* (February 6, 1979), 1A, 7A; "Asesinado jefe de la mafia en Santa Marta," *El Tiempo* (March 3, 1979), 1A 6A; "Multa de $1.5 millones a piloto: Dos muertos al caer avión de E.U.," *El Tiempo* (March 10, 1979), Última D; "8 muertos al caer 2 avionetas," *El Tiempo* (March 24, 1979), 6A; "Asesinado official de la Armada," *El Tiempo* (April 3, 1979), 6B; "Se estrelló avioneta: Dos muertos," *El Tiempo* (April 5, 1979), 7A; "Muertos dos militares y 2 traficantes en Guajira," *El Tiempo* (April 6, 1979), 1A, 6C; "Muertos 5 mafiosos," *El Tiempo* (April 25, 1979), 7C; "6 los muertos: Agresores eran narcotraficantes [*sic*]," *El Tiempo* (May 15, 1979), 15A; "Venganza de indios guajiros," *El Tiempo* (May 17, 1979), Última A.

43. For an analysis of twentieth-century Colombia as a case of anomie, see Daniel Pécaut, "Pasado, presente y futuro de la violencia," *Análisis Político* 30 (January–April 1997): 20–21.

44. María Clemencia Ramírez, "Maintaining Democracy in Colombia through Political Exclusions, States of Exception, Counterinsurgency, and Dirty War," in *Violent Democracies in Latin America,* ed. Enrique Desmond Arias and Daniel M. Goldstein (Durham, NC: Duke University Press, 2010), 84. See also Mauricio García Villegas and Rodrigo Uprimy, "El control judicial de los estados de excepción en Colombia," in *¿Justicia para todos? Sistema judicial, derechos sociales y democracia en Colombia,* ed. Mauricio García Villegas, César A. Rodríguez Garavito, and Rodrigo Uprimy (Bogotá: Editorial Norma, 2006), 531–69; and Cristina Rojas and Daniel Tubb, "La Violencia in Colombia, through Stories of the Body," in *Murder and Violence in Modern Latin America,* ed. Eric A. Johnson, Ricardo D. Salvatore, and Pieter Spierenburg (Chichester, UK: Wiley-Blackwell, 2013), 136, 150.

45. Giorgio Agamben, *State of Exception* (Chicago: University of Chicago Press, 2005), 2–6.

46. Mary Roldán, "End of Discussion: Violence, Participatory Democracy, and the Limits of Dissent in Colombia," in *Violent Democracies in Latin America,* 80.

47. On "survival imperative," see Kenney, *From Pablo to Osama,* 121.

48. Mauricio Cárdenas and Roberto Steiner, "Introducción," in *Corrupcion, Crimen y Justicia: Una perspectiva económica,* ed. Mauricio Cárdenas and Roberto Steiner (Bogotá: Tercer Mundo Editores, 1998), 6; Luis Jorge Garay and Eduardo Salcedo-Albarán, "Captura del Estado y reconfiguración cooptada del Estado," in *Narcotráfico, corrupción y Estados: Cómo las redes ilícitas han reconfigurado las instituciones en Colombia, Guatemala y México,* ed. Luis Jorge Garay Salamanca and Eduardo Salcedo-Albarán (México, DF: Random House Mondadori, 2012), 33.

49. Thoumi, *Illegal Drugs, Economy, and Society in the Andes,* 178.

50. Carlos, interview by the author, no. 2.

51. Carlos, interview by the author, no. 1.

52. "Hablan marimberos: No a la legalización," *Alternativa.*

53. Carlos, interview by the author, no. 2.

54. "Mafia en la Costa: De mano con la ley," *Alternativa* 209 (April 1979): 16–17.

55. "Gobernador de la Guajira critica a militares," *El Tiempo* (April 22, 1979), 6A.

56. "Los peces gordos están sueltos," *El Tiempo* (January 22, 1979), 7A.

57. José Francisco Socarrás, "Los penalistas y la delincuencia," *El Tiempo* (March 28, 1979), 5A.

58. Mary Roldán, "Afterword," in *Meanings of Violence in Contemporary Latin America,* ed. Gabriela Polit Dueñas and María Helena Rueda (New York: Palgrave Macmillan, 2011), 236.

59. Camacho Guizado, *Drogas, corrupción y poder,* 92.

60. Here I take inspiration from Gabriela Polit Dueñas, *Narrating Narcos: Culiacán and Medellín* (Pittsburgh: University of Pittsburgh Press, 2013), 8.

61. "Entonces, ¿cuál es la vaina? / ¿Qué es lo que pasa con nuestro pueblo? / El gobierno no da nada / y nos censura por lo que hacemos, / lo que nos da es mala fama / por sus periódicos embusteros." Romualdo Brito, "Yo soy el indio," in Diomedez Díaz and Colacho Mendoza, *Los profesionales* (1979).

62. Michael Taussig, "Shamanism, Colonialism, and the Wild Man: A Study in Terror and Healing," in *On Violence: A Reader,* ed. Bruce B. Lawrence and Aisha Karim (Durham, NC: Duke University Press, 2007), 518.

63. "El terror reina en Barranquilla," *El Tiempo* (March 4, 1979), 3A. On death threats against Cervantes Angulo, see "Las mafias amenazan a corresponsal de EL TIEMPO," *El Tiempo* (March 23, 1979), 1A, 6A. See also "Mafia en Barranquilla: Las culebras se matan por la Cabeza," *Alternativa* 104 (October 1976): 8.

64. Juan de Onis, "Colombia Cracks Down but the Marijuana Gets Through," *New York Times* (March 23, 1979), 2.

65. "¿Por qué son violentos los guajiros?" *El Tiempo* (May 27, 1979), 1B, 4B.

66. Here I take inspiration from Gabriela Polit Dueñas and María Helena Rueda, "Introduction," in *Meanings of Violence in Contemporary Latin America,* 3.

67. Karl, *Forgotten Peace,* 148–81.

68. Igor Goicovic Donos, "Los modelos interpretativos en el studio de la violencia," in *Escrita con sangre: Historia de la violencia en América Latina, Siglos XIX y XX,* ed. Igor Goicovic, Julio Pinto, Ivette Lozoya, and Claudio Pérez (Santiago, Chile: Ceibo Ediciones, 2013), 10–13. See also Álvaro Camacho Guizado, Álvaro

Guzmán, María Clemencia Ramírez, and Fernando Gaitán, *Nuevas visiones sobre la violencia en Colombia* (Bogotá: FESCOL, IEPRI, 1997).

69. Karl, *Forgotten Peace,* 223.

70. Barbero, "The City," 27. See also Camacho Guizado, *Drogas, corrupción y poder,* 94.

71. Ortiz Sarmiento, *Estado y subversión en Colombia,* 22.

72. On violence as the language of politics, see María Victoria Uribe, *Matar, rematar y contramatar: Las masacres de* La Violencia *en el Tolima, 1948–1964* (Bogotá: CINEP, 1990); Ortiz Sarmiento, *Estado y subversión en Colombia,* 291–93; Daniel Pécaut, *Orden y violencia: Evolución sociopolítica de Colombia entre 1930 y 1953* (Bogotá: Editorial Norma, 2001), 589; and Gonzalo Sánchez, "The Violence: An Interpretative Synthesis," in *Violence in Colombia: The Contemporary Crisis in Historical Perspective,* ed. Charles Bergquist, Ricardo Peñaranda, and Gonzalo Sánchez (Wilmington, DE: Scholarly Resources, 1992), 88–91.

73. "Créditos especiales a guajiros," *El Tiempo* (May 21, 1979), Última D.

74. "En Palomino, la 'bolsa de la yerba,'" *El Tiempo* (May 15, 1979), Última A. On "the sea of marijuana," see "Mar de marijuana hallado en la Guajira," *El Tiempo* (May 8, 1979), 1A, 6A.

75. Arango and Child, *Narcotráfico,* 52–60.

76. For a comparative analysis of the marijuana and cocaine businesses in the late 1970s in terms of visibility and social reach, see Andrés López Restrepo, "Narcotráfico, ilegalidad y conflicto armado en Colombia," in *Nuestra guerra sin nombre: Transformaciones del conflicto en Colombia,* ed. Fracisco Gutiérrez, María Emma Wills, and Gonzálo Sánchez (Bogotá: IEPRI, Universidad Nacional, 2006), 416.

77. Arango, *El impacto del narcotráfico en Antioquia,* 100; Fabio Castillo, *Los jinetes de la cocaína* (Bogota: Editorial Documentos Periodísticos, 1987).

78. Arango, *El impacto del narcotráfico en Antioquia,* 100.

79. Castillo, *Los jinetes de la cocaína;* Thoumi, *Illegal Drugs, Economy, and Society in the Andes,* 96; Eduardo Sáenz Rovner, "Los colombianos y las redes del narcotráfico en Nueva York durante los años 70," *Innovar* 24, no. 53 (2014): 223–34; *Cocaine Cowboys,* motion picture directed by Billy Corben (2006).

80. Alejandro Reyes Posada, "La violencia y la expansion territorial," in *Economía y política del narcotráfico,* ed. Juan G. Tokatlian and Bruce M. Bagley (Bogotá: Ediciones Uniandes, CEREC, 1990), 125–27.

81. "Los años de Hernán Giraldo en la Sierra Nevada," *verdadabierta.com,* November 19, 2010, https://verdadabierta.com/los-anos-de-hernan-giraldo-en-la-sierra-nevada-de-santa-marta/.

82. Castillo, *Los jinetes de la cocaína.*

83. Meco, interview by the author, January 17, 2005, San Juan del Cesar, Guajira, Colombia.

84. Silvio, interview by the author.

85. Carlos, interview by the author, no. 2.

86. Carlos, interview by the author, no. 1.

87. "15 muertos en batalla campal entre mafiosos," *El Tiempo* (April 22, 1979), 1A, 5B.

88. José Cervantes Angulo, "La noche de las luciérnagas," *El Tiempo* (May 16, 1979), 8A.

89. Enrique Herrera Barros, interview by the author.

90. Guillermo Velandia, interview by the author.

91. Viveros Vigoya, "Masculinidades."

92. Chucho, interview by the author.

93. Velandia, interview by the author.

94. Ann Twinam, *Miners, Merchants, and Farmers in Colonial Colombia* (Austin: University of Texas Press, 1982), 109.

95. James Parsons, *Antioqueño Colonization in Western Colombia* (Berkeley: University of California Press, 1949), 19; María Teresa Uribe, *Poderes y regiones: Problemas en la constitución de la nación colombiana, 1810-1850* (Medellín: Universidad de Antioquia, 1987).

96. Frank Safford, "Significación de los antioqueños en el desarrollo económico colombiano: Un ensayo crítico de las tesis de Everett Hagen," *Anuario colombiano de historia social y de la cultura* 3 (1965): 54. See also Álvaro López Toro, "Migración y cambio social en Antioquia durante el siglo XIX," *Estudios Demográficos y Urbanos* 2, no. 3 (1968): 351–403; María Teresa Uribe, *La territorialidad de los conflictos y de la violencia en Antioquia* (Medellín: Universidad de Antioquia, 1990).

97. Bergquist, *Labor in Latin America*, 328.

98. Ann Farnsworth-Alvear, *Dulcinea in the Factory: Myths, Morals, Men, and Women in Colombia's Industrial Experiment, 1905–1960* (Durham, NC: Duke University Press, 2000), 181–208.

99. Mary Roldán, *Blood and Fire:* La Violencia *in Antioquia, Colombia, 1946–1953* (Durham, NC: Duke University Press, 2002), 36–41.

100. Arango, *El impacto del narcotráfico en Antioquia*, 93–94.

101. Arango and Child, *Narcotráfico*, 129; Thoumy, *Illegal Drugs, Economy, and Society in the Andes*, 84.

102. Forrest Hylton, "The Cold War That Didn't End: Paramilitary Modernization in Medellin, Colombia," in *A Century of Revolution: Insurgent and Counterinsurgent Violence during Latin America's Long Cold War*, ed. Greg Grandin and Gilbert M. Joseph (Durham, NC: Duke University Press, 2010), 347.

103. Carlos, interview by the author, no. 1.

104. "Unclassified memorandum from American Embassy in Bogota to Secretary of State in Washington," December 1985, in NSA, box Colombia.

105. Henry Salgado Ruiz, "Conflicto agrario y expansión de los cultivos ilícitos en Colombia," in *Análisis histórico del narcotráfico en Colombia: VIII Cátedra anual de historia Ernesto Restrepo Tirado* (Bogotá: Museo Nacional de Colombia, 2014), 255, http://www.museonacional.gov.co/imagenes/publicaciones/analisis-historico-del-narcotrafico-en-colombia.pdf.

106. On authorities burning confiscated cargos in 1986, see Ardila Beltrán, Acevedo Merlano, and Martínez González, "Memoria de la bonanza marimbera en Santa Marta," 64–65.

107. On the violent legacies of the marijuana boom, see Montes Castilla et al., *Memorias y Narrativas,* 75-76.

108. Paul Eddy, Hugo Sabogal, and Sara Walden, *The Cocaine Wars* (New York: W. W. Norton, 1988), 146–70.

109. On Marx and Arendt, see Arno Meyer, *The Furies: Violence and Terror in the French and Russian Revolutions* (Princeton, NJ: Princeton University Press, 2000), 77, 83.

110. Here I take inspiration from Meyer, *The Furies,* 96–99, 111.

111. Meyer, *The Furies,* 116.

112. On "particular regulatory scale," see Abraham and van Schendel, "Introduction," 17.

APPENDIX

1. On the difference between social history and archival approaches to oral history, see Grele, "Oral History as Evidence," 34–40.

2. Here I take inspiration from Portelli, *The Death of Luigi Trastulli,* 1–28; and Elizabeth Jelin, *State Repression and the Labors of Memory* (Minneapolis: University of Minnesota Press, 2003), 56–59. See also Jeffrey K. Olick, Vered Vinitzky-Seroussi, and Daniel Levy, "Introduction," in *The Collective Memory Reader,* ed. Jeffrey K. Olick, Vered Vinitzky-Seroussi, and Daniel Levy (Oxford: Oxford University Press, 2011), 43–44; Renita Coleman, "Oral and Life Histories: Giving Voice to the Voiceless," in *Qualitative Research in Journalism: Taking It to the Streets,* ed. Sharon Hartin Iorio (Mahwah, NJ: Lawrence Erlbaum, 2004); and Paula Hamilton and Linda Shopes, "Introduction: Building Partnerships between Oral History and Memory Studies," in *Oral History and Public Memories,* ed. Paula Hamilton and Linda Shopes (Philadelphia: Temple University Press, 2008).

3. Daniel James, *Doña María's Story: Life History, Memory, and Political Identity* (Durham, NC: Duke University Press, 2000), 137.

BIBLIOGRAPHY

PUBLIC AND PRIVATE ARCHIVES

Archivo General de la Nación, Bogotá, Colombia.
Archivo Histórico del Cesar, Valledupar, Colombia.
Center for Creative Photography, University of Arizona, Tucson, Arizona.
Centro de documentación, Fundación ProSierra Nevada, Santa Marta, Colombia.
Echeverri, Rodrigo, personal archive, Carmen de Viboral, Antioquia, Colombia.
El Espectador photographic archive, Bogotá, Colombia.
Gilberto Alzate Avendaño Library in Political History, Bogotá, Colombia.
Hemeroteca, Biblioteca Luis Ángel Arango, Bogotá, Colombia.
Hemeroteca, Biblioteca Nacional, Bogotá, Colombia.
Jimmy Carter Presidential Library, Atlanta, Georgia.
National Security Archive, Washington, DC.
Rare Book and Manuscript Library, Columbia University, New York City.
Special Collections, Vanderbilt University Library, Nashville, Tennessee.
Tamiment and Fales Libraries, Bobst Library, New York University, New York City.
US National Archives and Records Administration, College Park, Maryland.
Vives, Luz Marina, personal archive, Santa Marta, Colombia.
Widener, Houghton, and Law School Libraries, Harvard University, Cambridge,
   Massachussetts.

NEWSPAPERS AND MAGAZINES

Alternativa, Bogotá
Austin Statesman, Austin, Texas
Consumer Reports, Yonkers, New York
Diario del Norte, Riohacha, Colombia
Diario Oficial, Bogotá
Drug Enforcement, Washington, DC

El Espectador, Bogotá
Hollywood Reporter, Los Angeles, California
New York Times, New York City
Life Magazine, New York City
El País, Cali, Colombia
Revista del Festival de la Leyenda Vallenata, Valledupar, Colombia
Semana, Bogotá
El Tiempo, Bogotá
Time Magazine, New York City
Wall Street Journal, New York City

PUBLISHED WORKS

Abello Roca, Antonio. "El algodón en Colombia." In *El sector agropecuario en el desarrollo de la Costa Caribe: Memorias del foro,* edited by Uriel Ramírez Bolívar. Bogotá: Fondo de Publicaciones, Universidad del Atlántico, 1999.

Abello Vives, Alberto, ed. *Un Caribe sin plantación.* San Andrés: Universidad de Colombia y Observatorio del Caribe, 2006.

Abraham, Itty, and Willen van Schendel. "Introduction: The Making of Illicitness." In *Illicit Flows and Criminal Things: States, Borders, and the Other Side of Globalization,* edited by Itty Abraham and Willen van Schendel. Bloomington: Indiana University Press, 2005.

Acosta, Amylkar. *Glosas al contrato de El Cerrejón.* Medellín: Editorial Lealon, 1981.

Acosta Medina, Ángel. "El hombre guajiro: Descubrimiento y nacionalización." In *La Guajira, pluriétnica y multicultural.* Riohacha, Colombia: Fondo Mixto para la Promoción de la Cultura y las Artes de La Guajira, 2000.

Agamben, Giorgio. *State of Exception.* Chicago: University of Chicago Press, 2005.

Aguirre, Carlos, and Ricardo D. Salvatore. "Writing the History of Law, Crime, and Punishment in Latin America." In *Crime and Punishment in Latin America: Law and Society Since Late Colonial Times,* edited by Gilbert Joseph, Carlos Aguirre, and Ricardo D. Salvatore. Durham, NC: Duke University Press, 2001.

Análisis histórico del narcotráfico en Colombia: VIII Cátedra anual de historia Ernesto Restrepo Tirado. Museo Nacional de Colombia, Bogotá, 2014. http://www.museonacional.gov.co/imagenes/publicaciones/analisis-historico-del-narcotrafico-en-colombia.pdf.

Anderson, Patrick. *High in America: The True Story behind NORML and the Politics of Marijuana.* New York: Viking, 1981.

Andreas, Peter. *Smuggler Nation: How Illicit Trade Made America.* Oxford: Oxford University Press, 2013.

Andreas, Peter, and Joel Wallman. "Illicit Markets and Violence: What Is the Relationship?" *Crime, Law and Social Change* 52, no. 3 (September 2009): 225–29.

Appelbaum, Nancy. *Mapping the Country of Regions: The Chorographic Commission of Nineteen-Century Colombia.* Chapel Hill: University of North Carolina Press, 2016.

———. *Muddied Waters: Race, Region, and Local History in Colombia, 1846–1948.* Durham, NC: Duke University Press, 2003.

Arango, Gonzalo. *Obra Negra.* Bogotá: Plaza & Janés, 1993.

Arango, Mariano. *Café e industria, 1850–1930.* Bogotá: Carlos Valencia Editores, 1981.

———. *El café en Colombia, 1930–1958: Producción, circulación y política.* Bogotá: Carlos Valencia Editores, 1982.

Arango, Mario. *El impacto del narcotráfico en Antioquia.* Medellín: J. M. Arango, 1988.

Arango, Mario, and Jorge Child. *Narcotráfico: Imperio de la cocaína.* Medellín: Editorial Percepción, 1987.

Araoz, Santiago. *Historia del Frente Nacional y otros ensayos.* Bogotá: Editorial Presencia, 1977.

Araújo Calderón, Antonio. *Cuaderno de la historia provincial.* Bogotá: Contraloría General de la República, 1978.

Araújo Noguera, Consuelo. "Vallenatología: Orígenes y fundamentos de la música vallenata." In *Trilogía vallenata.* 1973. Reprint, Bogotá: Ministerio de Cultura, 2002.

———. "Rafael Escalona, el hombre y el mito." In *Trilogía vallenata.* 1988. Reprint, Bogotá: Ministerio de Cultura, 2002.

Arciniegas, Germán. "Eduardo Santos." In Tirado Mejía, Melo, and Bejarano, *Nueva Historia de Colombia,* Volume 1.

———. *The Knight of El Dorado: The Tale of Don Gonzalo Jiménez de Quesada and His Conquest of New Granada, Now Called Colombia.* 1939. Reprint, New York: Viking Press, 1942.

Ardila Beltrán, Esperanza, Álvaro Acevedo Merlano, and Luis Martínez González. "Memoria de la bonanza marimbera en Santa Marta." *Oraloteca* 5 (2013): 55–79.

Arias, Enrique Desmond, and Daniel M. Goldstein, eds. *Violent Democracies in Latin America.* Durham, NC: Duke University Press, 2010.

Arizmendi, Aimar, and Jacquelyn Kovarik. "'Birds of Passage': Indigenous Communities Rewrite the Drug War." *NACLA* (North American Congress on Latin America), March 11, 2019, https://nacla.org/news/2019/03/11/%E2%80%9Cbirds-passage%E2%80%9D-indigenous-communities-rewrite-drug-war.

Arrieta, Carlos G., Luis J. Orjuela, Eduardo Sarmiento Palacio, and Juan G. Tokatlian, eds. *Narcotráfico en Colombia: Dimensiones políticas, económicas, jurídicas e internacionales.* Bogotá: Tercer Mundo Editores, Ediciones Uniandes, 1990.

Asencio, Diego. *Our Man Is Inside: Outmaneuvering the Terrorists.* Boston: Little, Brown, 1982.

Asociación Nacional de Instituciones Financieras (ANIF). *Marihuana: Legalización o represión.* Bogotá: Biblioteca ANIF de Economía, 1979.

———. *La legalización de la marihuana.* Bogotá: Serie Estudios ANIF, 1980.

Astorga, Luis Alejandro. *Mitología del narcotraficante en México.* México, DF: Plaza y Valdes, 1995.

————. *El siglo de las drogas: El narcotráfico, del Porfiriato al nuevo milenio.* México, DF: Plaza & Janés, 2005.

Astorga, Pablo, Ame R. Berges, and Valpy Fitzgerald. "The Standard of Living in Latin America during the Twentieth Century." *Economic History Review* 58, no. 4 (November 2005): 765–96.

Ayala, César Augusto. "Fiesta y golpe de Estado en Colombia." In *Anuario Colombiano de Historia Social y de la Cultura.* Volume 25. Bogotá: Departamento de Historia, Universidad Nacional de Colombia, 1998.

————. *El populismo atrapado, la memoria y el miedo: El caso de las elecciones de 1970.* Medellín: Universidad Nacional de Colombia, La Carreta Ediciones, 2006.

————. *Resistencia y oposición al establecimiento del Frente Nacional: Los orígenes de la Alianza Nacional Popular, ANAPO, Colombia, 1953–1964.* Bogotá: Universidad Nacional de Colombia, 1996.

Bagley, Bruce. "Colombia and the War on Drugs." *Foreign Affairs* 67, no. 1 (1988): 70–92.

————. "Myths of Militarization: Enlisting Armed Forces in the War on Drugs." In *Drug Policy in the Americas,* edited by Peter H. Smith. Boulder, CO: Westview Press, 1992.

Balán, Jorge. "Introduction." In Rotker, *Citizens of Fear.*

Balderstone, Daniel, Mike Gonzalez, and Ana M. López, eds. *Encyclopedia of Contemporary Latin American and Caribbean Cultures* (New York: Routledge, 2000)

Barba Jacob, Porfirio. *Poesía completa.* Bogotá: Arango Editores, El Áncora Editores, 1988.

Barbero, Jesús Martín. "The City: Between Fear and the Media." In Rotker, *Citizens of Fear.*

Barr-Melej, Patrick. *Psychedelic Chile: Youth, Counterculture, and Politics on the Road to Socialism and Dictatorship.* Chapel Hill: University of North Carolina Press, 2017.

Barrera Monroy, Eduardo. *Mestizaje, comercio y resistencia: La Guajira durante la segunda mitad del siglo XVIII.* Bogotá: Instituto Colombiano de Antropología e Historia, 2000.

Becker, Howard S. "Marijuana Use and the Social Context." In *Marijuana,* edited by Erich Goode. New York: Atherton Press, 1970.

Beckert, Sven. *Empire of Cotton: A Global History.* New York: Alfred A. Knopf, 2014.

Bejarano, Jesús Antonio. "Industrialización y Política Económica 1950–1976." In *Colombia Hoy,* edited by Jorge Orlando Melo. Bogotá: Imprenta Nacional, 1996.

Belk, Russell. "Yuppies as Arbiters of the Emerging Consumption Style." *Consumer Research* 13 (1986): 514–19.

Bell Lemus, Carlos. "Barranquilla y la modernización del delta del Río Magdalena, 1842–1935." *Revista M* 11, no. 1 (January–June 2014): 52–65.

Bell Lemus, Gustavo, ed. *La región y sus orígenes: Momentos de la historia económica y política del Caribe colombiano.* Bogotá: Maremagnum, 2007.

Berger, Mark T. *Under Northern Eyes: Latin American Studies and the U.S. Hegemony in the Americas, 1898–1990.* Bloomington: Indiana University Press, 1995.

Bergquist, Charles. *Coffee and Conflict in Colombia, 1886–1910.* Durham, NC: Duke University Press, 1978.

———. *Labor in Latin America: Comparative Essays on Chile, Argentina, Venezuela, and Colombia.* Palo Alto, CA: Stanford University Press, 1986.

Berman, William C. *America's Right Turn: From Nixon to Clinton.* Baltimore: Johns Hopkins University Press, 1998.

Bermúdez, Egberto. "Beyond Vallenato: The Accordion Traditions in Colombia." In *The Accordion in the Americas: Klezmer, Polka, Tango, Zydeco, and More!* edited by Helena Simonett. Urbana: University of Illinois Press, 2012.

———. "¿Qué es y qué no es vallenato?" In Martínez Durán and Sánchez Mejía, *Historia, identidades, cultura popular y música tradicional en el Caribe colombiano.*

———. "Qué es y qué no es vallenato? Una aproximación musicological." In *Ensayos: Historia y Teoría del Arte* 9 (2004): 11–62.

Bermúdez Torres, César Augusto. "La doctrina *respice polum* ('Mirar hacia el norte') en la práctica de las relaciones internacionales de Colombia durante el siglo XX." *Memorias: Revista digital de historia y arqueología desde el Caribe colombiano* 12 (July 2010), 189–222.

Bernal Castillo, Fernando. *Crisis algodonera y violencia en el departamento del Cesar.* Bogotá: PNUD, 2004.

Bértola, Luis, and José Antonio Ocampo. *The Economic Development of Latin America since Independence.* Oxford: Oxford University Press, 2012.

Betancourt, Darío, and Martha Luz García. *Matones y cuadrilleros: Origen y evolución de la violencia en el occidente colombiano, 1946–1965.* Bogotá: Tercer Mundo Editores, 1990.

———. *Contrabandistas, marimberos y mafiosos: Historia social de la mafia colombiana, 1965–1992.* Bogotá: Tercer Mundo Editores, 1994.

Blanco Arboleda, Darío. "De melancólicos a rumberos . . . de los Andes a la costa: La identidad colombiana y la música caribeña." *Boletín de Antropología Universidad de Antioquia* 23, no. 40 (2009): 102–28.

Bocarejo, Diana. "Thinking with (Il)legality: The Ethics of Living with Bonanzas." *Current Anthropology* 59, no. 18 (April 2018).

Bolinder, Gustaf. *Indians on Horseback.* London: Dennis Dobson, 1957.

Botero Gómez, Fabio. *La ciudad colombiana.* Medellín: Ediciones Autores Antioqueños, 1991.

Bourne, Peter. *Jimmy Carter: A Comprehensive Biography from Plains to Postpresidency.* New York: Scribner, 1997.

Bosemberg, Luis Eduardo. "The U.S., Nazi Germany, and the CIA in Latin America during WWII." In Rockefeller Archive Center, *Publications Research Reports: Research Reports Online.* New York: Rockefeller Archive Center, 2009.

Bourdieu, Pierre. *Distinction: A Social Critique of the Judgement of Taste.* Cambridge, MA: Harvard University Press, 1984.

Bouvet, Françoise. "*Leopardo al sol:* La monstruosidad desvelada de la Colombia del narcotráfico." *Amerika* 11 (2014), https://journals.openedition.org/amerika/5538.

Braden, Spruille. *Diplomats and Demagogues: The Memoirs of Spruille Braden.* New Rochelle, NY: Arlington House, 1971.

Bronfman, Alejandra. *Isles of Noise: Sonic Media in the Caribbean.* Chapel Hill: University of North Carolina Press, 2016.

Britto, Lina. "El eje guajiro: Nazis, contrabandistas y diplomáticos durante la Segunda Guerra Mundial, Riohacha, 1940–1943." In *Pensamiento Poscolonial: Cambio social y relaciones subalternas en América Latina,* edited by Ricardo Oviedo. Pasto, Colombia: Universidad de Nariño, 2014.

———. "'Legalización o represión': How a Debate in Colombia Steered the Fate of the 'War on Drugs.'" *Social History of Alcohol and Drugs* 33, no. 1 (spring 2019): 88–112.

———. "La venganza guajira." *Universo Centro* 101 (October 2018): 12–13.

Bucheli, Marcelo. *Bananas and Business: The United Fruit Company in Colombia, 1899–2000.* New York: New York University Press, 2005.

———. "La crisis del enclave bananero del Magdalena en los 60s." *Historia Crítica* 5 (1991): 107–24.

———. *Empresas multinationals y enclaves agrícolas: El caso de United Fruit en Magdalena y Urabá, Colombia (1948–1968).* Bogotá: Universidad de los Andes, Tercer Mundo Editores, 1994.

Bucheli, Marcelo, and Luis Felipe Sáenz. "Export Protectionism and the Great Depression: Multinational Corporations, Domestic Elite, and Export Policies in Colombia." In *The Great Depression in Latin America,* edited by Paulo Drinot and Alan Knight. Durham, NC: Duke University Press, 2014.

Bushnell, David. *Eduardo Santos and the Good Neighbor, 1938–1942.* Gainesville: University of Florida Press, 1967.

———. *The Making of Modern Colombia: A Nation in Spite of Itself.* Berkeley: University of California Press, 1993.

Cadavid Orozco, Iván, and Hugo Molina Muñoz. *El delito de contrabando.* Bogotá: Editorial Súper, 1979.

Calderón Guerra, Will. *Bonanza y crisis del algodón en el Cesar, 1950–2010.* Valledupar, Colombia: Imagen Visual Ltda., 2010.

Camacho Guizado, Álvaro. *Drogas, corrupción y poder: Marihuana y cocaína en la sociedad colombiana.* Cali, Colombia: Universidad del Valle, CIDE, 1981.

———. *Droga y sociedad en Colombia: El poder y el estigma.* Bogotá: CEREC, CIDSE, Universidad del Valle–Fondo Editorial, 1988.

Camacho Guizado, Álvaro, and Andrés López Restrepo. "Perspectives on Narcotics Traffic in Colombia." *International Journal of Politics, Culture, and Society* 14, no. 4 (2000): 151–82.

Camacho Guizado, Álvaro, Álvaro Guzmán, María Clemencia Ramírez, and Fernando Gaitán. *Nuevas visiones sobre la violencia en Colombia.* Bogota: FESCOL and IEPRI, 1997.

Campbell, Horace. *Rasta and Resistance: From Marcus Garvey to Walter Rodney.* Trenton, NJ: Africa World Press, 1987.

Campos, Isaac, and Paul Gootenberg. "Toward a New Drug History of Latin America: A Research Frontier at the Center of Debates." *Hispanic American Historical Review* 91, no. 1 (February 2015): 1–35.

Candelier, Henry. *Riohacha y los indios guajiros.* 1892. Reprint, Riohacha: Gobernación de la Guajira, 1994.

Cárdenas, Nicolás, and Simón Uribe. *La guerra de los Cárdenas y los Valdeblánquez: Estudio de un conflicto mestizo en la Guajira.* Bogotá: Universidad Nacional de Colombia, IEPRI, 2007.

Cárdenas, Mauricio, and Roberto Steiner. "Introducción." In *Corrupción, Crimen y Justicia: Una perspectiva económica,* edited by Mauricio Cárdenas and Roberto Steiner. Bogotá: Tercer Mundo Editores, 1998.

Carey, Elaine. *Women Drug Traffickers: Mules, Bosses, and Organized Crime.* Albuquerque: University of New Mexico Press, 2014.

Carrasquilla Baza, Deibys. "Entre las tradiciones de la tierra y los sonidos industrializados: Música tradicional e industrias culturales en el Caribe colombiano." In *Pensando la región: Etnografías propias para la construcción de un discurso regional,* edited by Fabio Silva Vallejo. Santa Marta: Universidad del Magdalena, 2007.

Carrier, Jerry. *Hard Right Turn: The History and the Assassination of the American Left.* New York: Algora, 2015.

Carter, Jimmy. "Drug Abuse Message to the Congress." Washington, DC, August 2, 1977. *The American Presidency Project.* https://www.presidency.ucsb.edu /node/243653.

Cartwright, Gary. *Dirty Dealings: A True Story of Smuggling, Murder, and the FBI's Biggest Investigation.* Cambridge, MA: Atheneum Press, 1984.

Castillo, Fabio. *Los jinetes de la cocaína.* Bogotá: Editorial Documentos Periodísticos, 1987.

Castillo Castro, Héctor. "Música de acordeón, frontera y contrabando en La Guajira, 1960–1980." *Educación y Ciencia* 10 (2007): 73–88.

Castro Castro, Pepe. *Crónicas de la Plaza Mayor.* Bogotá: Cargraphics, 1998.

———. *Crónicas y cuentos.* Bogotá: La Silueta Ediciones, 2005.

———. *Crónicas del Valle de Upar.* Bogotá: Zona Ltda., 2000.

———. *Crónicas de Pepe.* Bogotá: El Malpensante, 2002.

———. *El cuento de Pepe.* 2 volumes Bogotá: Tradelink Ltda., 2003.

———. *Iglesia Nuestra Señora de la Concepción y familia vallenata:* Bogotá: Tradelink Ltda., 2007.

Castro Monsalvo, Pedro. *Un campesino previno al país.* Bogotá: Ediciones Tercer Mundo, 1972.

Castro Monsalvo, Pedro, Raimundo Emiliani Román, and Benjamín Burgos Puche. *El INCORA y la ejecución de la Reforma Agraria. Informe de la Comisión del Senado.* Bogotá: Senado de la República, 1967.

Castro Socarrás, Álvaro. *Episodios históricos del Cesar.* Bogotá: Plaza & Janés, 1997.

————. "Mitos, leyendas y tradiciones vallenatas," *Desarrollo Indoamericano* 34 (2000): 67–73.

Centro de Investigación y Educación Popular, ed. *Campesinado y capitalismo en Colombia*. Bogotá: Centro de Investigación y Educación Popular, 1981.

Cervantes Angulo, José. *La noche de las luciérnagas*. Bogotá: Plaza & Janés, 1980.

Chaplin, Tamara, and Jadwiga E. Pieper Mooney. "Introduction." In *The Global 60s: Convention, Contest, and Counterculture*, edited by Tamara Chaplin and Jadwiga E. Pieper Mooney. New York: Routledge, 2018.

Chapman, Peter. *Bananas: How the United Fruit Company Shaped the World*. New York: Canongate, 2007.

Chasteen, John Charles. *Getting High: Marijuana through the Ages*. New York: Rowman & Littlefield, 2016.

Chaves, Milciades. "La Guajira: Una región y una cultura de Colombia." *Revista Colombiana de Antropología* 1 (1953): 123–95.

Chomsky, Aviva, Garry Leech, and Steve Striffler. *The People behind Colombian Coal*. Bogotá: Casa Editorial Pisando Callos, 2007.

Ciro Gómez, Bernardo A. "'Murió don Heriberto y los tambores y los cantos cesaron': Una aproximación a la tambora en el contexto de las políticas culturales de la Revolución en Marcha en Colombia, 1930–1946." *Trashumante: Revista Americana de Historia Social* 14 (2019).

Coatsworth, John. "The Roots of Violence in Colombia." *ReVista: Harvard Report on the Americas* 2, no. 3 (spring 2003): 8–12.

Cobbs-Hoffman, Elizabeth. *All You Need Is Love: The Peace Corps and the Spirit of the 1960s*. Cambridge, MA: Harvard University Press, 1998.

Cocks, Catherine. *Tropical Whites: The Rise of the Tourist South in the Americas*. Philadelphia: University of Pennsylvania Press, 2013.

Coleman, Bradley Lynn. *Colombia and the United States: The Making of an Inter-American Alliance, 1939–1960*. Kent, OH: Kent State University Press, 2008.

Coleman, Renita. "Oral and Life Histories: Giving Voice to the Voiceless." In *Qualitative Research in Journalism: Taking It to the Streets*, edited by Sharon Hartin Iorio. Mahwah, NJ: Lawrence Erlbaum, 2004.

Comité Nacional de Cafeteros. "El contrabando de café. Comunicado de la Secretaría del Comité Nacional de Cafeteros, Diciembre 14 de 1956." *Revista Cafetera de Colombia* 13, no. 130 (1957): 62.

Conde Calderón, Jorge. "Identidades políticas y grupos de poder en el Caribe colombiano, 1828–1848." In Martínez Durán and Sánchez Mejía, *Historia, identidades, cultura popular y música tradicional en el Caribe colombiano*.

Concha-Eastman, Alberto. "Urban Violence in Latin America and the Caribbean: Dimensions, Explanations, Actions." In Rotker, *Citizens of Fear*.

Cordovez, Mónica. "Transfer of Technology to Latin America." MA thesis, McGill University, 1991.

Coronil, Fernando. *The Magical State: Nature, Money, and Modernity in Venezuela*. Chicago: University of Chicago Press, 1997.

Corso, Adriana Mercedes. "El gravamen bananero: Un caso de historia política en el departamento del Magadalena" *Investigación y Desarrollo* 7 (1998): 89–103.

———. "Santa Marta, la habilidad para sobrevivir." In Abello Vives and Giaimo Chávez, eds., *Poblamiento y ciudades del Caribe colombiano.*

Cotter, Joseph. *Troubled Harvest: Agronomy and Revolution in Mexico, 1880–2002.* Westport, CT: Praeger, 2003.

Courtright, David T. *Sky as Frontier: Adventure, Aviation, and Empire.* College Station: Texas A&M University Press, 2005.

Craig, Richard B. "Colombian Narcotics and United States–Colombian Relations." *Journal of Inter-American Studies and World Affairs* 23, no. 3 (August 1981): 243–70.

———. "Mexican Narcotics Traffic: Binational Security Implications." In *The Latin American Narcotics Trade and U.S. National Security,* edited by Donald J. Mabry. New York: Greenwood, 1989.

———. "Operation Intercept: The International Politics of Pressure." *Review of Politics* 42, no. 4 (October 1980): 556–80.

Currie, Lauchlin, and Julio Bejarano. *El algodón en Colombia: Problemas y oportunidades.* Bogotá: Federación Nacional de Algodoneros y Fundación Para el Progreso de Colombia, 1963.

Dallanegra Pedraza, Luis. "Claves de la política exterior de Colombia." *Latinoamérica: Revista de Estudios Latinoamericanos* 54 (August 2012): 37–73.

Dangond Castro, Jorge. *Tierra nuestra: Crónicas de frontera.* Barranquilla, Colombia: Editorial Antillas, 2001.

Dangond Daza, Jorge. *De París a Villanueva: Memorias de un vallenato.* Bogotá: Plaza & Janés, 1990.

———. *Renacimiento de Valledupar. Así nació el Cesar.* Barranquilla, Colombia: Editorial Antillas, 2002.

Dangond Ovalle, Jaime. *El Cesar, hijo del amor: En el veinte aniversario del Departamento del Cesar.* Barranquilla, Colombia: Gráficas del Litoral, 1987.

Dávalos, Liliana, and Adriana Bejarano. "Conservation in Conflict: Illegal Drugs and Habitat in the Americas." In *State of the Wild, 2008–2009: A Global Portrait of Wildlife, Wildlands, and Oceans,* edited by Wild Life Conversation Society. Washington DC: Island Press, 2008.

Davis, Mike. *Ecology of Fear: Los Angeles and the Imagination of Disaster.* New York: Vintage Books, 1999.

Daza Noguera, Yin. *Itinerario de un periodista.* Bogotá: Colección de Autores Guajiros, Secretaría de Educación-Divulgación Cultural, Departamento de la Guajira, 1983.

Daza Sierra, Guillermo José. "Marihuana, sociedad y estado en la Guajira." Honors thesis, sociology, Universidad Nacional de Colombia, 1988.

Daza Villar, Vladimir. *La Guajira: El tortuoso camino a la legalidad.* Bogotá: Naciones Unidas, 2003.

Del Castillo Mathieu, Nicolás. "El léxico negro-africano de San Basilio de Palenque." *Thesaurus* 39, nos. 1–3 (1984): 80–169.

Dillman, Jefferson. *Colonizing Paradise: Landscape and Empire in the British West Indies*. Tuscaloosa: University of Alabama Press, 2015.

Domestic Council Drug Abuse Task Force. *White Paper on Drug Abuse: A Report to the President*. Washington, DC: US Government Printing Office, 1975.

Donos, Igor Goicovic. "Los modelos interpretativos en el studio de la violencia." In *Escrita con sangre: Historia de la violencia en América Latina, Siglos XIX y XX*, edited by Igor Goicovic, Julio Pinto, Ivette Lozoya, and Claudio Pérez. Santiago, Chile: Ceibo Ediciones, 2013.

Doyle, Kate. "Operation Intercept: The Perils of Unilateralism." *The National Security Archive*. Posted April 13, 2003. http://www.gwu.edu/~nsarchiv/NSAEBB /NSAEBB86/.

Dufton, Emily. *Grass Roots: The Rise and Fall and Rise of Marijuana in America*. New York: Basic Books, 2017.

Dunkerley, James. "Preface." In *Studies in the Formation of the Nation-State in Latin America*. London: University of London Press, 2002.

Echeverri, Marcela. "Antropólogas pioneras y nacionalismo liberal en Colombia, 1941–1949." *Revista Colombiana de Antropología* 43 (2007): 61–90.

Edberg, Mark Cameron. *El Narcotraficante: Narcocorridos and the Construction of a Cultural Persona on the US-Mexico Border*. Austin: University of Texas Press, 2004.

Eddy, Paul, Hugo Sabogal, and Sara Walden. *The Cocaine Wars*. New York: W. W. Norton, 1988.

Escamilla, Oscar. *Narcoextravagancia: Historias insólitas del narcotráfico*. Bogotá: Aguilar, 2002.

Escamilla Morales, Julio, Efraín Morales Escorcia, and Grandfield Henry. *La canción vallenata como acto discursivo*. Barranquilla, Colombia: Universidad del Altlántico, 2005.

Escobar, Arturo. *Encountering Development: The Making and Unmaking of the Third World*. Princeton, NJ: Princeton University Press, 1995.

Euraque, Dario. *Reinterpreting the Banana Republic: Region and State in Honduras, 1870–1972*. Chapel Hill: University of North Carolina Press, 1997.

Evans, Peter, Dietrich Rueschemeyer, and Theda Skocpol, eds. *Bringing the State Back In*. New York: Cambridge University Press, 1985.

Ezpeleta Ariza, Benjamín. *La verdadera historia de Riohacha*. Riohacha, Colombia: Aarón Impresores, 2000.

Fajardo, Darío. "Fronteras, colonizaciones y construcción social del espacio." In *Fronteras y poblamiento: Estudios de historia y antropología de Colombia y Ecuador*, edited by Chantal Caillavet and Ximena Pachón. Bogotá: Instituto Francés de Estudios Andinos (IFEA), Instituto de Investigaciones Amazónicas, Sinchi, Ediciones Uniandes, 1996.

———. *Para sembrar la paz hay que aflojar la tierra*. Bogotá: Universidad Nacional de Colombia, 2002.

Farapi, SL. *Drogas y género*. Vitoria-Gasteiez, Basque Country, Spain: Emakunde, Instituto Vasco de la Mujer, 2009.

Farnsworth-Alvear, Ann. *Dulcinea in the Factory: Myths, Morals, Men, and Women in Colombia's Industrial Experiment, 1905–1960*. Durham, NC: Duke University Press, 2000.

Fernández Gámez, Ismael Darío. *Romualdo Brito: Vivencias de un compositor vallenato*. Barranquilla, Colombia: Editorial Antillas, 1999.

Fernández Gámez, Ismael Darío, and Dilia Rosa Gnecco de Daza. *Historia de la radiodifusión en La Guajira*. Barranquilla, Colombia: Editorial Antillas, 2002.

Ferreira, Carmén Adriana. *Región, historia y cultura*. Bucaramanga, Colombia: Universidad Industrial de Santander, 2003.

Figueroa, José Antonio. *Del nacionalismo al exilio interior: El contraste de la experiencia modernista en Cataluña y los Andes americanos*. Bogotá: Convenio Andrés Bello, 2000.

———. "Excluidos y exiliados: Indígenas e intelectuales modernistas en la Sierra Nevada de Santa Marta." In *Modernidad, identidad y desarrollo: Construcción de sociedad y recreación cultural en contextos de modernización,* edited by Martha Lucía Sotomayor. Bogotá: Instituto Colombiano de Antropología e Historia (ICANH), 1998.

———. *Realismo Mágico, vallenato y violencia política en l Caribe colombiano*. Bogotá: Instituto Colombiano de Antropología e Historia, ICANH, 2009.

Fleetwood, Jennifer. *Drug Mules: Women in the International Cocaine Trade*. London: Palgrave Macmillan, 2015.

Fluharty, Vernon Lee. *Dance of the Millions: Military Rule and the Social Revolution in Colombia, 1930–1956*. Pittsburgh: University of Pittsburgh Press, 1957.

Foote, Nicola, and Michael Goebel. *Immigration and National Identities in Latin America*. Gainesville: University Press of Florida, 2014.

Ford, Gerald R. "Special Message to the Congress on Drug Abuse," Washington DC, April 27, 1976. Gerald R. Ford Presidential Library and Museum. https://www.fordlibrarymuseum.gov/library/speeches/760368.htm.

Franco, Jorge. *Rosario Tijeras*. Bogotá: Editorial Norma, 1999.

Frankema, Ewout. "The Expansion of Mass Education in Twentieth-Century Latin America: A Global Comparative Perspective." *Revista de historia económica/ Journal of Iberian and Latin American Economic History* 3 (winter 2009): 359–96.

Friedman, Max Paul. "Specter of a Nazi Threat: United States–Colombian Relations, 1939–1945." *The Americas* 56, no. 4 (2000): 563–89.

———. *Nazis and Good Neighbors: The United States Campaign against the Germans of Latin The America in WWII*. Cambridge: Cambridge University Press, 2003.

Frydl, Kathleen J. *The Drug Wars in America, 1940–1973*. Cambridge: Cambridge University Press, 2013.

Fundación ProSierra Nevada de Santa Marta. *Los cultivos de marihuana en la Sierra Nevada de Santa Marta: Una reflexión sobre los métodos de erradicación*. Santa Marta, Colombia: Fundación ProSierra, November 1993.

———. *Historia y geografía de la Sierra Nevada de Santa Marta*. Santa Marta, Colombia: Fundación ProSierra, 1991.

Galán, Luis Carlos. *Los carbones de Colombia*. Bogotá: Editorial Oveja Negra, 1982.

Galbraith, John Kenneth. *The Affluent Society*. 1958. Reprint, Boston: Houghton Mifflin, 1998.

Gale, Laurence. *Education and Development in Latin America, with Special Reference to Colombia and Some Comparison with Guyana, South America*. London: Routledge & Kegan Paul, 1969.

Galeano, Eduardo. *Memory of Fire*. Volume 3: *Century of the Wind*. New York: W. W. Norton, 1988.

Galeano, Juan Carlos. "El Nadaísmo y 'La Violencia' en Colombia." *Revista Iberoamericana* 59, no. 164 (July 1993): 647–58.

Galvis, Silvia, and Alberto Donadío. *Colombia Nazi, 1939–1945*. Bogotá: Editorial Planeta, 1986.

Garay Salamanca, Luis Jorge, and Eduardo Salcedo-Albarán. "Captura del Estado y reconfiguración cooptada del Estado." In *Narcotráfico, corrupción y Estados: Cómo las redes ilícitas han reconfigurado las instituciones en Colombia, Guatemala y México,* edited by Luis Jorge Garay Salamanca and Eduardo Salcedo-Albarán. México, DF: Random House Mondadori, 2012.

García, Clara Inés, ed. *Fronteras: Territorios y metáforas*. Medellín: Instituto de Estudios Regionales (INER), 2003.

García García, Jorge. *El cultivo de algodón en Colombia entre 1953 y 1978: Una evaluación de las políticas gubernamentales*. Documentos de trabajo sobre economía regional 44. Cartagena de Indias: Centro de investigaciones económicas del Caribe colombiano, Banco de la República, 2004.

García Márquez, Gabriel. *Cien años de soledad*. Buenos Aires: Editorial Sudamericana, 1967.

García Villegas, Mauricio, and Rodrigo Uprimy. "El control judicial de los estados de excepción en Colombia." In *¿Justicia para todos? Sistema judicial, derechos sociales y democracia en Colombia,* edited by Mauricio García Villegas, César A. Rodríguez Garavito, and Rodrigo Uprimy. Bogotá: Editorial Norma, 2006.

Gaviria, Víctor. *El pelaíto que no duró nada*. Bogotá: Editorial Planeta, 1991.

Geidel, Molly. *Peace Corps Fantasies: How Development Shaped the Global Sixties*. Minneapolis: University of Minnesota Press, 2015.

Gilard, Jacques. "Vallenato, ¿cuál tradición narrativa?" *Huellas, Revista de la Universidad del Norte* 19 (1987): 59–68.

———. "¿Crescencio o don Toba? Falsos interrogantes y verdaderas respuestas sobre el vallenato." *Huellas, Revista de la Universidad del Norte* 37 (1993): 28–34.

Gingeras, Ryan. *Heroin, Organized Crime, and the Making of Modern Turkey*. Oxford: Oxford University Press, 2014.

Gómez, Hernando José. "La economía ilegal en Colombia: Tamaño, evolución, características e impacto económico." *Coyuntura Política* 18, no. 3 (1988): 93–113.

González, Hector. *Vallenato: Tradición y comercio*. Cali, Colombia: Programa Editorial Universidad del Valle, 2007.

González Cuello, Jorge Alejandro. *Aquel Corral de Piedras: Un legado de la humanidad.* Bogotá: Editorial Carrera 7a, Ltda., 2003.

González Plazas, Santiago. *Pasado y presente del contrabando en la Guajira: Aproximaciones al fenómeno de ilegalidad en la región.* Bogotá: Centro de Estudios y Observatorio de Drogas y Delitos, Facultad de Economía, Universidad del Rosario, 2008.

González Zubiría, Fredy. *Crónicas del cancionero vallenato.* Riohacha: Dirección Departamental de Cultura de la Guajira, 2011.

———. *Cultura y sociedad criolla de La Guajira.* Riohacha, Colombia: Gobernación de La Guajira; Fondo Mixto para la Promoción de la Cultura y las Artes de La Guajira, 2005.

———. "Lisímaco Peralta y su 'Lluvia de verano.'" *Arte y Parte* 11–12 (January–February 2010): 12–15.

———. *Manuel Boy Magdaniel: Alegría, canto y parranda.* Riohacha, Colombia: Fondo Mixto para la Promoción de la Cultura y las Artes de la Guajira; Dirección de Cultura y Juventud Departamental, 2010.

Goode, Erich, and Nachman Ben-Yehuda. *Moral Panics: The Social Construction of Deviance.* 1994. Reprint, Malden, MA: Wiley-Blackwell, 2009.

Gootenberg, Paul. *Andean Cocaine: The Making of a Global Drug.* Chapel Hill: University of North Carolina Press, 2009.

———. "Talking like a State: Drugs, Borders, and the Language of Control." In *Illicit Flows and Criminal Things: States, Borders, and the Other Side of Globalization,* edited by Willem Van Schendel and Itty Abraham. Bloomington: Indiana University Press, 2005.

Gootenberg, Paul, and Isaac Campos. "Toward a New Drug History of Latin America: A Research Frontier at the Center of Debates." *Hispanic American Historical Review* 91, no. 1 (February 2015): 1–35.

Gossaín, Juan. *La mala hierba.* Bogotá: Plaza & Janés, 1981.

Gould, Jeffrey, and Aldo Lauria-Santiago. *To Rise in Darkness: Revolution, Repression, and Memory in El Salvador, 1920–1932.* Durham, NC: Duke University Press, 2008.

Grahn, Lance. *The Political Economy of Smuggling: Regional Informal Economies in Early Bourbon New Granada.* Boulder, CO: Westview Press, 1997.

Grandin, Greg. *Empire's Workshop: Latin America, the United States, and the Rise of New Imperialism.* New York: Henry Holt, 2007.

———. "Off the Beach: The United States, Latin America, and the Cold War." In *A Companion to Post-1945 America,* edited by Jean-Christophe Agnew and Roy Rosenzweig. Malden, MA: Blackwell, 2002.

Green, John W. *Gaitanismo, Left Liberalism, and Popular Mobilization in Colombia.* Gainesville: University Press of Florida, 2003.

———. "'Vibrations of the Collective:' The Popular Ideology of Gaitanismo on Colombia's Atlantic Coast, 1944–1948." *Hispanic American Historical Review* 76, no.2 (1996): 283–311.

Grele, Ronald J. "Oral History as Evidence." In *History of Oral History: Foundations and Methodology,* edited by Thomas L. Charlton, Lois E. Myers, and Rebecca Sharpless. New York: Altamira Press, 2007.

Gross, K. "Hawkeye." *Reefer Warrior: How My Friends and I Found Adventure, Wealth, and Romance Smuggling Marihuana—Until We All Went to Jail.* Boulder, CO: Paladin Press, 1998.

Gruzinski, Serge. *The Mestizo Mind: The Intellectual Dynamics of Colonization and Globalization.* New York: Routledge, 2002.

Gudmundson, Lowell. "Peasant, Farmer, Proletarian: Class Formation in a Smallholder Coffee Economy, 1850–1950." In *Coffee, Society, and Power in Latin America,* edited by William Roseberry, Lowell Gudmundson, and Mario Samper Kutschbach. Baltimore: Johns Hopkins University Press, 1995.

Guhl, Ernesto, ed. *Indios y blancos en La Guajira: Estudio socioeconomico.* Bogotá: Tercer Mundo Editores, 1963.

Guerra Curvelo, Wilder. *La disputa y la palabra: La ley en la Sociedad Wayúu.* Bogotá: Ministerio de Cultura, 2001.

———. "Riohacha: Ciudad inconclusa." In Abello Vives and Giaimo Chávez, eds., *Poblamiento y ciudades del Caribe colombiano.*

Guerrero, Arturo. "Algodón: la historia de un largo esfuerzo frustrado," *Nueva Frontera* 380 (1982).

Gutiérrez, Tomás Darío. "Los conflictos sociales en la historia de la cultura vallenata." In Martínez Durán and Sánchez Mejía, *Historia, identidades, cultura popular y música tradicional en el Caribe colombiano.*

———. *Cultura vallenata: Origen, teoría y pruebas.* Bogotá: Plaza & Janés, 1992.

———. *Valledupar: Música de una historia.* Bogotá: Editorial Grijalbo, 2000.

Gutiérrez de Pineda, Virginia. "Organización social en la Guajira." *Revista del Instituto Etnológico Nacional* 3, no. 2 (1948): 1–255.

Guzmán Campos, Germán, Orlando Fals Borda, and Eduardo Umaña Luna. *La Violencia en Colombia. Estudio de un proceso social.* Bogotá: Círculo de Lectores, 1963.

Guzmán Lengua, Víctor Hugo, Rosa Esther Pacheco Núñez, and Hermana Josefina Zúñiga Deluque. *Historia de la música en la ciudad de Riohacha, siglos XIX y XX.* Riohacha, Colombia: Fondo Mixto de Promoción de la Cultura y las Artes de la Guajira, 1998.

Hamilton, Paula, and Linda Shopes. "Introduction: Building Partnerships between Oral History and Memory Studies." In *Oral History and Public Memories,* edited by Paula Hamilton and Linda Shopes. Philadelphia: Temple University Press, 2008.

Hansen, Helena. "The 'New Masculinity': Addiction Treatment as a Reconstruction of Gender in Puerto Rican Evangelist Street Ministries." *Social Science and Medicine* 74, no. 11 (June 2012): 1721–28.

Harrison, David. *The Sociology of Modernization and Development.* New York: Routledge, 1988.

Harvey, Penelope, and Peter Gow, eds. *Sex and Violence: Issues in Representation and Experience.* New York: Routledge, 1994.

Helg, Aline. *Liberty and Equality in Caribbean Colombia, 1770–1835.* Chapel Hill: University of North Carolina Press, 2004.

Henderson, James D. *Colombia's Narcotics Nightmare: How the Drug Trade Destroyed Peace.* 2012, Reprint, Jefferson, NC: McFarland, 2015.

———. *Las ideas de Laureano Gómez.* Bogotá: Ediciones Tercer Mundo, 1985.

Henríquez Torres, Guillermo. "La música del Magdalena Grande en el siglo XIX: Eulalio Meléndez." In Martínez Durán and Sánchez Mejía, *Historia, identidades, cultura popular y música tradicional en el Caribe colombiano.*

Hernández Salgar, Óscar. "Colonialidad y postcolonialidad musical en Colombia." *Latin American Music Review* 28, no. 2 (2007): 242–70.

Herrera, Martha Cecilia. "Historia de la educación en Colombia: La República Liberal y la modernización de la educación, 1930–1946." *Revista Colombiana de Educación* 26 (1993).

Herrera Ángel, Marta. *Ordenar para controlar: Ordenamiento especial y control político en las llanuras del Caribe y en los Andes centrales neogranadinos, siglo XVIII.* Bogotá: Instituto Colombiano de Antropolgía e Historia, 2000.

Herrera Araújo, Fernando. "Prólogo." In Bernal Castillo, *Crisis algodonera y violencia en el departamento del Cesar.*

Herrera de Turbay, Luisa Fernanda. "La actividad agrícola en la SNSM (Colombia): Perspectiva histórica." In *Studies on Tropical Andean Ecosystems/Estudios de ecosistemas Tropoandinos,* Volume 2: *La Sierra Nevada de Santa Marta,* edited by Thomas Van Der Hammen and Pedro M. Ruiz. Berlin: J. Cramer, 1986.

Hobsbawm, Eric. *Primitive Rebels: Studies in Archaic Forms of Social Movement in the 19th and 20th Centuries.* Manchester: Manchester University Press, 1959.

Hylton, Forrest. "The Cold War That Didn't End: Paramilitary Modernization in Medellín, Colombia." In *A Century of Revolution: Insurgent and Counterinsurgent Violence during Latin America's Long Cold War,* edited by Greg Grandin and Gilbert M. Joseph. Durham, NC: Duke University Press, 2010.

———. *Evil Hour in Colombia.* London: Verso, 2006.

———. "'The Sole Owners of the Land': Empire, War, and Authority in the Guajira Peninsula, 1761–1779." *Atlantic Studies* 13, no. 3 (2016): 315–344.

Immerwahr, Daniel. *How to Hide an Empire: A History of the Greater United States.* New York: Farrar, Straus & Giroux, 2019.

———. *Thinking Small: The United States and the Lure of Community Development.* Cambridge, MA: Harvard University Press, 2015.

Informe del Grupo de Memoria Histórica. *La masacre de Bahía Portete: Mujeres Wayuu en la mira.* Bogotá: Comisión Nacional de Reparación y Reconciliación, Taurus Editores, 2010.

Institute of Medicine, Division of Health Sciences Policy. *Marijuana and Health.* Washington DC: National Academy Press, 1982.

James, Daniel. *Doña María's Story: Life History, Memory, and Political Identity.* Durham, NC: Duke University Press, 2001.

Jaramillo Uribe, Jaime. "Nación y región en los orígenes del Estado nacional en Colombia." In *Ensayos de Historia Social, Temas Americanos y Otros Ensayos.* Volume 2. Bogotá: Tercer Mundo Editores, Ediciones Uniandes, 1989.

Jaramillo Uribe, Jaime, Leonidas Mora, and Fernando Cubides. *Colonización, coca y guerrilla*. Bogotá: Universidad Nacional de Colombia, 1986.

Jelin, Elizabeth. *State Repression and the Labors of Memory*. Minneapolis: University of Minnesota Press, 2003.

Jian, Chen, Martin Klimke, Masha Kirasirova, Mary Nolan, Marilyn Young, and Joanna Waley-Cohen, eds. *The Routledge Handbook of the Global Sixties: Between Protest and Nation-Building*. New York: Routledge, 2018.

Jiménez, Margarita, and Sandro Sideri. *Historia del desarrollo regional en Colombia*. Bogotá: Fondo Editorial CEREC, 1985.

Jiménez, Michael F. "At the Banquet of Civilization: The Limits of Planter Hegemony in Early-Twentieth-Century Colombia." In Roseberry, Gudmundson, and Kutschbach, *Coffee, Society, and Power in Latin* America.

———. "From Plantation to Cup: Coffee Capitalism in the United States, 1830–1930." In Roseberry, Gudmundson, and Kutschbach, *Coffee, Society, and Power in Latin America*.

Johnson, Eric A., Ricardo D. Salvatore, and Pieter Spierenburg, eds. *Murder and Violence in Modern Latin America*. Chichester, UK: Wiley-Blackwell, 2013.

Joseph, Gilbert. "Close Encounters: Toward a New Cultural History of US–Latin American Relations." In *Close Encounters of Empire: Writing the Cultural History of US-Latin American Relations*, edited by Gilbert Joseph, Catherine C. LeGrand, and Ricardo D. Salvatore. Durham, NC: Duke University Press, 1998.

Joseph, Gilbert, and Daniel Nugent, eds. *Everyday Forms of State Formation: Revolution and the Negotiation of Rule in Modern Mexico*. Durham, NC: Duke University Press, 1994.

Joseph, Gilbert, Catherine C. LeGrand, and Ricardo D. Salvatore, eds. *Close Encounters of Empire: Writing the Cultural History of US–Latin American Relations*. Durham, NC: Duke University Press, 1998.

Junguito, Roberto, and Carlos Caballero. "La otra economía." *Coyuntura Económica* 8, no. 4 (1978): 101–41.

Kalmanovitz, Salomón. "La economía del narcotráfico en Colombia." *Economía Colombiana* 226–27 (1990): 18–28.

———. *Economía y nación: Una breve historia de Colombia*. Bogotá: Siglo Veintiuno Editores, 1988.

Kalmanovitz, Salomón, and Enrique López Enciso. *La agricultura colombiana en el siglo XX*. Bogotá: Fondo de Cultura Económica y Banco de la República, 2006.

Kalmanovitz, Salomón, Ricardo Vargas, and Camilo Borrero, eds. *Drogas, poder y región en Colombia*. Bogotá: CINEP, 1994.

Kamiénski, Lucasz. *Shooting Up: A Short History of Drugs and War*. Oxford: Oxford University Press, 2016.

Kamstra, Jerry. *Hierba: Aventuras de un contrabandista de marihuana*. 1974. Reprint, México, DF: Editorial Grijalbo, SA, 1976.

Karl, Robert. *Forgotten Peace: Reform, Violence, and the Making of Contemporary Colombia*. Oakland: University of California Press, 2017.

————. "From 'Showcase' to 'Failure': Democracy and the Colombian Developmental State in the 1960s." In *State and Nation Making in Latin America and Spain: The Rise and Fall of the Developmental State,* edited by Miguel A. Centeno and Agustin E. Ferraro. Cambridge: Cambridge University Press, 2018.

Kennedy, John F. Democratic National Convention Nomination Acceptance Address (July 15, 1960). *American Rhetoric.* http://www.americanrhetoric.com/speeches/jfk1960dnc.htm.

Kenney, Michael. *From Pablo to Osama: Trafficking and Terrorist Networks, Government Bureaucracies, and Competitive Adaptation.* University Park: Pennsylvania State University Press, 2007.

Kinder, Douglas Clark. "Nativism, Cultural Conflict, Drug Control: United States and Latin American Antinarcotics Diplomacy through 1965." In *The Latin American Narcotics Trade and U.S. National Security,* edited by Donald J. Mabry. New York: Greenwood Press, 1989.

King, Stephen A. *Reggae, Rastafari, and the Rhetoric of Social Control.* Jackson: University Press of Mississippi, 2002.

Kirk, Robin. *More Terrible than Death: Massacres, Drugs, and America's War in Colombia.* New York: PublicAffairs, 2003.

Klimke, Martin, and Mary Nolan. "Introduction: The Globalization of the Sixties." In Jian et al., *The Routledge Handbook of the Global Sixties.*

Kline, Harvey F. *The Coal of El Cerrejón: Dependent Bargaining and Colombian Policy-Making.* College Park: Pennsylvania State University Press, 1987.

————. *Colombia: Portrait of Unity and Diversity.* Boulder, CO: Westview Press, 1983.

Klubock, Thomas Miller. *La Frontera: Forests and Ecological Conflict in Chile's Frontier Territory.* Durham, NC: Duke University Press, 2014.

Knight, Alan. "War, Violence, and Homicide in Modern Mexico." In Johnson, Salvatore, and Spierenburg, *Murder and Violence in Modern Latin America.*

————. "The Weight of the State in Modern Mexico." In *Studies in the Formation of the Nation-State in Latin America,* edited by James Dunkerley. London: University of London Press, 2002.

Kofas, Jon V. *Dependence and Underdevelopment in Colombia.* Tempe: Arizona State University, 1986.

Kuzmarov, Jeremy. *The Myth of the Addicted Army: Vietnam and the Modern War on Drugs.* Amherst: University of Massachusetts Press, 2009.

Lafaurie Acosta, José Vicente. "El desarrollo del Cesar." In *Cesar, 20 años, 1967–1987.* Valledupar, Colombia: Impresos de la Costa Ltda., Gobernación del Cesar, 1988.

Larraín, Jorge. *Identity and Modernity in Latin America.* Malden, MA: Blackwell, 2000.

Larson, Brooke. *Trials of Nation Making: Liberalism, Race, and Ethnicity in the Andes, 1810–1910.* Cambridge: Cambridge University Press, 2004.

Latham, Michael. *Modernization as Ideology. American Social Science and Nation*

Building in the Kennedy Era. Chapel Hill: University of North Carolina Press, 2000.

———. "The Cold War in the Third World, 1963–1975." In *The Cambridge History of the Cold War,* edited by Melvyn P. Leffler and Odd Arne Westad. Cambridge: Cambridge University Press, 2010.

Lauderbaugh, George M. "Bolivarian Nations: Securing the Northern Frontier." In *Latin America during World War II,* edited by Thomas M. Leonard and John F. Bratzel. New York: Rowman & Littlefield, 2007.

Lauriére, Christine. "Padre fundador de la etnología francesa, americanista apasionado, verdadero colombianista: Paul Rivet, un antropólogo polifacético." In *Arqueología y etnología en Colombia: La creación de una tradición científica,* edited by Carl Henrik Langebaek and Clara Isabel Botero. Bogotá: Uniandes-Ceso, Museo del Oro, Banco de la República, 2009.

Lázaro Diago, Julio. *Riohacha, fénix del Caribe.* Riohacha, Colombia: Fondo Mixto para la Promoción de la Cultura y de las Artes de la Guajira, 2005.

Leal, Francisco. *El oficio de la guerra: La seguridad nacional en Colombia.* Bogotá: Tercer Mundo Editores and IEPRI, 1994.

———. *La inseguridad de la seguridad: Colombia, 1958–2005.* Bogotá: Planeta, 2006.

Lefebvre, Henri. *The Production of Space.* Malden, MA: Blackwell Publishing, 1991.

LeGrand, Catherine. *Frontier Expansion and Peasant Protest in Colombia, 1830–1936.* Albuquerque: University of New Mexico Press, 1986.

———. "Living in Macondo: Economy and Culture in a United Fruit Company Banana Enclave, Santa Marta, Colombia, 1890–1930." In Joseph, LeGrand, and Salvatore, *Close Encounters of Empire.*

Levine, Daniel H. *Constructing Culture and Power in Latin America.* Ann Arbor: University of Michigan Press, 1993.

Lewis, Linden. "Caribbean Masculinity at the Fin de Siècle." In *Interrogating Caribbean Masculinities: Theoretical and Empirical Analyses,* edited by Rhoda E. Reddock. Kingston, Jamaica: University of the West Indies Press, 2004.

Liddy, G. Gordon. *Will: The Autobiography of G. Gordon Liddy.* New York: St. Martin's, 1991.

Litwak, Robert S. *Détente and the Nixon Doctrine: American Foreign Policy and the Pursuit of Stability, 1969–1976.* Cambridge: Cambridge University Press, 1984.

Llano Parra, Daniel. *Enemigos públicos: Contexto intelectual y sociabilidad literaria del movimiento nadaísta, 1958–1971.* Medellín: Universidad de Antioquia, 2015.

Lleras Restrepo, Carlos. *Borradores para una historia de la República Liberal.* Bogotá: Editorial Nueva Frontera, 1975.

Llerena Villalobos, Rito. *Memoria cultural en el vallenato: Un modelo de textualidad en la canción folclórica colombiana.* Medellín: Centro de Investigaciones, Facultad de Ciencias Humanas, Universidad de Antioquia, 1985.

Logsdon, Gene. "The Importance of Traditional Farming Practices for a Sustainable Modern Agriculture." In *Meeting the Expectations of the Land: Essays in*

Sustainable Agriculture and Stewardship, edited by Wes Jackson, Wendell Berry, and Bruce Colman. San Francisco: North Point Press, 1984.

López de la Roche, Fabio. "Cultura política de las clases dirigentes en Colombia: Permanencias y rupturas." *Controversia: Ensayos sobre cultura política colombiana,* nos. 162–63 (1990).

———. "Tradiciones de cultura política en el siglo XX." In *Modernidad y sociedad política en Colombia,* edited by Miguel Eduardo Cárdenas Rivera. Bogotá: FESCOL, IEPRI, Ediciones Foro Nacional por Colombia, 1993.

López González, Martín. "Cambios en los procesos académicos, políticos y culturales de la sociedad riohachera producto de la bonanza marimbera, 1975–1985." MA thesis, Universidad Nacional Abierta y a Distancia (UNAD), 2008.

López Hernández, Karen Beatriz. "Sociopatología de la vida cotidiana en tres tiempos." In *La Guajira, pluriétnica y multicultural.* Riohacha, Colombia: Fondo Mixto para la Promoción de la Cultura y las Artes de la Guajira, 2000.

López Michelsen, Alfonso. "Buscando el rostro de mi abuela." *Revista del Festival de la Leyenda Vallenata* 29 (1996): 68.

———. *Colombia en la hora cero.* Bogotá: Ediciones Tercer Mundo, 1963.

———. *El Gobierno del Mandato Claro.* Volume 3. Bogotá: Imprenta Nacional, 1976.

———. *El Gobierno del Mandato Claro.* Volume 4. Bogotá: Imprenta Nacional, 1980.

———. "Prólogo." In Pepe Castro Castro, *Crónicas de la Plaza Mayor.* Bogotá: Cargraphics, 1998.

López Restrepo, Andrés. "El control del cannabis: De las políticas nacionales al régimen global" (forthcoming).

———. "Narcotráfico, ilegalidad y conflicto armado en Colombia." In *Nuestra guerra sin nombre: Transformaciones del conflicto en Colombia,* edited by Fracisco Gutiérrez, María Emma Wills, and Gonzálo Sánchez. Bogotá: IEPRI, Universidad Nacional, 2006.

López Toro, Álvaro. "Migración y cambio social en Antioquia durante el siglo XIX." *Estudios Demográficos y Urbanos* 2, no. 3 (1968): 351–403.

Lorek, Timothy W. "Imagining the Midwest in Latin America: U.S. Advisors and the Envisioning of an Agricultural Middle Class in Colombia's Cauca Valley, 1943–1946." *Historian* 75, no. 2 (summer 2013): 283–305.

Losonczy, Anne Marie. "De cimarrones a colonos y contrabandistas." In *Afrodescendientes en las Américas,* edited by Claudia Mosquera, Mauricio Pardo, and Odile Hoffman. Bogotá: Universidad Nacional de Colombia e Instituto Colombiano de Antropología e Historia (ICANH), 2002.

Machado, Absalón. *Problemas agrarios colombianos.* Bogotá: Corporación de Estudios Ganaderos y Agrícolas, 1986.

Maffesoli, Michel. *The Time of the Tribes: The Decline of Individualism in Mass Society.* London: SAGE, 1996.

Mallon, Florencia. *Peasant and Nation: The Making of Postcolonial Mexico and Peru.* Berkeley: University of California Press, 1995.

Manzano, Valeria. *The Age of Youth in Argentina: Culture, Politics, and Sexuality from Perón to Videla*. Chapel Hill: University of North Carolina Press, 2014.

Marez, Curtis. *Drug Wars: The Political Economy of Narcotics*. Minneapolis: University of Minnesota Press, 2004.

Markarian, Vania. "To the Beat of 'The Walrus': Uruguayan Communists and Youth Culture in the Global Sixties." *Americas* 70, no. 3 (January 2014): 363–92.

Martínez Durán, Leovedis, and Hugues Sánchez Mejía, eds. *Historia, identidades, cultura popular y música tradicional en el Caribe colombiano*. Valledupar, Colombia: Ediciones Unicesar, 2004.

Martínez Fonseca, Juan Manuel. "Santa Marta en la Independencia: Entre el pragmatismo y la insurrección." *Folios* 32 (2010): 61–72.

Martínez Zuleta, Aníbal. *Escolios y croniquillas del país vallenato*. Tefa Comercializadora, 1999.

Mayorga García, Fernando. *Alfonso López Michelsen: El retrato del intelectual*. Bogotá: Editorial Universidad del Rosario, 2008.

Mazuera Navarro, Alejandro. "Una charla con el gurú de la Santa Marta Golden, la marihuana colombiana por excelencia" *Cartel Urbano,* September 28, 2017. https://cartelurbano.com/420/una-charla-con-el-guru-de-la-santa-marta-golden-la-marihuana-colombiana-por-excelencia.

McCann, Bryan. *Hello, Hello Brazil: Popular Music in the Making of Modern Brazil*. Durham, NC: Duke University Press, 2004.

McCormick, Ken. "Duesenberry and Veblen: The Demonstration Effect Revisited." *Journal of Economic Issues* 17, no. 4 (1983): 1125–29.

Medina, Medófilo. *Juegos de rebeldía: La trayectoria política de Saúl Charris de la Hoz*. Bogotá: Universidad Nacional de Colombia, CINDEC, 1997.

Medina Sierra, Abel. "El cachafuera: Radiografía de un estilo de vida." *Jepiriana* 2, no. 2 (1999): 8–12.

———. "Escalona y su aventura en La Guajira." *Aguaita* 21 (December 2009): 105–12.

———. "El otro discurso de nuestra música emblemática." In *Primer Encuentro Nacional de Investigadores de Música Vallenata*. Valledupar, Colombia: Universidad Popular del Cesar; La Piedra en el Zapato, 2012.

———. *Seis cantores vallenatos y una identidad*. Riohacha, Colombia: Fondo Mixto para la Promoción de la Cultura y las Artes de la Guajira, 2004.

———. *El vallenato: Constante espiritual de un pueblo*. Riohacha, Colombia: Fondo Mixto para la Promoción de la Cultura y las Artes en la Guajira, 2002.

Meisel Roca, Adolfo. 2005. "Ciénaga: La economía después del banano." In *Economías locales en el Caribe colombiano: Siete estudios de caso,* edited by María M. Aguilera Díaz. Bogotá: Banco de la República.

Mejía Vallejo, Manuel. *El hombre que parecía un fantasma*. Medellín: Biblioteca Pública Piloto, 1984.

Melo, Jorge Orlando. "The Drug Trade, Politics, and the Economy: The Colombian Experience." In *Latin America and the Multinational Drug Trade,* edited by Elizabeth Joyce and Carlos Malamud. New York: Palgrave Macmillan, 1998.

Menezes Bastos, Rafael José de. "Situación del músico en la Sociedad." In *América Latina en su música,* edited by Isabel Aretz. México City: Siglo XXI, 1980.

Mercado, Yoleida, Seili Quintero, and Yenis Sierra. *Riohacha en tiempos de marimba.* Honors thesis, ethno-education, Universidad de la Guajira, 2000.

Merchant, Carolyn. *Reinventing Eden: The Fate of Nature in Western Culture.* London: Routledge, 2003.

Mesa Valencia, Andrés Felipe. "El papel de Colombia en la Segunda Guerra Mundial: Desde el inicio de la conflagración haste el ataque japonés a Pearl Harbor," *Historia Caribe* 10, no. 26 (January–June 2015): 291–319.

Meyer, Arno. *The Furies: Violence and Terror in the French and Russian Revolutions.* Princeton, NJ: Princeton University Press, 2000.

Mitchell, Nancy. *The Danger of Dreams: German and American Imperialism in Latin America.* Chapel Hill: University of North Carolina Press, 1999.

Molano Bravo, Alfredo. *Aguas arriba: Entre la coca y el oro.* Bogotá: El Áncora Editores, 1990.

———. *Selva adentro: Una historia oral de la colonización del Guaviare.* Bogotá: El Áncora Editores, 1987.

Molano, Alfredo, Fernando Rozo, Juana Escobar, and Omayra Mendiola. "Diagnóstico de la Sierra Nevada de Santa Marta, Área Social: Aproximación a una historia oral de la colonización de la SNSM, Descripción testimonial (Agosto 1988)." Documento de Trabajo (unpublished manuscript). Fundación ProSierra Nevada de Santa Marta, 1988.

———. "Diagnóstico de la Sierra Nevada de Santa Marta, Área Social: Aproximación a una historia oral de la colonización de la SNSM, Recuento analítico (Agosto 1988)." Documento de Trabajo (unpublished manuscript). Fundación ProSierra Nevada de Santa Marta, 1988.

Molina, Gerardo. *Las ideas liberales en Colombia,* Volume 2, *1915–1934.* Bogotá: Tercer Mundo Editores, 1978.

Montenegro, Armando, and Carlos Esteban Posada. "Criminalidad en Colombia." *Borradores de Economía* 4 (October 1994): 1–26.

Montes Castilla, Adriana, Luis Martínez González, Nestor Martínez González, William Renán Rodríguez, and Fabio Silva Vallejo. *Memorias y Narrativas: Tres décadas del conflicto armado en el Magdalena Grande.* Santa Marta, Colombia: Editorial Unimagdalena, 2014.

Moore, Henrietta. "The Problem of Explaining Violence in the Social Sciences." In Harvey and Gow, *Sex and Violence.*

Mörner, Magnus. *Race Mixture in the History of Latin America.* Boston: Little, Brown, 1967.

Muir, Edward. *Mad Blood Stirring: Vendetta in Renaissance Italy.* Baltimore: Johns Hopkins University Press, 1993.

Muñoz, Catalina. "'A Mission of Enormous Transcendence': The Cultural Politics of Music during Colombia's Liberal Republic, 1930–1946." *Hispanic American Historical Review* 94, no. 1 (2014): 77–105.

Musto, David, and Pamela Korsmeyer. *The Quest for Drug Control: Politics and Federal Policy in a Period of Increasing Substance Abuse, 1963–1981.* New Haven: Yale University Press, 2002.

Nieves Oviedo, Jorge. *De los sonidos del patio a la música mundo: Semiosis nómadas en el Caribe.* Bogotá: Convenio Andrés Bello, 2008.

Nixon, Richard. "Special Message to the Congress on Control of Narcotics and Dangerous Drugs." Washington, DC, July 14, 1969. *The American Presidency Project.* https://www.presidency.ucsb.edu/node/239611.

———."Remarks about an Intensified Program for Drug Abuse Prevention and Control." Washington DC, June 17, 1971. *The American Presidency Project.* https://www.presidency.ucsb.edu/documents/remarks-about-intensified-program-for-drug-abuse-prevention-and-control#axzz1PCJydjl5.

Nugent, Walter. *Crossings: The Great Transatlantic Migrations, 1870–1914.* Bloomington: Indiana University Press, 1992.

O'Bryan, Lee. "The Cost of Lacoste: Drugs, Style, and Money." In *Big Deal: The Politics of the Illicit Drug Business,* edited by Anthony Henman, Roger Lewis, and Tim Malyon. London: Pluto Press, 1985.

Ocampo, José Antonio, and Santiago Montenegro. *Crisis mundial, protección e industrialización.* Bogotá: CEREC, 1984.

Ocampo López, Javier. *Qué es el conservatismo colombiano.* Bogotá: Plaza & Janés, 1990.

Ochoa Gautier, Ana María. "García Márquez, Macondismo, and the Soundscapes of Vallenato." *Popular Music* 24, no. 2 (2005): 207–22.

———. "Sonic Transculturation, Epistemologies of Purification, and the Aural Public Sphere in Latin America." *Social Identities* 12, no. 6 (2006): 803–25.

Offner, Amy C. *Sorting Out the Mixed Economy: The Rise and Fall of Welfare and Developmental States in the Americas.* Princeton, NJ: Princeton University Press, 2019.

Olick, Jeffrey K., Vered Vinitzky-Seroussi, and Daniel Levy, "Introduction." In *The Collective Memory Reader,* edited by Jeffrey K. Olick, Vered Vinitzky-Seroussi, and Daniel Levy. Oxford: Oxford University Press, 2011.

Oñate Martínez, Julio. *El ABC del vallenato.* Bogotá: Tauros Editores, 2003.

Orjuela, Luis Javier. "Tensión entre tradición y modernidad (1904–1945)." In *Historia de las ideas políticas en Colombia: De la independencia hasta nuestros días,* edited by José Fernando Ocampo. Bogotá: Instituto de Estudios Sociales PENSAR y Taurus, 2008.

Orozco Daza, Enrique, Oswaldo Villalobos Hincapié, and Alberto Yurcowiez Melendez. "Implicaciones socio-económicas del cultivo del algodón en la zona de San Juan del Cesar, Guajira." Honors thesis, agricultural economy, Universidad Tecnológica del Magdalena, Santa Marta, 1983.

Orsini Aarón, Giangina. *Poligamia y contrabando: Nociones de legalidad y legitimidad en la frontera guajira, siglo XX.* Bogotá: Ediciones Uniandes, 2007.

Ortega Cantero, Nicolás. "El viaje iberoamericano de Élisée Reclus." *Eria: Revista de Geografía* 28 (1992): 125–33.

Ortiz Sarmiento, Carlos Miguel. *Estado y subversión en Colombia: La Violencia en el Quindío, años 50*. Bogotá: CIDER-Uniandes; Fondo Editorial CEREC, 1985.

Palacios, Marco. *Between Legitimacy and Violence: A History of Colombia, 1875–2002*. Durham, NC: Duke University Press, 2006.

———. *¿De quién es la tierra? Propiedad, politización y protesta campesina en la década de 1930*. Bogotá: Universidad de los Andes y Fondo de Cultura Económica, 2011.

———. *Parábola del liberalism*. Bogotá: Grupo Editorial Norma, 1999.

Page, Christine. "A History of Conspicuous Consumption." In *Meaning, Measure, and Morality of Materialism,* edited by Floyd W. Rudmin and Marsha Richins. Provo, UT: Association of Consumer Research, 1992.

Parra Sandoval, Rodrigo. *Ausencia de futuro: La juventud colombiana*. Bogotá: Plaza & Janés, 1978.

Parsons, James. *Antioqueño Colonization in Western Colombia*. Berkeley: University of California Press, 1949.

Partridge, William. "Banana County in the Wake of United Fruit: Social and Economic Linkages." *American Ethnologist* 6, no. 3 (1979): 491–509.

———. "Exchange Relations in a Community on the North Coast of Colombia, with Special Reference to Cannabis." PhD dissertation, University of Florida, 1974.

Pastor, Robert. *The Carter Administration and Latin America: A Test of Principle*. Atlanta: Carter Center of Emory University, 1992.

Pécaut, Daniel. *Crónicas de cuatro décadas de política colombiana*. Bogotá: Editorial Norma, 2006.

———. *Orden y violencia: Evolución socio-política de Colombia entre 1930 y 1953*. 1986. Reprint, Bogotá: Editorial Norma, 2001.

———. "Pasado, presente y futuro de la violencia." *Análisis Político* 30 (January–April 1997): 1–43.

Pembleton, Matthew. "The Voice of the Bureau: How Frederic Sondern and the Bureau of Narcotics Crafted a Drug War and Shaped Popular Understanding of Drugs, Addiction, and Organized Crime in the 1950s." *Journal of American Culture* 38, no. 2 (June 2015): 113–29.

Perkins, John H. *Geopolitics and the Green Revolution: Wheat, Genes, and the Cold War*. Oxford: Oxford University Press, 1997.

Pérez Gómez, Augusto, ed. *Sustancias psicoativas: Historia del consumo en Colombia*. 1988. Reprint, Bogotá: Tercer Mundo Editores, 1994.

Pérez Reverte, Arturo. *La Reina del Sur*. Madrid: Alfaguara, 2002.

Perrin, Michel. *The Way of the Dead Indians: Guajiro Myths and Symbols*. 1976. Reprint, Austin: University of Texas, 1987.

Pettersson, Lotta, and Christoffer Carlsson. "Sex, Drugs, and Masculinities: A Life-Course Perspective." In *Masculinities in the Criminological Field. Control, Vulnerability and Risk-Taking,* edited by Ingrid Lander, Signe Ravn, and Nina Jon. Burlington, VT: Ashgate, 2014.

Piccato, Pablo. *City of Suspects: Crime in Mexico City, 1900–1931*. Durham, NC: Duke University Press, 2001.

Pineda Giraldo, Roberto. "Informe preliminar sobre aspectos sociales y económicos de la Guajira: Expedición 1947." *Revista del Instituto Etnológico Nacional* 3, no. 1 (1947): 1–160.

Pizarro Leongómez, Eduardo. *Las FARC (1949–1966): De la autodefensa a la combinación de todas las formas de lucha*. Bogotá: Tercer Mundo Editores, 1991.

Polit Dueñas, Gabriela. *Narrating Narcos: Culiacán and Medellín*. Pittsburgh: University of Pittsburgh Press, 2013.

Polit Dueñas, Gabriela, and María Helena Rueda, eds. *Meanings of Violence in Contemporary Latin America*. New York: Palgrave Macmillan, 2011.

Pollan, Michael. *The Botany of Desire: A Plant's-Eye View of the World*. New York: Random House, 2001.

Polo Acuña, José. *Indígenas, poderes y mediaciones en la Guajira en la transición de la colonia a la república*. Bogotá: Universidad de los Andes, 2012.

Portelli, Alessandro. *The Death of Luigi Trastulli and Other Stories: Form and Meaning in Oral History*. Albany: State University of New York Press, 1991.

Porter, Jayson Maurice. "Plagas, pesticidas y ciencias agrícolas entre revoluciones." *Boletín* 89 (September–December 2018): 1–44.

Posada Carbó, Eduardo. *The Colombian Caribbean: A Regional History, 1870–1950*. New York: Oxford University Press, 1996.

———. "Fiction as History: The Bananeras and Gabriel García Márquez's *One Hundred Years of Solitude*." *Journal of Latin America Studies* 30, no. 2 (May 1998): 395–414.

———. "Progreso y estancamiento, 1850–1950." In *Historia económica y social del Caribe colombiano*, edited by Adolfo Meisel, Nicolás del Castillo Mathieu, et al. Barranquilla: Ediciones Uninorte and ECOE Ediciones, 1994.

Posada Giraldo, Consuelo. *Canción vallenata y tradición oral*. Medellín: Universidad de Antioquia, 1986.

Pratt, Mary Louise. "Arts of the Contact Zone." *Profession* (1991): 33–40.

Putnam, Lara. *The Company They Kept: Migrants and the Politics of Gender in Caribbean Costa Rica, 1870–1960*. Chapel Hill: University of North Carolina Press, 2002.

Quintero, Marina. *Identidad vallenata*. Medellín: Facultad de Educación, Universidad de Antioquia, 2006.

Quiroz Otero, Ciro. *Vallenato, hombre y canto*. Bogotá: Icaro Editores, 1983.

———. "Prólogo." In *Crónicas del Valle de Upar*, Pepe Castro Castro. Bogotá: Zona Ltda, 2000.

Rabe, Stephen G. *The Most Dangerous Area in the World: John F. Kennedy Confronts Communist Revolution in Latin America*. Chapel Hill: University of North Carolina, 1999.

Ramírez, María Clemencia. "Maintaining Democracy in Colombia through Political Exclusions, States of Exception, Counterinsurgency, and Dirty War." In

Violent Democracies in Latin America, edited by Enrique Desmond Arias and Daniel M. Goldstein. Durham, NC: Duke University Press, 2010.

Randall, Stephen. *Colombia and the United States: Hegemony and Interdependence.* Athens: University of Georgia Press, 1992.

———. *The Diplomacy of Modernization: Colombian-American Relations, 1920–1940.* Toronto: University of Toronto Press, 1977.

Rapport, Joanne. *The Politics of Memory: Native Historical Interpretation in the Colombian Andes.* Durham, NC: Duke University Press, 1990.

———. *The Disappearing Mestizo: Configuring Difference in the Colonial New Kingdom of Granada.* Durham, NC: Duke University Press, 2014.

Reclus, Élisée. *Viaje a la Sierra Nevada de Santa Marta.* 1869. Reprint, Bogotá: Biblioteca Popular de Colombia, 1947.

Reddock, Rhoda E., ed. *Interrogating Caribbean Masculinities: Theoretical and Empirical Analyses.* Kingston, Jamaica: University of the West Indies Press, 2004.

Reeves, Michelle Denise. "The Evolution of 'Narcoterrorism': From the Cold War to the War on Drugs." In *Beyond the Eagle Shadow: New Histories of Latin America's Cold War,* edited by Virginia Garrard-Burnett, Mark Atwood Lawrence, and Julio E. Moreno. Albuquerque: University of New Mexico Press, 2013.

Reichel-Dolmatoff, Gerardo. "Los Kogis: Una tribu indígena de la Sierra Nevada de Santa Marta." *Revista del Instituto Etnológico Nacional* 1–2 (1950–51).

Reichel-Dolmatoff, Gerardo, and Alicia Reichel-Dolmatoff. *The People of Aritama: The Cultural Personality of a Colombian Mestizo Village.* Oxford: Routledge, 1961.

Restrepo, Laura. *Leopardo al sol.* 1989. Reprint, Bogotá: Grupo Editorial Norma, 1997.

Restrepo Arteaga, Juan Guillermo. *El Caribe colombiano: Aproximación a la región y el regionalismo.* Barranquilla: Universidad del Norte, 2000.

Reuter, Peter. "Systemic Violence in Drug Markets." *Crime, Law and Social Change* 52, no. 3 (September 2009): 275–84.

Reyes Posada, Alejandro. "La violencia y la expansión territorial." In *Economía y política del narcotráfico,* edited by Juan G. Tokatlian and Bruce M. Bagley. Bogotá: Ediciones Uniandes, CEREC, 1990.

Riches, David. "The Phenomenon of Violence." In *The Anthropology of Violence,* edited by David Riches. New York: Basil Blackwell, 1986.

Rivera Cusicanqui, Silvia. *Política e ideología en el movimiento campesino colombiano: El caso de la ANUC, Asociación Nacional de Usuarios Campesinos.* Bogotá: Instituto de Investigaciones de las Naciones Unidas para el Desarrollo Social, UNRISD; Centro de Investigación y Educación Popular CINEP, 1987.

Rodríguez Ruíz, Jaime Alejandro. "Deconstrucción de códigos modernos: *Cuatro años a bordo de mí mismo.*" *Universitas Humanistica* 53, no. 53 (2002): 49–61.

Rodríguez Torres, Álvaro. "Eliseo Reclus: Geógrafo y anarquista." *Revista Credencial Historia* 35 (November 1992).

Rodríguez Vargas, Francisco. "Las organizaciones del sector cafetero colombiano." *Innovar* 7 (1996): 7–26.

Rojas, Cristina, and Daniel Tubb. "*La Violencia* in Colombia, through Stories of the Body." In Johnson, Salvatore, and Spierenburg, *Murder and Violence in Modern Latin America.*

Rojas, Diana. "La Alianza para el Progreso en Colombia." *Revista Análisis Político* 23, no. 70 (September–December 2010): 91–124.

———. "Colombia como 'vitrina' de la Alianza para el Progreso." In *50 años de la Alianza para el Progreso: Lecciones para el Presente, Relatoría del evento.* Documentos del Departamento de Ciencia Política 11. Bogotá: Universidad de los Andes, 2011.

Roldán, Mary. "Afterword." In Polit Dueñas and Rueda, *Meanings of Violence in Contemporary Latin America.*

———. *Blood and Fire:* La Violencia *in Antioquia, Colombia, 1946–1953.* Durham, NC: Duke University Press, 2002.

———. "Cocaine and the 'Miracle' of Modernity in Medellín." In *Cocaine: Global Histories,* edited by Paul Gootenberg. London: Routledge, 1999.

———. "End of Discussion: Violence, Participatory Democracy, and the Limits of Dissent in Colombia." In Arias and Goldstein, *Violent Democracies in Latin America.*

Roorda, Eric Paul. "The Cult of the Airplane among U.S. Military Men and Dominicans during the U.S. Occupation and the Trujillo Regime." In Joseph, LeGrand, and Salvatore, *Close Encounters of Empire.*

Rosado, Jairo. "El proceso industrial, terapéutico y biológico del dividivi." In *Memorias del foro el dividivi como árbol y el dividivi como festival.* Riohacha, Colombia: Fondo Mixto para la Promoción la Cultura y las Artes de la Guajira, 1994.

Roseberry, William. *Anthropologies and Histories: Essays in Culture, History, and Political Economy.* New Brunswick, NJ: Rutgers University Press, 1994.

———. "Hegemony and the Language of Contention." In Joseph and Nugent, *Everyday Forms of State Formation.*

Roseberry, William, Lowell Gudmundson, and Mario Samper Kutschbach, eds. *Coffee, Society, and Power in Latin America.* Baltimore: John Hopkins University Press, 1995.

Rostam-Kolay, Jasamin. "'Beautiful Americans': Peace Corps Iran in the Global Sixties." In Jian et al., *The Routledge Handbook of the Global Sixties.*

Rotker, Susana, ed. *Citizens of Fear: Urban Violence in Latin America.* New Brunswick, NJ: Rutgers University Press, 2002.

Rubin, Vera, and Lambros Comitas. *Ganja in Jamaica: A Medical Anthropological Study of Chronic Marijuana Use.* The Hague: Mouton, 1975.

Ruiz, Hernando. "Implicaciones sociales y económicas de la producción de la marihuana." In ANIF, *Marihuana.*

Russi Laverde, Germán. "Notas para una investigación etnológica sobre una situación de cambio económico y social en la comunidad indígena de la Guajira." Honors thesis, anthropology, Universidad Nacional de Colombia-Medellín, 1972.

Sáenz Rovner, Eduardo. "Los colombianos y las redes del narcotráfico en Nueva York durante los años 70." *Innovar* 24, no. 53 (2014): 223–34.

————. "Estudio de caso de la diplomacia antinarcóticos entre Colombia y los Estados Unidos (gobierno de Alfonso López Michelsen, 1974–1978)." *Documento Escuela de Administración y Contaduría* 13 (July 2012): 7.

————. "Industriales, proteccionismo y política en Colombia: Intereses, conflictos y violencia." *Historia Crítica* 3 (January–June 1990): 85–105.

————. *La ofensiva empresarial: Industriales, políticos y violencia en los años 40 en Colombia.* Bogotá: Universidad Nacional de Colombia, CES, 2007.

————. "La prehistoria de la marihuana en Colombia: Consumo y cultivos entre los años 30 y 60." *Cuadernos de Economía* 26, no. 47 (2007): 207–22.

————. "La prehistoria del narcotráfico en Colombia." *Innovar* 8 (July–December 1996): 65–92.

Saether, Steinar. "Independence and the Redefinition of Indianness around Santa Marta, Colombia, 1750–1850." *Journal of Latin American Studies* 37, no. 1 (February 2005): 55–80.

Safford, Frank. "Significación de los antioqueños en el desarrollo económico colombiano: Un ensayo crítico de las tesis de Everett Hagen." *Anuario colombiano de historia social y de la cultura* 3 (1965): 49–69.

Safford, Frank, and Marco Palacios. *Colombia: Fragmented Land, Divided Society.* Oxford: Oxford University Press, 2002.

Saganogo, Brahiman. "Nadaísmo colombiano: Ruptura socio-cultural o extravagancia expresiva." *Espéculo: Revista de Estudios Literarios* 38 (March–June 2008). http://webs.ucm.es/info/especulo/numero38/nadaism.html.

Salazar, Alonso. *La cola del lagarto: Drogas y narcotráfico en la sociedad colombiana.* Medellín: Corporación Región, 1998.

————. *No nacimos pa semilla.* Bogota: CINEP, 1990.

Salcedo Ramos, Alberto. *La eterna parranda: Crónicas 1997–2011.* Bogotá: Aguilar, 2011.

Salgado Ruiz, Henry. "Conflicto agrario y expansión de los cultivos ilícitos en Colombia." In *Análisis histórico del narcotráfico en Colombia: VIII Cátedra anual de historia Ernesto Restrepo Tirado.* Bogotá: Museo Nacional de Colombia, 2014. http://www.museonacional.gov.co/imagenes/publicaciones/analisis-historico-del-narcotrafico-en-colombia.pdf.

Samper, Adlai Stevenson. "El vallenato en tiempo de difusión." *Huellas: Revista de la Universidad del Norte* 67–68 (2003): 55–64.

Samper Pizano, Ernesto. "Marihuana U.S.A." In ANIF, *La legalización de la marihuana.*

Sanabria, Harry. *The Anthropology of Latin America and the Caribbean.* New York: Pearson Education, 2007.

Sánchez, Gonzalo. "The Violence: An Interpretative Synthesis." In *Violence in Colombia: The Contemporary Crisis in Historical Perspective,* edited by Charles Bergquist, Ricardo Peñaranda, and Gonzalo Sánchez. Wilmington, DE: Scholarly Resources, 1992.

Sánchez, Gonzalo, and Donny Meertens. *Bandoleros, gamonales y campesinos: El caso de* La Violencia *en Colombia.* Bogotá: El Áncora Editores, 1983.

Sánchez, Sonia. "Causas y manifestaciones del delito en la costa norte del país: departamentos del Atlántico, Magdalena y Guajira." Honors thesis, sociology, Universidad Nacional de Colombia, Bogotá, 1978.

Sánchez Baute, Alfonso. *Líbranos del bien*. Bogotá: Alfaguara, 2008.

Sánchez Mejia, Hugues R. "De bundes, cumbiambas y merengues vallenatos: Fusiones, cambios y permanencias en la música y danzas en el Magdalena Grande, 1750–1970." In *Música y sociedad en Colombia: Traslaciones, legitimaciones e identificaciones*, edited by Mauricio Pardo Rojas. Bogotá: Editorial Universidad del Rosario, 2009.

Sanders, Jerry W. *Peddlers of Crisis: The Committee on the Present Danger and the Politics of Containment*. Boston: Sound End Press, 1983.

Sargent, Daniel. *A Superpower Transformed: The Remaking of American Foreign Relations in the 1970s*. New York: Oxford University Press, 2015.

Sarmiento, Libardo, and Carlos Moreno. "Narcotráfico y sector agropecuario en Colombia." *Economía Colombiana* 226–27 (1990): 29–37.

Scott, James. "Foreword." In Joseph and Nugent, *Everyday Forms of State Formation*.

Schoulz, Lars. *Beneath the United States: A History of U.S. Policy toward Latin America*. Cambridge, MA: Harvard University Press, 1998.

Schulzinger, Robert D. "Détente in the Nixon-Ford Years, 1969–1976." In *The Cambridge History of the Cold War*, edited by Melvyn P. Leffler and Odd Arne Westad. Cambridge: Cambridge University Press, 2010.

Schwartz, Stuart B. *Sea of Storms: A History of Hurricanes in the Greater Caribbean, from Columbus to Katrina*. Princeton, NJ: Princeton University Press, 2015.

Secretary of Health, Education, and Welfare and Subcommittee on Alcoholism and Narcotics. *Marijuana and Health: Second Annual Report to Congress*. Washington DC: US Government Printing Office, 1972.

Segovia, Rodolfo. "El contrabando en el Nuevo Reino de Granada, 1700–1739." *Boletín Cultural y Bibliográfico* 39, no. 61 (2002): 34–55.

Serje, Margarita. "El 'Almirante Padilla' en Corea: Una crónica del legendario buque de la Armada Nacional de Colombia." *Expedición Padilla,* May 2012, https://www.academia.edu/3792656/El_Almirante_Padilla_en_Corea_Una_crónica_del_legendario_buque_de_la_Armada_Nacional_de_Colombia.

———. "La invención de la Sierra Nevada." *Antípoda: Revista de Antropología y Arquelogía* 7 (July 2008): 197–229.

———. "El mito de la ausencia del Estado: La incorporación económica de las 'zonas de frontera' en Colombia." *Cahiers des Ameriques Latines* 71 (2012): 95–117.

———. *El revés de la nación: Territorios salvajes, fronteras y tierras de nadie*. Bogotá: Ediciones Uniandes, 2005.

Simonett, Helena. "Narcocorridos: An Emerging Micromusic of Nuevo LA." *Ethnomusicology* 45, no. 2 (2001): 315–37.

Smith, David E., ed. *The New Social Drug: Cultural, Medical, and Legal Perspectives on Marihuana*. Englewood Cliffs, NJ: Prentice Hall, 1970.

Smith, Joseph. *The United States and Latin America: A History of American Diplomacy, 1776–2000.* New York: Routledge, 2005.

Solórzano, Betty, and Frida de Dangond. "Implicaciones socioeconómicas de la cannabiscultura en los departamentos del Magdalena y de la Guajira." Honors thesis, agricaltural economy, Universidad Tecnológica del Magdalena, 1978.

Somoza Rodríguez, Miguel. "Educación y movimientos populistas en América Latina: Una emancipación frustrada." *Historia de la Educación* 29 (2010): 157–75.

Stares, Paul. *Global Habit: The Drug Problem in a Borderless World.* Washington, DC: Brookings Institution Press, 1996.

Stern, Steve. "The Decentered Center and the Expansionist Periphery: The Paradoxes of Foreign-Local Encounter." In Joseph, LeGrand, and Salvatore, *Close Encounters of Empire.*

Stewart, Herbert, et al. "El desarrollo agrícola de Colombia: Informe de la Misión organizada por el Banco de Reconstrucción y Fomento a solicitud del Gobierno de Colombia." *Revista Cafetera de Colombia* 13, no. 30 (January 1957).

Stodder, Joseph H., and Kevin F. McCarthy. *Profiles of the Caribbean Basin, 1960–1980: Changing Geopolitical and Geostrategic Dimensions.* Santa Monica, CA: RAND Corporation, 1983.

Stoller, Richard. "Alfonso López Pumarejo and Liberal Radicalism in 1930s, Colombia." *Journal of Latin American Studies* 27 (1995): 367–97.

Striffler, Luis. *El río Cesar: Relación de un viaje a la Sierra Nevada.* 1876. Reprint, London: British Library, 2001.

Striffler, Steve, and Mark Moberg, eds. *Banana Wars: Power, Production, and History in the Americas.* Durham, NC: Duke University Press, 2003.

Tate, Winifred. *Drugs, Thugs, and Diplomats: U.S. Policymaking in Colombia.* Stanford, CA: Stanford University Press, 2015.

Taussig, Michael. *The Devil and Commodity Fetishism in South America.* 1980. Reprint, Chapel Hill: University of North Carolina Press, 2010.

———. "Shamanism, Colonialism, and the Wild Man: A Study in Terror and Healing." In *On Violence: A Reader,* edited by Bruce B. Lawrence and Aisha Karim. Durham, NC: Duke University Press, 2007.

Taylor, William. "Between Global Process and Local Knowledge: An Inquiry into Early Latin America Social History, 1500–1900." In *Reliving the Past: The World of Social History,* edited by Olivier Zunz. Chapel Hill: University of North Carolina Press, 1985.

Teague, Aileen. "Mexico's Dirty War on Drugs: Source Control and Dissidence in Drug Enforcement." *Social History of Alcohol and Drugs* 33, no. 1 (spring 2019): 63–87.

Thompson, Paul. "The Voice of the Past: Oral History." In *The Oral History Reader,* edited by Robert Perks and Alistair Thomson. New York: Routledge, 1988.

Thoumi, Francisco. *Economía política y narcotráfico.* Bogotá: Tercer Mundo Editores, 1994.

———. *Illegal Drugs, Economy, and Society in the Andes.* Washington, DC: Woodrow Wilson Center Press; Baltimore: Johns Hopkins University Press, 2003.

Thoumi, Francisco, et al., eds. *Drogas ilícitas en Colombia: Su impacto económico, político y social.* Bogotá: Editorial Ariel, 1997.

Tickner, Arlene, and Carolina Cepeda, "The Role of Illegal Drugs in Colombia-US Relations." In *Anti-drug Policies in Colombia: Successes, Failures, and Wrong Turns,* edited by Alejandro Gaviria and Daniel Mejía. 2011. Reprint, Nashville: Vanderbilt University Press, 2016.

Tickner, Arlene, and Sandra Borda. "Las relaciones internacionales en Colombia: Creación, consolidación y producción disciplinaria." In *Relaciones internacionales y política exterior de Colombia,* edited by Sandra Borda and Arlene Tickner. Bogotá: Universidad de los Andes, 2011.

Tirado, Thomas Charles. "Alfonso López Pumarejo: His Contribution to Reconciliation in Colombian Politics." PhD dissertation, Temple University, Philadelphia, 1977.

———. *Alfonso López Pumarejo, el conciliador: Su contribucion a la paz política en Colombia.* 1977. Reprint, Bogotá: Editorial Planeta, 1986.

Tirado Mejía, Alvaro. *Aspectos políticos del primer gobierno de Alfonso López Pumarejo, 1934–1938.* Bogotá: Instituto Colombiano de Cultura, 1981.

———. "Cambios económicos, sociales y culturales en los años sesenta del siglo XX." *Historia y Memoria* 12 (January–June 2016): 297–316.

———. "López Pumarejo: La Revolución en Marcha." In Tirado Mejía, Melo, and Bejarano, *Nueva Historia de Colombia,* vol. 1.

———. "Violence and the State in Colombia." In *Colombia: The Politics of Reforming the State,* edited by Eduardo Posada Carbó. London: Institute of Latin American Studies, University of London; Macmillan Press, 1998.

Tirado Mejía, Álvaro, Jorge Orlando Melo, and Jesús Antonio Bejarano, eds. *Nueva Historia de Colombia,* Volume 1, *Historia Política, 1886–1946.* Bogotá: Editorial Planeta, 1989.

Tokatlian, Juan G. "La polémica sobre la legalización de drogas en Colombia, el Presidente Samper y los Estados Unidos." *Latin American Research Review* 35, no. 1 (2000): 37–83.

Tokatlian, Juan G., and Bruce Bagley, eds. *Economía y política del narcotráfico.* Bogotá: Ediciones Uniandes, 1990.

Topik, Steven C., and Allen Wells, eds. *The Second Conquest of Latin America: Coffee, Henequen, and Oil during the Export Boom, 1850–1930.* Austin: University of Texas Press, 1998.

Torres Duque, Óscar, ed. *El mausoleo iluminado: Antología del ensayo en Colombia.* Bogotá: Presidencia de la República, 1997.

Torres, Guillermo Henríquez. *Cienaga: La música del otro valle; Zona bananera del Magdalena, siglos XVIII, XIX, XX.* Barranquilla, Colombia: Editorial La Iguana Ciega, 2013.

Tovar Pinzón, Hermes. *Grandes empresas agrícolas y ganaderas: Su desarrollo en el siglo XVIII.* Bogota: Ediciones Ciec, 1980.

Turbay Ayala, Julio César. *Memorias de un Cuatrenio, 1978–1982.* Volume 5. Bogotá: Editorial Presencia, n.d.

Turino, Thomas. "Nationalism and Latin American Music: Selected Case Studies and Theoretical Considerations." *Latin American Music Review* 24, no. 2 (2003): 169–209.

Twinam, Ann. *Miners, Merchants, and Farmers in Colonial Colombia.* Austin: University of Texas Press, 1982.

United States v. Cadena. 585 F.2d 1252. *American Journal of International Law* 73, no. 2 (1979): 302–4.

United States v. Cortes. 588 F.2d 106. *American Journal of International Law* 73, no. 3 (1979): 514–15.

United States v. Warren. 578 F.2d. 1058. *American Journal of International Law* 73, no. 1 (1979): 143–44.

United States v. Williams. 589 F.2d 210. *American Journal of International Law* 73, no. 4 (1979): 701–2.

Urbina Joiro, Hernán. *Lírica vallenata: De Gustavo Gutiérrez a las fusiones modernas.* Bogotá: Convenio Andrés Bello, 2003.

Uribe, María Teresa. *Poderes y regiones: Problemas en la constitución de la nación colombiana, 1810–1850.* Medellín: Universidad de Antioquia, 1987.

———. *La territorialidad de los conflictos y de la violencia en Antioquia.* Medellín: Universidad de Antioquia, 1990.

Uribe Tobón, Carlos Alberto. "Pioneros de la antropología en Colombia: El padre Rafael Celedón." *Boletín Museo del Oro* 17 (1986): 3–31.

———. "De Gran Jaguar a padre simbólico: La biografía 'oficial' de Gerardo Reichel-Dolmatoff." *Antípoda. Revista de Antropología y Arquelogía* 27 (January-April 2017): 35–60.

Uribe, María Victoria. *Matar, rematar y contramatar: Las masacres de* La Violencia *en el Tolima, 1948–1964.* Bogotá: CINEP, 1990.

US House of Representatives, Select Committee on Narcotics Abuse and Control. *Problems of Law Enforcement and Its Efforts to Reduce the Level of Drug Trafficking in South Florida.* Report to the 95th Congress, 2nd sess. Washington, DC: US Government Printing Office, 1978.

US Senate, Committee on the Judiciary. *Controlled Dangerous Substances Act of 1969: Report of the Committee on the Judiciary, United States Senate, Together with Additional Views.* June 6, 1969. Washington, DC: US Government Printing Office, 1969.

Vallejo, Fernando. *Barba Jacob el mensajero.* México: Editorial Séptimo Círculo, 1984.

Van Vleck, Jennifer. *Empire of the Air: Aviation and the American Ascendancy.* Cambridge, MA: Harvard University Press, 2013.

Vega Seña, Marcos Fidel. *Vallenato: Cultura y sentimiento.* Bogotá: Universidad Cooperativa de Colombia, 2005.

Vélez, Hugo. *El debate en gráficas de Nacho Vives ante el Senado.* Bogotá: Hugo Vélez O, 1969.

Vidal Joiro, Orlando Essau. *Cuentos, relatos y personajes de mi tierra.* Riohacha, Colombia: Editorial Antorcha Guajira, 2000.

Vidal Perdomo, Jaime. *La región en la organización territorial del estado.* Bogotá: Universidad del Rosario, 2001.

Viloria de la Hoz, Joaquín. *Acordeones, cumbiamba y vallenato en el Magdalena Grande: Una historia cultural, económica y política, 1870–1960.* Santa Marta, Colombia: Editorial Unimagdalena, 2018.

———. *Café Caribe: La economía cafetera en la Sierra Nevada de Santa Marta.* Cartagena de Indias: Centro de Investigaciones Económicas del Caribe Colombiano, Banco de la República, 1997.

———. *Empresarios del Caribe colombiano: Historia económica y empresarial del Magdalena Grande y del Bajo Magdalena, 1870–1930.* Bogotá: Colección de Economía Regional, Banco de la República, 2014.

———. *Historia empresarial del guineo: Empresas y empresarios bananeros en el departamento del Magdalena, 1870–1930.* Cuadernos de historia económica y empresarial 23. Bogotá: Banco de la República, 2009.

———. *Sierra Nevada de Santa Marta: Economía de sus recursos naturales.* Cartagena de Indias: Centro de Estudios Económicos Regionales, Banco de la República, 2005.

Viveros Vigoya, Mara. "Masculinidades: Diversidades regionales y cambios generacionales en Colombia." In *Hombres e identidades de género: Investigaciones desde América Latina,* edited by Mara Viveros, José Olavarría and Norma Fuller. Medellín: CES, Universidad Nacional de Colombia, 2001.

Vives, Alberto Abello, and Silvana Giaimo Chávez, eds. *Poblamiento y ciudades del Caribe colombiano.* Bogotá: Observatorio del Caribe Colombiano y Editorial Gente Nueva, 2000.

Vives, José Benito. *Pepe Vives cuenta su vida.* Santa Marta, Colombia: Editorial Mejoras, 1981.

Vives, José Ignacio. "Las banderas no se encarcelan." *Seneca* 9 (October 1969).

———. *La Guajira ante el Congreso de Colombia: Historia de un proceso.* Bogotá: Senado de la República, Imprenta Nacional, 1965.

Wade, Peter. *Blackness and Race Mixture: The Dynamics of Racial Identity in Colombia.* Baltimore: John Hopkins University Press, 1993.

———. "Man the Hunter: Gender and Violence in Music and Drinking Contexts in Colombia." In Harvey and Gow, *Sex and Violence.*

———. *Music, Race, and Nation: Música Tropical in Colombia.* Chicago: University of Chicago Press, 2000.

———. "Racial Identity and Nationalism: A Theoretical View from Latin America." *Ethnic and Racial Studies* 24, no. 5 (2001): 845–65.

Wagner Medina, Marcela. "Las huellas ambientales del oro blanco: La expansión algodonera en el vallle del río Cesar, 1950–1980." MA thesis, Universidad de los Andes, 2011.

Washington Office for Latin American Affairs (WOLA). *La aspersión de cultivos de usos ilícitos en Colombia: Una estrategia fallida.* Washington, DC: WOLA; Bogotá: Instituto de Estudios para el Desarollo y la Paz, 2008.

Wasserman, Abby. "PCVs and Wayuu Blamed for Drug Trade." *Worldview Magazine* (Spring 2019): 20–23.

Weimer, Daniel. *Seeing Drugs: Modernization, Counterinsurgency, and U.S. Narcotics Control in the Third World, 1969–1976.* Kent, OH: Kent University Press, 2011.

Weston, Julian A. *The Cactus Eaters.* London: H. F. & G. Witherby, Ltd., 1937.

White, Judith. *Historia de una ignominia: La United Fruit Co. en Colombia.* Bogotá: Editorial Presencia, 1978.

Williams, William Appleman. *The Tragedy of American Diplomacy.* Cleveland: World Publishing, 1959.

Wollaston, A. F. R. "The Sierra Nevada of Santa Marta, Colombia." *Geographical Journal* 66, no. 2 (1925): 97–106.

Wright, Angus. *The Death of Ramón González: The Modern Agricultural Dilemma.* Austin: University of Texas Press, 1990.

Zalamea Borda, Eduardo. *Cuatro años a bordo de mí mismo: Diario de los cinco sentidos.* 1935. Reprint, Medellín: Editorial Bedout, 1976.

Zambrano Pantoja, Fabio. *Colombia, país de regiones.* Bogotá: CINEP, 1998.

———. "Historia del poblamiento del territorio de la región Caribe de Colombia." In Abello Vives and Giaimo Chávez, *Poblamiento y ciudades del Caribe colombiano.*

Zamosc, Leon. *The Agrarian Question and the Peasant Movement in Colombia: Struggles of the National Peasant Association, 1967–1981.* Cambridge: Cambridge University Press; Geneva: United Nations Institute for Social Development, 1986.

Zapata, Blanca Nubia. "Empresas comerciales del municipio de Valledupar, 1950–1980." In *Becas culturales en investigación sociocultural en historia regional y/o local del Departamento del Cesar.* Bogotá: Observatorio del Caribe Colombiano, 2006.

Zolov, Eric. "Introduction: Latin America in the Global Sixties." *The Americas* 70, no. 3 (January 2014): 349–62.

INTERVIEWS CONDUCTED BY THE AUTHOR

Aguilar Epieyú, Germán, January 28, 2011, Maicao, Guajira, Colombia.

Arroyo, Bienvenido, February 4, 2011, Pueblo Bello, Cesar, Colombia.

Barros, Germán, July 2, 2006, Riohacha, Guajira, Colombia.

Bermúdez, Roger, March 11, 2005, Riohacha, Guajira, Colombia.

Britto, Rafael Enrique "Arique" (no. 1), January 16, 2005, San Juan del Cesar, Guajira, Colombia.

——— (no. 2), February 23, 2005, San Juan del Cesar, Guajira, Colombia.

——— (no. 3), February 24, 2005, on road Villanueva–San Juan del Cesar, Guajira, Colombia.

——— (no. 4), December 5, 2014, on road La Junta–San Juan del Cesar, Guajira, Colombia.

Bourne, Peter, May 26, 2014, questionnaire via email.

Bueno Suárez, Lenín, February 10, 2005, Riohacha, Guajira, Colombia.

Callo, March 18, 2005, Riohacha, Guajira, Colombia.

Carlos (no. 1), March 9, 2005, Riohacha, Guajira, Colombia.

——— (no. 2), March 11, 2005, Riohacha, Guajira, Colombia.

Castro Castro, Pepe. February 1, 2011, Valledupar, Cesar, Colombia.

Chucho, July 4, 2005, La Paz, Bolivia.

Daza Noguera, Yim, March 24, 2005, San Juan del Cesar, Guajira, Colombia.

De Andreis, Pedro, January 20, 2011, Santa Marta, Magdalena, Colombia.

Deluque, Wilfredo, March 18, 2005, Riohacha, Guajira, Colombia.

Echeverri, Rodrigo, March 15, 2010, Carmen de Viboral, Antioquia, Colombia.

Elber, February 24, 2005, Villanueva, Guajira, Colombia.

Ferrucho Padilla, Edgar (no. 1), February 16, 2005, Riohacha, Guajira, Colombia.

——— (no. 2), February 18, 2005, Riohacha, Guajira, Colombia.

Gutiérrez Cabello, Gustavo, February 4, 2005, Riohacha, Guajira, Colombia.

Hernández Pimienta, Édison, February 10, 2005, Riohacha, Guajira, Colombia.

Herrera Barros, Enrique, February 8, 2005, Riohacha, Guajira, Colombia.

Irma, March 30, 2005, Buritaca, Magdalena, Colombia.

Ismael, January 30, 2005, Santa Marta, Magdalena, Colombia.

Josefina, July 4, 2006, Riohacha, Guajira, Colombia.

José Luis, January 17, 2005, San Juan del Cesar, Guajira, Colombia.

Lineros, Manuel, January 21, 2011, Santa Marta, Magdalena, Colombia.

Llaguna, José Agustín, Febraury 28, 2005, Conejo-Fonseca, Guajira, Colombia.

López González, Martín, February 14, 2005, Riohacha, Guajira, Colombia.

López Hernández, Miguel Ángel, March 10, 2005, Riohacha, Guajira, Colombia.

Mantequilla, March 11, 2005, Riohacha, Guajira, Colombia.

Martínez, Ariel, January 21, 2011, Santa Marta, Magdalena, Colombia.

Meco, January 17, 2005, San Juan del Cesar, Guajira, Colombia.

Medina Sierra, Abel, June 28, 2006, Riohacha, Guajira, Colombia.

Mejía, Jacobo "El Pano," August 8, 2008, San Juan del Cesar, Guajira, Colombia.

Mendoza, Justiniano, February 23, 2005, San Juan del Cesar, Guajira, Colombia.

Melo, Meña, August 2, 2008, Riohacha, Guajira, Colombia.

Moya Molina, Sergio, February 3, 2011, Valledupar, Cesar, Colombia.

Orth, Maureen, January 10, 2019, questionnaire via email.

Palacio Tiller, Manuel, July 7, 2006, Maicao, Guajira, Colombia.

Pebo, June 25, 2006, Taganga, Magdalena, Colombia.

Quintero, Marina, October 19, 2010, Medellín, Antioquia, Colombia.

Raúl, March 16, 2005, Riohacha, Guajira, Colombia.

Rojas, Germán, March 28, 2005, Riohacha, Guajira, Colombia.

Ruiz, Hernando, February 16, 2010, Bogotá, Colombia.

Silvio, March 15, 2005, Riohacha, Guajira, Colombia.

Velandia, Guillermo, February 12, 2005, Riohacha, Guajira, Colombia.

Vieira, Juan "Ios," March 30, 2005, Santa Marta, Magdalena, Colombia.

Vives, Luz Marina, January 24, 2011, Santa Marta, Magdalena, Colombia.

Wasserman, Abby December 23, 2018, phone interview.
———, January 9, 2019, questionnaire via email.
Zuñiga, Doris Paulina, August 11, 2018, San Juan del Cesar, Guajira, Colombia.

FILMS AND TV SHOWS

La bacanería, un estilo de vida. Directed by Hugo González Montalvo. Colombia, 1999.
Cocaine Cowboys. Directed by Billy Corben. United States, 2006.
Diomedes, el cacique de la Junta. Produced by RCN Televisión. Colombia, 2015.
Guajira. Produced by RCN Televisión. Colombia, 1996.
La mala hierba. Produced by Caracol Televisión. Colombia, 1982.
Maria Full of Grace. Directed by Joshua Marston. United States, 2004.
Pájaros de verano. Directed by Ciro Guerra and Cristina Gallego. Colombia, 2018.

RECORDINGS

Brito, Romualdo. "El Marimbero." In Roberto Torres, featuring Daniel Santos, *La Charanga Vallenata,* 1981.
———. "Yo soy el indio." In Diomedez Díaz and Colacho Mendoza, *Los profesionales,* 1979.
———. "Los ojos no mienten." In Binomio de Oro, *Superior,* 1985
Bueno Suárez, Lenín. "Soy parrandero y qué." In Los Hermanos Zuleta, *Dos estrellas,* 1977.
———. "La parranda es pa' amanecer." In Binomio de Oro, *Enamorado como siempre,* 1978.
Carrillo, Isaac "Tijito." "Mi primo." In Hermanos Zuleta, *Dinastía y folclor,* 1979.
Coronado, Euclides Enrique. "Adiós a un amigo." In Hermanos Zuleta, *Dinastía y folclor,* 1979.
Daza, Octavio. "Dime Pajarito." In Binomio de Oro, *Clase Aparte,* 1980
Díaz, Diomedes. "El profesional." In Diomedes Díaz and Colacho Mendoza, *Los profesionales,* 1979.
———. "Mi compadre." In Diomedes Díaz and Juancho Rois, *El cóndor herido,* 1989.
Durán, Alejo. "La perra." In Alejo Durán, *Lo Mejor de Alejo Durán,* n.d.
Escalona, Rafael. "El almirante Padilla." In Bovea y sus Vallenatos, *Los cantos vallenatos de Escalona,* 1962.
———. "El hambre del liceo," 1948.
Gómez, José María "Chema." *Compae Chipuco,* 1938.
Chijo. "Recordings," tapes 1 to 7; each tape, sides A and B. Family archive, n.d.

Marín, Hernando. "El gavilán mayor." In Diomedes Díaz y Colacho Mendoza, *Dos Grandes,* 1978.

———. "Lluvia de verano." In Diomedes Díaz y Juancho Rois, *La locura,* 1978.

Movil, Máximo. "Mujer conforme." In Jorge Oñate, *La parranda y la mujer,* 1975.

Moya Molina, Sergio. "La celosa." In Hermanos Zuleta, *Río crecido,* 1974.

Oñate Martínez, Julio. "La profecía." in Hermanos Zuleta, *Tierra de cantores,* 1978

Rois, Juancho. "Homenaje sincero." In Jorge Oñate and Juancho Rois, *Ruiseñor de mi valle,* 1981.

Serrano, Álvaro. "Yo tenía mi cafetal." In Los Melódicos, *Los Melódicos en vallenato,* 1980.

Zabaleta, Armando. "Jaime Luis." In Hermanos Zuleta, *Volumen 12,* 1979.

INDEX

Prisoners' Welfare Committee, 179
Proclaimed List, 36
"La profecía" (Oñate Martínez), 126, 265n51
"El profesional" (Díaz), 137, 268n95
public works. See infrastructure
Puerto López, 22f, 31, 34, 58f, 62–63, 90f
Pulowi (god), 67
Pupo Martínez, Ciro, 30

Quintero, Marina, 135–36

race, 6–9, 77, 80, 118, 122–27, 198, 204–5,
  217. See also class; gender; indigenous
  groups; mestizaje
Radio Valledupar, 45
Reclus, Élisée, 5–6
Registro Padilla, 25
Reichel-Dolmatoff, Gerardo, 6
reign of terror, 3, 183–209, 217
Respice Polum, 25
Restrepo, Laura, 192, 282n37
Revolutionary Armed Forces of Colombia
  (FARC), 159, 208, 217
Revolutionary Independent Labor Move-
  ment (MOIR), 161
Revolutionary Liberal Movement (MRL),
  51–52, 122, 157
Revolution on the March plan, 29–34
Reyes, Rafael, 24–27
Riohacha: about, 7, 25, 52; decline of mari-
  juana and, 161, 193, 200; emergence of
  marijuana and, 77–79, 84; emergence of
  tropical commodities and, 31–36, 39, 42,
  52; maps of, 16f, 58f, 90f; music and,
  119–21; smuggling of marijuana and,
  94–95, 103, 109
Rivet, Paul, 6
Rocha Molina, Hugo, 128
Rockefeller Organization, 5
Rodríguez, Crisóstomo, 69
Rodríguez, Damaso, 69
Rodríguez, Santos, 69
Rois, Juancho, 138f
Rojas, Germán, 84, 130–31
Rojas Pinilla, Gustavo, 42, 46, 63–67,
  74–75, 159
Roldán, Mary, 196, 205
Rondón Group, 64

Roosevelt, Franklin D., 29, 32
Rostam-Kolayi, Jasamin, 101
Ruiz, Hernando, 93, 177–78

Sáenz Rovner, Eduardo, 74
Safford, Frank, 205
Salazar, Parménides, 99
SALT, 150
Samper Pizano, Ernesto, 176–77, 189
Sánchez, César, 72
Sánchez, Gonzalo, 75
Sánchez, Sonia, 190
Sanders, Terry, Jr., 35–36
Sandinistas, 173
San Juan del Cesar, 12, 42, 57–58, 64,
  69–71, 102–3, 129–30, 135–37, 142, 219
Santa Marta: about, 7; decline of marijuana
  and, 186–88, 193; emergence of tropical
  commodities and, 22–24, 30–32, 39,
  45–47; maps of, 22f, 58f, 90f; marijuana
  boom and, 91–98, 103; music and, 118,
  121; smuggling and, 77–80
Santa Marta Gold, 91–96, 100, 113–14
Santoro, Billy, 96
Santos, Daniel, 121, 133
Santos, Eduardo, 32–35, 39
Santos, Juan Manuel, 217
SCADTA, 35
Security Statute, 174, 179, 195–96, 200
Serje, Margarita, 99
Sierra Nevada de Santa Marta: about,
  4–8, 256n27; cocaine and, 200–202,
  206–8; criminalization of marijuana
  and violence in, 183–209; decline of
  marijuana and, 148–49, 153, 162, 168–
  69, 174–75, 184–87, 192–93, 207–8;
  emergence of marijuana and, 1, 72–74,
  84; emergence of tropical commodities
  in, 21–24, 60–64; maps of, 58f, 90f; the
  marijuana boom and, 89–103, 107, 111,
  213, 216
Siglo, El (newspaper), 39
smuggling, 10–12, 32–36, 55–85, 98–99,
  109–13, 167–70, 183–209, 213–16. See
  also marijuana
Socarrás, José Francisco, 195–96, 198
Socarrás, Silvestre (Tite), 63
Socialist party, 26

Venezuelan National Guard, 160
Vieira, Juan (Ios), 80
Vieja Sara, 119
Vietnam war, 148–50
violence and criminalization of marijuana, 3, 183–209, 217
Vives, José Benito, 26
Vives, José Ignacio (Nacho), 49–55, 79–81, 244n196, 244n199
Vives de Andreis family, 26
Vives family, 23–24
Vives Ferrer, Salvador, 24, 27, 32, 48
Vives v. Fadul & Peñaloza, 53

Wade, Peter, 118
War of a Thousand Days, 21, 24, 37, 127, 198
war on drugs, 1–2, 76, 141, 148–64, 172–81, 213–14. *See also* violence and criminalization of marijuana

Wasserman, Abby, 94f, 97, 101
Wayuu people, 10, 13, 25, 30–32, 36–38, 66–71, 78, 109, 192, 198. *See also* indigenous groups
White Paper on Drug Abuse (Ford), 164
"Why Are Guajiros Violent" (El Tiempo), 198
Wolff, Lester, 169–70, 178–79
World War I, 33
World War II, 32–39

"Yo soy el indio" (Brito), 283n61
"Yo tenía mi cafetal" (Los Melódicos), 100, 258n47
Yunai. *See* United Fruit Company

Zalamea Borda, Eduardo, 4–5
Zenón, Mocho, 72
Zuleta clan, 119, 140

Founded in 1893,
UNIVERSITY OF CALIFORNIA PRESS
publishes bold, progressive books and journals
on topics in the arts, humanities, social sciences,
and natural sciences—with a focus on social
justice issues—that inspire thought and action
among readers worldwide.

The UC PRESS FOUNDATION
raises funds to uphold the press's vital role
as an independent, nonprofit publisher, and
receives philanthropic support from a wide
range of individuals and institutions—and from
committed readers like you. To learn more, visit
ucpress.edu/supportus.